John Wyclif

A Lion Book
an imprint of
Lion Hudson plc
Wilkinson House, Jordan Hill Road,
Oxford OX2 8DR, England
www.lionhudson.com
ISBN 978 0 7459 5291 8

First hardback edition 2005
First paperback edition 2007
10 9 8 7 6 5 4 3 2 1 0

Picture Acknowledgments
p. 13 Oxford in 1400, showing the colleges, parish churches and monastic precincts. Map of Medieval Oxford from "The History of the University of Oxford, Volume 2: Late Middle Ages" by Catto (1992). Used with permission.
p. 91 New College: the Warden and Scholars. Taken from the Chaundler manuscript. Reproduced with permission of New College and by courtesy of the Bodleian Library.
p. 149 A medieval friar preaches to his congregation in the open air from a moveable pulpit (circa 1500). Photo by Hulton Archive/Getty Images.
p. 195 Macclesfield Psalter. Miniature of King David and the fool; portrait busts and ploughing scene. Copyright © The Fitzwilliam Museum, University of Cambridge. Reproduced with permission.

A catalogue record for this book is available
from the British Library

Typeset in 11.5/14 BerkOldsty Bk BT
Printed and bound in Malta
by Gutenberg Press

The text paper used in this book has been made from wood
independently certified as having come from sustainable forests.

John Wyclif

G. R. EVANS

LION

Acknowledgments

Workman's biography of 1926 has stood the test of time remarkably well. But it is time for another *Life*. A biographer of the twenty-first century must acknowledge an enormous debt to scholars without whose patient uncovering of the evidences this book could not have been attempted. Their work underpins the end notes to each chapter and informs such enlarged understanding of Wyclif and what he did as is now possible. I am especially grateful to Patrick Hornchurch for reading and criticising an earlier draft, and to Margaret Harvey for friendly discussion.

I should also like to thank David Bygott, a quite exceptional copy-editor with a salutary wry humour.

Contents

Part III The Troubles Begin

Part IV Coping with Failure

Preface

> 'To Wyclif we owe… our English language, our English Bible, and our reformed religion… Expand that three-fold claim a little further. It means nothing less than this: that in Wyclif we have the acknowledged father of English prose, the first translator of the whole Bible into the language of the English people, the first disseminator of that Bible amongst all classes, the foremost intellect of his times brought to bear upon the religious questions of the day, the patient and courageous writer of innumerable tracts and books, not for one, but for all the different classes of society.'[1]

Montagu Burrows made these great claims for John Wyclif (or Wiclif or Wycliffe; there are over twenty spellings) when he gave a series of lectures at Oxford in 1881. It has become apparent in the last century and a quarter that none of them stands up, yet lingering hero-worship still surrounds the figure of Wyclif. A new biography is almost bound to be controversial.

Although there are hints that he had considerable personal charm when he chose to exert it, Wyclif was not a man who put himself out to be likeable when something aroused his indignation. And a great deal made him indignant. He knew nothing of the tact which disarms an opponent and turns him into an ally. He wrests from his readers a protesting admiration for his honesty, coupled with an irritation that he could repeatedly be so silly and self-defeating. It is hard not to be caught up in the story of a life lived with energy and on principle and reckless of personal consequences. Wyclif is 'heroic' in these ways, if not as Burrows thought.

Wyclif's story begins with half-obliterated footprints. The evidence that has come down to us is full of gaps and uncertainties. There is no cosy nursery world in Wyclif's story. Little is known in his case about that stage of life which generally gets the reader reading on from the beginning of a biography, the account of the childhood and early youth of the subject. There is barely enough to allow us to put a face to him and sketch the distinctive roundnesses and roughnesses of individuality – almost no surviving letters and no memorials from devoted personal friends to preserve the touching vulnerabilities and moments of humour which define a person as surely as the major events of a life and its achievements. Wyclif had no Boswell to record what he said; there is no equivalent of Luther's *Table Talk*. Wyclif himself was no stylist. His writing is almost wholly without elegance, awkward and often unclear,[2] and he lacked the urge to discuss his inner self which makes Augustine's *Confessions* still a gripping read despite their prolixity and the frequent interruptions while Augustine breaks off to have a conversation with God.

On the other hand, we know a good deal about the Oxford in which Wyclif spent most of his life, the academic rivalries and conflicts and the way his thinking was formed by his studies and the arguments he had with his colleagues. Here he and his environment really come to life. The controversial reputation he actually acquired in his lifetime was in reality probably not much different from that of other Oxford figures who got into trouble with the authorities. Troublesome academics were quite a common feature of medieval Europe, once the universities came into being in the course of the twelfth century. Wyclif was among the first 'academic experts' to be brought in by a Government as an adviser, with consequences which resemble those which may be read about in newspapers today (for example, conflict of interest and favours returned).

Modern biography presents the life of an individual in its particularity, attempting to render as exactly as possible the man or woman in the circumstances. The typical medieval biography is a saint's *Life*[3] and hagiography had its own strong conventions, which have more to do with norms than with the peculiar features of individual lives. For example, it is common for the subject's mother to have had a vision when pregnant of the future greatness of her child. The purpose of hagiography was edification and to that end it sought to depict its subject as an example to others. It did not confine itself to the kinds of event which find a place in modern biography, for it took its subject to be holy to a degree which manifested itself in miracles, and supernatural events are taken to be testimony to the sanctity of the subject. Lessons are drawn so that the reader may not fail to be led in the right direction by his or her reading, which is envisaged as a form of devotional exercise. No one tried to canonize Wyclif, but there were energetic attempts to make him a hero or a villain. In this respect he was made a 'type', an example (of good or bad).

A modern biography of Wyclif has to resolve challenging questions of genre. It must avoid becoming a hagiography while making room for the fact that Wyclif became a hero of the call for a return to Scripture and the resistance to the abuse of power in the Church. It also needs to provide a sufficient context to give the modern reader a sense of the realities of the world of fourteenth-century Oxford in which abstruse academic debates could sometimes generate enough heat and interest to spill over and eventually become linked in people's minds with things which concerned them in their own lives. There is a social and political as well as a theological story to tell alongside the personal, the life of the man. Above all, a judgment has to be arrived at about the scale of Wyclif's personal achievement within the trends and movements with which his name became associated. Some Wycliffite and Lollard ideas were Wyclif's own; some later flowed from his work; some were given currency by his friends and followers rather than Wyclif himself.

The perspectives given to things by religious factionalism are not merely a phenomenon of the modern world. They bedevilled Wyclif's story in his own day and they have coloured the way he has been seen since. The case which was put for the highly coloured Wyclif by the enthusiasts of the sixteenth century, and after, must now be looked at in the context of the evidence, before we can decide whether to declare him still in any sense the 'Morning Star of the Reformation'.[4]

> 'Until within the last few years, England has been singularly ungrateful to the memory of one of her greatest men. She seems to have forgotten that not only is John Wiclif the father of her prose but that he was also the first to do battle for the maintenance of evangelical faith and English freedom with a foreign power that openly denied to Englishmen the privilege of both.'[5]

Thus warmly wrote Rudolf Buddensieg, the Dresden schoolmaster who gave up all his leisure for a quarter of a century to his great project of bringing the writings of his hero into print. He stimulated the Wyclif Society to undertake the nineteenth-century edition of Wyclif's works, which has still not been superseded by a more accurate, modern version. Did Buddensieg, like Burrows, long to restore for Wyclif a reputation he never deserved? And if so, what balance is to be struck now between criticism and admiration? There is 'a popular fallacy that biographers fall in love with their subjects. Such a cosy presumption… . Writing biography… can, just as easily as not, be an act of contempt. Think of Sartre writing on Flaubert… . And… who could *love* Ezra Pound?'[6] Wyclif may not be lovable, but he deserves sympathy and a kind of respect. What kind, and for what, the reader may judge from the following pages.

G.R. Evans

Part I

The Master of Arts

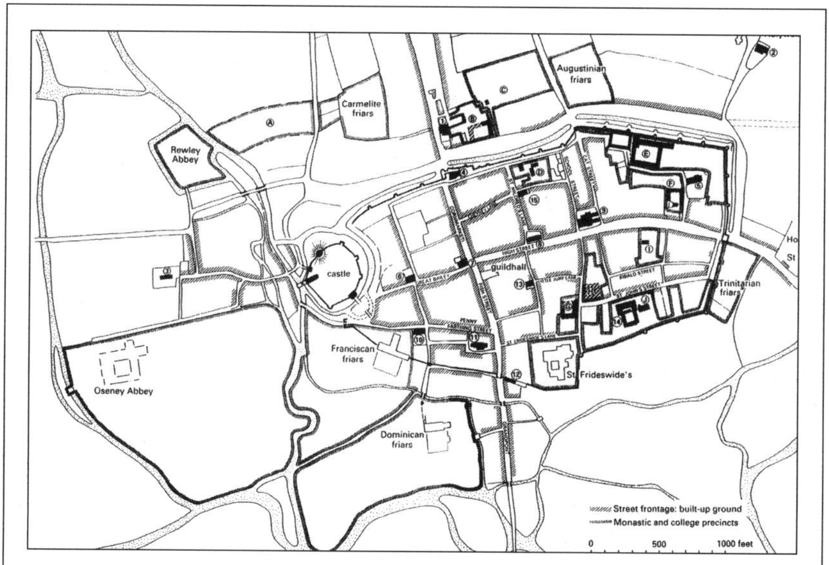

Chapter 1

Going to Oxford

i. From Yorkshire

About 1372, one of those who challenged Wyclif to public intellectual duels in an Oxford 'disputation', gave it as his opinion that Wyclif was 'deep', spoke well and with distinction and was a solemn and learned figure both in speech and in knowledge.[1] Wyclif himself says that he has not always lived an ascetic life. He admits that 'in excess of eating and clothing' he has not set the priestly example he should have done. He has consumed goods which might have benefited the poor.[2] He admits to losing his temper easily. 'I have often lapsed into indignation or irritation.'[3] He says he prays about this and tries to break himself of the habit.[4] In 1407 William Thorpe, a 'Lollard' who had been in Oxford from about 1377, described John Wyclif to the Archbishop of Canterbury who was 'examining' him on his own beliefs. Wyclif, he said, was spare, thin, a man of moderate and harmless habits and able to win the affection of those who knew him. 'They loved him dearly,' he said.[5] Thorpe, who had been in prison all summer, had had time to think what he would say to give the impression he wanted when he was brought before Arundel. Nevertheless, his comments have a convincing air of strong, personal recollection and they remain, though a mere thumbnail sketch of the person who is the subject of this book, one of the few close-up pictures we have.

John Wyclif was born into a family which is first heard of as quite humble, mere undertenants on the land in Yorkshire from which they took their name, a few miles north-north-west of Richmond. As late as 1286–87, Robert de Wyclif held a mere 'knight's fee', the minimum for a 'gentleman's family'. This was the way in which the royal armies were manned, members of the knightly classes providing so many days' military service in return for their use of a property on which they and their families and households and workers could live as farmers. Wyclif's ancestor acquired some additional land, perhaps to enable him to provide for his family. Descendants of the family were still living there until early in the nineteenth century.[6]

Robert de Wyclif also had the advowson (right to nominate the priest) of a church, which was granted by Robert, Prior of Markby, 'for himself and his heirs for ever' on 6 May 1263. This was the right to make a 'presentation' to a 'living'. The holder of the advowson gave the local bishop a name and the bishop would appoint the nominee to be rector or vicar of a parish and to receive the income which went with the position, whether or not he actually discharged the duties. This could have enabled his family to ensure that John Wyclif, when he decided to be a priest, had (in every sense) a 'living'. The living was worth £13 6s 8d in 1291. That is £13 and a third of a pound in the currency used in England until the mid-twentieth century. It should be compared with the annual salary of a modern clergyman. This income could also have been used to support our John Wyclif as a student, although no evidence survives that it was.

The family was coming up in the world. A Robert de Wyclif was a freeholder in 1286–87. A Roger de Wyclif had got the manor of Wyclif in his own name by 1303. He had died by 1316, for at that date another Robert was lord of the manor. A further Roger, possibly this Robert's brother, and his wife Catherine, whom he married in 1319, were our Wyclif's parents.

Our John Wyclif was possibly not born for a decade or more after his parents' marriage. Wyclif's father Roger was still alive in 1347–48. It is not known when he died, although it must have been before 1362 when John Wyclif's mother is recorded as associated with the bestowing of the family living to a Robert de Wyclif in 1362. Though John's name does not appear in the record on that occasion, he would have become patron of the living on his father's death. This assumes that he was the eldest or only son, but there is no way of knowing whether he was.

At some point in this period William de Wycliffe held the manor but by 1363 the manor was held by John de Wycliffe, for he is recorded as the patron of the family benefice, presenting it to William de Wycliffe in 1363 and Henry Hugate in 1369. A John de Hugate appears among the Fellows of Balliol and followed our Wyclif as Master (that is, head) of the college, although the name is sufficiently common for it to be possible that he had no connection with the Henry Hugate who enjoyed the family's patronage.

So there were other clerics in the family beside John: a Robert, a William and possibly another John, son of a Simon de Wyclif. A John Wyclif was ordained in 1351, Deacon at St Mary's in York and Priest at York Minster, when William de la Zouche was Archbishop. This is not likely to be our John Wyclif, because the minimum age for ordination to the priesthood under canon law was twenty-five. Although the rule was quite commonly ignored, it took influence and an important reason such as a particular act of patronage to get it waived. Our John Wyclif was to graduate only in the late 1350s and it would have been unusual for a student to begin his basic undergraduate studies at such an advanced age as twenty-five; and unlikely that an obscure fourteen-year-old would have been ordained a priest. Soon after his ordination the John Wyclif priested in 1351 was to be found in the household of the new Archbishop, John Thoresby, who had risen to his primacy by way of many diplomatic missions for Church and state and who would have made a useful patron for the young man.[7] William Wyclif the priest may well have been the William Wyclif who was a Fellow of Balliol in 1361, and appointed by John to the family living as an act of patronage.[8] Perhaps he was a cousin. He held the benefice for six years. In 1365 he was granted a licence to be non-resident for two years so that he could study at Oxford, so perhaps he followed the John Wyclif who is our subject in deciding to study Theology. Robert Wyclif is mentioned in a letter of John of Gaunt in 1373, in which he instructs one of his foresters to deliver a deer to Sir Robert de Wyclif. Robert was parish priest of Holy Cross, York in 1378. He entered the king's service and appears as 'the king's clerk' in 1379. In 1380 he was placed second in the queue for when a canonry at Dublin fell vacant. He moved in due course to the living of Kirkby Ravensworth in north Yorkshire, which was a parish in which the Wyclif family had some lands. In 1382 he exchanged that living for the one at St Ronald Kirk and then moved to the wealthy living of Hutton Rugby from 1392 until he died. He was a friend of the Bishop of Durham, Walter Skirlaw, and his name appears frequently in connection with legal business of one kind or another in the region. He was evidently an able man, one on whom others relied for the transaction of business. He had no compunction in taking part in the conduct of the trials of a suspected Lollard.

This was a busy and influential family, then, climbing the ladder of preferment and patronage, adding to its wealth, making influential friendships, possibly already possessing a useful fund of goodwill with John of Gaunt. It was not one of the first families in the land by any means, but in Yorkshire it carried weight.[9] But the John Wyclif whose life we are exploring was decisively 'formed' not in this family context, but by his time in Oxford.

ii. Wyclif arrives in Oxford

A young man with his way to make, Wyclif arrived in Oxford probably sometime late in the 1340s or early 1350s. Term began on 9 October, the feast of St Denys. Boys would travel to Oxford in the company of a 'bringer' who acted like a human school bus and collected up pupils at points along the route.[10] They might stay the first night at an inn, of which some of the originals still survive (for example, the Mitre).[11]

The outline of Oxford was, and still is, shaped by the complex system of rivers and tributaries of Isis and Cherwell, eventually running together to form the head of the Thames, and the large areas of marshy ground around them. The main roads on firm ground ran north beyond the city walls through St Giles, still site of the annual fair in early September, and there were routes to the other points of the compass over causeways and bridges.[12]

The town would have looked quite different from today, although features from Wyclif's time are still to be seen. The street level was perhaps twelve feet lower than it is now. The modern High Street was a narrow lane; the modern Broad, the town ditch with walls on one side and Balliol College on the other. St Mary's, the University church, stood not in the handsome square of today, surrounded by golden buildings, but in a tangle of narrow dark lanes where a boy could easily be set upon by muggers. Oxford was a market town with several markets. It is based on an intersection of streets meeting at Carfax. Each of these, the High Street, the Cornmarket, Queen Street, St Aldate's, which runs steeply down the only hill, had a medieval market. Behind each street ran lanes criss-crossing one another, and fronting onto each street were shops and workshops, narrow but going back some way behind each front. Inside the city walls were the parish churches of thirteen parishes and four big churches for the communities of friars. Some of the church towers, such as that of St Michael at the North Gate, were part of the city wall, but they all stood up high above the level of most of the houses and shops, which were generally of only two storeys.

It is not impossible that Wyclif was there first as a schoolboy, for the Queen's College, with which he was to be associated for much of his later life, ran a boys' school from 1341 and a John Wyclif, who could have been a relative, was there as a boy thirty years later. Wyclif knew the local children's talk of the town well enough to remark on some of the names the boys had for parts of it.[13]

If Wyclif asked to be directed to 'the University' on arrival no one would have known how to answer him. The University was not a group of buildings; it had almost no buildings yet to call its own. There was no faculty building for the Masters of the Theology Faculty. They gave their lectures in one of the religious houses, or in the schools near the University Church of St Mary the Virgin, possibly in one of the halls or colleges.[14] The University was not even a 'place', for the group of Oxford scholars who decamped to Cambridge in 1208 after a quarrel had shown clearly enough that they could 'become a university' elsewhere. It was a community of people organized as a 'corporation' and living under rules of its own devising, though under royal and papal protection.

Today a prospective university student in England sends for a prospectus. The student arriving at a modern university is unlikely to know much about its internal administrative arrangements, for there will have been little or nothing about that in the prospectus. The prospective student perhaps goes to an 'Open Day', fills in an application form, may be interviewed. There may be an offer of a place conditional on obtaining sufficiently high grades in secondary or high school examinations. Wyclif did not have to 'get a place'. He 'went to Oxford' in the simple literal sense that he travelled there. Although it was open to all comers, the University was in many ways a closed society, and it is very difficult to guess what rumours of what it had to offer would reach Wyclif's boyhood home in the north of England. It is hard to know how much he can have understood in advance about the course he was to follow, what was involved in getting a degree, how long it would take, and the careers it would equip him to follow. He may have been told something by former students he had known at home. But there was no prospectus, no handbook for new students, no systematic provision of information. Yet, then as now, education provided a ladder to a distinguished career for those without wealthy or influential families. 'We commonly see that the sons of the rich and powerful do not learn and the sons of the simple poor are raised to the highest ecclesiastical dignities by reason of their behaviour and knowledge,' remarked one of Wyclif's older contemporaries encouragingly in a sermon.[15]

Before we try to get a picture of Wyclif's student life and what he studied, we must try to answer the question what this fiercely independent and still fairly new entity known as the University of Oxford actually was.

iii. The academic 'craft'

Universities were quite a new invention. They had existed for less than two hundred years when Wyclif arrived in Oxford, and there had been nothing quite like them in the ancient or earlier medieval world to form a model. They had to invent themselves and work out what they were for and set their own rules. They also had to arrive at a *modus vivendi* with the inhabitants of any town or city where they wished to settle and grow.

The driving force in their beginning in the twelfth century was student demand, for it was already apparent that there were career ladders for ambitious young men to climb from a good education to influential positions in Church and state. This was a world very like the modern one in the way it confronted the prospective student with the problem of financing his course. There were tuition fees to pay and maintenance costs to find. There was the carrot of a better-paid career at the end of it, but no certainty. Perhaps Wyclif had all this in mind when he arrived in Oxford. Intellectual curiosity and the sheer interestingness of advanced study should not be discounted as a motivation capable of driving graduates back into study and keeping grown men, including Wyclif, arguing into old age. He eventually entered into the spirit of the place entirely.

We shall see how ambition grew in him while he was getting his degree and after. The man with a higher education might aspire to high office in the Church, for example, a bishopric, which carried secular power and influence and considerable wealth. Or he might enter the ecclesiastical or state civil service. This could lead to high honours too, just as in modern Britain senior civil servants have long had a better chance of a knighthood than other categories of worker. Another possible career was as a teacher in the university world. The student hunger for high-level teaching had encouraged the multiplication of such 'Masters' throughout the twelfth century, for some of those who began as students found that what they really enjoyed best was study and they could make a living and a reputation just as well by staying in the schools and teaching the next generation. That way could lead to a bishopric as well as any other. In the twelfth century, the English John of Salisbury left the schools for the papal civil service; he moved on to the civil service of the King of England, Henry II. Eventually he became Bishop of Chartres.[16] Closer to Wyclif's own time, six or seven of the Bishops of Lincoln from 1209–1362 were 'Oxford men'. Wyclif's ambition took him away only briefly, once, at the beginning of his career.

The student–master arrangement was the basic structural element of the first 'schools' which were to mutate into universities such as Wyclif's Oxford. In its first, informal, shape, it allowed students to pay fees to those they themselves chose to be their teachers, and to move on freely when they thought they had learned all they could from one particular Master, or when a new one arrived locally and they were told he was worth hearing. It encouraged Masters and would-be Masters to congregate in towns and cities where others were already teaching because that was where they could find prospective students for themselves and try to win them over from their rivals. This is exactly the process described by Peter Abelard when, at the end of the eleventh century, he went to listen to the lectures on the Bible of the most famous theologian of the day, Anselm of Laon. Where he expected to see a tree full of leaves he found bare branches, he claims in his autobiographical 'letter' describing all this. He threw down a challenge. He would give a lecture himself, on Ezekiel, acknowledged to be the most difficult of the prophets to interpret, and he would do it the very next day. Naturally, Anselm's students flocked to hear him, and he complains that he became the subject of Anselm's resentment because he was jealous.[17] So the stirrings of academic rivalry among the Masters were noticeable from the very beginning, before universities formally existed at all.

A similarly vivid personal account of this early world of students choosing their teachers and Masters vying for students is to be found a generation later in John of Salisbury's *Metalogicon*, and it gives us a glimpse of the way a syllabus gradually established itself. John was an Englishman who spent twelve years hearing lectures at Paris. He gives a list of some of the Masters he chose to 'hear'. 'I attached myself to Master Alberic,' he reports. He seems to have had a general plan, but he felt free to go backwards and forwards among the subjects of what would gradually become the 'arts' course. Petrus Helias was famous as a teacher of grammar, which was the foundation study, but John went to him after he had studied under other Masters. And he 'went back' after three years to Gilbert of Poitiers, whose lectures he heard on both Logic and Philosophy.[18]

The result, for most of the twelfth century, had been a libertarian atmosphere in which students could largely do as they pleased, and where there were considerable numbers in a town or city, it is not surprising that there was some friction with the townspeople. Students had a reputation for drunkenness and also for never having enough money, even before universities had properly come into existence.[19] In a satirical poem of the twelfth century one student at Paris is described as often at the table or in his cups.[20] There follows some gentle mockery of the difficulty of learning with a hangover, of seven years of studies leading to nothing very much by way of the acquisition of knowledge.

Well before there was a university in the town, wandering teachers are known to have taught in Oxford. Theobald of Étampes was there for four years about 1117 with as many as fifty pupils, which would have made a sizeable 'school'.[21] Robert Pullen (who is thought to have taught in Paris too) and the lawyer Vacarius taught in Oxford in the 1130s and 1140s.[22] Englishmen as well as scholars from abroad were teaching there: Robert Crickslade and Walter, Archdeacon of Oxford.[23] In 1167 the King, Henry II, forbade the English to study abroad and this may have been the prompter for some consolidation of the efforts of the Masters who were teaching in Oxford. The important point is that it was the Masters themselves who decided to cooperate, and to begin to formalize what they were offering to students. Names of a few individuals connected with Oxford in this early period of its organization survive: Daniel of Morley (1175–1200), John of Constantine (1186–90), Alexander Neckham (1192–1197/1202).[24] It has been calculated that there were over a hundred identifiable working scholars teaching in Oxford in the century up to the crisis of 1208–09, when the scholars walked out in indignation.[25] By 1201 its first official 'Master' appears in the list.[26]

Surviving records of the very earliest lectures given in northern France show lecturers referring to one another's opinions in a derogatory way. A lecturer will seem to anticipate the waving hand of a student anxious to point out that a different Master has another opinion and explain that this other Master is wrong. This competitiveness was natural enough if students could be won for one's own courses and kept from paying their fees to one's rivals. The first important change towards institutionalizing such 'schools' and turning them into universities, at least in northern Europe, at Paris and Oxford, was the decision of the Masters to formalize the status of approved lecturers, form themselves into a gild (or guild) and work together. This enabled them to defend their common interests and define the features of the teaching and learning and assessing in which the informal community had been engaged. It institutionalized the rivalry to some degree by arranging for the resolution of disputed questions to take place in formal disputations. A different model emerged at the Italian University of Bologna, where graduate student lawyers ran the University for their own convenience, hiring their lecturers and making the rules themselves.

Universitas is another word for gild; and the essential character of the university was that of a corporation of Masters, much like any other medieval gild or combined professional association and trade union, in that it had apprentices (the undergraduates) and journeymen, or bachelors, craftsmen who had not yet proceeded quite so far as to become masters of their craft, much as a fishmonger did when gutting fish as a member of the Fishmongers' Gild.[27] The masters in the craft of scholarship set and monitored the standards to be attained, not so much by requiring a level of attainment in students as in setting the content of the courses to be taught, their length and the number of series of lectures a student must have attended before he could graduate.

Oxford was known as a *universitas* before it is certain that it was yet a true corporation. However, in 1231 the Crown made the first grant of privilege to it as a corporation, with the Chancellor acting as the recipient, so that the grant was made to the University in his 'person'.[28] Being a 'corporation' meant that the body of Masters could be regarded as a legal person. Legally, it was a 'body' which could act like a human person in law, suing and being sued as a litigant.[29] The University was a 'body' in a fuller sense, too, a sense which was very important to the medieval way of thinking. The University 'was' the free association of the established scholars in a gild (*universitas*) or corporation. It 'was' the people who made it up, and they choose who to admit to membership of their 'body'.

'We had... hand-picked ourselves or each other. Nobody in the world could wish a colleague on us,'' [30] comments a character in *Full Term*, J.I.M. Stewart's modern novel about Oxford. This underlines the importance of autonomy in the basic structure, which has been preserved in all Oxford and Cambridge Colleges and the two Universities themselves ever since these medieval principles were established.

When they were 'being the University', the scholars were acting as a kind of 'body politic'. This was an image familiar from the New Testament[31] and much beloved by medieval political theorists. It makes it possible to speak of the body acting as an entity while recognizing that, like a human body, it has parts which have different functions. The foot is used for walking, not the hand. Moreover, the health and proper functioning of the whole body depends on the cooperation of the parts. A rebellious eye should be cut out, advises the New Testament.[32] In a sermon preached at Oxford by John Shirborne a little after Wyclif's time,[33] the image of the body politic is adapted to fit the 'body' of the university. 'In our mother [the university] over which the multitude of doctors and masters presides it is apparent that they have different duties just like the different members of a single body. But there is a single Chancellor like the head; the same law, the statutes and privileges; and the whole has a single purpose, that is the strengthening and increasing of the faith in the one civil body [of the state]. So the professors of sacred theology, like eyes, fitly preside like those who contemplate the divine secrets the more clearly because they are not held back by the limitations of what can be perceived by the senses. The lawyers are like ears pricked for higher things judging between the just and the unjust. The medical doctors, like hands, protect the whole body against dangers to the bodily members, and provide remedies. The feet are the masters of the philosophical liberal arts and they support the whole body.'

If the internal rules of the community of scholars were largely of their own devising, they had the additional authority and protection of state and Church which was invoked or challenged as occasion required. The battle for autonomy was fought with a shrewd eye on the fact that the ecclesiastical and secular authorities which were protecting or confirming the liberties could be powerful allies for the university against one another if there was a dispute with one of them.

The idea of a university

Scholars were, technically, members of the clergy, as well as being 'clerks'. In the medieval hierarchy that placed them under obedience as individuals.

Monastic students and those who were members of religious orders obeyed their abbot or his equivalent. Secular clergy obeyed the bishop. Normally, bishops expected to control the right of clerks (clergy) to preach and by implication also the right to teach, because they had pastoral responsibility to ensure that their flocks were not led astray to the peril of their souls. The local Bishop was at Lincoln, a very long way from Oxford; there was no diocese of Oxford yet. For twenty years during a crucial period of the University's formation, the bishopric of Lincoln was vacant (1166–86), so the natural interest of the ecclesiastical authorities was not able to be as vigilant as it might have been. Where Paris and other cities had long had cathedral schools attached to them, and the new universities in such places had to establish their position in relation to these existing schools, Oxford's new University had no cathedral school to distinguish itself from, for there was no cathedral, until the sixteenth-century foundation of Christ Church. It centred on what became the 'University Church' of St Mary's, behind what is now the Radcliffe Camera.

Papal generosity extended to the making of a grant of liberties to the University by Innocent IV in 1254. There was a political context to this. Robert Grosseteste, Oxford's former Chancellor and later Bishop of Lincoln,[34] had been succeeded by a new Bishop of Lincoln, who was hostile to Oxford. The Pope appointed the Bishop of London and the Bishop of Salisbury as protectors of the rights, liberties and immunities of the University, who were to make sure that the scholars were not troubled.[35] That set up fresh eddies and cross-currents in the power games involving the Church in England, the Church in Rome and the community of scholars. In 1362, 1367 and 1369, the King repeated the ban which prevented those condemned in the Chancellor's court from appealing to the Pope. The University's courts were to be free from interference by the courts of the realm[36] and by royal judges. Kings too confirmed the privileges of the University at intervals: for example, in 1378 and 1380. In 1380 and 1381 the University was exempted from paying the parliamentary subsidy which had been levied in 1377. Henry IV began his reign by confirming and enlarging the University's privileges, even pardoning those members who had committed offences against the Crown. In the episodes where the University sought the protection of Pope or King, it was engaged in an inherently dangerous, but a surprisingly successful strategy, because it set the great powers at loggerheads. In that way the University obtained a long series of grants of privilege and confirmations of privilege, which enabled it to stand up to local challenges to its freedoms.

The powerful sense of the importance of defending its own autonomy the University developed from the beginning was undiminished in Wyclif's day, and it signally affected developments in his own life. But it was very far from being a determination to allow everyone to do what he liked. The University made rules for itself and for its students and it became as firm about internal discipline as about the right for its scholars to trial in the University's courts and not the Church or the secular courts if they got into trouble with the townspeople. All this gave the scholars tremendous self-confidence when they acted as a body, even if as individuals they could be timid (or aggressive or defensive or quite unreasonable, especially with one another). As a modern novelist has put it:

> 'I would have described the majority of my colleagues as being, individually, diffident men, who through their intellectual endowment were very sufficiently aware of the perplexingness and treachery and uncontrollability of things in general. But collectively they had a serene confidence in themselves.'[37]

iv. Town and gown

Foxe's *Book of Martyrs* took a dim view of the Oxford where Wyclif arrived as a student probably about 1350, a few years before our earliest definite glimpse of him in 1356. 'The state of religion amongst the divines was in a deep lethargy,' Foxe says. Wyclif, his hero, was a great intellectual leader, but only insofar as the contemporary state of learning allowed. 'He... was for the rude time wherein he lived, famously reputed for a great clergyman, a deep scholar, and no less expert in all kind of philosophy.'[38] Foxe was far out in his assessment of the state of learning in the university when Wyclif arrived there. That will become obvious as we follow Wyclif through his youthful studies.

Nor was he right about the lethargy. Roger Bacon remarked in the thirteenth century that wherever clerics congregate, in Oxford or in Paris, there were disturbances and warfare and the laity were scandalized.[39] The story of medieval Oxford is the story of repeated disputes between town and gown, some mere street brawls; some involving more substantial warfare. Squabbling between scholars and townspeople and drunken brawls involving students and the young men of the town was natural. The students were not locals. Their dress was distinctive.[40] They were resented for being 'different' as readily as they were welcomed for being a useful source of income to the townspeople. This was an age when people carried knives and violence in the streets could easily lead to deaths.

There was a further concern. Robert de Stratford, Archdeacon of Canterbury, wrote to the University of Oxford, about the summer of 1337, on the subject of the 'dangerous dissidents' in the University, a list of whom had been sent to the King by one William Trussell late in 1335. His subject is the 'subversion of the University', his concern that a ringleader can lead the scholars astray and even carry them off to Stamford in Lincolnshire to 'false study'.[41] The great fear in Oxford was of the departure of the students, who could easily decamp elsewhere, to the considerable financial loss of the tradespeople of the town. Stamford might as easily have become a university town as Cambridge – it was beginning to acquire halls and religious houses full of potential students.

The University complained in 1346 that the town authorities were using force of arms to keep the University from the 'assizes' when ordinances regulating weights and measures were officially fixed so as to ensure that things were sold in agreed quantities and buyers were not swindled. In 1348 the Archbishop of Canterbury and the Bishop of Chichester were still trying to bring about agreement of the embattled town and gown about this; and a 'concord' in the administrative Norman French (which was about to give way to English for official documents) preserves the agreement eventually reached between the town and the University.[42]

While Wyclif was an undergraduate, before he appears in person in this story, there had been brawls in the town between scholars and townspeople. He must have been a witness, if not a participant. They took place on 10 February 1355 and came to be known as the St Scholastica's Day riots. It began with an argument in a tavern, a fourteenth-century pub brawl which escalated to such a pitch that it went on for three days. The townspeople had a good many long-standing grievances to vent and they seized the moment to sack University lodgings and beat up the scholars. The bells of the University Church of St Mary's were rung to summon the academics, and those of St Martin's Church to call out the townspeople and the two gangs met face to face in the High Street. Supporters for the townspeople were brought in from the countryside round Oxford. They looted and burned some of the academic halls and many of the students and scholars were injured or killed.[43]

A contemporary verse records 'the University's Complaint' about these events.[44] This kind of 'complaint' poem was quite a popular form, and often it was used to point a finger at general abuses. But this Complaint was most particular. In the poem, the Scholar begins by asking his 'mother', the University, why she is so sad. She points to the ungrateful Mayor of Oxford, John de Bereford, whom she rescued from an unpromising and disadvantaged boyhood and allowed to become a servant to her scholars. He rose to local prominence as a result. Yet the townspeople he now leads have attacked her scholars and many have been slain in the riots of the last two days. The Scholar tries to reassure the University with the promise that she has a royal protector and the miscreants are to be punished. But the University is not much comforted. She says that the number of scholars is diminishing, there is fraud and bribery, and the clerics of the University dress effeminately and provoke quarrels with the laity. Do not lose faith in us, pleads the Scholar! The older scholars are not like this and the younger ones will soon learn how to behave.

The indignant University authorities turned for protection to the King and the Bishop of distant Lincoln, in whose enormous diocese Oxford then lay, and who had pastoral responsibility for the local people. As it happened, the King was staying at Woodstock just outside Oxford and he sent judges to Oxford to hold hearings and sentence the ringleaders. The Mayor and some of his colleagues found themselves in prison. The King followed this up with a settlement. The townspeople were to give all the plunder back to the academics and pay a large fine. There was to be a charter for the University, setting out its privileges.

The charter of 27 June 1355[45] added new rights for the University to the ones it had previously enjoyed. The Chancellor of the University was to have exclusive jurisdiction over the selling of food in Oxford and he was to have the profits of the judicial process there. And in future each new Sheriff of Oxford was to take an oath to defend the University's privileges and to protect the Masters and the students from violence. King Edward's letter of 11 June 1355 speaks of the danger of shipwreck the University has been in, promises it the restoration of its privileges and the royal protection, and regrets that it has not been possible for the scholars to dare to resume their lectures and carry on with their 'scholarly acts' (*actus scolasticos*) for fear of the townspeople.[46]

The Bishop placed the whole town under an interdict, which meant that it was barred from the celebration of the Eucharist and the souls of everyone in it were considered to be in peril if anyone died while the excommunication lasted. It lasted a year. It was eventually lifted only on condition that the townspeople performed an act of penance every year for ever, when the Mayor, the bailiffs and sixty of the inhabitants must pay for a Mass to be said in the University Church for the souls of those who had been killed in the riot, and attend it themselves, and each put a penny into the offertory.

These draconian punishments for the town would have done little for mutual goodwill, for the University 'gangs' had been pardoned and no one could call the settlement even-handed. But they show at the outset of our story that Wyclif was not only arriving in a university town which was far from the lethargy Foxe describes, but also in a university which stood high in the royal and ecclesiastical order of priorities, and was important enough to Church and state to be able to expect active protection when it needed it. The University was useful in the wider world. It educated those who would become parish priests. It provided a higher education for those who might become bishops and senior civil servants and provided a convenient pool of names for patrons to draw from in making such appointments. It trained lawyers, who could be helpful to a king when he needed a treaty drafted or a marriage contract written so that it constituted an advantageous property deal, or someone to send on a mission to the papal Court. Its masters provided a pool of expertise for the king or the Church to draw on in a high-level political argument.[47] From the very beginning academic experts were drawn in by the state when it had a political difference of opinion to settle and a battle to win. The story of Wyclif is the story of a key stage of the development of this complex dual life in Oxford, its corporate confidence and independence and its ability to contain within it able and articulate individuals who would take their disputes outside and rouse national and international concern and provoke attempts to interfere. Wyclif made a difference here.

By Wyclif's time a good deal had been done, at least in theory, to regularize what had begun, if not as a free-for-all, certainly as a 'free market' contest for advantage between students and townspeople. For resent them though they might, the townspeople were well aware that the students were a useful source of income. They needed lodgings and food and taverns and books, they needed to be able to arrange loans, and there was a profit to be made from all these things. There was a general sense that poor students deserved support. After a riot or dispute was settled, if it was found that the town had been at fault, the townspeople might be expected to make some contribution by way of alms to assist poor scholars. In 1240 the Bishop of Lincoln was trying to make provision for money deposited by the burgesses of Oxford in amendment of and satisfaction for a public affront against the scholars of the University of Oxford, to be used regularly for the relief of such students.[48]

And, although it is far from easy to guess at numbers, the early thirteenth-century academic community may have been almost as large as that of the townspeople. Those who wanted their readers to believe that things had declined sadly since their young day were given to declaring enormous figures for the numbers of students in the past and comparing them with the small current numbers at the University. Richard FitzRalph claimed in 1357 that there had once been as many as 30,000 students but, because the friars had put people off with their dubious methods of recruiting students as members of their religious orders, there were now only 6,000. Wyclif himself contributed to this habit of exaggeration in the 1370s, with a figure of 60,000 for the good old days and less than 3,000 in his own.

An outbreak of the Bubonic Plague (the 'Black Death') ran throughout England in 1348–49. In rural districts and places where the poor were huddled in close proximity the death rate seems to have reached 40 per cent. The upper classes and the professional classes died off at a rate nearer 25 per cent.[49] The impact of the Black Death in Oxford[50] may be traced in part by the list of deaths in office and the frequent need for replacements. In 1349 there were three mayors; three priests were lost at All Saints, two at St Ebbe's, one at St Giles, with the University Church of St Mary's also suffering the loss of clergy.[51] Undoubtedly a proportion of Oxford's lecturers as well as its students fell victim to the sudden and usually fatal fever.[52] But the lecturers were mostly young, at least those in the arts, and their required 'stint' was short; they could be relatively easily replaced by the next generation. It was in the countryside, in grammar schools, that serious gaps of educated manpower seem to have appeared after the Black Death, perhaps affecting the educational standards of university entrants of a subsequent generation.[53]

Wyclif himself was probably just passing from school to university when the plague struck and there is no way of knowing which stage he was at or how he and his family were affected by the disease. He arrived in an Oxford depleted of some students and some teachers but by no means diminished or seriously undermined as an academic institution by its losses.

Whatever allowance is made for the effect of the Black Death, it is only necessary to look at the map of medieval Oxford to see that none of this talk of huge numbers in 'earlier days' can have been true. Numbers like the ones which were looked back on with such nostalgia, if servants and ordinary townspeople were added, would take the population of Oxford above its modern level. Yet the town was so small that it was possible to walk across it in a few minutes. Even colleges which are now thought of as lying in the heart of Oxford, such as St John's College and Magdalen College, lie outside the medieval city walls. The real figures, and they were large enough to make the academics and their servants and the associated trades swell the town to an uncomfortable degree, were probably a few thousand at most and frequently fewer. Better ways of counting involve looking at the number who graduated or at the number and size of the known halls and lodgings. Since each student spent many more than the modern three years at the University, especially those like Wyclif who went on being students well into middle age so that they could graduate in Theology or Law or Medicine, the numbers in each 'year' would be small enough for it to be likely that everyone knew everyone else.

The students and lecturers led the life of a community within a community. They were highly visible only when they became a provocation, but perhaps always an irritant and something of a challenge. Alongside them, not of their number but indispensable to the functioning of the University, were stationers and bookbinders and caterers and launderers and, for the richer students, personal servants, in that uneasy economic interdependency which was always ready to erupt into trouble.[54]

v. The religious orders in Oxford

A Monk there was, a fair for the maistrye,
An out-rydere that lovede venerye;
A manly man, to been an abbot able.[55]

A Frer there was, a wantown and a merye,
A limitour, a ful solempne man.
In ale the orders four is noon that can
So much of daliaunce and fair langage.[56]

Wyclif was unusual in that he seems to have had no vocation to join the orders of monks or friars who were sending considerable numbers of students to the University. He arrived as an independent student, and remained a 'secular'. But the friars in particular were to loom very large in his life and we need to set them in their context in Oxford at the outset.

A poem of the mid-fourteenth century begins with an encomium on the University, where all literature is studied and all intellectual problems solved. It gives light to the mind just as the sun lights up the world. But the University grows lax and does not correct its children. Monks gad about and some scholars preach heresy and win others to follow them.[57] The religious orders stirred unease. They played a part in the teaching and even the governance of the University and yet were never fully assimilated into its structures. Indeed, they could be a source of strife. A request from the University to the Bishop of Winchester in 1366 for help against the 'unheard-of' threatening behaviour of the friars has a distinct edge to it.[58] In some respects they appeared rather in the light of the scientists, the 'Adullamites', of Francis Cornford's satire of academic life at the very beginning of the twentieth century, the *Microcosmographia Academica*:

> 'The Adullamites are dangerous, because they know what they want; and that is, all the money there is going... They say to one another, 'If you scratch my back, I will scratch yours; and if you won't, I will scratch your face.' [59]

Many of Wyclif's contemporaries, the young members of the religious orders, were sent to Oxford with the built-in system of support and the guarantee of somewhere to live which the religious orders could provide. A number of the 'halls' where students lived in Wyclif's Oxford were run by religious communities. The religious orders made their presence felt by acquiring and setting themselves up in properties all over the town.

As well as sending their own young members to Oxford,[60] the religious orders were active in recruiting from the students in Oxford. The friars in particular were so keen to recruit in the universities that their efforts caused controversy and hostility, and Wyclif must almost certainly have resisted enticements to join them. Why he did so when he was still young and had not conceived the hearty dislike of his later years remains a puzzle.

The religious orders had been founded to provide a way of life in which members could achieve holiness by self-denial and obedience. But their reputation was mixed. Chaucer, Wyclif's contemporary, had a shrewd idea what would strike a chord with his readers and he pulls no punches in *The Canterbury Tales*. He mocks both monks and friars for their unchastity and worldliness. He adds his Pardoner to the list of dubious friar confessors in medieval literature – which includes Sir Penetrans Domos[61] (Enter-Houses) in Piers Plowman and Faus Semblant (False Seeming) in the *Roman de la Rose*.[62] The 'Penetrators of Houses' were a recognized 'type'.[63] Anti-establishment dissidents had been asking awkward questions for a century or two when they saw bishops riding about on fancy horses and wearing expensive clothes. It is true that the Benedictine vow of poverty was personal, not communal, and communities of Benedictine monks depended to some degree on gifts of land and property to provide them with means of support. But the incompatibility of the self-indulgence and conspicuous consumption which went on in reality with the simplicity and poverty of life – the 'apostolic life' which, critics cried, surely members of the religious orders should be living if anyone should – prompted criticisms of the 'hypocrisy' of much religious life.

The Benedictines, known as the Black Monks because of the colour of their habits, were supposed to be contemplatives, who followed the Rule which had been drawn up by Benedict of Nursia in the sixth century. His monks were to live in poverty, chastity and obedience to the Abbot. They were to remain in the house where they took their vows. They were to spend their lives in prayer, reading and manual labour. It was a life which was open to abuses and subject to a repeating cycle of reform and subsequent falling away from the ideal again and again in the history of the Benedictines throughout the Middle Ages.

'Visitation articles' for English Benedictines survive from the mid-1360s, which give a fair idea where there was likely to be laxity. When they were 'inspected' the monks in a given community were expected to be able to show that they were all in chapel for the series of 'Hours' or appointed times of worship during the day, and also for Mass; that they all made the required weekly confession of their sins; that their chapel was duly appointed and properly furnished; that, if they had a duty to say special Masses or prayers for the souls of their founders or other benefactors, they did so regularly and properly; that they lived 'according to the main points of the Rule, that is, obeying their superiors in all things lawful and honest, practising continence and denying themselves property'; and that there was no one among them who is a known criminal or a disturber of the peace of the community.[64] There were five houses of Benedictine monks near Oxford,[65] at Abingdon and Eynsham and Godstow, Littlemore and Studley, the last three being houses of nuns, but major property-owners in Oxford like the communities of monks. The Benedictines opened houses of study not only in Oxford, but in Gloucester College in 1283, Durham College in 1286 and Canterbury College in 1361.

The Cistercians, a new order which had had its heyday in the twelfth century, also followed the Benedictine Rule, but with the difference that they sought to avoid the danger of decadence the Benedictines had fallen into, by building their houses in remote places. They did not live where farmland was rich and productive and tried to avoid material prosperity with its seductive inherent dangers to the simplicity of their way of life. The Cistercians were represented among the religious houses of Oxford from 1282, when they opened a school or *studium* for their own monks.[66]

An example of a Benedictine monk–student who was nearly Wyclif's contemporary is the preacher Thomas Brinton. He had become a monk in Norwich, at the Cathedral Priory, in a community which was enthusiastic about education, and regularly sent young monks to university, especially in the years just after the Black Death. Adam Easton, the bibliophile who was probably responsible for reporting Wyclif to Rome for heresy, is another Benedictine monk who appears in Wyclif's story.[67] Brinton and Easton would have learned their Latin and got their basic education in the school there. There was also an exceptionally good library in the monastery, both in its size and in its diversity, no doubt whetting Easton's lifetime appetite for the acquisition of books.[68] Brinton says he went to Cambridge as well as to Oxford,[69] but he is known to have studied in Oxford in the 1360s when Adam Easton was there. These two are examples of the student 'religious', who did not have to find lodgings. They could be accommodated in Gloucester College, which was the main Benedictine house in Oxford, now Worcester College.[70] Easton's patron Langham opposed Wyclif, as we shall see, during the Canterbury Hall affair.

Another twelfth-century development was the founding of new orders of 'regular canons', that is, canons living under a Rule. There had long been canonries attached to cathedrals, and since the time of Charlemagne cathedrals had been required to maintain schools and ensure that their canons had a reasonable standard of education. Canons were priests, and could therefore discharge parish duties if needed. Twelfth-century orders such as the Victorines in Paris and the Premonstratensians tended to follow the Rule which was believed to have been devised by Augustine of Hippo.[71] There were Augustinian canons in Oxford in Wyclif's time. The House of Augustinian Canons at Osney had begun in 1129 as a Priory but by 1154 it had become successful enough to be an Abbey. During the thirteenth century it steadily added to its wealth and influence, acquiring properties in Oxford and receiving gifts and endowments, until that kind of thing was stopped by the Statute of Mortmain in 1279, which prevented the conveyancing of real property to religious houses. By then the Abbey owned a tenth of Oxford and was gathering in the rents from more Halls and Schools than any other landlord. A second Augustinian House, the Priory of St Frideswide, founded in 1122, was also successful in this kind of profiteering, but not on such a large scale.

The third broad category of 'religious' comprised the friars or mendicants. These new-style religious orders had come into being at the beginning of the thirteenth century, inspired by Francis of Assisi, who founded the Friars Minor or Franciscans, and Dominic, who founded the order which came to be known as the Dominicans or Friars Preacher. Led by Francis, the Franciscans set out to rediscover the apostolic life, the life to which Jesus had sent out his disciples, of wandering ('mendicancy') in poverty, preaching the Gospel. Dominic's vision was rather different. He identified for his Order of Preachers a specific task of bringing back to the fold the heretical lost sheep of northern Spain and southern France.

Friars differed from monks in that they were not expected to remain within the houses where they were 'professed' (took their oath as religious), but on the contrary, considered it their calling to go about and preach. They settled in towns, in contrast to the rural preferences of the Benedictines and the preference for remote rural places of the Cistercians. Preaching required education, and from the first these new orders, particularly the Dominicans, placed a heavy emphasis on the intellectual training of those who joined them.

The two new orders of Friars, the Dominicans and Franciscans, came to Oxford at almost the same time, the Friars Preacher in 1221 and the Friars Minor in 1224. They did not open schools at once. In 1229–30 there was a general arrival of scholars from their respective houses in Paris.[72] Their numbers grew so that both orders had to move from their original sites. The Dominicans did so in 1236, acquiring additional land until by 1358 they had fifteen acres. The Franciscans extended their lands across the city wall and took over the lands briefly occupied by the ephemeral order of the Friars of the Sack (1261–62), who were suppressed by the Council of Lyons in 1274, until they had acquired up to eight acres.

The Augustinian Friars followed the Rule of Augustine but their origin, like that of the Carmelites, lay in the hermit life. A series of papal directives brought orders of hermits under this Rule in the thirteen century until in 1244 Innocent IV brought the Tuscan hermits to follow it. These various congregations were united in 1256 by Pope Alexander IV. The 'Austin' Friars came to Oxford in 1266–67, and they too set about acquiring land and extending their domain until they had about six acres in 1335.[73]

The Carmelites were also eventually accepted as belonging to the category of 'friars', but they first came into being in the late twelfth century as the order of the brothers of Our Lady of Mount Carmel, and their original inspiration was eremitical and they lived in the deserts of the Middle East. In 1247 the Pope granted approval for them to live in towns and cities and to preach, and also for them to live in communities and eat together. In 1256 the Carmelites arrived in Oxford and in 1317 they acquired the Palace of Beaumont because King Edward II had vowed that if he escaped after the battle of Bannockburn he would build a priory for the Carmelites. They sold their first site to the Benedictines in 1320–21 and moved. But they went on acquiring land and property.[74]

There were heated disputes among these newcomer religious orders and with the ones established in Oxford longer,[75] including a quarrel between the Austin Friars and Merton College lasting from 1335[76] and which Wyclif must have been aware of when he became a Fellow of Merton in the mid-1350s.

There was criticism of the conspicuously large buildings of the Friars.[77] There was a story of the ghostly appearance of a dead friar warning the Franciscans that they stood at risk of severe punishment, if not damnation, for their excesses in building.[78] But much more troublesome to the University was the intrusion of the friars and their recruits into the life of the scholars.

The friars as educators

Under their Rule, every priory of Dominicans was a school and each of them had to have a Doctor of Theology in residence. By contrast, Francis had at first been inclined against encouraging his friars to study, and he had still been against it in the final version of his Rule. However, rivalry between the Dominicans and Franciscans became intense at an early stage and by 1254 the Franciscans too had adopted the practice of insisting that each house of the order had a resident Doctor of Theology. In both orders, the role of this *lector* was to teach Theology to the members.

Recognition needed to go both ways when the friars set up schools in their Oxford houses. The friars had decided that a degree was worth having. Both Franciscans and Dominicans recruited actively in Oxford, to the point where parents became reluctant to allow their sons to go there in case they were tempted into one of these orders. In 1358 the University made a statute forbidding either order of friars to receive any student under eighteen or even to try to recruit such a student.[79]

For its part, the University created requirements to ensure that the Regent Masters[80] had at least a toehold in the religious orders. In Oxford the Franciscans had to wait for a Regent Master, Robert Bacon, to become a member of their order before they were regarded as members of the University.[81] Robert Grosseteste was the first such *lector* for the Franciscans.[82] He was himself a pioneering scholar, studying Greek, and also subjects in the area of the modern sciences, and in due course he became Oxford's Chancellor and then Bishop of Lincoln. Once he was Bishop he was influential in encouraging the parishes in his charge to accept friars of both the main orders as preachers and confessors. His idea seems to have been that in that way the people would receive sound and wholesome teaching from well-educated priests.

A need for 'quality assurance' was noted from an early stage in Oxford, with particular reference to the doings of the friars. For the friars were wont to try to obtain concessions for the young friars, so that they need not complete the full course in the Arts before going on to study the theology they needed to equip themselves as preachers. There was a further reason for the University to look askance at all this capturing of students for the increasingly full houses of the friars in the city. As Roger Bacon, a Franciscan and therefore an insider, seems to have complained in 1271 in his *Compendium Studii*:

> 'There have arisen some in the Universities who have made themselves doctors and masters of theology and philosophy, though they have never learned anything of real value. They are boys inexperienced in themselves, in the world, in the learned languages, Greek and Hebrew; ... they are ignorant of all parts and sciences of mundane philosophy, when they venture on the study of theology... . They are the boys of the two student orders, like Albert and Thomas and others, who enter the orders when they are twenty years old or less... many thousands enter who cannot read the Psalter or Donatus, and immediately after making their professions, they are set to study theology.'[83]

There was plenty of 'scandal' in Oxford about the way the friars allegedly exploited young persons coming to join them, and used their influence to get special arrangements made in their favour. There was the accusation in the mid-fourteenth century that Friar Richard Lyminster was allowed to incept (as a master) in Theology only because he had letters from a royal patron, and so ignorant was he that this was in effect to be an honorary inception only. His predecessor was to continue to do the actual lecturing. Friar Giuliortus de Limosano claimed to be secretary to the King of Sicily and 'extorted' a similar 'qualification' from the University by means of letters from the King.[84] Whether such things regularly happened is hard to say, but Wyclif was ready enough to shout that Masters' caps were to be had at the request of lords.[85]

It is a further question whether the 'special arrangements' were compromising academic standards in the University even when they 'fast-tracked' the intellectually genuinely well-equipped. The friars did have schools for young boys where a basic grounding was provided, but certainly in the early years of the two main orders their attraction for the most able young men was strong. This conflict about the maintenance of standards and the making of concessions for members of the religious orders rose to a climax in connection with the Theology course, as we shall see later.

Yet, manifestly, academic standards were not low among the friars. They were attracting some of the most able recruits, their products included the leading intellects of the time. In the generation or so before Wyclif there were probably seventy or eighty living in the Oxford Franciscan house.[86] Their training was in reality lengthy and rigorous and the young men sent to study at Oxford by their home communities could be expected to be well grounded in the arts. At Oxford they spent six years, not the four expected of the secular students, hearing lectures on the Bible. These were called 'cursory' lectures not because they were shallow or brief, but because they went through the Bible painstakingly in sequence and thus formed a 'course'. Nevertheless, the University was keen to pin things down. No member of a religious order who had not been a Regent Master in Arts was allowed to lecture on the *Sentences* until he had been an opponent for a year in public disputations, and not against any member of his own order, so that there could be no collaborative 'fixing'.[87] The records do not seem to suggest that the requirements of two-year gaps were taken very seriously. Until the registers begin about 1450 it is hard to judge how closely the statutes were obeyed; but, once there is a record, it shows that assertions of numbers of years of preceding study by the same individual could be highly variable. [88]

It may be that this internal warfare in Oxford first roused in Wyclif the negative feelings about the friars which became such a dominant theme in his last works. Richard FitzRalph was incensed by the invasion of parish ministry by the friars. At some point Wyclif took a settled dislike to the religious orders, a negative stance which grew stronger in the course of time and eventually became almost an obsession. The decision not to become a friar while he was a student progressed in the course of a few years to the decision to rail against them as a polemicist.

vi. The practicalities of student life

Finding somewhere to live

> '[Jago] The first undergraduates lived in the town and looked after themselves and did what they chose. One can picture them reeling hilariously through the streets, full of the wild hopes of youth. And so the boarding-houses appeared, to keep the young men out of mischief, and this college of ours was founded, towards the end of the fourteenth century, by taking over a simple rooming-house. It gives one a glow to think that if a fourteenth-century member of the College were to be dropped in our first court today, he would be instantaneously at home.'
>
> '[Sir Horace] You're a romantic, Dr Jago. You love this place.'[89]

We have not yet considered where Wyclif would live, as a new student who was apparently determined not to become a monk or a friar. He could not have become a member of a college, as a student at Oxford would have to do today. The first colleges were usually restricted to graduates. There may well have been no one to make sure he had a bed to sleep in and adequate food. Wyclif arrived at a time in the evolution of Oxford's practical arrangements when students lived about the town, wherever they could get lodgings, and the townspeople were free to make what profit they could out of them. In the century before Wyclif's arrival there had already been some tightening up of the rules. One particularly dramatic episode in 1208, when townspeople killed some of the scholars, had led to the mass exodus which created what has become the modern University of Cambridge. Some scholars went to Reading. They left, possibly on the orders of their new head, the Chancellor, to make a point. Oxford's townspeople were to learn that its prosperity would shrink if the University went elsewhere, as it showed it could easily do when it simply packed its bags and left. The eventual submission of the town to the papal legate led to a legatine ordinance that for the next ten years, from 1214, half of the rents from lodgings let to students were to go to the scholars and that academics and burgesses (or townspeople) were to be jointly responsible for the fixing of appropriate rents. This by no means settled the matter, but control of the excessively 'free' market in student rooms was gradually achieved and there was the beginning of supervision of the lodgings 'market'.

Wyclif's arrival as a student had coincided with several significant developments in the constitution of the University, both in the way it saw itself and in the practical arrangements it made for supervising its students and making it less likely that they would get themselves and the University into trouble. The trend was clear and was about to become fixed. For in the early fifteenth century, a generation or so after Wyclif, it was decided to require the students to live in approved academic halls with a Regent Master or other approved principal in charge. The statutes of the University made under Henry V in 1421 decreed that all scholars and their servants were to be under the authority of principals, who were to be prudent men[90] and formally approved by the Chancellor and Regents.[91]

The process of setting out rules for the conduct of halls had, however, been experimental at first. Before 1313 the University had established rules for Principals of halls, imposing a duty on them to supervise students and ensure that their behaviour remained within reasonable bounds.[92] The Principals at this stage were not necessarily senior figures, nor were they all even Regent Masters. Bachelors could set themselves up as Principals, with permission, or even manciples, the caterers who dealt with the practical arrangements for feeding the resident scholars; so could Non-Regent Masters, who had already taken the degree of Master of Arts but who were not lecturing in the arts because they were continuing their studies in one of the 'higher degree' subjects.[93]

Halls of the kind found in Wyclif's Oxford, and even the more closely regulated ones of the fifteenth century, might be short-lived projects. There was a community of sorts, although not one possessing property. Halls needed a sufficiently large number of students to apply to live in them and they needed to be able to find someone who could be approved to act as Principal. Students voted with their feet in Wyclif's day, moving from one hall to another if they did not like the conditions of residence imposed upon them, and this may have encouraged Principals to hold the reins very loosely. There was natural resentment if a Principal was too relaxed in allowing poor scholars to get away with not paying their dues, when others were paying regularly. By 1412 there had been a tightening up in this respect, too. The University insisted from that date that if a scholar was expelled from a hall he was not allowed to move into another one until the Chancellor or the University had looked into the reason for his expulsion and had guarantees of future good behaviour.

Halls may have specialized quite early on in the types of student they took in. By the mid-fifteenth century, some would cater for students in the Arts, others for students in Law. A list was drawn up by Rous, Chaplain of Warwick, in which he counted five halls for young boys studying Grammar, that is learning sufficient Latin to enable them to begin their Arts studies. He says there were twenty-one halls for students of the Arts when he counted and thirty-three for students of Law.[94] The number of lawyers is striking, for these were postgraduate students who had to have means to support themselves through a lengthy course. But it is also likely that there were more halls for them because, in the nature of things, they would not accept such crowded conditions and expected better food and service than their juniors.[95]

In Wyclif's time it was not yet a requirement that scholars should live in approved communities, and many poor scholars could not afford to live in a hall. We do not know what Wyclif himself did. Of Wyclif's early experience of finding a lodging nothing is known, but we shall come a little later to his time at various colleges and what happened to him there once he had his first degree.

Teaching arrangements and pastoral care

The University had taken to itself the authority and the mechanisms of control to ensure that an approved syllabus was properly and comprehensively taught and examinations conducted to an appropriate standard. This was one of the practices which turned the schools of the twelfth-century town from a casual meeting-place for wandering teachers and their shifting crowd of students into a 'university' with a capacity to last from generation to generation. The purpose of study for the paying student could have remained informal. He could have gone on as many did in the twelfth century to set up as a Master in his own right when he thought he was ready, with student opinion the only test of whether he could make a living at it. But even in the twelfth century there was a burgeoning need for a 'recognized qualification' as a means of entry to a 'career', in the ecclesiastical or state 'civil service'.

And there was the question of the 'licence to teach'. An episcopal licence was required for preaching in any diocese and in the young University of Paris there was internal warfare between the gild of Masters and the Chancellor about the right to grant a licence.[96] Oxford Masters too wanted to control examinations, decide who passed and failed and who should be allowed to lecture as a qualified person. A lecturer, like a preacher, was a potential stumbling block to the faithful and it was important to the defence of the faith that those who were allowed to address people in large numbers and influence their thinking should be people the Bishop could trust not to be talking heretically. That in its turn raised the question of academic autonomy, for this was also a matter on which the Masters wanted to have the last word.

All this was important in determining what Wyclif had to learn and how he was to demonstrate in the end that he had learned it sufficiently well to get an Oxford degree. It appears that the requirements evolved, rather than being laid down formally from the first, because there are references to 'custom', 'approved customs' and the way the University 'usually' does things (or has done them 'of old'). The first detailed information about the requirements survives from a generation or two after Wyclif, in the first register of the University of 1448–63,[97] but it almost certainly reflects quite closely the requirements he had to meet. A statute of 1431 insists that no one was to be a Master in any Faculty until he had demonstrated over a period of time that he had studied the subject and was competent. In the case of the Faculty of Arts this meant that he must study all seven liberal arts and three philosophical subjects for eight years (and each term must include at least thirty days of lectures).[98]

'The Chancellor requires that every scholar has his own Master from among the Regents, in whose register the student's name shall appear. Each registered student must hear a daily lecture from his Master.[99] Unless he is registered, no student shall enjoy the privileges of the University.'[100]

This was the rule from before 1231. So Wyclif had to get himself put on the register of a Regent Master and attend his lectures regularly. There would be a check to ensure that he had done so. Another thirteenth-century statute required the Master to read out the names of the students on his personal register at the beginning of every term.[101]

Under the supervision of these lecturers taught the probationers, the Bachelors, discharging the periods of lecturing they were required to carry out before they could graduate as Masters. New graduates were required to lecture for a period after they became Masters, and some carried on much longer than the required minimum, as Wyclif seems to have done. These Regent Masters retained the prerogative of giving official academic instruction on behalf of the University. There was no guarantee that they did it well, or that a poor performance would damage their future career prospects. In the twelfth century, the controversial academic Gilbert became Bishop of Poitiers despite his reputation for giving lectures which were more obscure than the texts they were intended to clarify.[102]

Numbers in Wyclif's day were probably small enough to ensure that a student did not have a sense of being a blank face in a crowd. Nevertheless, a need was obviously felt for some form of pastoral support. A patron or a religious house could arrange for tutorial support for one or more students. For instance, a monk–scholar of a college could be hired to ensure that someone's protégés were looked after and financial and disciplinary aspects of their lives attended to.[103] Individual tuition to supplement 'lectures' began to be called for almost at the outset of Oxford's becoming a recognized *studium generale*. This kind of teacher was provided on a more informal basis by the college or hall. Or it could involve arrangements made or paid for directly by a student's patron and financial supporter. In 1220 the Bishop of Chichester was providing maintenance for at least one student on the Arts course and ensured that he had a tutor in the person of a Canon of St Frideswide's known as Elias.[104]

During Wyclif's century the proliferating halls probably became places where teaching could take place, as well as providing living quarters. Teaching within halls is likely to have been restricted to those living in them, in contrast to the public lecturing which took place in the 'schools', which were open to students from any hall. Each teaching Master had to rent or borrow rooms to lecture in. This required delicate negotiation with the town. One of the University's earliest statutes[105] tried to ensure that any such room, once it had been used for the purpose of teaching, could be reclaimed for a similar academic use in the future. This had the natural consequence of making landlords reluctant to let rooms for teaching purposes at all. One way of getting round this was to grant a special licence allowing someone to teach in his own living quarters without the 'change of use' making that henceforth an official lecture-room.[106]

What it cost to be a student

If the student who arrived to study at Oxford did not have to 'get a place', he did not remain so free for long. (It was always a he. Girls did not go to university.) He had to pay his way. The University was not insensitive to the problems faced by poor students and the need for Masters to make allowances. The *De disciplina scolarium*, a very popular thirteenth-century work which pretended to be by Boethius, the sixth-century author of the *Consolation of Philosophy*, contains a section on the effects of poverty on a student's ability to study to the best effect.[107] But we do not know where Wyclif got the money he needed.

The Master on whose register he was required to be put would have expected a fee. There were no overall tuition fees, but a good many particular fees had to be found. The student had to pay for the compulsory lectures. The fee in 1333 was 12d a year for lectures in Logic, which was one of the first basic subjects everyone had to study.[108] For lectures on the slightly more advanced *libri naturales*, or scientific books of Aristotle, the charge was 18d for each year. Those who went on to study Canon Law for a higher degree each paid the Doctor whose lectures he heard in 1350 at least 40d. The student had to be able to find fees at this rate for many years, for these were not three-year degree courses. They lasted considerably longer.

Once the course had been completed and the examination passed, a fee had to be paid to graduate. These fees could be varied, at the instigation of an influential parent or a religious order; or by the permission of the University. This was not necessarily to ensure that poor students paid less. There was a good deal of effort to ensure that members of the religious orders were dispensed from some of the requirements for completion of the degree, which could save them money as well as time. In the mid-fifteenth-century those taking degrees are recorded as paying anything from 4d to 16d. Buying a 'grace',[109] to make a dispensation to allow the student to be let off some of the requirements, could, however, be a lot more expensive than simply taking the examination and then paying the graduation fee. Then there were 'gratuities' expected by the proctors, the bedels and other officers of the University – very probably personal tips rather than fees formally due to the University.[110] The University was quite capable of deliberately exploiting its right to charge fees, when it came to getting the most it could from members of the religious orders. There was a dispute in 1428 because Oxford was charging Benedictine monks 6s 8d as the regular fee to hear the lectures of their Regent Master in Arts. But the religious orders were wealthy.

The student also had to be able to support himself while he studied. Maintenance costs had to be found, as well as tuition fees. The expenses of a young student who was still an undergraduate and studying for his first degree in Arts would be less than those of a graduate student working towards a higher degree, particularly in the case of lawyers, who were older, whose servants expected to be better paid for the provision of meals, and who had to have their own copies of the main textbooks. This last was an enormous potential expense. A copy of the *Code* of Justinian or the *Digest* might be 6s 8d, a figure which should be compared with a whole year's lecturing fee for Logic of 12d a year. It is also one-fortieth of the 'living' of the priest whom Wyclif's family could appoint.

It is possible to get some idea of the total annual expenditure of a student who was careful and not extravagant. In the early fifteenth century, lodgings and lecture fees and money for books and the odd gratuity could probably have been kept under 50s. But the calculation on which that figure is based probably omits the cost of University lectures because it comes from the records of a hall.[111] About Wyclif's time the expenses of the kinsfolk of the founder of Merton College, where Wyclif became a Fellow once he had completed his first degree, have been costed at about £2 5s 6d.[112]

Chapter 2

A degree in the liberal arts

i. First principles

We can only guess at the education Wyclif already had when he arrived in Oxford. Information about local schooling in England in the middle of the fourteenth century is patchy.[1] There were no entrance requirements for the University, and no fixed age to begin, although a statute of the University before 1350 mentions the possibility of a query arising about someone's age, in which case it would have to be referred to the Congregation of the Masters.[2] Boys could arrive in their early teens, perhaps at twelve (although such extremely youthful beginnings began to be discouraged) or at fourteen, not at the modern age of eighteen.

In some ways going to Oxford was like going to a secondary school, at least in the first years. It was usual to spend up to seven years of adolescence on the first course in the 'Arts' which led to the Bachelor's degree, so a graduate would complete his degree at about twenty-one, the usual modern age. (The Latin for 'degree' is *gradus*, 'step' or 'stage'.) Everyone began in the same place with the basic course in the Arts. In Wyclif's Oxford, there was no division between 'Arts' and 'Sciences', for all subjects at the first level, including one called 'Physics', were studied in the Arts course. Some climbed up the 'steps' to the higher degrees, choosing among the approved 'higher degree' subjects of Theology, Law and Medicine.

'Arts' is now sometimes called 'Humanities'. It broadly excludes subjects such as Physics and Chemistry, which are now classified as 'Sciences'. It includes subjects which reflect the intellectual and social fashions of the modern world such as 'Media Studies', as well as a traditional list of subjects such as English Literature and History, which are in fact comparatively recent, having been accepted as appropriate subjects for university study only in the nineteenth century.

Most students in modern England work for a BA or a BSc degree (Bachelor of Arts or a Bachelor of Science), choosing a particular subject or combination of subjects. In the USA a student will normally 'major' in a particular field or fields. Wyclif's Arts degree did not allow him this kind of choice – or any choice at all. He had to study the whole syllabus of 'the Arts' in order to get a BA degree and later an MA (Master of Arts). Wyclif could not choose his subject of study as a beginner and specialize in any way. The *artes* were divided into *the trivium* or 'three ways' (Grammar, Logic and Rhetoric) and the *quadrivium*, or 'four ways' (Arithmetic, Music, Geometry and Astronomy). The word *quadrivium* had been coined by Boethius in the sixth century to provide a collective noun for the 'mathematical' subjects which would make a convenient pair for the word *trivium*. By Wyclif's time, as we shall see, some philosophical topics had been added to an expanded syllabus.

The modern question which has to be answered before a degree course can be set up is whether the area of knowledge to be studied contains enough substance and is of sufficient difficulty for it to be appropriate for a university to grant degrees in it without compromising its intellectual integrity. The usual assumption is that there ought to be some substantial theoretical element. For example, a contemporary degree in 'Surf Studies' might need to feature Oceanography and the Economics of Tourism to make it respectable.

C.P. Snow's 'two cultures' of the 1950s identified a modern divide.[3] From a medieval point of view there was no reason for the separation of what we should now call Arts and Sciences for first-degree study, not least because there was no difference in the resources required. There was no bench-based laboratory work, no experimental science in the syllabus; everything was studied as theory by means of lectures and exercises in which the students learned to argue for and against various opinions.

The medieval idea of a suitable subject was different. The subjects selected for study as 'Arts' subjects were on a rather longer list which had been prescribed in ancient Rome by Varro, refined for Christian study by Boethius and Cassiodorus in the sixth century and then by Isidore of Seville in the seventh century, and now reduced to the 'seven Liberal Arts' with the addition of some Philosophy. The student was expected to cover them all, though not in equal detail, for some had been real growth areas in the Middle Ages and some had not.

So fundamental were these subjects imagined to be that Wyclif even asks whether they were studied in the Garden of Eden. His idea is that before they fell into sin, Adam and Eve had no need of such studies, nor of the mechanical arts which accompanied them in the classical portfolio of subjects. Adam was 'a great philosopher without art'. He did not need to study Hebrew grammar when he was called upon to name the animals.[4] The words came to him naturally. In Eden there was no need to learn Mathematics, for example, so as to study the stars and foretell when pestilences would come; nor was there any need for human laws, which curb bad behaviour, for there was no bad behaviour.[5] This little excursion of Wyclif's is a useful reminder that he, like his contemporaries, took the story of the creation in Genesis to be straightforward history.

Had he known more classical history, he would have been more aware that the Arts were described by the Romans as 'liberal' (*liberales*) because they were thought of as fit subjects for the study of free men (*liberi*), not slaves. But they maintained their position as requirements for centuries, since nothing better emerged to replace them. In the Middle Ages they were on the list because they were regarded as fundamental disciplines for all scholars, the starting point of all serious intellectual endeavour. At the end of the sixth century Gregory the Great had stressed their value as helps to the more subtle understanding of Scripture.[6] The Benedictine Rupert of Deutz at the beginning of the twelfth century commented that no one could truly (*veraciter*) be a physician (*medicus*) 'unless he was skilled in all the liberal arts'.[7]

The Arts were also considered fundamental because they were thought of as distinct 'disciplines', irreducible subdivisions of knowledge. Each was believed to have its own distinctive truths which were its special first principles. This idea became increasingly important in the later Middle Ages under the influence of Aristotle's *Posterior Analytics*.

Wyclif's Oxford certainly thought it was equipping its students of the Arts with all-purpose intellectual tools. Robert Kilwardby, future Archbishop of Canterbury, was Provincial (that is, regional head) of the English Dominican friars from 1261. He had strong ideas on the design of courses and what they should contain. Before he joined the friars, Kilwardby himself completed the Arts course at the University of Paris and gave lectures there in the 1230s and 1240s; then he arrived in Oxford, where as a new recruit to the Dominicans, he began to study Theology. He wrote an introduction to help the student understand the origins of the branches of knowledge and the way they are related to one another. It gives a helpful picture of the way Wyclif's teachers understood what they were doing and why. Kilwardby discusses the 'science of language'.[8] He explains that the subject matter of study in the Arts and the relevant skills the Arts teach antedate the framing of the 'disciplines' or formal areas of study with which students are now expected to be familiar. Before there was Arithmetic people counted things and before there was Music they sang.

Before there was Geometry they measured fields and before there was Astronomy they told the time by the movement of the stars. The drawback to trying to use such skills and such knowledge without a proper system of instruction is that it is inefficient and may even corrupt the subject matter; moreover, it allows for disagreements about the way things should be understood.

Of all the Arts the most important in keeping the others in order is the art of reasoning (*ars ratiocinandi*) known as Logic or Dialectic (*logica* and *dialectica* can be used more or less interchangeably). From human speech was devised the 'part of philosophy' which 'teaches the artistry of' (*docet artificialiter*) speaking, writing and reasoning. This must be fundamental, he thinks, because all teaching and learning about language is done with or in language. 'It is the same with logic.' Logic is a means of judging the probability of the assertions made in other subjects, such as Physics or Ethics. It will be more than apparent by now that this was no light syllabus for the average boy, and that it was heavy with abstractions and intellectual difficulties.

ii. Grammar

No one in fourteenth-century Europe spoke Latin as a native language. Nevertheless, the academic community throughout Europe treated it as their common language. It remained vividly alive, growing and developing far beyond its classical patterns and vocabulary, becoming an increasingly exact vehicle for philosophical and theological discourse, until with the sixteenth century and the ambitious attempt to revive it in its classical forms the development toppled over into excess. Erasmus and others achieved for Latin the status of a dead language at last, a thousand years after the fall of the Roman Empire which had given it birth.

The student of Wyclif's generation had to learn the Latin language at least well enough to be able to use it to hear lectures and to speak it to fellow-students. The method of instruction was evidently effective, since the whole 'clerical' class became capable of reading and writing and doing all their business in Latin. Not everyone became a good stylist or even capable of expressing himself with exactness and lucidity. Wyclif himself wrote a convoluted Latin. He anglicizes, and invents words and phrases, and it is sometimes hard to be sure that he is really thinking in Latin at all, but despite his awkwardness he automatically employs it as his working language.[9]

In the absence of any form of school-leaving or qualifying examination or any test to be passed on entry, some students must have arrived in need of remedial teaching in Latin before they could follow the lectures. We have no way of knowing whether Wyclif was one of these. The University could not ignore its responsibilities. The early statutes suggest that some lecturers specialized in the basics of Grammar. Before 1350 the statutes prescribe rules for those lecturing in Grammar at this level, possibly because this was the subject where it was most likely that rival teachers, coming from the lower schools which prepared future students by giving them a grounding in Latin, might try to obtrude themselves into the University's teaching without being full Regent Masters in Arts. There were no rules, it seems, to prevent anyone 'tutoring' privately and it would be natural enough for such teachers to try to offer 'university' lectures as well if they could get away with it.[10] It is provided (*provisum est*) that no one is to lecture on Grammar without the Chancellor's licence to do so. That licence will not be granted until the prospective lecturer has been examined in writing verse and letters and in his knowledge of the Latin authors and the parts of speech. He will then be expected to observe the statutes and customs of the University as laid down by its 'Lord' Chancellor, but it sounds as though this is a provision for a particular category of teacher whose members were not necessarily Masters of Arts; for, if they were, there would be no need for such special rules. They were, however, known as Regent Masters in Grammar. The first known example, William Forster, died in 1401 and another, Edward Roos, was alive at the beginning of the fifteenth century,[11] so these Masters were probably at least beginning to be visible during Wyclif's time in Oxford. If one of these comparative outsiders dies, the Masters are expected to attend his funeral.[12]

This suggests that other practical basic skills were normally taught under the heading of 'Grammar'. On this more 'literary' side of the laying of grammatical foundations the University regulations placed the art of writing letters (*ars dictaminis*). This has a claim to be a 'rhetorical' art'[13] rather than strictly a branch of Grammar, because it taught the letter-writer to imitate the structure of a classical speech. Manuals of instruction in this art had begun to appear at the end of the eleventh century to meet the growing need for a literate civil service in both state and Church, to whom a busy potentate could say, 'write a letter for me' and expect it to be done to a professional standard. By now it was an established 'business skill'.

A few of Wyclif's own letters survive, but they were mainly written in a desperate attempt to protect his position, as controversy put him on the defensive. They are stilted and platitudinous.[14] We do not see Wyclif as a letter-writer at leisure, a social being, corresponding with his friends on pleasure or business, outside that extreme and dangerous context in which he gradually found himself, and there is no evidence that he ever did so. Enthusiastic medieval letter-writers often collected their correspondence. When Wyclif set about reworking his writings towards the end of his life he might have been expected to do the same, but there is no hint of this.

The literary grounding in Grammar also included at least a smattering of the art of poetry. This was a second 'medieval rhetorical art', which had had its heyday in the twelfth century. There is no evidence that Wyclif was a poet, or even that he sometimes experimented with rhyme for fun, so we cannot judge how well he mastered this skill. His known later preference was for 'plain speaking on what was relevant'.[15]

Once the student could get along in Latin he was expected to turn to the real meat of the grammar part of the syllabus, the study of the deep structure of language in general, those features of speech which make it 'language'. The main textbook used for this purpose was by the late Roman grammarian Priscian.[16] It covered the 'parts of speech'. These are the same eight as in English grammar (which was modelled on Latin) except that, in Latin, nouns and adjectives are counted as the same part of speech and participles are regarded as a part of speech in their own right, not merely a subdivision of the class of 'verbs'. The Latin list consists of nouns, verbs, participles, pronouns, adverbs, prepositions, conjunctions, interjections. Students practised reading approved 'authors' such as Cicero and Virgil as examples while learning Latin and they would have been used to their Grammar Masters requiring them to parse what they were reading (that is, identify the part of speech of each word in sample passages). The practical usefulness of learning the parts of speech was that it enabled the reader of Latin as the 'foreign language' it was to everyone at the beginning to analyse what he read, and work out the meanings of sentences by applying grammatical principles.

Grammar had a theoretical, indeed a philosophical, aspect too. Parts of speech had to be put together not only so as to satisfy the structural rules of grammar but also so as to ensure that they made up propositions which could be used in arguments. That takes us into the study of Logic or Dialectic, which was the second of the Arts of the trivium, and by far the most exciting area of growth and development in the arts between the eleventh century and Wyclif's lifetime. The importance of these foundation studies in the formation of his lifetime's habits of thought cannot be overestimated.

iii. Logic

The student had to learn which parts of speech are indispensable in a sentence or proposition and were thought to be capable of standing alone; and which modify or qualify those essential elements but could be removed, while still leaving a complete sentence or proposition. Latin has no definite article, so the word *regina* means 'the-Queen'. 'The-Queen reigns' is a complete sentence, grammatically speaking. All it needs is the noun and the verb. It is also a proposition which could be put into a formal argument as it stands. Nouns and verbs were known as 'categorical' (*categoremata*) because they needed no assistance from other words to make complete sense in this way. 'The present Queen still reigns over us' has acquired a number of additional parts, an adjective, an adverb, a preposition, a pronoun, and so on, but they are not necessary to make the resulting sequence of words a sentence (or a proposition), though it may still be a sentence and a proposition if they are added. These other parts of speech, have to be associated with *categoremata*, that is, to be *syncategoremata* ('joined-with categories'), in order to convey meaning or to be properly understood. For example, if I say 'all elephants', you will know that I am referring to all members of the class of pachyderms. If I merely say 'all', your full understanding of what I am talking about will wait upon my telling you all of 'what' noun or name of a substance I am referring to. It is the same with 'both', 'neither', with conjunctions ('if', 'unless', 'and', 'or'), and with the other parts of speech which are not categorematic.[17] All this is the logician's concern. But the grammarian has a concern too. He is familiar with a rule that 'every' or 'all' must be used of at least three things if it is to be used correctly (grammatically) in a sentence or correctly (logically) in a proposition.[18] Students were expected to achieve a thorough grasp of such things as they moved from Grammar into the study of Logic. Logic had the kind of importance in the minds of educators which Mathematics now enjoys. Reasoning was the process by which problems were addressed and uncertainties and contradictions were resolved in all branches of medieval study. It was a 'basic' subject because without competence in Logic students could not reason without being in danger of falling into fallacies.

Wyclif could be critical of the seductiveness of the claim that logicians were possessed of tools with which they could do anything, intellectually speaking. He mocked 'disciples in logic' and discusses the pros and cons of taking the actual words literally.[19] He was also wrily aware that there were fashions in the study of Logic and what was up to the minute in Oxford at one time might be grossly out of date twenty years later.

> 'For, as is obvious in Oxford, a fashion is brought in in logic which lasts barely twenty years, and it all keeps changing, so that there are as many logics as teachers of logic. But the logic of the Bible is eternal, founded as it is in unchanging truth and independent of human fame or favour.'[20]

Logic was taught in both Paris and Oxford according to the outlines provided by 'introductory' textbooks such as those of the thirteenth-century William of Sherwood.[21] Surviving manuals for beginners in Logic used in Oxford at the end of the thirteenth century and the beginning of the fourteenth give an idea of the kind of textbook Wyclif may have learned from himself when he started the subject.[22] The first, an elementary Logic textbook known from its first words as the *Logica: Ut dicit*, gives a definition of an 'art' which it (wrongly) claims comes from Cicero. It says that an 'art' is a 'collection of many first principles or precepts, leading to a single end',[23] no arbitrary construct of human syllabus-builders, but formed on first principles which existed in their own right and were special to the discipline in question.

Cum sit nostra are the opening words of another elementary textbook for Logic students used in Oxford at about the same period.[24] There were certainly others, and it may be that a number of masters provided such helpful guides for their students.[25] The chapter headings of simple introductory textbooks such as the *Logica: Ut dicit* take us immediately into the contents of the course a student like Wyclif would be expected to follow. The first was 'categories' (*predicamenta*). The second was 'universals'. The third was 'propositions'. The fourth was 'syllogisms'. The fifth was 'topics'. The sixth was 'supposition'. But before we look at what Wyclif would have learned under these headings we need to go back a step and see what underlay the choice of areas of the logic syllabus for study in Wyclif's Oxford.

In Logic as in Grammar – and every other area of medieval study – the practice was to begin if at all possible by studying a set text, an 'authority', preferably from the early Christian or the classical world. In the case of the Arts the secular authors of ancient Greece or Rome were the main authorities. But, whereas Priscian had written his Latin grammar in Latin in the first place, Aristotle, chief ancient authority on Logic, had written in Greek. Few spoke Greek in the West after the end of ancient world. Until the late twelfth and early thirteenth century, scholars were dependent on a limited range of Aristotle's works which happened to have been translated into Latin by Boethius in the sixth century, together with some textbooks he had written to assist beginners in Logic.[26] Consequently, the Middle Ages received its Logic textbooks in three batches.

Those Boethius had made available in Latin were known as the 'old logic' (*logica vetus*). The first of these was Aristotle's *Categories* (*Praedicamenta*), the subject of the first chapter of the little book for Oxford student beginners. The second batch arrived in Latin in the form of the remainder of Aristotle's books on Logic in the twelfth century and were called the 'new logic'. The last were newly composed textbooks, the 'modern logic'.

a. The old logic

Let us say that I have a portrait of the Victorian novelist Charles Dickens. If Dickens were still alive I could point to him or to the portrait, and say 'that is a man'. But I shall not mean that the portrait itself is a man. Exactness in such matters is essential to the proper construction of arguments, as Aristotle shows.

Aristotle sets out to do a number of things in the *Categories* and medieval scholars were inventive at finding additional things, things he perhaps never intended at all, but which were significant in their own studies. The full list of *praedicamenta* or categories identified by Aristotle is ten. Aristotle taught students to ask what something essentially 'is', what its unalterable substance is, and then to consider a variety of things which may be said about it ('predicated' of it) which are changeable. For example, an apple may be green or red (quality), large or small (quantity), here or there (place), present or past (time).

Christian theologians who tried to apply this method found themselves asking whether God too was a substance with a number of variable qualities or whether he was fundamentally different. If we say a human being is good, we recognize that this is an attribute which may change on a 'bad day'. But goodness is not a mere quality of God; it is of his essence or substance to be good. The category of 'relation', too, posed special questions for the Christian theologian. A human father and son have not always been father and son because there was a time before the father begot the son. But the Father and Son in the Trinity are in an eternal 'relation'.

One doctrinal development which was formulated as the result of an argument about these 'predicates' was to prove immensely important in Wyclif's later life. Towards the end of the eleventh century and running on into the twelfth there had been a debate, triggered by the disputatious grammarian Berengar, about what exactly happened when the priest said the words of consecration of the bread and wine in the Eucharist.[27] Were Jesus's words 'This is my body' (*Hoc est corpus meum*), in Mark 14:22 and Luke 22:19, to be taken to mean that the bread literally became his body as he uttered them? If so, the 'categories' were turned on their head. Ordinary bread may change in outward appearance as it grows stale and mouldy but Aristotle would say that it is still in substance bread. The consecrated bread of the Eucharist looks exactly the same as it had before it was consecrated. The accidents or properties have not changed. Yet it was being asserted that the substance had altered. After a century when scholar after scholar contributed his monograph on the subject, the doctrine of 'transubstantiation' was accepted. Wyclif said it took him a long time to grasp it; and his ultimate rejection of it was to be the occasion of his final departure from Oxford in 1381.

The *Introduction* (*Isagoge*) of Porphyry had also been translated into Latin by Boethius, because it was used in his own day as a basic textbook for beginners.[28] From this the student learned the art of classification by identifying the genus and then the species to which something belonged, until a definition was arrived at which would identify the individual exactly. We can identify fruit, say, as a genus. In logic, one species of fruit is the apple. This has various subspecies (say, Cox's Orange Pippins and Bramleys). This particular apple is a Bramley with a bruise which fell off the tree into my hand at three o'clock this afternoon, and there is only one apple which fits that category.

Porphyry wrote the book not only as an 'introduction for beginners' but also partly to try to persuade the Platonists of his own time that they should take Aristotle's logic seriously. Porphyry's *Isagoge* was still being taught as part of the foundation for Logic in Wyclif's day.[29] By then much of its original rationale as an elementary manual on classification had slipped into the background because its larger philosophical implications had captured the interest of academics. Wyclif found the topic profoundly challenging, not because it was difficult – though it was – but because he thought it was important. Looked at as a textbook of Metaphysics, the *Isagoge* is concerned with the deepest being of things, what they are.

This is a huge, perennially recurring and extremely difficult question of Metaphysics to introduce to the young student of Logic at the stage when he was merely trying to get the hang of drafting propositions in a watertight way. Wyclif was probably still of what would now be secondary school age when he was introduced to all this as a student himself, as were his contemporaries. We have no means of knowing what such young minds made of it all.

Wyclif's own book 'On Universals' (*De Universalibus*) was probably written about 1368–69, ten years after he had graduated in Arts,[30] so it was evidently of importance and interest beyond the level at which the beginner needed to understand the basics. The book demonstrates that Wyclif was not averse to relying on the work of at least some of the friars. In his *De Universalibus* Wyclif borrows from the Franciscan Robert Grosseteste, (who was something of a favourite with him), his list of the five kinds of universal, which is to be found in the *Commentary* Grosseteste wrote on Aristotle's *Posterior Analytics*.[31] The first 'and supreme' is the 'reason' or 'exemplary idea' in God. This is the Christian version of the Platonic 'idea'. Universals, the forms or patterns or ideas of things in the divine mind, are stamped on each thing of this kind that God creates. So the human observer has an idea of an elephant and all elephants are like it. That is how he knows they are elephants.

Porphyry challenges the *Categories* in his *Introduction* (I.3–16) with a discussion of the 'existential status' of genera and species. Are they mere conveniences of classification, no more 'real' in their own right than, to use modern examples, a card index or a computer file, certainly not 'real' in the same way as the things they contain? Or is 'mammal' a 'real' something, even though it is impossible to point to it in the way a particular elephant or mouse or other example of a mammal can be pointed to?

The dispute between Platonists and Aristotelians in the late antique world turned partly on the question of the place in the 'hierarchy of being' of genus and species on the one hand, and the particular exemplifications of the things in those genera and species on the other. Aristotelians tended to say that the most 'real' were the individual examples. Platonists preferred the view that the genera and species were more 'real'. This debate was still in vigorous progress in Wyclif's day under the heading of 'universals'. Wyclif took the view that universals were more real than particular concrete things, which made him a 'realist'. Those of the opposite persuasion were known as 'nominalists', because they took genus-words and species-words and so on to be merely verbal conveniences, classificatory devices.

The student who has mastered the preliminaries and learned to define his terms can then construct propositions such as 'an apple is a fruit', and practise putting them together in pairs to see what conclusion may be drawn. This he learned to do according to the guidelines laid down in Aristotle in *On Interpretation* (*Perihermeneias*), which was the second of Aristotle's works of logic to have been translated by Boethius. It begins with a discussion of the way a noise or sound becomes a word, by having signification attached to it. Students had already learned some rather different ideas about what a word was in the Grammar course.

But *On Interpretation* is mainly concerned with the elements of constructing formal sequences of argumentation. The propositions have to be put together into pairs according to rules which the student would be expected to learn. A conclusion could then be drawn. These were known as 'syllogisms'. In a syllogism there has to be a common 'middle term', a word or phrase which appears in both propositions so as to make a bridge to allow a conclusion to be drawn when they are placed side by side. No conclusion would follow from putting together two propositions such as 'an apple is a fruit' and 'an elephant is an animal'. The syllogism must have a pattern something like this:

A is B
B is C

And then it will follow that A is C.

Nowadays 'an apple is a fruit' could go together with 'all fruits contain Vitamin C' to allow the conclusion to be drawn that an apple contains Vitamin C. A standard example used in Wyclif's day ran thus:

Socrates is a man.
All men are mortal.
Therefore Socrates is mortal.

It will be apparent that this all becomes much more difficult as soon as the verb in the proposition (the *copula*, which links the terms) moves from the present tense to the past or to the future, or the 'all' turns into a 'some', or the debater introduces an 'if' into his propositions and makes them conditional.

On Interpretation deals with matters which turned out to have implications as significant for Christian theologians as some aspects of the *Categories*. For example, it ends with a discussion of the truth of statements that have verbs in the future tense. How can it be possible to know whether such a statement is true, when we mortals cannot see into the future? And if the truth of the propositions or premises of a syllogism is in question, the syllogism's conclusion, however valid in the sense that it follows logically from the premises, cannot be known to be true.

Wyclif must have lectured on this problem at some time when he himself became a Regent Master. There is an autobiographical reference in his record of the sort of thing he said. Wyclif is discussing whether a statement which is false at present could become true with the passage of time. It is false (at present), he says, 'that I have lived for forty years'. But this is evidently something which could become true in the future. It is to be expected that it was quite obvious to his students that he was not yet forty, or the example would have lost some of its point and not engaged their amused interest. So perhaps it is a useful indication that he was really quite young when he gave these lectures, perhaps in his mid-twenties.[32]

But this is obviously not a mere problem of logic. If everything in the universe is determined in advance I can make a statement in the future tense which is or is not true, although I do not know which at the time I make it. If things are not so determined, any statement I make in the future tense is not true or false. Its truth or falsehood can only be conditional upon what, as it turns out, is actually going to happen. For that is not yet fixed.

Although this had been a problem for Aristotle long before the Christian era, it became a far more complex one for Christian thinkers. The Christian God is omniscient (which means he knows the future), and omnipotent (so the future cannot turn out to be any different from the way he knows it will happen). But then there is the doctrine of human free will, which seems to allow for the possibility that we as human beings must be free to change our minds; and the doctrine of divine grace, which says that God may as an act of free generosity intervene as he wishes to alter anything.

The controversy about all this had never entirely died away in the Middle Ages, but from time to time it reawoke quite violently, as it did in fourteenth-century Oxford. Thomas Bradwardine was one of a group known as the Mertonian Calculators. He appears at Merton in 1325 acting as Proctor in one of the University's disputes over jurisdiction, and it is likely that Wyclif was aware of at least some of his work. Bradwardine was notorious enough for Chaucer to make a joking reference to him in the *Nun's Priest's Tale*, in the evident expectation that his English-speaking readers would be able to 'place' him:

That in scole is gret altercacioun
In this matere, and greet disputisoun,
And hath ben of an hundred thousand men.
But I ne can not bulte it to the bren,
As can the holy doctour Augustyn,
Or Boëce, or the bishop Bradwardyn… [33]

In his *De Causa Dei* Bradwardine explores the theme that God is the immediate and omnipotent efficient cause of every effect.[34] Wyclif himself was to get into trouble over his teaching on predestination.

So from the 'old logic' had flowed a number of controversies of a kind highly relevant to Christian theology.

b. The new logic

The medieval study of Logic had advanced a good deal beyond these topics covered in the textbooks of the 'old logic' (*logica vetus*) even by the mid-twelfth century, when there arrived in the West and in Latin the *logica nova*, the remaining four works of Aristotle's set of logic manuals (collectively known from the sixteenth century as the *Organon*). These contained more advanced instruction in the construction of syllogisms, a treatise on spotting fallacious arguments, and 'topics', as well as the ideas on first principles discussed in the opening sections of the *Posterior Analytics*.[35]

The most advanced and difficult of the books of the 'new logic' was generally found to be the *Posterior Analytics*. Many who tried it said so. John of Salisbury commented disparagingly in the middle of the twelfth century, when it had just become available for study, that many found it opaque and challenging, and said there must be mistakes in the translation, although he seems to have considered himself well able to understand it. 'There are as many obstacles to understanding this book as there are chapters.'[36] There is confirmation from elsewhere that lecturers were afraid at first to attempt to teach from the book, so hard was it to understand and so suspicious were they that this was partly because there were errors in the translation.[37] The *Posterior Analytics* dealt with the demonstrative method, the method of argument which begins from first principles which are themselves self-evident, and proceeds by watertight proofs to establish other principles or theorems. Its advantage is that its conclusions can be regarded as 'necessary', while those arrived at by ordinary syllogisms are merely probable. Demonstrative argument was much aspired to in the Middle Ages, and various attempts were made to apply it to a wide range of subject matter, although it is possible it will really work only for Euclidean Geometry. A useful textbook or commentary could survive in use for generations.[38] Grosseteste's *Commentary* on the *Posterior Analytics*[39] was cited by Wyclif in the *De Universalibus*, not only so as to allow him to borrow the fivefold division of types of universal, but also in several other places.[40]

c. Modern logic

The *Logica: Ut dicit* we are taking as a reference book to the kind of thing Wyclif would have learned as a young student of Logic includes the sphere of 'modern logic' (*Logica Moderna*). That included work in areas not covered by Aristotle: for example, 'terminist logic' (or 'the logic of terms'), a branch of logic described in Wyclif's Oxford as neither 'old' nor 'new' but 'modern' (*logica modernorum*). A word comes to have a general meaning (*significatio*) by a process of 'imposition'. There was some discussion of the passage in Genesis where Adam names the animals,[41] but interest in the problem of the way imposition occurs was not confined to Christian scholarship. In a given context, within perhaps a specific sequence of argumentation, the user of a word or term gave it an actual meaning, its *suppositio*,[42] and it was very important to be clear what the *suppositio* was or the argument would not 'work' and conclusions would not 'follow'. Wyclif uses the word *suppositio* a good deal.

Within this arena of 'modern logic' a series of further topics would have been studied by a student in Wyclif's day: *insolubilia* (paradoxes); *exponibilia* (propositions containing statements that something begins or ends); consequences (treatises concerned with the way inferences may be drawn from *exponibilia*); obligations.

Insolubilia afforded endless scope for serious analysis but also for fun. The 'Cretan liar' paradox is the most famous example of the genre. The Cretan says, 'All Cretans are liars,' but if he is telling the truth he is telling a lie and if he is lying all Cretans are not liars, so he is telling the truth.[43] The passage in Amos where the prophet says, 'I am not prophet',[44] is not exactly analogous but it provided an interesting example in Scripture.[45] Wyclif mentions it in his lectures on Amos, getting quite cross and calling those who thought differently 'frivolous', while insisting that Amos has the spirit of prophecy he was denying because unless he had been a prophet he would not have said what he did.[46] Wyclif himself wrote a treatise on 'insoluble propositions', which he says was composed 'for the instruction of the young' and almost certainly belongs with the first books he wrote while he was fulfilling the graduation requirement to lecture for a few years on the Arts.[47]

Exponibles bring us back to the tantalizing closing passages of Aristotle's *On Interpretation* and the question how it is possible to know whether a statement in the future tense is true. The underlying questions are again much deeper than an elementary Logic course could cope with, and their immense importance to Christian theologians kept the interest of scholars much more senior than undergraduates. William of Ockham, in the generation before Wyclif, was against treating statements in the future tense as somehow neutral as to their truth or falsehood until they moved into the present tense or the past tense and it was possible to find out whether they had in fact been true or false. He attempted to move the question of the effect of God's knowledge to Theology, where he said it belonged.[48] The energetic Oxford debates on all this take us close to Wyclif's time as a student and it is unlikely that he can have graduated in Arts without hearing something about them, for those involved were debating at Merton as well as in the university at large. Walter Burley finished his commentary on the 'old logic' only in 1337, disagreeing with Ockham and maintaining that some future events remained contingent, that there was such a thing as chance and human free choice.[49] Thomas Buckingham thought that things which exist necessarily exist, but he was not willing to build into his scheme any antecedent necessity in God.[50] Bradwardine chimed in. The stories of the arguments may still have been part of the local legends at Merton when Wyclif became a Fellow of Merton himself in the 1350s. The issues they were raising took him deep into yet another area of Theology, though we must wait to follow them there until we get to Wyclif's time as a Theology student.[51]

'Consequences' was the art of drawing inferences from exponibles. 'Obligations' was a game or, more accurately, a method of practising certain skills. The way it was played conveys something of the spirit of the Logic courses. They were difficult and demanding and a good deal of dull effort was required to master the concepts and rules. But the students were young and the lecturers were young and there was ample opportunity for the brighter students to tease: for example, by asking questions which would trap the teacher in a contradiction or a fallacy. An *obligation* is an expression which requires someone to respond either positively or negatively. The game begins when one combatant says, 'I put it that... .' This could be something quite hypothetical: for example, 'I put it that Martians are green.' The respondent admits this as a starting point (*concedo*). Or he might choose to deny it as a starting point. If he decides to admit it, he is 'obliged' to say *concedo* to everything his opponent says which is consistent with that original assertion. Similarly, if he gives up that assertion at the outset, he has to accept everything his opponent says which is consistent with his having denied it. The aim of the game is to make the respondent deny what he accepted in the first place, or vice versa. It will be plain that this is a good game and an excellent way of motivating the students to concentrate on ensuring that each step of an argument is properly constructed.

Although there are several examples of treatises on how to conduct a disputation of this kind, no actual examples of these exercises are known to survive.[52] It would have been like preserving a game of noughts and crosses for posterity. The 'obligations' disputations were not about anything that mattered. They were probably regarded as preliminary training for real disputation about 'questions', particularly theological questions, of which innumerable examples survive. By Wyclif's time a skill in formal disputation was essential. It had to be demonstrated before anyone could graduate, and presiding over disputations was one of the defining acts of the master.

Logic seems to have been recognized to need the kind of 'remedial' tutorial teaching we glimpse in the special provision in the statutes for specialist Grammar Masters to be included within the the University's arrangements and brought under its control. That was not because it was a subject in which boys should have got up to a reasonable standard before they came, but because some (with good reason) found it difficult. William Wheatley, Master of Stamford School from 1309, probably studied at Paris and also at Oxford. He left an account[53] in which a picture emerges of students near to graduation and close to becoming Regent Masters taking students privately in their rooms to give them tutorials in Logic. The nearly-qualified student got useful practice. The younger student got teaching, of unpredictable quality.[54]

On the other hand, Logic was always a subject which lent itself to the fulfilment of the ambitions of able young scholars. It was possible to become extremely proficient, to challenge the best understanding of mature experts, rather as is the case with Mathematics or Computer Programming today, where youth can be a positive advantage, intellectually speaking. Oxford had a particular line in the teaching of Logic for which it was known in the fourteenth century.[55] It is suggested – and this fits in with the timetable of an academic's career – that it was probably the Bachelors of Arts who were the authors of the new work and the additional and experimental textbooks in the field of Logic.[56]

Wyclif himself wrote a book on Logic, probably his very first book, written about 1360, soon after he had become a Master of Arts and while he was still lecturing.[57] It shows very clearly the limitations of a young man who has only just mastered his subject matter. Wyclif promises to cover a series of topics: terms and their properties, universals and the categories, the method of reasoning, including suppositions, consequences and obligations, ending with a discussion of epistemology. There is in reality little in the treatise beyond a bare outline of the elements of the traditional Logic course. Yet it is not without its ambitions, and it indicates the direction in which his interest was moving. Wyclif begins with a preface in which he says he has written it 'moved by certain friends of the Law of God' and that it is a 'logic of Holy Scripture' (*logica sacre scripture*) intended to help those who take up the study of logic in order to understand the law of God better.[58] This making of a conscious effort to apply the study of Logic to the study of the Bible by someone who has not yet studied Theology was nothing new, and it had previously led to controversy. Peter Abelard had set out to do exactly the same thing in the late eleventh and early twelfth century and had been put on trial twice by the ecclesiastical authorities.[59] But it was bold for a non-theologian to do it, and it may have been perceived as the throwing down of a gauntlet, although in fact the book contains no thoroughgoing attempt to apply the skills of the logician to the study of Scripture.

Chapter II, on universals, affords a comparison of Wyclif's understanding of the matter at this early date with what he thought later when he wrote his mature work *On universals*. In about 1360 he recognized three kinds of universal: 'causative' universals, such as God, sun, moon; universals which lend their universality to a number of individuals, such as human nature, which 'is communicated to all individuals of the human species'; and universals 'by representation', such as 'man' when it is used to refer to the whole of humanity.[60] The emphasis is mainly upon the logical not the metaphysical aspects of the problem of universals.

In chapter XXII Wyclif comes to obligations.[61] He goes through the basic principles already outlined. He gives examples which are valuable in themselves, in the absence of such things in the general literature of obligations, and because they indicate that this student game could involve the consideration of profound logical difficulties and matters of serious logical or even theological import. One is a *sophisma*. The opponent is asked to concede that 'no proposition is put to you' (*nulla proposicio est tibi proposita*). He accepts that. He is then faced with 'a proposition is put to you', which naturally he denies, since it is incompatible with the first, which he accepted. The challenger then says, 'But that proposition was put to you, and that proposition is a proposition, so a proposition is put to you.' Naturally the opponent is foxed. He can neither affirm nor deny without contradicting himself.[62] The example is like the Cretan Liar paradox, self-referential and internally contradictory. Another of Wyclif's examples is theological. 'I put it to you that God is man' (*quod deus sit homo*). That is admitted by the opponent 'because it is true'. Then it is proposed that 'God is immortal.' But Christ, God who is man, is mortal. The opponent is trapped into indecision once more, for it is not easy to say which is compatible with 'God is man', the proposition that God is mortal or the proposition that God is immortal.

In his *Logice continuatio*,[63] probably written not long after the 'Logic' and while he was still lecturing on the arts, Wyclif says he is responding to the request of his students that he write something more to assist them in their studies.[64] This strongly suggests that this was the art in which he specialized as a young lecturer.

iv. Rhetoric

The third subject of the *trivium* was Rhetoric. This had been the most important subject of all in late antiquity, because the educational system was geared chiefly to the creation of public speakers who could act as advocates in court, who could make a political speech, or who could, if occasion demanded, turn a panegyric to flatter an emperor. Rhetoric was comparatively neglected in the medieval Arts course for a number of reasons. The three medieval rhetorical arts, of letter-writing, poetry and preaching, had moved into different parts of the syllabus, the first two into Grammar, the third into Theology. Preaching was for the theologians, the most senior of the University's scholars, and not for boys.

In any case, in Wyclif's day there were still comparatively few rhetorical textbooks from the classical period to use as a basis for study. Cicero's *On invention* is about the finding of arguments, that is, the methods to be used in the collection and retrieval of materials appropriate for use in particular speeches. The *Rhetorica ad Herennium*, wrongly believed to be by Cicero, purported to be a more comprehensive textbook, and contained material on the choice of style, as did part of Quintilian's *Institutes of Oratory* of the first century AD. The remainder of his vast and more than comprehensive manual was not 'discovered' until the complete text came to light in the fifteenth century,[65] after Wyclif's death. The 'Ciceronian rhetorics' had, by Wyclif's day, been largely taken over by the teachers of Logic, who were interested in what he had to say about argumentation and not in the idea of public speaking. A new textbook had arrived on the scene with the new Latin translations of Aristotle, and his *Rhetoric* is listed in the Oxford statutes among the set books. But the inclusion of books which are really literary, and would have been encountered by many students in their preliminary grammar studies, is an indication of the comparative poverty of rhetorical studies in the syllabus. Certainly there was nothing to compare with the deep and extensive interest that Logic was triggering. The 'fun and games' of the student's intellectual life which, to judge by Quintilian's exercises, were once to be found in rhetoric, had now moved to Logic.

Topics

The study of 'Topics' was nothing new in Rhetoric, nor in Logic, although it was a novelty from the twelfth century to be able to study it in Aristotle's *Topics*. The textbooks which had been known in the West from ancient times without a break were by Cicero and Boethius.[66] Ancient orators used to be trained to memorize stock arguments and stock illustrations and quotations and examples. When they had to make a speech, whether as an advocate in court or in a political context, they could then draw upon these resources to enable them to put their thoughts in order and to illustrate and support their points. It was the stock patterns of argumentation which most interested logicians and which formed the basis of the 'topics' part of the Logic course long after ancient Rhetoric had ceased to be taught in any depth or to be practised in the old way. The *Logica: Ut dicit* begins by quoting Boethius' definition of a topic as a 'seat of argument' (*sedes argumenti*).

v. Mathematics and philosophy

Wyclif learned Mathematics as part of the Arts course. The *quadrivium* or 'four ways' consisted of subjects regarded as mathematical: Arithmetic (the study of number), Geometry (the study of magnitudes), Music (which was treated as though it was about the movement and interrelationship of numbers, as on one level it is); and Astronomy (which was regarded as the study of the movement and relationships to one another of the 'magnitudes' of the cosmos).[67] There is no evidence that Wyclif took fire as a mathematician.

Some Oxford scholars did, and made significant discoveries. Thomas Bradwardine of the Mertonian Calculators was the author of a book, *On Proportions*, in which he attempted to apply mathematical principles to the study of the natural world. He devised a useful formula to express the relationship of a force, a resistance impeding the force and the resultant velocity. This allows one quantity to be expressed as a relation between two others.[68] Bradwardine's work, and that of others in the Oxford community who followed him, led to fresh thinking about the nature of quantity, motion, the forming and changing of forms, infinity.

The applications were not only to Physics or what we would now call Natural Science. They could be theological, too, and that was where Wyclif's interest was engaged. It was postulated by another Mertonian, William of Ockham, in his lectures of 1318 on the *Sentences* of Peter Lombard, that God can annihilate any matter which exists, but if he does so the matter is still 'there' as it was 'before', for God does not cause the past not to be. He cannot do so, for he is omniscient and cannot be mistaken and the thing that was once there was known by him. This had disturbing implications for the doctrine of the transubstantiation in the theology of the Eucharist. If, when the priest says the words of consecration, the bread and wine cease to be bread and wine and 'really' become the body and blood of Christ, 'where' are the former bread and wine? Wyclif was drawn disastrously into this area of controversy at the end of his life.[69] Is annihilation the supreme punishment? This was a theme which interested Wyclif too.[70] It was his view that God punishes only in order to make things better, which would appear to rule out the possibility that he would cause a creature to cease to be.[71] He refers to Augustine. No one disagrees with Augustine except some *moderniores*, he notes.[72] Yet in his *De tempore*, an early treatise, Wyclif says that 'nothing is incapable of annihilation' (*nichil est anichilabile*).[73]

Philosophy

The level of technical difficulty and the highly abstract nature of the study did not diminish as the Arts student moved on to Philosophy. For, from the early thirteenth century, additional 'philosophical' parts had been added to this already onerous set of requirements in the traditional liberal arts. The arrival in Latin of Aristotle's works of Science and Metaphysics proved an irresistible temptation to lecturers in the Arts Faculties of Paris and Oxford. For Natural Philosophy (three terms of a year were prescribed in Oxford) there was the *Physics*, the *On heaven and earth*, or another of Aristotle's books of Natural

Science. For Moral Philosophy there was Aristotle's *Ethics* or *Politics*. For Metaphysics, the set book was Aristotle's *Metaphysics*.[74] Wyclif wrote on the *Physics*,[75] almost certainly at the time when he was lecturing in the Arts, and also a monograph on 'matter and form'.[76]

Not everything in Aristotle fits into the system of explanation of the nature of things which had by now been very fully worked out in Christian thought. For example, Augustine insisted that God had created everything from nothing and that there had therefore been a time when the universe was not. Genesis appears to support that explanation. But in Aristotle there is talk of the eternity of the universe and a notion that God merely acts within an eternal 'framework'. There are also significant differences between the ideas Aristotle puts forward on the soul and those of Christian theology. To introduce these new notions became a dangerous attraction, and it led to comparing of notes and mutual challenge by rival Masters well before Wyclif's time. For example, Johannes Blund died in 1248. He had taught the Arts in Oxford for a time, but most of his teaching career until he entered the civil service of Henry III of England in 1227 was spent in Paris in such debates. He and Alexander Neckham have very similar concerns about the soul within such a context, with Neckham probably borrowing from John, although John was younger than Alexander.[77] Students liked to be fashionable, to hold the latest opinions, and in any case it was amusing to challenge a lecturer's statements with a contradictory authority. Aristotle could be put in his place which was, since he was a mere secular philosopher, a much lower place in the hierarchy of authorities than that of the text of Scripture or even of a Christian authority such as Augustine. But it went against the grain of medieval scholarship to ignore him once copies of his works were available and the academic urge was to try to form a synthesis and reconcile the irreconcilable.

These 'new' books of Aristotle had caused a good deal of disturbance when they got to Paris early in the thirteenth century. At the University of Paris a series of unsuccessful attempts was made to suppress erroneous ideas. Books were condemned in 1210, lists of ideas later in the century. For example, in 1270 the Bishop of Paris published a list of thirteen propositions and banned those who taught them or even said them aloud. They included the ideas that the world is eternal, that God does not know individual things or indeed anything other than himself, and that there was never a 'first man'.[78] Oxford was not entirely free of censorship. In the 1270s, in the same decade as an attempt was being made to suppress undesirable opinions arising out of the study of the new works of Aristotle in Paris, Robert Kilwardby published thirty propositions which must not be taught at Oxford.[79] This method of suppressing ideas by listing them and forbidding people to entertain them was going to be used against Wyclif, too. Possibly Oxford did not suffer so much disruption of study as a consequence of the arrival of the new philosophy. It was less alarmist about it, anyway, and by Wyclif's time these books no longer appeared dangerous novelties.

Robert Grosseteste may have been important in encouraging a less anxious attitude on the part of the Oxford authorities,[80] for he was himself very interested indeed in the new Aristotle and the new science. Wyclif certainly read him on such subjects and approved of what he read to the point where he quotes Grosseteste as an authority. For example, Grosseteste's *Commentary* on the *Physics* is cited in the Wyclif's *De Universalibus*,[81] also Grosseteste's commentary on the *De Divinis Nominibus* of Dionysius the Pseudo-Areopagite[82] and Grosseteste's *Hexaemeron*.[83] Grosseteste's commentary on the *Physics* suggests that the way to arrive at first principles is to begin from universals and proceed downwards through the hierarchy by division of the universals into species, and so on.[84] There is some evidence that from late in the thirteenth century Oxford specialized in the 'three philosophies' and its Arts students would have considered those to be important parts of the course. In any case, he is prepared to defend the use of Philosophy on the grounds that the Holy Spirit's prompting lay – at least sometimes – behind the analysis of the 'philosophers'.[85] Wyclif appears to have lectured on at least one philosophical subject. His *On the Acts of the Soul*[86] begins with a hint that he was continuing from previous remarks, perhaps previous lectures.[87] He refers forward, too, to other writings of his own, for example to his treatise on insolubles.[88]

On the Acts of the Soul concerns the soul, and might therefore be expected to deal with the issues brought into the arts syllabus by the arrival of Latin texts of Aristotle's controversial 'On the Soul'. It is in fact concerned partly with questions arising out of the study of Geometry, one of the mathematical arts of the *quadrivium*, and especially with Optics. Wyclif expected his students to know, possibly even to have in front of them, the *Perspective* of a Polish scholar called Witelo, which seems to have been well established as a Geometry textbook for use in the Arts course.[89] He refers to it several times, not by name,[90] but pointing his students to particular passages.[91] The soul moves the body and the body moves about in space, and Wyclif is also concerned with the problem, part physics, part metaphysics, of the way in which the soul 'knows that it knows'.[92]

There are hints in Wyclif's writings that it was usual for lecturers to specialize to some degree. He discusses in his book on the Ten Commandments how 'a professor in each Faculty teaches the rules of his own specialist discipline; the arithmetician concentrates on the laws of number; the geometer on the rules governing figures; the astronomer on the laws of celestial motion; the natural philosopher on the laws of natural bodies, and so on with the others.'[93] Among the prominent names of the mid-fourteenth-century Faculty of Arts in Oxford some are best known as logicians: William of Sherwood and Simon of Faversham alongside Grosseteste and Kilwardby. Some were famed in mathematical studies: Richard of Campshall, Thomas Bradwardine, William Heysbury, Thomas Buckingham, John Dumbleton, William Sutton, Richard Billingham, Simon Bredon, John Ashenden, Richard Swyneshead the Calculator, among whom were those noted as logicians as well as for their mathematical writings (Dumbleton and Swyneshead, for example). Swyneshead and Rede had reputations as both mathematicians and astronomers.[94] Rede, who had influential connections, particularly with the Arundel family, lived until 1385, through the period of Wyclif's rise to fame and condemnation. Wyclif may have liked Logic best, but he cannot be ranked with these 'great names' of the times in the subject.

Even this brief journey through some of what Wyclif's first experience of university life exposed him to, demonstrates that Arts teaching, at least at the hands of some Masters, allowed a fairly flexible and stimulating pedagogical juxtaposition of elements from the traditional separate 'disciplines'. The syllabus was eventually set out for each of these traditional 'liberal arts' subjects in the Oxford statutes, with the length of time a student was required to spend hearing lectures on each set book. The late Roman grammarian Priscian provided the textbook for Grammar. For Rhetoric (three terms of a year) Aristotle's *Rhetoric* or the fourth book of Boethius' *Topics* or Cicero's 'new' Rhetoric or Ovid's *Metamorphoses* or Virgil's poetry. For Logic (three terms of a year) Aristotle's *Perihermeneias*, the first three books of Boethius' *Topics* or the *Prior Analytics* or Aristotle's *Topics*. For Arithmetic and Music (a year each) Boethius on these subjects. For Geometry and Astronomy (two terms of a year each) Euclid's *Elements* and Ptolemy's *Almagest*.[95]

There was a possibility of some optional extras for those who were interested. Students were not required by the statutes of the University to cover more than this range of subjects and set books in order to graduate in Arts, but there were possible additional areas of study. Grosseteste and Bacon set about learning Greek, although there is no evidence that Wyclif tried. The attraction for his precessors lay in the wish to get access to Aristotle rather than in any notion of reading the New Testament in the original Greek.[96]

These were preliminary studies, but also studies of great sophistication, capable of being applied to the resolution of problems arising in the higher studies of Theology, Law and Medicine. Wyclif has something to say on this subject in his books on Logic. He is, he says, moved to compile a treatise because it is possible to see many turning to logic who propose to know the

Law of God that way.[97] But boys and those merely learning should not get ahead of themselves. The logicians play equivocation in a manner designed to bring them personal glory.[98] It is a good idea to have knowledge of both 'schools', Logic and Theology. For the young student the study of Theology is burdensome.[99] There are drawbacks, too, for the theologian who uses Logic; for it is easy to be let into trivial disputes and sophistries and mistakenly to think that one is addressing serious questions of the condition of man, the kinds of thing which are the proper subject matter of that school. Wyclif considers himself 'too much an old man' now to allow himself to be imprisoned in that 'first school'.[100]

Chapter 3

John Wyclif, Regent Master

i. Examinations and assessment

When Wyclif had 'graduated' as a Bachelor of Arts and then as a Master of Arts, he was entitled to become one of the Regent Masters, with a vote and an active role – if he chose to play it – in the life and business of the University.

He did not have to pass an examination of the modern sort. The would-be graduates had had to meet the course requirements of the Faculty, which included 'determination' (presiding over the disputations at which the younger undergraduates practised arguing for and against set questions). The first three years, the student was a *scolaris* and a *sophista* (student disputant). In disputation practice he spent a year first 'questioning' and then, when he had got some practice at that, 'responding'. The purpose of this practice was to ensure that the student had mastered all the arguments which could be advanced 'for' and 'against' on any given question. A student who had spent four or five years of study could set about graduating as a Bachelor of Arts. The Bachelors of Arts who aspired to become Masters were also required to give some lectures for junior students, under supervision.[1] The successful candidate was 'presented' to the Chancellor in the words which are still used at graduation, assuring him that he was 'suitable' in both learning and conduct to 'qualify', and the Chancellor granted him a licence.[2]

The method of 'incepting' in Arts survives as set out in December 1431, in the form of a 'statute' drafted by the Proctors with the agreement of senior scholars.[3] The holder of the new licence sent to each Master of Theology the information that he intended to hold his *vesperies* (or 'evening before' ceremony). This he could do on any day which was appointed for the giving of lectures in the Arts, that is, any ordinary teaching day; inception was not allowed in the vacation. In the thirteenth century the inception could take place in a friar's own community's house. But from the beginning of the fourteenth century it became a requirement that inceptions should take place in the University Church of St Mary.[4] There might not be a large attendance, for the Masters were not obliged to attend, but the church could be full for the inception of someone likely to be exciting or controversial and it seems that the inceptor could choose the subjects for disputation, with the other Masters present putting in their arguments in turn. This was intended to give the new Master the opportunity to show off his talents and perhaps attract students to his future lectures.

When the disputation was concluded the presiding Master made a speech praising the new Master.[5] Two speeches of congratulation from the end of the thirteenth century survive in a manuscript of mixed academic material, where they have been copied in on two spare pages.[6] One speech praises the incepting Master especially for his prowess as a mathematician. The other emphasizes how he profited particularly from the teaching at Oxford on the Natural Sciences and he was fired with such a passion for Philosophy that he was even willing to go into exile to continue his studies and accordingly went to Paris for the purpose.[7] The admission as a Master was signified by allowing the new member to wear the academic cap and by formally 'giving' him the insignia of his office: a ring and a book held open.

It was an expensive business to incept, because it was customary to throw a dinner, even a feast, for all the Masters of the guild, which could cost hundreds of pounds. Wyclif criticizes the mendicants for throwing lavish feasts. Certain 'gifts' were also expected, though the statutes discouraged bribery.[8] In the fifteenth century payment was commuted into a 'composition fee' to the University.[9] In the fourteenth century, the friars could be very helpful to one another when it came to finding the considerable amount of money it cost to incept. The Franciscan William Woodford was on his way back to Oxford to incept in Theology with £40 for the purpose when he was mugged and lost it all.[10] He says, 'I have never found greater charity anywhere than among the friars when one of them has to incept in Theology.'[11] How he afforded it himself is not known.

An exhortation of Wyclif's given at the inception of a Doctor sets out his personal idea of the academic calling.[12] A scholar, especially a theologian, should be honest (*fugere debet mendacia*). When he speaks or writes he should ask himself the three questions listed by Bernard of Clairvaux: *an liceat, an deceat, an expediat*. Is it allowed? Is it appropriate? Is it profitable?[13] Profitableness in this context Wyclif construes to mean 'edifying to one's neighbour'. When the scholar praises someone he should not speak falsely, even in jest (*iocose*). Wyclif is rather against joking with one's audience. He thinks it harmful to the soul, though physically pleasurable, to laugh.[14] His idea of what is 'academic' is solemn and consistent and purposeful. He praises an 'inceptor' for completing what he begins, and for *upholding the truth* (*observancia veritatis*).[15] And the upholding of the truth may well mean defending it against its enemies, the sophists, those ashamed of the truth, those keeping silent about it.[16]

The new Master was then required to lecture for a period as a 'Regent', which Wyclif certainly did.

ii. Academic politics

> 'Never allowing anyone to act without first consulting at least twenty other people who are accustomed to regard him with well-founded suspicion... twenty independent persons, each of whom has a different reason for not doing a certain thing, and no one of whom will compromise with any other, constitutes a most effective check upon the rashness of individuals.'[17]

Apart from some brief excursions outside Oxford, Wyclif's life was now going to be spent in the heated atmosphere of the internal politics of the University. From the moment of his inception, he became an insider in a fourteenth-century *Microcosmographia* which, in all its essentials, closely resembled the Cambridge version Francis Cornford wrote about in 1908.

The Chancellor

Chris Patten, former Governor of Hong Kong, was inducted as Chancellor of Oxford in 2003. He had been elected in an open vote of all the graduate 'members' of the University of Oxford, many of whom, of all ages, turned up in person to vote in the election. The office was by then mainly ceremonial and the working head of the University had long been the Vice-Chancellor, not the Chancellor. A Vice-Chancellor appears only once in Wyclif's story, when he briefly took Wyclif's place in prison. The office was that of a mere deputy in Wyclif's day.

Several Chancellors were important in Wyclif's life, and their roles in his story reflected the development of the considerable powers of the office. It was instituted in about 1214, probably as quite a modest position, with no stipend attached. A humble official, such as the Chancellor was at first, would not perhaps expect preferment. This was not, at least at first, a route to a top job in later life. But it grew to be very important indeed, and even in modern times, when it is a mainly ceremonial office, the election of Oxford's Chancellor can be fiercely fought for. By Wyclif's time, Oxford's Chancellor had extensive disciplinary and supervisory powers. He could arrest and imprison in the local king's prison. He was given jurisdiction in any litigation involving Oxford's scholars, both students and teachers. He supervised the schools. He could deprive a teacher of his licence to teach. A petition of the reign of Edward II, or possibly of Edward III, grants a privilege for five years which would allow the Chancellor of Oxford to certify directly to the Chancellor of England the names of persons who have been excommunicated for offences they have committed in Oxford, in order that they may seized to be punished by the secular authorities.[18]

The Chancellor presided at meetings of the Congregation of the Masters, for he was the head ('Head Master'). It was an office in which a complex balance of power had to be contrived. In 1327 a statute decrees that the Chancellor, or if there is a vacancy, even the Senior Proctor, has powers to order the Masters to stop lecturing, but only when they have held a meeting and voted through an ordinance to that effect.[19] It is not impossible that as early as the indignant defection from Oxford in 1208-09 the scholars were acting under some such instructions on which their leader could call them all out on strike. But that was certainly the rule in Wyclif's own day.

At first the Chancellor of the University was probably thought of as the equivalent of the Chancellor of a cathedral. This was the member of a cathedral chapter who ran the cathedral's school. Oxford needed an additional figure to be its own peculiar Chancellor because the cathedral of the diocese at Lincoln was well over a hundred miles away and the Chancellor of Lincoln could not possibly oversee the affairs of the University in Oxford on a day-to-day basis. It is suggested that there was a pragmatic acceptance at Lincoln that this was a sensible arrangement.[20] Chancellor of Oxford is therefore an innovative form of a familiar title. It was probably not the first title to be used for what was in effect already the office of 'Oxford's Chancellor'. John Grim in 1201 is referred to as the 'Master of the scholars', a title which would have been used by a headmaster of a school. St Paul's Cathedral in London had a *Magister scholarum* of the cathedral school, who began to be referred to as *Cancellarius* at the beginning of the thirteenth century.[21] The Chancellor was required to be a senior scholar; he had to be one of the Masters of Theology or Law, which were the higher degree subjects.

The term of office of a Chancellor was fixed by statute closer to Wyclif's time, in 1322, limiting it to two years. The limit was not always adhered to, any more than the rule that the Chancellor should be present in Oxford from October to July, with not more than a month away.[22] John Gilbert may scarcely have been seen in Oxford. If the choice proved to be disastrous he could be deposed by a decree of the Congregation of the entire University, if the Congregation of Regent Masters asked. A vote of no-confidence would lead to the Proctors calling on the Chancellor to resign. His main functions were internal and involved presiding over the 'Congregations' at which the Masters democratically decided policy and practice. It was he who announced what had been decided (the *acta*) and dissolved the Congregation. (Only in exceptional circumstances could he call one, for that was the task of the Proctors). He presided when the Masters gave testimony about the suitability of a new Master to join them, as well as granting the licence to teach.

The Bishop agreed in 1281 that the Chancellor could impose any necessary disciplinary penalties in the University, and the Archdeacon of Oxford resigned still more of the Church's natural authority over the University in 1346. But the diocese was reluctant to let go completely. Adam Tonworth was Chancellor from 1369 to 1371 and again in 1377, Wyclif's *annus horribilis*. He was 'cited' (summoned before the Bishop) twice, on 4 May 1369 and 23 June 1369, with the allegation that he had not been properly elected because his election had not been ratified by the Bishop's approval, depite the fact that recent papal letters had stated that that approval was no longer required.[23]

The Masters

Yet, even if he had jurisdiction over all its members (from a disciplinary point of view), the Chancellor was never the supreme authority in the University. The Masters made it plain from the start that they expected to choose the individual the Bishop of Lincoln would 'appoint', and for some decades this had been allowed without any clear rule about the right to do so being articulated. In 1295 the leaders of the University went to see the Bishop about the next Chancellor as usual, but this time they announced that they had already elected their choice. The Bishop was politically adroit enough to allow them the person they wanted, but he insisted that the choice was in fact his.[24] A prolonged battle of wills, in which attempts were made to distinguish between the 'nomination' (by the Masters) and the 'election' (by the Bishop of Lincoln), was concluded by the Pope in 1367, when he removed the requirement of episcopal confirmation and allowed the Masters to make themselves a Chancellor by their own direct decision. This was at the time when Wyclif was a new Master of Arts and certainly aware of the innovation. It took another generation before, in 1433, it was decided that a majority vote would be a simple numerical majority, and not a majority of the Faculties, which could have given very different results.[25]

That did not alter the fundamental principle that the Chancellor was given a commission by the Bishop, and was acting as his deputy, for example, in granting a new Master his licence to teach (*licentia docendi*).[26] The fact that it was really the Bishop's grant was not really noticeable when the Chancellor was, to all appearances, the University's choice and acting in its name.

The Proctors

Proctors (*procuratores*) were the legal officers of the University. They sat on either side of the Chancellor at meetings of the Congregation of the Masters, with the most senior Doctors (of Theology and Canon Law) flanking them. The other higher studies, Civil Law and Medicine, had lower status and those who were Doctors in these subjects sat against the walls. Those who were plain Masters of Arts probably sat in the middle of the room, facing the Chancellor and the Proctors. The Proctors conducted the Congregation, calling out the items on the agenda, ensuring that votes were counted properly and there was no cheating, reading out the result of the count, keeping the record and reading out any statute to be promulgated. It was the duty of the Proctors, with the Chancellor, to keep a register of any new statutes which were made. Oxford did not have a Registrar to do that until a few generations after Wyclif.[27]

There were only two Proctors at Oxford because they represented the two English equivalents of the groups which were known as 'Nations' (*nationes*) at Paris. The modern idea of 'nationhood' barely existed as yet. As a concept and a reality it belongs to the period since the nineteenth century. The meaning of the classical Latin term is closer to 'race' or 'people'. In Paris the 'nations' represented groups of students from the same area who had a sense of 'gang' loyalty. It was a little like supporting the local football team. Oxford recognized two, the Northerners (*Boreales*) and the Southerners (*Australes*), with England notionally divided at the river Nene in modern Northamptonshire. If a student came from Scotland, he was classed with the Northerners. If he came from Wales or Ireland or was French, or from anywhere else at all, he was classed with the Southerners.[28]

The majority of Oxford's student body in the Middle Ages seems to have been English and the pressures and tensions which made the affairs of the

Nations in Paris so lively were largely absent. Nevertheless, the division of students at Oxford into what were really two gangs presented disciplinary problems. The gangs fought one another and disturbed the peace. Sometimes students were killed in such battles: for example, some Irish scholars had died in 1273 in a dispute between Northerners and Southerners.[29] By 1274 it had become apparent that it would be sensible to unite the groups. 'Northerners' and 'Southerners' were officially spoken of no longer. The two Proctors continued, however, to be drawn one from each group, and they continued to be needed to keep order. The Northerners and Southerners went on fighting each other,[30] and they triggered riot and street-fighting with the townspeople. Disciplinary matters arose.

So the Proctors were in the first instance the officers of the Arts Faculty. But gradually they became the University's executive officers. As *pro-curatores* they 'took care' of things 'on behalf' of the University. Together with the Chancellor they formed the administration of the University in the centuries before the registrar and other administrative officers came into being (from the sixteenth century). They could supervise public disputations, summon congregations, pronounce the passing of graces, supervise the election of the Chancellor and the bedels (executive officers with ceremonial functions), assist the Chancellor in his judicial and academic functions and depose him if necessary.[31] They first appear on the record in 1248 successfully representing the University in a hearing before the King, which resulted in a grant of privileges to prevent any repetition of the injuries to the University's interests which they were complaining of. They appear in 1252 taking an oath on behalf of the University to maintain the peace.

In 1257 they were given authority to suspend from lecturing Masters who had broken their oath to obey the statutes (*alioquin magistrorum et scolarium eis societas subtrahatur*).[32] Wyclif is not known to have been accused of that or to have tangled with the Proctors directly on his own account.

Direct democracy: Congregations

Despite the development of these rotating administrative offices, the powers of the University remained in the hands of the Masters in Congregations. This was direct democracy, the meeting of the Masters to debate and make decisions about their common affairs and the way the University was to be run.[33] There is a stipulation that all Masters must have their names on the roll (matriculation). The Masters probably did not hold formal meetings very often or regularly at first.[34] Realization that power to govern themselves was important to their various individual and group interests was – and remains – essential to getting busy people involved. Regent Masters were those actually engaged in teaching. Non-Regent Masters were those who had completed the requirements for their degrees in Arts and were studying again, on their way to a higher degree in Law or Theology.

The *universitas regentium* or the *coetus magistrorum regentium* was the sole governing body until the mid-thirteenth century when the difference between Regent (teaching) and Non-Regent Masters was clarified and the Non-Regents were given certain rights and powers.[35] The Congregation would meet in the University Church of St Mary's until 1320, when Thomas Chobham, Bishop of Worcester 1317-27, gave money to be used to build a Congregation House. This was to be in a two-storey addition at the north end of the church, with a library upstairs and the lower part a room for the Masters to meet. Meetings were held on official lecture days, beginning at six or nine o'clock in the morning, so that there could be no excuse for the Masters not to attend, and indeed, they were required to come, properly dressed in their habits or academic dress. As a compensation they were not required to lecture on the day after a meeting of a Congregation.[36]

At a Congregation the Regent (teaching) Masters and the Non-Regent Masters would meet separately for initial discussions. From 1314 the Regents and the Non-Regents met together as the Great Congregation (later called the Convocation) and the Regents formed the working Congregation which discharged ordinary business, for they were the Masters with practical responsibility for ensuring that teaching was given regularly and properly.[37] The leadership of the Arts Faculty was strengthened by its pre-eminence in numbers. A Congregation of the Artists, meeting in St Mildred's Church, is mentioned in 1325.

The Regents dealt with more of the minor detailed business, but on their own they could create only ordinances, that is, subordinate legislation. To create a statute a decision of the full Congregation was required. It began to make a bid for supreme power in the University at the time Wyclif arrived. In 1357 it tried to claim a right of veto on motions brought before the full Congregation. This idea was rejected by the Non-Regents and also by the Regents in Theology and Civil Law.[38]

Making the rules

Already in the early thirteenth century the University had begun to make rules for itself and, in order to give them authority and certainty, it had to distinguish proper legislative decisions from mere custom and practice. It was not practicable to expect the new member of the gild to take an oath to obey the domestic laws of the University on pain of being excluded from the society and its privileges, unless it was clear what they were.[39] The taking of that oath is known to have been a requirement by 1252.[40]

Possibly the first proper 'law of the University' to survive was the rule from before 1231 that 'the Chancellor requires that every scholar has his own Master from among the Regents, in whose register the student's name shall appear.' Each registered student must hear a daily lecture from his Master.[41] Unless he is registered, no student shall enjoy the privileges of the University.[42]

The first legislative acts were probably proclamations made in the name of the Chancellor.[43] Considering the immense importance the Oxford statutes were to have when there was a dispute about the ground rules of the place, the scholars were slow to put their domestic legislation in order. Registrum A was issued by Henry Harclay as Chancellor in 1312, leaving the statutes in a muddle, with duplications and omissions, and no clarity about the office of Chancellor, but at least making a preliminary attempt to draw the materials together.[44]

It seems to have been the friars who first raised serious concerns over the lack of certainty about the 'statutes'. In 1311 they were complaining that ordinances were being made which excluded them. They complained to the King, who tended to think they were right to say that this was unacceptable. They continued to press in 1366 and 1376, within Wyclif's time at Oxford, and in 1376 the dispute became so grave that Edward III appointed a commission to enquire into the statutes the friars were complaining about.[45] The petition – which now has a large piece torn away – is from the 'Doctors, Bachelors and scholars and students of Civil and Canon Law'. It complains of 'a malicious ordinance' made 'by the Chancellor, Proctors and Regents' against the Faculties of Civil and Canon Law, to which the Doctors of those Faculties had not agreed. Royal intervention had orded the University to keep to its old statutes and customs. It was ordained that Parliament was to be the final court of appeal in such matters (the 'final remedy' ordained). The University has made new statutes regardless. This is, says the petition, in 'great and horrible contempt of our lord the King'. There is an endorsement noting what is to be done in response. 'Let the Bishops of London, Ely, St David's, Chichester and Salisbury be deputed to make them agree.' If that does not work, the Archbishop of Canterbury is to insist on a final agreement.[46]

These were the structural and constitutional features of the Oxford Wyclif was now going to teach in. Their importance in forming his 'environment' of work and thought cannot be overstated. There is no record of what he did in meetings of Congregation, though he is clearly to be seen 'disputing' and 'determining' in the academic arena, and it is unlikely that he was any less involved in the business of the University when it touched on matters of importance to him. He was a 'participant' by nature and training, and this was his world.

iii. Pedagogical practice

Wyclif must have been lecturing as a Regent Master during the first years when he is visible as a Fellow of Merton College, because that was a requirement all new graduates had to fulfil. The style of teaching was combative and competitive. We have already had glimpses in his surviving writings of the kind of thing he chose to lecture on and his occasional self-indulgences as he let fly against a rival. Indeed, it is possible to put together quite a full picture of what this involved and how good he was at it. He would also have been presiding at and taking part in disputations. It seems to have been common for lectures and disputations to take place in the lecture rooms of the religious orders even when they were not presided over by one of their members. At the time of Wyclif's final condemnation,[47] there is a graphic depiction of the way the presiding Master sat in a seat for which the same Latin word is used as for the Bishop's seat in a cathedral. Those present at a disputation may have had to stand.[48]

The *De disciplina scolarium* pretended to be by the sixth-century Boethius, but it was in reality a popular thirteenth-century work which, describes the characteristics of a good teacher as they were reckoned in Wyclif's time. He should be learned, gentle, strict and conscientious; he must not be arrogant (*eruditus, mansuetus, rigidus, … nec necligens, non arrogans*). The need to make this list suggests that such characteristics were not always to be found in university lecturers. The ideal lecturer, says pseudo-Boethius, should also be 'old'; not 'old' in years, it is explained, but 'old' in learning (*antiquus in perpetuanti scientia*).[49]

The most striking feature of the lecture courses in Oxford in Wyclif's day to a modern attender would be the extreme youth of many of the lecturers. They were, literally, barely out of school themselves. It is true that one of the textbooks of Rhetoric which was routinely used, Cicero's *On Invention*, was itself the work of just such a young man, who had only recently finished learning the elements of the subject he was writing about. But that was not the norm with the set-book 'authorities' and it is striking that this youthful pedagogy was found acceptable. The most practical way of ensuring a supply of lectures for the youngest undergraduate students was to require new graduates to give a few years to the work before going on with their own careers. The reality was that this was the only cohort of prospective lecturers whose services could be compelled in Oxford. The statutes of Merton College, where Wyclif first appears as a young Fellow, required the Fellows to teach for three full years after 'inception', though they were free to continue indefinitely after that as lecturers in the Faculty of Arts, should they like the work or have no alternative career possibilities to take them away. The scene was not enormously different perhaps from that of nineteenth-century Oxford. There, Fellows of colleges were normally required by college statutes to be unmarried and commonly they were recent graduates. The most important effect was the creation of a gap between the young teachers of undergraduates and the much more senior 'Doctors' who taught the higher degree subjects of Theology, Law and Medicine.

The University behaved like any medieval gild in setting the rules for admission to membership, including rules for any exchange with members of other gilds. Before 1350 Oxford had a rule which stated that no one could discharge his lecturing requirement anywhere but Oxford and Cambridge. The lecturer had to take an oath to this effect, and also swear that he would not 'incept' anywhere else.[50] That meant he would not try to use his studies to obtain a qualification or membership elsewhere. The reason for the friendliness towards Cambridge may have lain in the events of 1208-09, since the founders of the University of Cambridge had been Oxford scholars. One of Thomas Brinton's sermons records him at Cambridge (*tempore quo studui Cantabrigie*), so there was some movement from one place to the other.[51] The statute of the fourteenth century forbids lecturing at Stamford, with which relations had been far from cordial. Every member of the University of Oxford who wished to be admitted to the degree of Bachelor of Arts was still required until 1827 to swear that he would not lecture or hear lectures at Stamford.[52] 'However, their dispute with the authorities was settled, and eventually they returned "home", but left on their Stamford door the brass knocker which they had brought from Oxford; it was not returned to Brasenose College until the closing decade of the nineteenth century.'[53]

Some left the University as soon as they were permitted on graduation and pursued careers in the ecclesiastical or state civil service or began to climb the ladder of patronage and preferment towards a bishopric. Wyclif chose to stay, to teach, to argue, and the peculiar qualities of an academic society entered into his bones.

Teaching methods: the lecturer's art

We can not only be sure that Wyclif would have been required to lecture; we can also get a picture of what lecturing would have involved for him. There were two main kinds of lecture, the bread-and-butter work of teaching the syllabus and the special performance. Gerald of Wales tells a story of his own prowess as a 'special performance' lecturer in the late 1180s. He gave a public reading of his 'Irish Places' (*Topographia Hibernica*). He had given a reading in Paris, too, and he compares the experiences.[54] Gerald had a classical model for this kind of reading as a 'display piece'. Pliny and his friends used to do something similar when one of them wanted to try out a new work on an appreciative but critical audience. Yet the context of Gerald's public lectures was decidedly not that of the classical world. It both was and was not an anticipation of the way university lecturing was to develop. What he was doing foreshadowed what new Masters were going to be expected to do in succeeding centuries, when they were expected to mark the successful completion of their degree studies with a public performance and a good dinner for those who had admitted him to their fellowship as Master and colleague. Gerald gave three dinners, one on each day of his three-day Oxford reading. The first day's dinner was, piously, for the poor and needy. To the second day's dinner he invited the most senior scholars, the *doctores* of the 'different Faculties' (*diversorum facultatum*) and their favourite and most promising pupils. To the third day's dinner he invited other scholars and the townsfolk. Underpinning this seems to have been some idea of the public lecture to the assembled clergy and people blended with the book launch of more modern times and Pliny's reading to a circle of friends.

The apparent success of his attempt in both the university towns of Paris and Oxford suggests there was a sizeable prospective audience for this kind of thing. Popular interest in the doings of the university and public lecturing to the clerics or scholars (*in publica cleri audientia*) is a familiar pattern in the history of medieval universities, and it was to be a significant factor in making Wyclif notorious.

Ordinary regular lecturing was a very different thing from Gerald of Wales's special performance. This staple of university teaching was called a 'lecture' from *lectio* or 'reading' (aloud) of a set text, with a commentary or explanation by the Master, which took the form of the patient exposition, phrase by phrase, of the text of a set book. The foundation of all study therefore was the 'set book'. It is not absolutely certain the Masters always read out every word, but some certainly did, and it may not then have been necessary for each student of the Arts to have the text before him when he 'heard' a lecture.[55] But it was obviously an advantage for a student to have his own copy. There are further practical questions, such as whether the Master would own his own copy of a set book on which he lectured, and whether Masters usually specialized in some portions of the Arts syllabus, which, as we have seen, was extensive and technically demanding.

Books and set books

A CLERK ther was of Oxenford also,
That un-to logik hadde longe y-go...
Ful thredbar was his overest courtepy;
For he had geten him yet no benefyce,
Ne was so worldly for to have offyce.
For him was lever have at his beddes heed
Twenty bokes, clad in blak or reed,
Of Aristotle and his philosophye,
Than robes riche, or fithele, or gay sautyre.[56]

The acquiring of books or getting access to them was largely a matter of private enterprise, and for a 'secular' like Wyclif this was an expensive requirement. Members of the religious orders seem to have had distinct advantages. In fact the Franciscan community at Oxford had two libraries, one of books for student use and one for the community in general. The main libraries were those of the mendicant houses, although some of the colleges held significant collections (Merton, Balliol, Oriel, University). Monastic and cathedral libraries are on record as having lent students books during the fourteenth century and it was even possible to deposit one book as security in order to borrow another. Nicholas Stenington borrowed a Bede *Historia Ecclesiastica* from St Frideswide's Priory in the 1380s and left a copy of Nicholas Trevet's commentary on Leviticus for them to hold until he brought it back.[57] Adam Easton, an eager book collector in later life, was one of Thomas Brinton's contemporaries among the Benedictine students at Oxford, where he is known to have been studying in 1363–64. The monastery records of his home 'house' of Holy Trinity, Norwich, note a large sum spent on providing him with books for his studies. He later left books to Norwich, including a Hebrew dictionary (now MS St John's 218), of which he may himself be the compiler.[58]

It appears that some of the friar students were less public-spirited and it could sometimes be difficult to get them to give back books which had been lent to them. Once they had finished with them the books were supposed to revert to the common stock (*remaneant in conventu*) to be made available to another student. In 1330 the Sheriff of Oxfordshire received a writ from the King requiring the Warden of the Oxford Franciscans and Friar Walter Chatton to give back to the Clerk, John de Penreth, immediately two books which he says they have no right to keep, which are worth forty shillings.[59]

College libraries became important as the colleges developed. A list of books returned to the Queen's College in 1378 includes a grammar, the *Decretals*,[60] a Bible, Gregory the Great's *Moralia on Job*, Richard of St Victor on the Trinity, Peter Lombard's *Sentences* and some commentaries on parts of the *Sentences*, and a few patristic works.[61] The notion of a university library, a *universitatis nostre libraria communis*, appears in the early statutes, in 1412,[62] but it was to take some time to be realized, longer than the period when Wyclif was a student. The intention was that a collection would be held on the upper floor of the Congregation House, from the time of the generous benefaction of Thomas Chobham, Bishop of Worcester, in 1320, which allowed the building of a place for meetings of Congregation to be held and above it a room in which his gift of his own books could be kept, for the use of poor scholars who could not afford their own, the books kept safely chained up. Chobham's wishes could not be carried out as he had intended because, when he died, his executors pawned them to pay for his funeral. They were redeemed from the pawnbrokers by the first Provost of the newly-founded Oriel College and it took nearly a century of warfare between the University and the College before the University could retrieve them and use them to start a University Library. This was the library which was to last until Duke Humfrey's Library superseded it in 1488 and the modern Bodleian Library was to follow.[63]

Beyond that provision, a student such as Wyclif who could not rely on a monastic house to help him might well have to fend for himself in the matter of getting hold of the books he needed for his studies. It is possible that the University Chest of Exemplars, mentioned in 1347, was exactly what its name suggests, and that it contained copies of set texts, probably divided into convenient sections, which could be borrowed for the making of a student's own copy.[64]

Students of 'higher degree' subjects could be required by the University's rules to possess the set books. Lawyers, for example, had to swear 'that they had all the books of both laws', civil and canon.[65] The University had to provide them not only with benches but also with desks to rest their books on. Again, they may have 'had' them only because they had borrowed them. The catalogue of Oriel College Library in 1375 lists nearly a hundred volumes belonging to the barely a dozen graduate Fellows engaged in higher degree studies and their Provost, forty in Theology and more than twenty on Philosophy. As befitted a society whose members had already completed their degrees in Arts, the collection is bare of the Latin classics, although translations of Aristotle were included.[66]

There was money to be made out of copying and selling books. Students may even have made money to support themselves by copying for sale. Students might make copies for themselves from borrowed manuscripts,[67] as Richard Calne did, probably while he was studying at Oxford (1412–21). He had copies made too, including treatises by current or recent Oxford Masters. Such a personal 'copying' business might include lecture notes.[68]

It is possible to trace a good number of tradesmen meeting that need in Oxford at the beginning of the thirteenth century, and the number is not likely to have diminished by Wyclif's day. One John Brown is recorded as an Oxford stationer who sold two volumes in the fourteenth century to Mr Thomas Cranley containing various works including a *Historia scholastica*. One of these survives as MS New College 104.[69]

There was a second-hand book trade run by the *editores librorum*. This could range from the finding to order of a particular book to the bulk purchase of a whole collection of set books, probably for the use of the monks of a particular house, for there was also some buying of books in Oxford for the libraries of abbeys.[70] Twenty-six books were bought by Thomas Westoe, a monk of Durham, about 1300.[71] The list suggests a serious attempt to bring together a library of major theological writing of the late thirteenth century, for there were books by Thomas Aquinas, Giles of Rome, Henry of Ghent, Robert Orford, William Ware. Durham's energetic procurement went on. Twenty years later Robert Graystanes was at Oxford, and he acquired books and had new copies made of works of Augustine which were already held at Durham.[72]

The influence of the friars on book provision in Oxford was very considerable.[73] Among the Franciscans each student friar was supposed to be provided with books for his own use.[74] Some of these were gifts to the community, but some had to be bought. Notes in surviving copies sometimes indicate the source: for example, one annotation says, 'From the books given for the use of any person in the community'.[75] 'John Ledbury of the order of the Friars Minor bought this book from Gilbert Hunderton, an act made possible by the generosity of his friends (1349).'[76] The other way of acquiring more books for the use of the community was for the friars in the community to make copies. It does not seem that the Oxford Franciscans had a proper *scriptorium*, although this was a recognized form of manual labour for the friars of the house to carry out. Merton College MSS 168, 169, 170 and 171 were surviving copies of works of Nicholas of Gorham. Friar William of Nottingham is said to have copied these at Oxford with 'weary carefulness', his brother Hugh of Nottingham paying the cost (presumably of the materials).

So valuable were books that they could be used as pledges if a student had to pawn something to raise money for his living expenses.[77] Then there were the stationers, who would take books which were pawned and, if the books were not redeemed by their owners' paying back the money they had borrowed, they would be sold on. Such stationer-pawnshops are reported in the period of the fourteenth century when Wyclif went to Oxford. A Master Robert had 'deposited' a copy of Peter Comestor's *Historia Scholastica* in the Turville 'chest'. The rules of the chest at the time were that a pledge not redeemed after a year could be sold. The book lay there for nearly two years (perhaps the pledge was renewed), but in 1359 the book was sold to Lewis Charlton, a rich man who was to become Bishop of Hereford three years later.[78] This example underlines another facet of this trade. A book was a good long-term investment, for this one had been written in the thirteenth century and it was still extremely valuable. Books already 200 years old were not the less desirable for their age.

Students sometimes had their books stolen from their rooms. This happened to Walter Thanet at Haberdasher Hall in 1343 and to John Pope in 1350 (when his were worth £20).[79] There was a trade in stolen books. We glimpse the expression of doubts as to whether a particular book had been come by honestly when it was clearly marked as someone else's property. In a Cambridge example from fifty years after Wyclif's time, MS Bodley 132 has the inscription of Robertsbridge Abbey, and there is a record of Bishop Grandisson claiming that, contrary to appearances, he purchased it in good faith.[80]

The University's control over this roaring trade seems to have been weak. In 1374, Oxford issued an ordinance against those who sold books against the will of the stationers (*contra voluntatem stationarii*). The 'will' of the stationers seems to have been against other booksellers being too numerous or too competitive or tempting prospective purchasers with gorgeous illumination (*exquisitis coloribus*), thus taking away their own profit. The University's ordinance was an attempt to require that only the 'public stationers' should sell books over a certain value, or those they legitimately permitted to do so on their behalf (*seu ab eis legitime deputatis*). Breach of this rule was to be punished by a fine.[81]

There is no direct surviving evidence about the actual copies of books Wyclif was able to acquire, or even read as a secular student. Nevertheless the sources with which he shows he was familiar tell a story about his reading far beyond the confines of set books, and the uses he felt free to make of it. For example, Anselm of Canterbury is mentioned in *De dominio divino*,[82] in a way which suggests Wyclif knew his work well enough to refer to its arguments without merely copying quotations.[83] There is plentiful evidence of his respect for and use of works of Robert Grosseteste.[84]

Lecturing on the book

The *accessus*[85] or 'formal introduction' was used automatically as the introduction even to the most difficult and advanced texts. The lecturer would begin by answering a series of standard opening questions about the text he was about to 'read' with the students, commenting as he went. Several different sequences of questions were in use, but each of them was designed to answer questions which would naturally be in a student's mind. Who is the author of this book? What was his purpose in writing it? What branch of study does it belong to? What is it about? In Grosseteste's commentary on the *Posterior Analytics*, the first words concern the 'intention of Aristotle in this book', which he says is 'to investigate and make apparent the essentials of demonstration'.[86]

The body of the lecture consisted of exposition. The comments of the lecturer could range from simply providing a synonym to help the students understand a difficult word to providing them with quotations from relevant passages in the authorities, so that they could form a sound view on a disputed point. From the mid-twelfth century students asking questions became a problem because it slowed the lecturer's progress through the text. A custom grew up of referring the more challenging questions to a separate session in the afternoon, when the arguments for and against would be discussed.[87]

The disputation

This was the beginning of a form of training and a method of resolving matters of disagreement which was to have a profound effect in the forming of the minds of medieval students and their teachers. By Wyclif's time it had become a requirement for the students to demonstrate competence in the resolving of disputed questions. The exercise required several student 'objectors' and a respondent, who would normally be a Bachelor of Arts. A Master presided and he would 'determine' the question.

An example from Thomas Aquinas's *Summa Theologiae* will show how this worked in the period when it came to its full development.[88] First the question would be posed (in Aquinas always the opposite way from the conclusion he was going to come to). Then a series of objections would be raised. Then the

Master would 'determine', that is, give the right answer. Then the Bachelor would deal one by one with the positions taken by the objectors. The methodology was still much the same at the University of Wittenberg in the fifteenth century. Some of the disputations which survive among Luther's Latin works could have been held in Wyclif's schoolroom too. 'Question: whether this proposition is philosophically true, "And the Word was made flesh".'[89] In 1537 Luther himself presided over a *promotions disputation* between Palladius and Tileman, still in spirit the doctoral graduation display piece of the medieval university. Luther, as presiding Master, introduced the topic with a *praefatiunculum* explaining its importance. 'The article of justification is the master and prince of all kinds of doctrine.' The first question is whether this is certain, for the Latin for the word used by Paul in the verse from Romans 3:28 is *arbitramur*, 'we think'. The Latin Vulgate was still being used as the text of Scripture on which such analysis would be done, but there is a discussion of the different connotation of the Latin word ('which includes some doubt and uncertainty') and the Greek *logisometha* which, it is explained, does not signify a mere opinion but a definition and conclusion.[90] This is still the world in which Wyclif, a century and a half earlier, mocked 'disciples in logic' for taking words literally in the wrong places.[91] This method of teaching made Wyclif and his opponents habitually adversarial in their problem-solving. John Usk, Abbot of Chertsey,[92] had sent a little treatise or pamphlet to Oxford and Wyclif's own short book on the duty or office of a king, *De officio regis*, may have been written in response.[93] As with many such pamphlets or tracts or treatises, this may well have begun as a live debate, subsequently turned into a published work. There is no need for further illustration here, for we shall see in succeeding chapters how difficult the scholars of Oxford found it to seek middle ground or creative solutions as they dispute about every question on which there was the slightest potential for disagreement.

Wyclif publishes his first books

The teaching prompted the writing of books. It has been widely assumed that Wyclif intended to compile a philosophical *summa*, and a good deal of effort has been expended on trying to work out an order for the surviving early writings which may be candidates for inclusion.[94] The real lesson to be drawn from Wyclif's enthusiastic composition of so many treatises based on his lectures in the Arts is probably rather different. These works show a habit of mind which never left him. He did not like to waste work, and when he had taught something he wanted to write a book based on his lectures. And the subject matter interested him. He had not graduated with any wish to put his notes away except when he was obliged to get them out again to fulfil his teaching requirements.

The lecturer would often hire one or two students to take notes as he spoke and give them to him afterwards as a *reportatio*,[95] from which he could work up what he had said for publication or in preparation for future lectures on the same material.[96] Wyclif himself seems to have done this. Some of his monographs were apparently first given as lectures, and the marks of the 'lecture' remain visible. 'I ask you, kind listeners, not to be sinister "reportators".'[97] The normal process of *reportatio* lent itself readily enough to spies maliciously taking advantage of the opportunity to copy down a lecturer's more shocking remarks and use them against him, at least that is what Wycliff alleges.[98]

But it looks as though he was working up his lectures into treatises on his own account too, in a steady stream. The requirement to lecture as part of the process of becoming a 'graduate' and for a short period afterwards as a 'Regent Master' meant that in the Arts at least relatively young and inexperienced scholars were likely to be producing the most publicly visible work. There was, too, such a rivalry between the 'secular' academics and those in the religious orders, that it becomes noticeable in the early fourteenth century that in theological studies especially the seculars were anxious to heighten their visibility by recording and publishing what they said in lectures,[99] and there is no reason to think this would not also be true in the arts. For there was 'research', original work and interpretation and criticism, intended by those who were involved in it to go far beyond the direct needs of the syllabus and the requirements of teaching. Wyclif's treatises on logic probably date from about 1360–63,[100] the treatise on the soul and the treatise on 'insoluble propositions' from perhaps 1365. Much effort has been put into reconstructing this presumed *summa* and identifying its completed and surviving parts,[101] yet it is by no means certain that Wyclif had any such systematically conceived and executed project clearly in mind.

Although good working copies of set textbooks could have wide margins and spaces between the lines to make space for commentary, university teachers' own books were usually written in a more heavily abbreviated and rapid hand than books for liturgical use or library copies. The copies of Wyclif which survive in Prague are like that. But we have no real idea how Wyclif liked his writings to look. Like others he used secretaries and paid students to take notes when he spoke so there are many unknown intermediaries between him and the actual copies we now have.

iv. John Wyclif, Fellow of Merton and Master of Balliol

Fellow of Merton College

Wyclif was moving into a new phase of life, as a graduate and – at least for a time – aspirant to prestigious or lucrative positions. The evidences for the first episodes of his adult life are frustratingly sketchy. Just when it would bring him forward as a three-dimensional figure, striding out into the word, the picture is at its most unsatisfactory.

We first come face to face with him in a college, one of the corporate institutions beginning to emerge from the motley collection of halls and lodgings we glanced at earlier. The informal 'lodgings-like' character of the 'halls', which most closely resembled modern halls of residence, went with an often rather ephemeral character. They came and went. Some which ultimately survived to become fully-fledged colleges were first called halls. Balliol College was Balliol Hall at first. One reason for their being called 'halls' may have been that they tended to retain the large room or 'hall' which would be found in big country houses.[102] The halls contained individual chambers, which would usually be shared by the more junior. In each would be a bed (in which more than one might have to sleep), perhaps small, partitioned sections with a table or sloping board to write on and a shelf for books so that each scholar could have private space to work, a chest or two and a chair or two completing the usual furnishings of the chambers.[103] Physical remnants of parts of such a hall survive at St Edmund Hall, which eventually became a college.

Before New College was founded the six secular colleges already in existence in Oxford had among them about sixty-three Fellows, fewer than a dozen each.[104] In 1379 New College came into existence on an entirely different scale, with provision for a Warden and seventy Fellows or scholars 'on the foundation'. Fellow is a translation of the Latin *socius*, and it connotes ideas of community living together, corporate life.

The Fellows of these early Oxford colleges were usually young clerics, and Fellows for only a short time. This is quite different from the modern picture, where the achieving of a college Fellowship is likely to set a scholar up for life, and where a pattern of intense lifetime college loyalties has grown up, with elderly, retired Fellows still coming in regularly to meals, whose eccentricities are tolerated with a kindliness the working Fellows do not always show to one another. Malice departs and the old man, once a fiercely combated rival, who now totters from the common table with a slice of the breakfast toast in his pocket, is looked on benignly.

Wyclif's youthful experience was of the tiny infant colleges of the mid-fourteenth century.[105] The great shift of practice which led to the colleges taking in undergraduates and housing them happened in the century after his death.[106] The Oxford colleges he knew resembled modern All Souls College and were exclusive little societies of senior members, which did not as a rule admit undergraduates. The founder of Merton College took over a house which had been rented by two student brothers from a wealthy family for the sole use of themselves and their servants.[107] Merton, where John Wyclif first appears in 1356 as a Fellow, had regarded itself as 'the' college in Oxford for a century after its foundation in 1264, with University College, Balliol, Exeter, Oriel and Queen's mere halls.[108] It originally occupied two sites but under the statutes of 1274, when the founder, Walter de Merton, revised his wishes in the light of the experience of the first few years of the College's existence, it was established in its present position, on land close to the river-meadows. The constitution arranged for by the founder consisted of an endowment of property, given with the stipulation that it was to be used for the support of an academic community and vested in the members of the community.[109] He would leave behind him for future generations a 'Visitor', such as all Oxford and Cambridge colleges still have, with authority to interpret statutes of the college and to adjudicate in disputes between its members. But it was no more free of internal warfare that the other early academic societies of Oxford. During the year when Wyclif was a probationer-fellow or immediately afterwards there occurred one of the disputes which have so often divided Oxford and Cambridge colleges, and still do. Archbishop Islip had to make a visitation.

Wyclif must have been a Bachelor of Arts in 1356, or he would not have been eligible for a Fellowship under the college's statutes, for this college was not yet open to undergraduates. He could in principle have found himself a Proctor now, for he was eligible. Two other Fellows of Merton College, John de Middleton and Nicholas de Redyng, were, respectively, the Northern and Southern Proctors for 1355–56 and John Joskin, another Fellow of Merton, was Proctor for the Southerners in 1357–58. Not until 1368 did a Fellow of Balliol appear in the lists in Wyclif's time,[110] although Balliol was founded especially for Northerners.

In Wyclif's Oxford, the colleges were still mostly very small communities, within a numerically modestly-sized University where everyone knew one another, and a young scholar could easily be fired by the interest of the work others were doing. Among Wyclif's predecessor Mertonians we have met Richard of Campshall, Thomas Bradwardine, William Heysbury, Thomas

Buckingham, John Dumbleton, William Sutton, Richard Billingham, Simon Bredon, John Ashenden, Richard Swyneshead the Calculator.[111] Wyclif was lecturing on Logic while he was at Merton; he continued some work which had been done by his older fellow-Mertonian Richard Billingham on the proving of propositions.[112]

It is possible to get a shadowy picture of other aspects of the early period of this ambitious little College. Merton went to some trouble to acquire books. Some Fellows of Merton appear in the book-buying records between about 1325 and 1350. A book from St Albans Abbey (whether deliberately sold by the Abbey or not) containing works of St Ambrose and written in the twelfth century, was bought by William of Harington.[113]

There is a record that Wyclif arranged for the expenditure of £4 7s 5 ½d to entertain eighteen guests of the college on Ascension Day, 1356 (2 June). Probably he was simply 'steward of the week' in the normal rotation among the Fellows. The steward apparently lightened the bursar's load by carrying out those duties which related to the provision of meals and hospitality.[114] This would have been in much the way the administrative duties involved in running the place rotate today among the Fellows of an Oxford college. Wyclif's duties were simply administrative. The money would not have come out of his own pocket. It would have been reimbursed by the bursar in due course. The Third Bursar at the time was Richard Billingham. That the Wyclif in question was our Wyclif is confirmed by a list prepared before 1422 by Thomas Robert, Third Bursar in 1411. His Old Catalogue gives a list of the Fellows of Merton arranged under the reigns of kings, and in alphabetical order. Annotations appear beside many names, including that of Wyclif. What is said about him is not flattering, for the note was made after he had made his dubious reputation. He is identified as 'a Doctor of Theology (which he was certainly not as early as 1356 when he was at Merton), who was too confident in his own abilities'. He is contradictorily also said never to have been a Fellow (*socius*) of Merton at all.[115] It cannot of course be true both that he was never a Fellow of Merton and that he did not complete a year as a Fellow.

Master of Balliol

The modern pattern of a lifetime's loyalty to a college entered at the time of first entering the University, of membership for life, was not the norm in medieval Oxford. Within a year or two of his appearance as a Fellow of Merton Wyclif is to be discovered not only as a Fellow, but as the Master of Balliol College, a little further to the north of the town.

John de Balliol, a northern landowner, had violently attacked the Bishop of Durham and his men. The Bishop imposed a penance. John de Balliol was to support sixteen poor scholars at Oxford. On his death in 1269 his widow gave an endowment to create a foundation. The procurators were to be a Franciscan friar and a secular Master and the students on the foundation were to read only for Arts degrees. If they went on to higher degree studies they would have to leave the house.[116] Balliol was one of the earliest true colleges to survive. It had its chapel built by 1309-28. And Balliol ran various provisions, for example, a School of Arts and a house to accommodate students on the corner of Brasenose Lane.[117] Among the early members of the College were some of the outstanding logicians and mathematicians whose names Wyclif would have known: Walter de Burley, Thomas Bradwardine, Adam de Pipewell.[118]

Today the Mastership of an Oxford or Cambridge college is a considerable prize and one rarely aspired to until late middle age. Yet by 1360–61 the still comparatively young John Wyclif, whom we have so only just heard of as a junior probationary Fellow of Merton College, is to be found in the records as Master of Balliol College, and a Master of Arts, and surrounded it seems by north country colleagues, for that was the founder's idea and remained the tradition of the place. The position of Master then was much closer to that of the tutor of a student hall of residence; it was the kind of responsibility which may now be undertaken by a relatively young academic or administrator in return for accommodation.

There are three documents in evidence of Wyclif's connection with Balliol.[119] The first one describes a dispute between the Master and Fellows of Balliol and Nicholas Marchaunt about property in St Lawrence Jewry. It records a court case. Johannes de Wyclyf, 'Master of the house of scholars at the hall known as Balliol in Oxford', was summoned to explain to the court why he had required pledges worth forty-eight shillings from Nicholas Marchaunt two months before, even though Nicholas had his tenement in Old Jewry freehold, he claimed. In the end Balliol established that it owned the property and it won its case. The second and third documents relate to another matter. The College appropriated to itself the church of Abbotsley and legal documents were created to establish the fact. One is a deed, dated 7 April 1361, to which the Master and ten Fellows were witnesses. The other is a notary's record which identifies the 'Master or Warden of the aforeseaid College (*Magister sive custos collegii predicti*) as John de Wykcliff.'[120]

Soon after these two brief forays into grown-up academic Oxford life, during which he was perhaps completing his lecturing requirements as a Master of Arts, Wyclif went off to be a parish priest in a parish Balliol made available to him. We do not know why or exactly when, but it is likely that he and the college regarded it as an appropriate next step in a promising career for a young 'secular'.

Part I

Ambition Thwarted

Chapter 4

A taste of parish life

'Francis Arabin... was the younger son of a country gentleman of small fortune in the north of England. [...] he went to Oxford... He became a member of a vigorous debating society... In due process of time he took his degree and wrote himself B.A., but he did not do so with any remarkable amount of academical éclat. He had occupied himself too much with... polemics, politics and outward demonstrations... When Mr. Arabin left Oxford, he was inclined to look upon the rural clergymen of most English parishes almost with contempt. It was his ambition... to do something towards redeeming and rectifying their inferiority.'[1]

Wyclif's resemblances to Trollope's nineteenth-century Mr Arabin underline how commonplace over many centuries it was for a young man who had been to Oxford to take the next step Wyclif was about to take. In May 1361 Wyclif was inducted into the Balliol College living of Fillingham in Lincolnshire, a few miles north of Lincoln beside Ermine Street. The college had livings in its gift, but those to whom they were given could not continue as Fellows, let alone occupy such an office as Master, so Wyclif was, in every sense, leaving Oxford. One of the main *raisons d'être* of the University of Oxford at this date was to provide adequately educated priests for parishes.

A good man was ther of religioun,
And was a povre Persoun of a toun;
But riche he was of holy thoght and werk,
He was also a lerned man, a clerk,
That Cristes gospel trewely wolde preche;
His parisshens devoutly wolde he teche...

He sette nat his benefice to hyre,
And leet his sheep encombred in the myre…
But dwelt at hoom, and kept wel his folde. [2]

Chaucer's Poor Parson has an extensive parish, in which the houses are scattered, but he visits them assiduously on foot with a staff. He is an example to his people. His own substance is small, but he gives to those in need. He lives according to the Gospel and he preaches the Gospel:

But Cristes lore, and his apostles twelve,
He taughte, and first he folwed it him-selve.[3]

Wyclif was beginning the career which had perhaps been mapped out for him by his family, or in his own mind, all along, for it makes sense of his remaining a 'secular' and not joining one of the religious orders. As far as it is possible to establish, he spent the next two years living in his 'living' and presumably performing his parish duties. This was his first experience of life as a parish priest and probably his longest time until the very end of his life when he was actually performing the duties which went with the 'cure of souls'.

The daily life of a young priest in a parish is not easy to reconstruct now. The expectations were probably not high. Even though Oxford existed (in part) to ensure that a sound theological education was available for parish priests, their educational levels varied. Wyclif was almost certainly much better educated than many who embarked on this life. It is hard to be sure how idealistic he was at this stage and how clearly he saw difficulties which were to become enormous for him as time went on. A summary of the 1370s survives which tells us what Wyclif probably thought about the role of a good priest in taking care of the needs of the souls in his charge. A priest, he believed, should be accountable, that is, subject to recall if he is unsatisfactory. He should be a good pastor to his flock, not a gambler or a huntsman, nor indeed a chess-player; he should not be a drinker; he should be a preacher of the Gospel with clarity and a man of prayer.[4] He has something to say about the duties of a priest in the book he wrote on 'The Pastoral Office', but that was not until early 1379,[5] and by then he had had many painful experiences and his ideas had moved on a long way. A pastor must be a good and virtuous man, he insists. He has a threefold duty. The first is to feed his sheep spiritually with the Word of God, as though to introduce them to the fields of heaven through the perpetual greenness of the fields in which he feeds them. His second duty is to purge his flock of spiritual scabies. His third duty is to defend his flock against the wolves which want to attack and hurt them.[6] There is more information about Wyclif's theology of ministry in his 'On Degrees of the Clergy',[7] perhaps written late in 1382 when he had returned to parish life and was once more living the life of a parish priest.

In this first period of his parish life, opportunities for heady talk of the kind he had enjoyed at Oxford, for real engagement with subtle and contentious minds, will have been few, although it is possible that he kept up some of the connections. The Master of Balliol who followed Wyclif, Master John Hugate, is not known to have taken up his post until 1366, but this does not mean that Wyclif would be able to linger in the College after he began to be a parish priest. It seems a fair inference that Wyclif did not find parish life completely satisfying, for it was not long before he was making plans to go back to Oxford and study for the higher degree which would eventually make him a Doctor of Theology.

If Wyclif wanted to become a theologian he had to find the funding to enable him to return to Oxford and continue his studies. There were neither student grants nor student loans. He had to set himself up with a better income. In practice that meant obtaining a sufficient 'living' (or number of livings), and also getting a licence from the local Bishop to enable him to be 'non-resident' once he was in charge of a parish, so that he could spend his time in Oxford and in study. These were the practical realities for a would-be graduate student in fourteenth-century Oxford. The problem of poverty was well recognized at this level, as it was for 'poor students' at undergraduate level. Balliol College used the revenue from a benefaction of Sir William Felton, some £40, to relieve poor scholars. Some of it was to be used to keep those who had graduated as Masters of Arts, until they could get preferment, for the Pope's licence to the College did not allow them to stay in the college after graduation.[8] In 1343 the College got the advowsons of Fillingham, Brattleby and Risholm.

Pluralism and absenteeism became proper objects of Wyclif's criticism in later life. Before that, his failure to obtain rewards he believed he deserved, caused him considerable personal disappointment and made a dispassionate and judicious view of the rights and wrongs of current practices by no means easy for him. He was not alone. Richard Ullerston was a Fellow of the Queen's College in 1391 and he served the College faithfully in various capacities, but more than a decade later he had still not been rewarded with a benefice.[9] Ullerston complained, as did others, including Wyclif, that the promotion he should have been able to expect was denied him.[10]

In 1362 Wyclif's name appears on the list of those who deserved to have some such provision made for them, which the University sent to Urban V (1309–70, Pope from 1362), the Pope-in-exile at Avignon (for this was one of the many periods of the Middle Ages when there was both a Pope and an anti-Pope, rivals for control of the See of Rome itself). The specific request on behalf of Wyclif was for a canonry at York. Wyclif also had reasonable hopes of the prebend (portion of the income) of Caistor, a canonry in Lincoln Cathedral, for he had obtained a papal 'reservation' which should have ensured that it fell to him when it next became vacant. The Pope did ensure that Wyclif got something, but it was the less prestigious prebend of Aust in Westbury-on-Trym, near Bristol, a collegiate church (one independent of diocesan control).

On 29 August 1363 John Buckingham, Bishop of Lincoln, granted Wyclif a licence to be non-resident at Fillingham. The non-residency licence was important. A priest without a licence, or one whose licence had run out, could find himself in trouble. Wyclif was 'cited' (summoned) to show reason why he should not be suspended from office and from his benefice for failing to provide a chaplain for the prebend of Aust while he held it. The situation was saved when in 1368 Wyclif was able to exchange the living of Fillingham for that of Ludgershall in Buckinghamshire, which was much closer to Oxford. Absenteeism and pluralism, the holding of several livings and benefices so that it was impossible to provide pastoral care personally in all of them, pose some serious ethical questions, as Wyclif eventually realized. The more conscientious might put in an impecunious curate to take pastoral care of the parishioners at a small fee. When Wyclif became a negligent absentee he was in good company, or at least numerous company.[11] Some of those who examined Wyclif's opinions and found them heretical at the Blackfriars meeting of 1381 can be shown to be shameless pluralists and absentees. John de Appleby, Dean of St Paul's, one of the Doctors of Law present also held the living of Rothbury, the Archdeaconry of Carlisle, prebends at Work and at Southwell and a pension from Durham of £100 a year. John Waltham, another lawyer, and Master of the Rolls, was made a Bishop and immediately handed over the work to two suffragans.[12]

We shall be able to observe Wyclif's changing position on benefices as the story unfolds.[13]

Chapter 5

At the Queen's College

> 'Academic persons, when they carry on study, not only in youth, as a part of education, but as a pursuit of their maturer years, become decidedly queer, not to say rotten; and... those who may be considered the best of them are made useless to the world by the very study which you extol.'[1]

When Wyclif returned to Oxford in 1363, he probably moved into rented rooms at the Queen's College, a relatively impoverished foundation which was glad of the income which could be got from such business, and could take in lodgers without admitting them to its Fellowship. The record shows that workmen did several days' work on rooms he lived in (referred to as Wyclif's 'chamber') in 1363–64. There is also a receipt for 40s for two years' rent for 1365–66.[2] So Wyclif paid a rent of £1 a year for his accommodation. A final surviving receipt, of 1374–75, is for another pound for a year's room-rent.[3] It is impossible to be certain whether he lived on in Queen's rooms throughout his years of growing fame and notoriety, but it seems very likely, since there is no hint of his living anywhere else, and he was apparently living at Queen's again in 1380–81.[4] What this meant for him in reality bears a moment's thought, for it shows us a Wyclif with no home but this rented bedsitter throughout all the years of strife which lay before him. Distractions from hard intellectual work and growing stress were few, and there was little hope of his being able to retreat for long from the artificial, intense and combative atmosphere of the University.

The link with the Queen's College presumably remained an informal business arrangement, but Wyclif would have had ample opportunity to make friends with others living in the house and to get to know about the various excitements and passages of arms at Queen's. Wyclif's long-time supporter Nicholas Hereford, whom we shall meet when he was under attack for his

Wycliffite ideas, was a Fellow of Queen's from 1369–75.[5] He had other acquaintances there who could have been responsible for securing for him the right to be a tenant in Queen's rooms. William Middleworth was elected a Fellow of Queen's in 1369, very soon after he had been expelled from Canterbury Hall with Wyclif.[6] Wyclif was not the only survivor of that episode to be taken in by Queen's. There is a record of a room being occupied by William Selby in 1380–81, during one of the periods when Wyclif is known to have had a room there too.[7] Robert Alington was Fellow of Queen's in 1381, at a time when Wyclif was still resident. And he and Matthew Willesthorpe (Fellow between 1379 and 1395) deposited a book with Wyclif as surety for a loan. Among his other sympathizers connected with Queen's towards the end of his time at Oxford were the former Fellows, John Trevila and William Middleworth who were, like Wyclif, renting rooms there.[8]

Ambitions for office

> 'I've been asked to let myself be a candidate for the Mastership. Those who asked me to stand are not a majority of the Fellows, but they represent a sound body of opinions. I don't approve of people who have to be persuaded to play, like the young woman who just happens to have brought her music.'[9]

Henry Whitfield, Provost (that is, the head) of Queen's 1361–62, and already eight years a Fellow when he was elected, remained Provost until 1377. The ostensible reason for his ultimate expulsion was that things were being proposed which were in conflict with the college statutes. Statutes were very important to a college, for they were its domestic laws and to infringe them was to undermine the College's very identity. The Queen's College statutes seemed to indicate that only someone born in Cumberland or Westmorland was eligible to be elected as its head. The internal wrangles became so heated that the Visitor had to be called in. He appointed a commission and after much litigation the decision went against Whitfield's party. His long service did not prevent his being expelled from the Fellowship in 1379 along with William Franck, R. Lydford and John Trevils for 'Wycliffism', although the record shows that he had also been making difficulties about the election of the next Provost on which the dispute had officially turned.[10]

That was not the end of the matter. The King tried to mediate to get the ejected Fellows forgiven and restored. But, as it proved, they had kept hold of the keys and the common seal of the college, papers and plate and books, and more legal proceedings were needed to get them back. The battle ran on at least until 1380, and Wyclif can hardly have been unaware of the commotion while living in his rooms at Queen's, although we do not know which side or part he took.

Chapter 6

John Wyclif, Doctor of Theology

i. The academic scene

> 'While you are young, you will be oppressed, and angry, and increasingly disagreeable. When you reach middle age, at five-and-thirty, you will become complacent, and, in your turn, an oppressor; [...] it will seem to you then that you grow wiser every day, as you learn more and more of the reasons why things should not be done, and understand more fully the peculiarities of powerful persons.'[1]

When Wyclif returned to Oxford from his parish life, he knew he was coming back to a contentious world, and events can only have strengthened that awareness. In August 1363 Wyclif obtained permission to study Theology. It was unusual for a Master of Arts who was a secular to do this, though not unprecedented.[2] The Canterbury Hall episode would demonstrate only too clearly that the seculars remained misfits.

Wyclif was now moving from the familiar tasks and already-mastered subject matter of a lecturer in the Arts to 'higher degree' studies. His objective was to become a Doctor of Theology. A modern graduate student who goes beyond the level of a 'Master's degree' aims to begin on 'research'; a 'taught' graduate course is largely a preparation for independent research and most of those who go on to 'doctorates' (the PhD) write a thesis which embodies original enquiry. The higher degree studies of medieval universities were not research degrees but taught courses. There were three options for a student in a medieval university who wanted to go on with his studies after completing the Arts course. He could study Medicine or Law or Theology, and the highest of these was universally recognized to be Theology. In Oxford, Law and Theology were by far the most important of the three. There was a Medical Faculty but it was small and undistinguished.[3]

It does not seem to have been questioned that the taught subjects on offer at this level were somehow inherently more advanced that the subjects studied in the Arts course. In modern Britain a student chooses from a list of courses on the assumption that all subjects are roughly equivalent. They can almost all be studied for a first degree and the study can continue, if the student seeks a higher degree, by doing more advanced work in the same subject. But there is little idea that the broad area of subject matter itself may be inherently higher or lower, that Mathematics is, for example, an inherently more 'advanced' subject to study than the French language.

Yet it must have been obvious to everyone in Wyclif's Oxford that the theory did not match the practice, that it was not really a simple hierarchy of study at all. We have already seen that the Arts subjects, especially Grammar and Logic, were conceived of as tools for use in the study of the intrinsically 'higher' studies of Theology, Law and Medicine. Wyclif's books on Logic are concerned with theological matters, including Trinity, transubstantiation, divine foreknowledge, futurity and eternity, necessary futurity, time as fourth dimension.[4] The *Logicae continuatio* is Wyclif's study of the logic of Scripture.[5] The problem of universals was still relevant now that he was going to be a theologian, for he was writing the *De Universalibus*, probably about the time of his inception as a Doctor of Theology in 1372 and the controversy with Cunningham,[6] taking forward the *Purgans errores circa universalia in communi*. No theologian could achieve a mastery of Theology without applying advanced and sophisticated principles from his Arts studies, while the young students of the Arts were being introduced to theological problems. There was considerable overlap of topics.

The friars, who were running their own 'preparatory schools' in the essentials of the Arts, were impatient with the requirement that their own students should complete the Arts course in the University too. The religious orders set up separate *studia* of their own for *naturalis philosophia* and *logica* (three years' study for each).[7] These they tried to get the University to accept in lieu of study in their own courses, rather like the modern 'transferable credits'. The lawyers too challenged the requirement to complete an Arts degree first on behalf of their members who wanted to go straight to Theology on arrival in Oxford. William Chynals applied for the degree of Bachelor of Civil Law after only two years, one term and two long vacations in the *artes*.[8] The Arts Faculty said the lawyers were in it only for the money.[9]

The numerical balance of power in the University was complicated by the fact that the Regent Masters were of two kinds and at two very different levels of seniority, the theologians and lawyers and Doctors of Medicine over against the young regent masters of arts. In the middle of the sandwich were other figures such as Wyclif was about to become, senior in age to the Masters of Arts, but not currently Regents, because they had given up lecturing to study for the higher degree. Relations between the young Regent Masters in the Arts – of which Wyclif had himself recently been one – and the senior scholars who studied and lectured in the higher degree subjects could be distinctly uncomfortable when it came to University politics and the conduct of the University's business. The Regent Masters of Arts might be more junior but they were more numerous, and in a direct democracy where the Regent Masters, that is, those actually lecturing, in Arts and higher subjects each had one vote, numbers counted. At one stage the Artists held as many as thirty-four of the University offices.[10] They thus had, *de facto*, a power of veto in the decision-making of the University which became more firmly established as time went on. The Faculty of Arts had a right to see any proposal before it was discussed by Congregation (*facultate arcium integre reclamante*).[11] So much did this impede business that in 1357 a declaration by the Non-Regents in the Faculties of Theology and Civil Law sought to deny the Regents in Arts the right to block discussion of business by Congregation.[12] The University statutes of the fourteenth century suggest that the Regents in Arts could in theory expel the Chancellors, Proctors and Doctors from Congregations.[13] It is true that the Chancellor was almost always a Regent Master in Theology in recognition that this was the most elevated faculty of all. But the Proctors were always Regent Masters of Arts.

Wyclif was familiar with the politics of the place, intimate with the leaders of factions, almost certainly already a member of cliques and interest groups, and capable of displaying to its fullest the petty territoriality characteristic of the academic mind. The disputatiousness normal to the academic world was sharpened in Wyclif's Oxford by the training in formal disputation everyone had as a basic degree requirement. There are descriptions of the *parvisus*, the place where disputations were held,[14] and where the friendly sparring of the student lion cubs readily turned into snarling battles for dominance.

We can identify some of the people Wyclif knew, but he must of course have known almost everyone in the small town with its active bustle of scholarly disputes and academic indignation, its rivalries and alliances. It is not easy to say whether Wyclif had close or true friends, certainly not possible to point to a loyal circle, either of equals or of pupils. Those who might have been loyal, some of whose names drift by on the tide of events, were perhaps frightened off, when Wyclif became notorious and began to be demonized, by threats of damage to their own prospects by the authorities. This difficulty in getting a picture of the network of his early allies continues into his last years, as we shall see.

William Woodford was ordained as a subdeacon in 1351, and priest in 1357, and at that time he would already have been a Franciscan friar for some years. He was studying Theology in Oxford by 1367, after a preparatory period studying at least selected selected elements of the liberal arts within the order. He remarks that the order chose which of its students to send to the University, presumably when it had formed a view of their abilities and capacity to benefit from higher education.[15] Woodford and Wyclif would not only have attended the same lectures. They even lectured on the *Sentences* together when they were Theology students, or possibly later when they were discharging their lecturing obligations as new graduates. Woodford would jot down arguments in a notebook and show them to Wyclif who would write his answers. William Woodford kept this document and had it by him when he referred to it many years later, in order to hint disapprovingly that, even at that date, Wyclif was showing signs of unsoundness of opinion.[16] He remarks, 'when I was giving a course of lectures with him at Oxford, Wyclif was already expressing certain opinions about the Eucharist' (*quando concurrebam cum eo Oxoniae*). [17] Wyclif later mentions Woodford, whom he describes as 'my reverend doctor Master William Woddford' by name, as a person holding rival opinions to his own on the subject of the civil dominion of the clergy'.[18] Woodford became a Bachelor of Theology at the same time as Wyclif in 1369. Woodford incepted as a Doctor of Theology in 1372 or 1373, close to the time when Wyclif did so. There is a world of difference between their friendly rivalry at first and the sour mockery and bitter condemnations of the later years.

Woodford provides a useful comparison with Wyclif from the point of view of the way each began his postgraduate career as a qualified 'theologian'. The friars were expected to work in the world to a degree the monks were not. William Woodford acted for two decades at least as confessor to a number of individuals, including the Countess of Norfolk, Margaret Marshal. Here was opportunity to influence the innermost counsels of the great of the land, for such intimacies gave one access to important ears (or the ears of those married to the important). He acted as reader (*lector*) in a cathedral church, possibly St Paul's Cathedral. He was probably a chaplain to a community of nuns. Offices of this sort again created opportunities to have an influence on those who were important in the secular world. Woodford was also much more adventurous in his journeying than Wyclif. Apart from his one trip to Bruges (in Flanders, nowadays part of Belgium), Wyclif seems to have stayed in England all his life and to have travelled no further afield from Oxford than his livings and London. But Woodford – as a friar with a bed available to him almost anywhere he went in the *studia* of Europe – was in Cologne in 1375. This wider knowledge of the world enabled him to observe that they do things differently in other countries. How many orders are there (*Quot sunt ordines*), he asks? It depends where you live. There are more in some countries than others. Similarly, 'begging' practices vary. Friars are not all to be found out on the streets doing their begging personally. In some parts of Italy it is the rule that only two or three of the friars of a large house will actually go out begging.[19]

A repeating pattern of contriving to cause lasting offence in the normal course of academic debate is found again and again in Wyclif's encounters with his fellow-students and colleagues. Among the Dominicans, Ralph Strode (fl. 1350–1400) was a Fellow of Merton before 1360. His main early interest was in Logic, though he also had a reputation as a poet. He is mentioned by Chaucer in *Troylus and Crysede* (written between 1372 and 1386), where he is 'the philosophical Strode'. When Wyclif began to speak and write about predestination he took issue with him strongly, on the grounds that a doctrine of predestination destroys hope. He believed apostolic poverty was a good, and a better way of life than that of the rich man, but he did not consider it intrinsically sinful for the clergy to possess wealth.

John Cunningham, with whom Wyclif was to have his first contentious public exchange as a theologian, was a Carmelite friar from Ipswich. He was a Doctor of Theology before Wyclif himself achieved that status in 1372. He was, like William Woodford, a confessor with important clients, indeed he was confessor to Wyclif's patron John of Gaunt. He was a mild man and gently spoken. But Cunningham too turned decisively against Wyclif at the last, attacking his teaching in the Blackfriars Council of 1381–82 and in the sermon he preached at St Paul's Cross afterwards. 'I know that I am not more really in God than the spire of St Mary's is in my soul.' Cunningham became a 'strenuous persecutor of the Lollards', who tangled with Wyclif over many years, enduring his 'corrosive' and 'mordant' language. [20]

Another of the younger Carmelites was Stephen Patrington, later Bishop of Chichester (d. 1417). He entered the Carmelite Order while he was a student at Oxford, one of those who were 'recruited' by the friars. At the stage when he was himself a Bachelor of Theology he sent a letter to John of Gaunt on behalf of the Oxford friars for the consideration of the 'Earthquake Council' in 1382.[21] He became in due course a leader of the anti-Lollards in Oxford, and was put under the protection of the Chancellor, Robert Rygge (who proved equivocal in these matters), because he was so useful to the University authorities in this connection. In 1389 he became a Doctor of Theology and soon left Oxford for his Order's house in London, where he won fame as a preacher.

Among the Benedictines with whom Wyclif publicly quarrelled is Uthred of Boldon.[22] He had probably been one of Wyclif's Masters when he was a student, for he addresses him as 'my reverend doctor and special Master Dom Uthred' and speaks of 'beautiful things he drew out of Scripture and the way he had of sowing the seeds of knowledge in the University'.[23] Uthred, sustaining the Benedictine position against that of the friars in Oxford, had had a serious difference of opinion with the Archbishop, Simon Langham, on the subject of poverty and he had withdrawn from Oxford in 1368. Wyclif's own pattern of leaving Oxford and coming back was far from unique.

The *Fasciculi Zizaniorum* (the 'Bundle of weeds' of Matthew 13:40),[24] gives a list of Masters who disputed with or determined against Wyclif,[25] and there are undoubtedly more[26] whose identities would have been clearer to contemporaries when they heard Wyclif mention them obliquely in a sermon or lecture.

These moments of illumination of the academic social scene within which Wyclif lived and worked do not help us to understand how close any of these friendships were. It is possible in university life to work with colleagues for long periods without close friendships forming, and who Wyclif knew remains a quite different question from who he liked and who liked him.

Canterbury Hall

> 'The political motive in the academic breast is honest enough. It is Fear – genuine, perpetual, heartfelt, timorousness.'[27]
>
> 'The principle of the dangerous precedent is that you should not now do an admittedly right action for fear you or your equally timid successors should not have the courage to do right in some future case.'[28]

There was one brief passage when Wyclif ventured elsewhere, and this episode lends a sharper flavour to the circumstances in which he did so. There has been some dispute as to whether this episode concerns our Wyclif, but it is more than probable that it does. Canterbury Hall (or College) was founded by Simon Islip, Archbishop of Canterbury, in 1361.[29] It was to be a community in which both monks and secular Fellows could live, the monks coming from the community at Christ Church, Canterbury. The idea had much to recommend it, as a method of providing for the needs of 'secular' scholars and breaking down the 'class barrier' between them and the members of the religious orders. The plan was for about a dozen, a dangerously small number perhaps because of the likelihood that they would get on top of one another and quarrel. It was stated in the eventual litigation that there were to have been four monks, one of whom was to be the Warden, and eight seculars.[30] In the ensuing squabbles between the monks, the Archbishop appointed Henry Wodehull, a monk of Christ Church, to be the first Warden. In the foreseeable quarrels between the monks and the secular scholars, the secular scholars drove the Warden out. Three more seculars, William Middleworth, Richard Benger and William Selby, among them friends or associates of Wyclif, moved in, in place of the ejected monks.[31]

Islip drew up new statutes to provide the community with a fresh constitution in which the balance of power was more clearly defined, with seculars in the ascendent. He appointed a John Wyclif to be the new Warden in 1365. It should be borne in mind that if this was our John Wyclif, he was probably still quite young, with his way to make, and Islip had not given him an easy step up in the world with this proposed solution to his residential problems.

This was an unsatisfactory state of affairs and it seemed to go against the principle that seculars should not enter monastic schools. The new Archbishop of Canterbury, Simon Langham, was himself a Benedictine monk. He was enthroned in March 1367 and promptly, within days, he intervened, as the statutes Islip had written for Canterbury Hall allowed the Archbishop to do. He appointed a monk of Canterbury, John de Redyngate, as Warden, and ordered the scholars in the college to obey him. Wyclif and his supporters were ejected in their turn. Redyngate lasted only three weeks; the Prior and Chapter of Christ Church, Canterbury, were soon sending in their own preferred names. The Archbishop reappointed the original Warden. By 1370 Canterbury Hall had become a mainly monastic society. The decision of Rome in 1384, when the ensuing lawsuit was finally resolved, was that the house must be either for monks or for seculars and could no longer be a mixture. The monks had it. In 1384 five undergraduates were allowed to live in as servants to the monk-fellows and to assist in the running of the chapel.[32]

Whatever the truth about this episode, it provides a valuable rare pointer to a key date in Wyclif's life. The final judgment on the Canterbury affair names Wyclif as a Bachelor of Theology for the first time (May 1370, possibly citing a text of July 1369). He incepted as a Master between January 1371 and the end of 1373.

William Woodford, the Franciscan, who used to collaborate with Wyclif in the preparation of lectures when they were both students,[33] commented that it was this episode which first turned Wyclif decisively against the religious orders,[34] (although he also says that Wyclif's anger was aroused by the public attack the mendicants made upon his teaching about the Eucharist; after that he spoke ill of them in many ways).[35]

ii. The Theology course

Becoming a theologian was probably not as lucrative as the career open to those who took higher degrees in Law. But the doctorate in either subject had the ring of the modern MBA in terms of the assistance it might give to the ambitious who wanted to climb an ecclesiastical or academic career ladder. The qualification of Doctor of Theology was most prestigious of all. That is implicitly recognized in the fierceness of the dispute about whether members of the religious orders should have special terms of entry. The friars complained in 1311 that they were being disadvantaged by the rule that no one could become a Master in Theology until he had graduated in Arts, for in their view their own students were well equipped to leap a stage or two. To protect its own standards, the University had decided that any dispensation from the requirement had to be a unanimous decision of the Masters. The friars protested that this meant that a single Master could prevent a friar being excused, even if he had had an ample grounding within the order. That power, it was alleged, was being abused. Having got the bit between their teeth, the University authorities took further actions to weaken the position of the Dominicans and other friars which suggest a certain lack of good faith.

In one episode, their Doctor of Divinity, Hugh of Sutton (or Dutton) has been expelled from the *consortio Magistrorum*. The bedel no longer includes him in his rounds to read and accept Notices from him. The other Masters are refusing to take part in disputations in which friars are involved, and that prevents the friars from taking their degrees.

There was a good deal of intimidation designed to prevent students attending the friars' lectures in Theology. The University persuaded the Archbishop of Canterbury to excommunicate the friars. The friars also voiced objections to the structure of the Theology course itself.[36] Challenge to these changes had been made more difficult by the fact that since the friars appealed against the new rules, a requirement had been introduced that all existing and new graduates must swear never to oppose the University or assist anyone to oppose it.[37] The University claimed that it was only seeking to maintain standards. It could not allow unqualified lecturers to teach,[38] any more than it could allow its students to graduate without completing all the requirements. The continuing heatedness of these arguments in Wyclif's time[39] is evident in the royal writ of 30 May 1379, to the Chancellor and Proctors, that the Friars Preacher shall not be hindered in their scholastic acts. The King says he is responding to a supplication by the Regent Master of the Dominicans and their Bachelors and students. He is struck by the difficulties the Dominicans are struggling under and he wants them to be allowed to perform their scholastic acts and to be permitted to proceed to their degrees.[40]

When he returned to Oxford in search of this desirable qualification, Wyclif began on a higher degree course which was unlike a modern research degree. It was more like a modern graduate taught-course. It followed a similar pattern to that of the undergraduate course in Arts, in that it involved hearing lectures on set texts and practising the required disputations, except that the students were older and were graduates. There is evidence that the course was being abbreviated in Oxford, no doubt under pressure from the religious orders who wanted their members to be able to graduate as early as possible, but the requirements were still fairly onerous. By 1313 a Bachelor's degree 'required lectures' on the Bible, one book of the Old Testament and one of the New, need not last more than a year and the student had to complete only two years of residence and disputation after his period of required lecturing on the *Sentences* before he could finally graduate. The lectures on the *Sentences* required were reduced between 1313 and 1407 to three terms of a single academical year, and the 'regency' period was also abbreviated. It remained, nevertheless, a long course for someone in early middle age who was expected to give up his lucrative Arts lecturing and other pursuits and return to the status of full-time student for a period of years. Some cut it short by not graduating.

In theory the student could not graduate as a Master of Theology before the seventh year of study or the age of thirty-five,[41] and during the two years or more after he had become a Bachelor he had to practise 'opposing' and 'responding' in the theological schools so as to demonstrate that he had the skills he would need as a Master. So the course and the examinations involved elements that modern higher education would call 'continuous assessment'. He also had to give public sermons (*publice predicare*), to demonstrate his competence in preaching, including an 'examination sermon' at the University Church of St Mary's, the *sermo generalis or examinatorius*.[42] Wyclif's progression through this lengthy process of qualification can be traced reasonably confidently. He is described first as *sacra theologia bacallarius* in May 1370 in a document in connection with the Canterbury Hall dispute. He is described in a similar way in January 1371 when Pope Gregory XI appointed him to a canonry at Lincoln Cathedral. But by 1373, when there was a renewal of the gift of the canonry on better terms, he is described as 'Magister'. He must therefore have incepted, though there is no way of knowing how he found the money. A Master of Theology seems to have been eligible to be referred to as a 'Doctor' when he had discharged his lecturing obligations and Wyclif did that too. It therefore took Wyclif some time to progress from the status of Master of Arts to his theological doctorate after he returned to Oxford in the autumn of 1363, more than the minimum period of seven years, but that is probably because he had to find the necessary tuition fees to pay for the required lectures. There is no evidence that he was ever an idle or half-hearted student.

It was perfectly possible to write and publish and make a name outside Oxford independently of the stage one had reached in this 'advanced' course of study in Theology, and whether or not one had formally graduated. A good example is William of Ockham in the generation before Wyclif. He had entered the Franciscan Order as a small boy, younger than fourteen. Ockham's Oxford career fell between 1307–08 and 1320. He was engaged in theological studies and lecturing on the *Sentences* in 1317–18, when he was thirty-two. Two or three years after that he would have completed all the requirements for his doctorate in Theology, including being at least thirty-five years old, and, if he got so far, he could have graduated, but he never incepted. It is probable that he returned to the Greyfriars' house in London when he left Oxford and that it is there that he wrote his first, largely non-political, published works. They were not, however, uncontroversial. His freedom to do this without apparent detriment to his chance of his work becoming known shows that the religious orders constituted a real challenge to the University as rival centres of scholarship and influence. For a 'secular' like Wyclif there was less flexibility.[43]

iii. The *Sentences* of Peter Lombard

Wyclif did complete the course. We must now try to get a picture of what it involved, as we did for the arts course, partly by looking at what he was expected to learn through the lens of what he went on to teach. His teaching helped to form his ideas, not least through the satisfactions of shocking an appreciative student audience. For when in the fifth year, after the four years of compulsory 'hearing' of lectures, three of them on the Bible, the student was admitted to the degree of Bachelor of Theology, he was then expected to lecture on ('read' to others) the *Sentences* of Peter Lombard as a Bachelor of Theology (or 'Divinity'), although he was not allowed to put in his own ideas or to challenge accepted views except in his opening and closing lectures.[44] One result – as with the spur to original work in the *artes* – was to encourage the beginners, the mere Bachelors, to be as original and adventurous as they dared, with the Masters of Theology apparently being much less productive and stimulating.

The *Sentences* of Peter Lombard achieved an extraordinary dominance in the medieval Theology curriculum.[45] They were the work of a mid-to-late twelfth-century Paris Master who had set about making an orderly compilation of the views of 'authorities', particularly that select band of important early Christian authors such as Augustine, who were by now beginning to be known as 'the Fathers', on the principal topics of a systematically arranged Christian theology. The use of established authorities was nothing new; the novelty lay in the attempt at orderly treatment, for that required the whole subject matter of Theology to be put in order. It was the beginning of modern 'systematic Theology'.

Peter Lombard explains in his Preface what he has tried to do. There are many whose learning is inadequate. (He modestly includes himself.) He proposes to assist his readers by gathering the key texts conveniently together for them in a short book (*brevi volumine*), 'so that it will not be necessary for them to look them up by turning over the pages of many books'. He has been conscious, as he worked, that there are many contradictions in these opinions.[46] His own attempts to put these thoughts of others in order unavoidably evinced opinions of his own, and here he ran into trouble. It is the more extraordinary that this became the standard textbook because to begin with Peter Lombard and his work were at risk of being condemned for heresy.

Walter of St Victor wrote a polemic (probably in 1177–78) against the 'four labyrinths of France'. Among them he includes Peter Abelard and Gilbert of Poitiers. Both were condemned by councils of the Church. He adds Peter Lombard and Peter of Poitiers, one of Peter Lombard's pupils.[47] This treatise on the 'four labyrinths' is an acknowledgment of the power of writing and teaching to influence minds and affect events. The work of the individuals labelled the 'four labyrinths' is causing alarm.[48] Walter's contention is that these are the 'modern heretics' (*novi heretici*). Peter Lombard, he says, even tries to drag all the Fathers into manifest heresy with him (*cogit secum omnes deficere*), making the very authorities tell his own unreliable story.

Yet this was the book which was to form the bedrock of Theology teaching for centuries to come. The *Sentences* found their place in the syllabus partly as a consequence of their being attacked by persons perceived to be even more dangerous than Peter Lombard himself. Joachim of Fiore (c. 1135–1202), the wild Calabrian Prophet and Abbot who foretold that the end of the world was at hand,[49] spoke out against Peter Lombard's views on the doctrine of the Trinity and did him the good turn of making his work more prominent and crystallizing opinion; after some wrangling and attempts to persuade the Church's authorities to take an official position, it was Joachim who was formally condemned by the Fourth Lateran Council,[50] and Peter Lombard's *Sentences* were discovered to be orthodox after all. The *Sentences* had their influence even in the vernacular. Richard Rolle the hermit wrote an English and a Latin psalter which made use of the text.[51]

By Thomas Aquinas's time, in the second half of the thirteenth century, Theology had resolved itself into innumerable 'questions', on all of which opposing views could be marshalled, supported by series of arguments, each with its authority or very good reason. Indeed, Aquinas says that his own reason for composing the *Summa Theologiae* is that this cloud of questions has become so dense and obscure that students find it impossible to see their way through. 'My plan in this work is to treat those things which pertain to the Christian religion in such a way as to meet the needs of those just beginning their studies. For I have reflected how novices in this branch of learning are greatly impeded by having to deal with so many authors, partly because of the multiplication of useless questions, articles and arguments; partly, too, that those matters which such students need to know are not taught according to the order of the subject, but according to the demands of the exposition of the set books, or as they prompt a disputation.' He concludes that this is creating a great deal of confusion in the minds of students, and he has accordingly set about arranging the things they need to know in order. Important though Aquinas's *Summa* was to become from the sixteenth century, especially within his own Dominican order, the *Sentences* kept their place.

Oxford was unusual in requiring the study of the *Sentences* before the study of the Bible.[52] Nothing should be read into this by way of any intention on the part of the Oxford authorities to make the *Sentences* more important than the Bible, but it makes it appropriate to begin with it here, because it was where Wyclif was obliged to begin, both as a student and as an apprentice lecturer.

In practice the *Sentences* were used as a jumping-off point. From about 1290 commentaries on this textbook were already becoming a principal vehicle for budding theologians who wanted to venture experimental opinions and make their names. They had to give their required lectures on the *Sentences* as part of the course. Effectiveness for this purpose was naturally the greater if the lecturer did not go through the whole text but concentrated on particular topics. That became the norm from about 1335. It was not even necessary to treat the text in the normal lecturer's way and produce a continuous 'commentary' on the parts selected. Something more like a monograph or treatise would do.[53] The *quaestio* could easily evolve into a treatise or monograph; it was simply a matter of length. *Sentences* commentaries from fourteenth-century Oxford are known (for example, those of Nicholas Aston, Osbert Pickingham, John Klenkok, Richard Brinkley),[54] but the Oxford record is bare in an era when the tradition of *Sentence* commentary at Paris was still quite rich.

Into the consideration of 'questions arising' were imported the technical assumptions of the day. We can get an idea of the way they were being used close to Wyclif's time from William of Ockham. Ockham drew 'questions' out of the very Preface to the *Sentences*: whether the understanding we have in this life can give us 'evident knowledge' (*notitia evidentia*) of theological truth; whether such *notitia evidentia* is strictly speaking science or knowledge; whether God is the subject of Theology; whether knowledge which is practical and that which is speculative are distinguished by their aims.[55] It is clear enough how the *Sentences* were being taken as a springboard.

A question is asked about the meaning of the statement that God begets God. It will be remembered that 'supposition' was taught as one of the elements of Logic in the Arts course, so it is natural for Ockham to approach the matter in this way. Ockham takes the opportunity[56] to argue that simple supposition does not merely involve the term standing for a particular thing in a given context. In his opinion it is also necessary to consider the *intentio animae*, the intention of the soul, as to what the term is to signify in that context on that occasion. Ockham cites various modern opinions with disapproval: that of Aquinas; that of Duns Scotus. Ockham had his supporters, especially outside Oxford, John Buridan, Marsilius of Inghen, Albert of Saxony.[57] There was controversy. But he also had his opponents at home in England.[58] Walter Burley began the longer version of his de *Puritate Artis Logicae* with an attack on Ockham's theory of simple supposition.[59] Another anti-Ockhamist treatise, the *De suppositionibus* by William Sutton, who was a Fellow of Merton between 1330 and 1346, rejects the Ockhamist principle.[60] Wyclif very probably knew at least the main points of this exchange.

'On the blessed Incarnation'[61] may well have derived from Wyclif's commentary on Book III of the *Sentences*. It contains an account of Wyclif's Christology as it probably stood at the time of this lecturing.[62] It takes the student through the elements of the traditional debates of Christian theologians on the divine and human natures of Christ. Wyclif accepts that there are numerous apparently contradictory passages in Scripture on these subjects which may confuse the beginner.[63] He offers a solution which is designed to make things easier for the (admittedly rather mature and sophisticated) beginners he is lecturing to and writing for. Christ has three natures. He is Godhead, body and soul: *deitas, corpus et anima*.[64] Wyclif is confident that the careful application of these distinctions will protect the student from confusion and error. For example, 'unless I am mistaken', he says, 'Scripture nowhere takes "to be created" to mean "to be begotten".'[65] But the potential for this turning out to be heretical is obvious. Had not Gilbert of Poitiers been condemned for saying they were four Gods when he spoke of *divinitas* as well as Father, Son and Holy Spirit?

Wyclif could be disparaging about modern trends. 'The schools, falling away from the old logic concerning universals, and from the correct metaphysics of substantial forms, the more modern doctors agree in denying [the old ideas about Christ's soul and his humanity].'[66] Theological subjects should be approached 'with diligence, reverence and fear'. With diligence, because no matter is more difficult to understand; with reverence, because no theological topic is more precious; and with fear because nowhere is it easier to go dangerously astray.[67]

There is no reason to think Wyclif – or many others bringing their study of the Arts to bear in what may now appear obscure and over-technical ways – had had any intention other than the pedagogical one of helping his students to see their way more clearly in the thickets of the orthodox formulations. As a new teacher of Theology, Wyclif faced extreme difficulty in explaining things without misleading his students. And rival lecturers were on the lookout for things to complain of. It was a cut-throat world.

The problems did not end with finding a way to express orthodoxy intelligibly, and before we move on to the study of the Bible in the Theology course it may be useful to take stock of some of the issues. Theology in fourteenth-century Oxford faced the dilemma which has to be resolved for all academic Theology courses. Was it to treat its subject matter with the same detachment as would be appropriate in the study of Grammar, looking only to questions of correctness and exactness and so on? Or was it to try to include the devotional and spiritual dimensions in recognition that the students were also on a 'spiritual journey'? In the modern world, this question is answered differently in universities and in theological colleges and seminaries; and differently again in different countries. In Germany and the USA, academic theological departments and faculties are often confessional (denominational). In British universities, as distinct from seminaries, the norm is to study Theology both non-denominationally and in a manner which leaves out the spiritual and devotional except insofar as those are proper subjects for academic study in themselves. In Wyclif's world and Wyclif's generation, the solution was to divert much of the study of such aspects to preaching, as we shall see. As we shall also see, the preacher, especially when he had a university congregation, was often tempted into asides of pure academic malice.

iv. Bible study

On the question of Wyclif's attitude to Scripture rests much of his reputation as 'Morning Star of the Reformation'. The legend that Wyclif put Scripture back at the centre of theological studies, and sought to make its text available for ordinary people to read in their own language, makes the stage of the Oxford Theology course which consisted in Bible study of especial interest.[68] Did Wyclif need to bring the study of the Bible back into a prominent position? Had it ever slipped from first place in theological studies? From before the time of its establishment as the 'canon' and throughout the Middle Ages, the Bible was held to be the most important of all texts and the one held in greatest reverence. Until at least the end of the twelfth century, *studium sacrae scripturae* (the study of Holy Scripture) was the term everyone naturally used to describe what is now called 'theology'.[69] In the thirteenth and fourteenth centuries, while 'Systematic Theology' was advancing to academic centre stage, the Bible kept its place there too. These modes of study remained complementary. The only real question is whether the accepted technicalities of method worked as well as everyone, including Wyclif, thought.

For Wyclif and his contemporaries, hearing lectures and then lecturing *biblice* was the other major element in the Theology course alongside the study of 'Systematic Theology' as represented in Peter Lombard's *Sentences*. Academic 'Bible study' involved the close study of the text word by word and phrase by phrase, in the same manner as was used in lecturing on other set books. Wyclif accepted the need for 'interpretation' and he had no real concerns about making use of the comments of earlier Christian authorities, although he insists that if the Bible contradicts human knowledge, one should not be ashamed to prefer what 'the Bible says'. Even the 'modern doctors' are prepared to do that when 'human knowledge' needs to be put in its place.[70] Scripture should be followed rather than any secular writing,[71] with the great early Christian writers such as Augustine having a certain accepted reliability. Wyclif points out that even an Augustine is not infallible, but some authorities are more acceptable than others: Augustine is more reliable than Plato or Aristotle and he is indeed outstanding among the authorities on Holy Scripture.[72] Wyclif has found no mistakes in Augustine's writings, none at least that he himself did not retract.[73]

The comments of the Fathers had been brought together into a standard commentary or *Glossa ordinaria* covering the whole Bible, which was nominally completed in the twelfth century.[74] It nevertheless went on evolving in the thirteenth century. 'Postills' (from *post illa*, 'after that') continued to be added. Hugh of St Cher[75] had contributed further material and Nicholas of Lyre had added more, completing his own revision of the *Glossa ordinaria* in the 1330s. *Postillatio and glossatio* were fancier and more advanced technical terms, but the old terminology perhaps came more naturally and we find mediaeval scholars routinely discussing the 'glosses'. Grosseteste writes that something in Galatians 3 [17] 'is sufficiently explained in the Master's Gloss'.[76] 'The gloss says that' appears again and again.[77]

By Wyclif's time there were two distinct vehicles of interpretation which could use this collected material and other 'authorities' to illuminate the text: sermons and academic lectures. In the early Christian centuries, they were probably not really seen as distinct. The Fathers preached at very great length – for hours, sermon after sermon – interpreting a chosen book, a word or a phrase at a time, and establishing the assumption that this minute scrutiny was the most appropriate and respectful way to do it. Some long series of such homilies survive: for example, Augustine's *Enarrationes* on the Psalms and Gregory the Great's homilies on Ezekiel. Such materials were used in medieval interpretation with no sense that they should be treated differently because they had originally been in sermons. University sermons were now, however, in Wyclif's time, rather different from lectures.

Wyclif apparently had, at first, nothing against continuing in the tradition of the lectures on the Bible he had himself so recently heard, and was now required to continue as part of the process of completing and taking his degree. He had nothing against it when, first as a Bachelor and then as a Master of Theology, he had to give his own required lectures. There was no expectation that he would produce entirely or even substantially original material, indeed the purpose of the routine lecturing was to provide the students with a grounding in what was familiar and accepted. On the other hand, the lectures, like those of the young practitioners in the arts, were display pieces and a lecturer might well choose to be provocative.

He probably lectured on the whole Bible between c. 1371 and 1376, for there are sufficient internal cross-references in his writings to indicate that he got all the way from Genesis to Revelation,[78] relying a good deal on what was in effect a crowd of 'intellectual intimates' of a very recent generation. Wyclif's chief source was probably Nicholas of Lyre.[79] Nicholas of Lyre met Richard FitzRalph, one of the instigators of the debate about dominion which was soon to take over Wyclif's life, and indeed they probably spent some time in the same place about similar business during the late 1330s. Wyclif also used the thirteenth-century Franciscan Robert Grosseteste most respectfully. He allowed himself some name-dropping of obscure authors. Then there were contemporaries, a mixed bunch. 'Love moves even the modern doctors, to make use of the magisterial words drawn from Scripture even if they seem to contradict human sciences,' says Wyclif, possibly with a twinkle at his students, for he was of course (or was soon to be) a 'modern doctor' himself.[80]

Wyclif's *Postilla* on the Old Testament was divided into eight parts, of which three survive variously in a series of Oxford manuscripts.[81] The commentary is in note-form, probably reflecting the *reportatio* of Wyclif's actual lectures. Spaces are left for references to be completed, and there is a concluding prayer for each, as was customary at the end of Oxford lecture courses.[82] There are two discussions of the Song of Songs, the second of which is the *principium*, or inaugural lecture Wyclif gave as a Doctor of Theology, and it probably also marks the stage he had reached in lecturing on the Bible as a Bachelor when he became entitled to incept as a Master in 1372. As he goes on through the Old Testament he becomes bolder and more willing to include his own opinions as befitted his growing standing.[83]

It is possible to get a flavour of these early commentaries from the surviving copies. His study of the Arts and Philosophy is still much in Wyclif's thoughts. In the introductory remarks to the Song of Songs, 'or rather to the whole of Scripture', he discusses the frame of mind, devotionally speaking, in which the reader ought to come to the Bible. Then he adds, 'but the philosopher may enquire what the disposition of the feelings has to do with the application of the intellect to the grasping of theological wisdom'.[84] Wyclif's own view is that Christian theology requires a different approach from any other subject, because it inquires into things beyond human understanding. To read the Bible unspiritually is to risk misunderstanding it. At the same time – in a characteristic balancing act – he insists that the arts of language, grammar, dialectic and rhetoric are extremely helpful to the interpretation of the Bible. 'Happy is he' who knows his literal and his figurative senses; 'happier' is he who knows how to resolve the Latin into the original Greek and Hebrew (which Wyclif himself was certainly not competent to do); and 'happiest' is he whose skills as a logician enable him to bring out what is hidden and make everything clear.[85] Augustine had written comprehensively about the problem of applying rhetorical theory in Bible reading, as Wyclif knew and explains. Logic had far more potential to cause difficulties in Wyclif's day than rhetoric had had in Augustine's fourth and fifth centuries, particularly when its areas of overlap with grammatical theory were brought into play. Scripture can be misinterpreted through the misapplication of human logic.[86] When he points out that the special language of Scripture has its own special 'way of speaking',[87] Wyclif is doing no more than echo Gregory the Great's sixth-century cry that the Holy Spirit is not constrained by the rules of [the grammarian] Donatus. 'The greater part of our disputation goes beyond the rules of the law of Christ,' says Wyclif reprovingly, for it is done for vainglory and not in love for the elucidation of Scripture.

There are already underlying disgruntlements with corrupt and misleading contemporary clerical practices, which surface in such comments as disapproval of the adoration of modern sculptures. These are mostly no more than commonplaces of a rich medieval literature of similar 'radical' grumbles. Wyclif could be a vivid speaker. He describes the golden hair, the sumptuous garments, the decoration of gold, silver and precious stones by which 'the foolish people are wretchedly misled', for they love what pleases the bodily eye. They are seduced into believing that the saints themselves take pleasure in the corruptible goods of this life. A statue of a well-dressed, wealthy woman is more appropriate for Diana of the Ephesians (Acts 19:24–28) than for the Virgin Mary. It is important to be clear what Wyclif is really saying in such passages; this does not mean that Wyclif disapproves of images, merely that he is suspicious of their misuse. 'Images were introduced into the primitive Church to be books for the laity,' he says.[88]

So Wyclif broadly accepted the norms and conventions of his training, but that did not mean he asked no awkward questions. The idea was abroad that 'glossing' or 'postillating' could adulterate or distort the meaning of the text of Scripture. This was not at all a new idea. Gregory the Great partly shared the concern 800 years earlier. A commentator is rightly called an adulterator of the Word of God (*recte adulterare verbum dei dicitur*), says Gregory, if he perversely desires to show off his own knowledge and does not defer to the text.[89] The interpreter should be humble in the face of the sacred text. Wyclif did not wish to end or sideline the tradition of gloss and commentary on the Bible in its contemporary form,[90] merely to ensure that the job was done properly and the faithful were not misled.

By Wyclif's time, *glossatio* certainly had a good and a bad meaning. In one sense it was simply interpretation. In another it was the ancestor of the modern English 'glossing over', the putting of an interpretation on things so as to bend the text in a particular direction. Similarly, *postillatio* could be taken to involve adulteration,[91] 'distorting Holy Scripture by giving it a new meaning'.[92] There is also a hint that Wyclif came to see that interpretation could be skewed by politicians for their own ends.[93] In the *On Apostasy* of late 1380, he refers to the casual way glossators can use their power to turn the old meaning of Scripture into a new meaning to suit themselves, deny the literal sense of the whole story of the actions of Christ and gloss the text as though it meant the very opposite, thus inserting into the Bible things which are not really there.[94] Here we begin to see the scale of the difficulty of understanding where Wyclif stood at any given point in his career, let alone in general. The pattern of his thinking usually involves beginning in the conventional place, and taking note of the debates going on around him, as he had to do to 'keep up' with his students and their questions, and to be in a position to comment on whatever his fellow-lecturers were saying when someone asked him to do so in one of his own lectures. Notions linger in the educated mind, are reflected on, polished, adjusted, fitted into a larger framework of related ideas. We can see that happening, and also how, as time went on, ideas became caught in the mesh of Wyclif's anger and frustration, or hurled intemperately at his enemies in later years.

Wyclif and the four senses

> 'The letter teaches what happened; allegory what you are to believe; the moral sense how you are to behave; and the prophetic sense tells you where you are going.'
>
> *Littera gesta docet; quid credas, allegoria;*
> *Moralis, quid agas; quo tendas, anagogia.*[95]

This little mnemonic to help the student rattle off the four senses of Scripture sums up neatly the exegetical methodology which underlay the use of figurative interpretation in the West from the time of Gregory the Great. (Augustine had not succeeded in reducing the list to four.) There were four ways of reading a given passage, though not all of them might be applicable. The first was to read it as saying what it appeared to say on the surface of the words. The second was to look for a transferred sense in which it meant something else, as when the Lion of Judah (Genesis 49:9) was understood to be Christ, not an actual lion. The third drew a 'moral'. The fourth pointed towards the heavenly future, and was 'prophetic' or anagogical.

Fables and figures were really only seriously disliked by Wyclif (and the Lollards) when it came to preaching by the friars, for their use of fables and figures could be seen to tempt many mendicant preachers away from the interpretation of Scripture on which their sermons ought to be concentrating. This eventually seems to have become the focus of any hostility he felt.[96] There was no question in Wyclif's mind that sometimes figurative interpretations were unavoidable. We should imitate Scripture's habit of clarity and not its passages of obscurity when we interpret it,[97] but the Bible is mysterious, enigmatic, and a plain meaning will not always do, he admits.[98]

The ideal of standing humbly under Scripture and not 'manipulating' it by one's interpretation was already being developed in Wyclif's *On the Truth of Scripture* (c. 1378). 'Holy Scripture says so and I, as its humble disciple, ought to speak under its authority, in accordance with what it says.'[99] Wyclif says this in full awareness of the well-known difficulty of knowing what the Bible 'means to say'. There is another pedagogic jest. 'Today I learned in school that contradiction in the sacred page has to be allowed for.'[100] There are obvious contradictions to be resolved.[101] The way this had traditionally been dealt with was to resort to the use of figurative interpretation.[102] That made it possible to get round apparent contradiction by showing that one or both passages could be taken to mean something other than its obvious literal sense. The head-on conflict could thus be made to disappear.

In his commentary on Luke 9:3 he discusses a debating point of the schools in this area. 'Some' allege that propositions of Scripture which are mystical or figurative are false in the force of the words. It behoves the 'deep logician' to put before him the pursuit of the saving truth and employ his skills in unravelling such puzzles so that that truth may become clear.[103] He has learned, when he meets a seeming contradiction, to address himself to it logically and grammatically until he has resolved it. It may be hiding a mystery and it is not for Christian critics to think themselves so far above the text of Scripture as to seek to put it right.[104] If we can tease it out, all knowledge is most fully present in Scripture. Augustine says so.

But here he takes a startling position. He cites commentators (both Augustine and Gregory) as 'authorities' for the view that the interpreter should not allow the actual wording of Scripture to get in the way of the clearest possible understanding of the text by the faithful. Better that the grammarians should criticize the words than that the people should not understand what they are truly saying. The words of Scripture are like leaves. If they obscure the sense, the fruit, they should be removed, interpreted figuratively, or otherwise adjusted.[105] He admits that he himself once had bad habits and was so eager to be famous for his skilful use of argument that he lost sight of this imperative.[106] He admits that he has, in his time, fallen away from a due adherence to the teaching of Scripture, desiring to look well in the eyes of his audience (*cupiens simul apparenciam fame in populo*).[107] This is not the stance of a fundamentalist, nor even of a reader of the Bible with a preference for its literal sense, but the working position of a professional teacher in an age when the complexities of these matters were understood in a particular way, which was bred into every such teacher in the Arts course.

The paradox of the 'figurative which is the literal' was familiar to Wyclif and his contemporaries. When Jesus speaks in parables, the literal meaning of what he says is, paradoxically, a figure. The 'story' is not being read into the words by human interpreters; the Word himself meant it to be a story, and his 'intention' makes the story 'literal'.

Wyclif thought about the issues here partly in terms of contemporary 'signification theory' as he had studied it in his Arts course. In his discussion of the Lion of Judah in the *De Veritate Sacrae Scripturae* he notes that it is a vexed question in scholastic circles whether the 'proper' reference is to 'Christ' or the yellow roaring beast.[108] One school of thought says that, if a 'creaturely' word is used for the Creator, that makes the 'proper' sense the one which speaks of the divine.[109] 'The Church and the holy doctors, after expounding the meaning of Scripture, concede its supreme truth by the power of the word, when it says that Christ is a lamb, or a sheep or a vine or a ram or a serpent or a lion or a worm, but in the mystical sense which is the most utterly literal.'[110] That will not work so well, however, when the allegory involves a transference of meaning away from God. Wyclif draws out the points of likeness between the lion and Christ so as to demonstrate that it is an appropriate comparison. 'This lion is the strongest in things spiritual.' And his roar is like the sound of the Last Trumpet, or the cry with which Jesus called Lazarus to rise from the dead, he comments.[111] But the lion can be compared to the Devil too, and here again there are points of similarity, for example, his rapacity.[112]

Truth and Scripture

In the light of all this, it is not difficult to see how Wyclif came to see as a continuum the questions of figurative interpretation, consideration of the application of signification theories to the reading of the Bible, and whether the Bible is true. Others among his contemporaries were making a similar journey. In Richard FitzRalph's *Summa in Questionibus Armenorum*, ('*Summa* of the questions Armenians ask') which was a product of the period when he could have been in contact with Nicholas of Lyre, a dialogue, takes place between two characters called 'John' and 'Richard'. It begins with John asking which should be taken to be the literal sense of Scripture. He argues that the common, workaday meanings of words cannot always be the required ones, because that leads to obvious nonsense in some passages, and thus draws the reader away from the truth. Isaiah 5:14 includes the assertion that hell has opened its mouth and hell does not literally have a mouth.[113] John 10:20 has the Jews accusing Jesus of having a devil. If the Bible says that Jesus was possessed by a devil does that have to be taken to be true?[114]

Wyclif's first public opponent on the subject of Scripture in about 1373, when he had barely graduated in Theology, was the John Cunningham or Kenningham who was later to be Provincial (local head) of the Carmelite Order and confessor to John of Gaunt. Here Wyclif first showed his controversial colours on the subject of the right way to read Scripture.[115] Perhaps the debate began with a *quodlibet* ('question on anything you like') or a determination in the schools by Wyclif, followed by a *responsio* by Cunningham.[116] Possibly there was then a response by Wyclif.[117] The Master's task in 'determining' in a disputation was to be authoritative, to make it clear that of all the pros and cons argued by his students and juniors his was the right and acceptable answer. It was, to a degree, an impersonal exercise, with the Master 'adjudicating' between the two sides. Yet the attack by Cunningham seems to have been far from impersonal and distinctly lacking in scholarly detachment. A question currently being debated in Oxford was whether Scripture was like a charter making a donation, where proof of its antiquity will do all that is necessary to establish its validity, and this or something like it they took as their theme.[118] Wyclif's position as described by Cunningham was that its antiquity – or, more strictly, its eternity – is indeed a 'cause' of Scripture being true.[119] (This should not be confused with the familiar idea of the sixteenth century that it was important to go back to the sources, *ad fontes*).[120]

The survival of this debate enables us to get a picture not only of the genre but of the level of skill and competence in it Wyclif had attained by the time of his graduation in Theology, which was still very recent when he entered the lists with Cunningham. Wyclif begins his own contribution almost whimsically. 'There are three nests in which I have been reared, with other Christian chicks which do not yet know how to fly.' The first is the logic nest, in which the chicks learn about universals and genus and species, by means of which Scripture often makes its meaning clear. The second nest is higher up, the nest of natural philosophy, in which the chicks learn about the nature and substance of things, and learn that Scripture is true; and there they also learn about the force of words. The third nest is highest of all. This is the nest in which the chicks learn metaphysics. They learn of the eternity and immensity of God, of past, present and future and God's presence in all. They learn how to resolve the puzzles of freedom of choice and necessity and contingent futurity, and they learn to uphold the truth of Scripture and the force of its words against the arguments of the sophists. To overturn one of these nests is not only to injure Wyclif the chick, but everyone who studies holy Scripture.[121]

He alleges that this is what Cunningham has done. He has let loose sharp arrows to try to bring down these nests, especially the last, not for the sake of attacking them but for mere exercise, just to see if he can. Wyclif now proposes to respond in a series of three linked determinations, one on each day, first to the arguments he has fired off to upset the first nest.[122] Wyclif adds an additional 'argument' to the ones he needs to refute Cunningham – at, he says, his insistence (*sed quod Doctor instat*). This is to fortify, by providing more than is really needed to establish the superiority of his own argument for the truth of Scripture.[123]

Wyclif's later *On the Truth of Holy Scripture* cannot give a clear picture of Wyclif's attitude to the Bible at the time when he was studying it for his Theology degree and completing the preliminary lecturing requirements to allow him to call himself a Master. It is, moreover, a work in which his digressive habits are very pronounced. But, with the Cunningham debate, it remains one of the best places to begin to unravel Wyclif's early thinking about these standard contemporary dilemmas over the study of the Bible, as he learned the accepted ground rules and then began to give lectures himself. For it was this process which brought him to the views he sets out in the *De Veritate Sacrae Scripturae*.

We must pause for a moment to note here that the edition of this text is the work of Buddensieg, Wyclif's devoted Dresden defender. He gave twenty-two years of his leisure to the preparation of this edition, he says, 'chiefly the outcome of holiday leisure and of work up to the small hours of the night', which was his only opportunity 'as the head of a large school'. His verdict on the work is that of a man who has made a huge investment in it. 'I think,' he says, '*De Veritate* before all other works of his has cast life-engendering seed into the furrows of time.'[124] 'It is a known fact that in Wyclif's time the scholastic theology… made the Bible the corpus vile of their petty-fogging subtleties and the aim of their scoff and scorn,' he writes.[125]

Wyclif opens his book with a bold challenge. In the Bible lies the safety of the faithful; there is the foundation of every orthodox opinion and the place to look for a refutation of every error. The slightest mistake in connection with Scripture is death to the Church.[126] On these assumptions he sets out to establish, but in true scholastic fashion, with every subtlety at his command, the truth of Scripture (1–8), its authority (9–14), its divine origin (16–19) and three theses (20–32): that Scripture is superior to all human writings; that all Christians have a right to read it; that the Bible is the best foundation for the organization of human life, secular and ecclesiastical. There is, he admits, room for a lot of argument about all this because the Bible offers many opportunities for dispute about what almost every passage means. He often speaks of 'the force of the word'.[127] The right way is to explain it plainly and clearly. It is by no means easy to say how that is to be done, and Wyclif runs with no small relish into many obscure corners of contemporary academic practice and the necessary technical skills of grammar and logic in the attempt to explain.

Wyclif gives every indication of having learned in his first introduction to Bible study that, however anxious he was to give the text a privileged status, it could not be read simply at its face value. The reality is far more complex than Foxe allowed, when he made his claim that 'Scripture, learning, and divinity, were known but to a few, and that in the schools only, and there also it was almost all turned into sophistry.'[128]

Where Wyclif's struggle with the real difficulties of Scripture took him we shall see in later chapters, when he caused his colleagues and contemporaries all kinds of problems.

University sermons and biblical exegesis

> 'The whole world was filled and overwhelmed with error and darkness. And no great wonder, for the simple and unlearned people, being far from all knowledge of the holy scripture, thought it sufficient for them to know only these things which were delivered to them by their pastors and shepherds; and they, on the other hand, taught nothing else but such things as came forth from the court of Rome, of which the greater part tended to the profit of their order more than to the glory of Christ.'[129]

This is John Foxe's brightly coloured but inaccurate picture of a positive 'priestly conspiracy' to keep ordinary people from knowing what the Bible had to teach them. Oxford existed partly to ensure that they were assisted to know precisely that, for it trained all its theologians to preach as a required part of their Theology course.

In the early Church the Bishop would preach from his *cathedra* (official seat in the church, from which the word 'cathedral' derives), and when he preached he was discharging what Gregory the Great saw as one of the principal episcopal functions, the maintenance and communication of the faith. Wyclif knew and approved of this idea. A Bishop ought first and foremost to concentrate on preaching and teaching the catholic faith, he says in one of his last works.[130] The ancient, normal context for the sermon was liturgical, and still in the Middle Ages, at each celebration of the Eucharist, a portion of a Gospel and a portion of an Epistle were read. If there was a sermon, the norm was for the preacher to expound a text from one of these. In his last years, Wyclif chose to put his sermon collection together in the order of the liturgical year, beginning with the sermons on the Gospels.[131] That was the natural sequence, the normal as well as the pastoral way of doing things. As so often, we must be careful here not to read into this the thinking of the sixteenth-century Reformation. When Wyclif says that the evangelization (*evangelizacio*) of the Word is more precious than the ministry of any sacrament of the Church (*preciosior quam ministracio alicuius ecclesiastici sacramenti*),[132] this is not a weighing of the sacramental and the pastoral ministry against one another in favour of the pastoral. For in the *Opus Evangelicum*, from which this is taken, one of his last works, he is also saying that Christ knew that evangelization is a more worthy ministry than the achieving of temporal dominion.[133] And in a sermon he balances it against the author's profession: 'It is better to work and to preach to the people in a live voice than to multiply many manuscripts.'[134] The preoccupation was subtly but importantly different; the supreme importance of the preaching of the Word is emphasized for the reasons of the fourteenth century not the sixteenth.

The patterns and assumptions of the ancient Church had shifted a good deal by the time of Wyclif. Preaching was no longer the preserve of bishops. An 'art of preaching' had been invented, and preaching was taught as part of the training not only of the mendicants but also of secular and monastic Doctors of Theology. The trainee preachers did have to give their practice sermons, so the 'preaching' element of the course was not merely a paper exercise. And, on formal occasions, the University was one of the contexts for the delivering of sermons by the leaders of the community as well as its students.

Wyclif did not greatly like the formal structure of the 'modern' art of preaching which had evolved from the end of the twelfth century, with the publication of a manual by Alan of Lille[135] and advice from Peter the Chanter.[136] Now, in Wyclif's own day, it was a well-polished method and had been developed by the friars. For the Dominicans in particular (for they were by definition the 'Friars Preacher'), the training which equipped them to preach was the *raison d'être* for their whole education and a main reason for their becoming students in Oxford. Some of the Benedictines or black monks made their names as preachers too, although strictly they should not have been involved in this ministry, since their vocation was to an enclosed life of contemplation. The General Chapter of the English Benedictines laid down in 1363 the Rule that Black Monks who were sent to Oxford to learn to preach should study to do so in Latin as well as the vernacular so there was clearly recognition that a purpose of their studies was to equip them as preachers.[137]

The preaching was coloured by the adversarial habits of the schoolroom.

Uthred of Boldon could command sizeable crowds when he preached on the subject of mendicant poverty (and, later, on the views of Wyclif and his followers).[138] Thomas Brinton, one of the noted Benedictine preachers of Oxford, was no friend of Wyclif's and he allowed that to show in his sermons. Just as Wyclif himself would let fly in his preaching and attack his personal enemies, so Brinton seems to have thought it not at all inappropriate to say what he thought about Wyclif. Several of his sermons were preached 'against' Wyclif.[139] The first of these, number 17, emphasizes how greatly the flock stands in need of the clergy's shepherding, for its own protection. It was probably preached to the convocation of the clergy held in November 1377, at the time of the first Parliament of the reign of Richard II. A second (85) of the time of the beginning of the Great Schism was preached to the London clergy in 1378 or 1379, with a similar message. Sermon 100 was preached at Ascensiontide in 1381, and it urges the clergy to try to protect their flocks from being influenced by *subtiles locutores*. By the time he was preaching Sermon 101, in July 1382 at Chobham, Thomas was able to comfort his listeners with the news that Wyclif's teaching had been condemned and to give them a list of the now officially unacceptable opinions he had been spreading. He speaks of pseudo-prophets, those who falsely preach and affirm concerning the sacraments and especially baptism that if a Bishop or priest is in mortal sin, he cannot administer the sacraments; they teach that if someone is genuinely contrite, outward confession is useless and superfluous; concerning the Eucharist, they teach that the substance of the bread and wine remain after consecration.[140] So the skills of the formal art of preaching were adaptable for use by all sides in the attempt to influence the faithful.

The preacher took a text as a starting point and divided the themes the text suggested, developing each with subdivisions. These could be discussed by analyzing the terminology and vocabulary or by using illustrations such as fables or quotations from poems. The first could lead to excesses of academic refinement and unintelligibility to those who had not done the Arts course. The second, overplayed, led to the kind of non-scriptural overload Wyclif deployed as an abuse of the licence to think figuratively. Contemporary Oxford manuals of preaching survive, including those of 'Bartholomew the Englishman' (Bartholomaeus Anglicus);[141] the Dominican John Bromyard with his homely, familiar examples taken from contemporary life as well as from the stock collections of the friars;[142] Robert Holcot;[143] Roger Rypon of Durham, Wyclif's contemporary.[144]

An example worth a closer look is the manual describing these techniques by the Dominican friar Thomas Waleys, who was in Oxford towards the end of his life, certainly in 1352 and probably for some years before that.[145] Wyclif could have known him when he was himself an arts student. Waleys' *On the method of composing sermons*,[146] begins with the assertion that it behoves the preacher to be an example in himself,[147] for the preacher's task is more angelic than human. He expects the sermon to have a theme. It is the common custom, and rightly approved by all preachers of modern times, that the preacher should first propose a theme for himself when he is going to address the people (*populum alloqui*). A theme is some authentic saying (*dictum... authenticum*) on which the preacher intends to base his sermon (*fundare*). This theme should be taken from Holy Scripture. Even though Augustine and other authors have much to say that is holy, a theme should come from the canon of the Bible. That is the surest way to ensure that there can be no doubt that it is in accordance with the faith.

The preacher should, where appropriate, use the Gospel or Epistle of the day 'according to modern custom', except on special feast-days when the Congregation is likely to be especially large. Then, in order to speak appropriately for the feast the preacher may take his theme from somewhere else in the Bible.[148] Further, it is the modern practice to keep the theme very short, as short as a single word, such as *surgite*, 'Arise!'[149]

When he comes to develop his theme, by division, the preacher should make sure that the divisions are consistent not only in appropriateness and relevance but also verbally (*in verbis*): thus he might link texts containing three or four words with same root, such as *iustis, iustitia, iuste, iustificatio*.[150] The divisions should be set out straight away, as soon as the theme has been introduced.[151] Waleys warns against excess in the 'modern' use of rhythmical colour.[152] But he sets out a 'beautiful and spacious' field of possibilities for illustration and enlargement. The 'saving' meaning which lay hidden in the parable would lodge the more forcibly in the memory in that way. For we are assisted to memorize by the artificial use of mnemonic devices, the 'topics' of the ancient rhetorical art of memory.[153]

Wyclif himself was not slow to make the most of novelties. In his generation spectacles began to be used quite commonly to enable older readers to read by magnifying the size of the writing, and he mentions this.[154] And Wyclif does just what Thomas Waleys says he should when he himself preaches. For example, in one sermon he examines the meanings and usages of 'seed' in the Bible. The seed can be compared to the Word of God. The power of the divine seed is astounding. It softens hard hearts and recalls people from beastly behaviour and turns them back into images of God. But today it is as though the seed has been killed and the consequences which follow are those already referred to: the friars play with examples and bits of poetry instead of solidly preaching the Word of God.[155]

The techniques of the formal 'art of preaching' could make a sermon delightful and amusing for the congregation, but Wyclif says that this should not tempt the preacher too far outside the Bible. Nor should the division be too minute. Nor should there be too much play with rhetorical 'colours' and other stylistic devices.[156] He identified this kind of thing with the style of the friars. 'They are not willing to preach the Gospel as a whole, but they do it in brief, lest they should be known to talk with Christ,'[157] he says, accusing them of making as minimal use of Scripture as they can. He could, however, make selective use of this methodology as well as anyone else.

It is true that some friars were fond of fables, perhaps overfond. This attracted the criticism of others who were anxious that the focus should not shift away from the Bible, and not only Wyclif. John Sheppey's[158] 'The Mirror of the Laity' of the thirteenth century preserves an English collection of examples. Its compiler in his prologue declares himself led by his sense of pastoral duty to write something for the instruction of the laity.[159] His collection includes patristic matter and portions of lives of saints and other matter from less august sources, arranged under topic headings such as 'Abstinence' and 'Penance'. Collections of handy stories and suchlike were frequently made by the friars,[160] and it must have been tempting to entertain a Congregation with them rather than press conscientiously on with the exegesis of the biblical text which has been taken as the theme of the sermon. There are grand themes to be drawn out in that way: for example, the notion which underlies the legend of the Fisher King, that the nation may be in a bad way because of its sins, with natural disasters, lawlessness, immorality and failure of military expeditions all linked.[161]

There can be no doubt about the popularity of preaching in an age comparatively starved of mass entertainment. A famous political sermon of Adam Orleton, Bishop of Hereford in 1326, was given at Oxford, probably taking as his text Genesis 3:15 ('I will put enmity between thee and the woman and between thy seed and her seed').[162] Uthred of Boldon drew large crowds, on poverty and why Wyclif was wrong and dangerous.[163] Something of the same popular thirst for excitement as brought the crowds to St Paul's in 1376 undoubtedly affected the attendance at sermons given by figures with 'reputations'. Thomas Brinton, who made his name partly as a preacher in London, preached a sermon on the fable of the rats who belled the cat at the beginning of the Good Parliament, in an undisguised attempt to sway public opinion.[164]

There seems to have been little or no sense that it might be inappropriate to discuss contemporary politics in sermons. This ensured that large numbers of lay people got to hear what was in the wind when there was political or theological controversy (and a good deal of fourteenth-century controversy was both). The call to take seriously the needs of simple and unlearned people and anti-establishment sentiment commonly went together in medieval dissent. Wyclif himself frequently gave way to the temptation to talk politics in his sermons, to deliver a stab at his enemies. In a sermon for Advent he explains the text in Zechariah 9:9 which contains the prophecy that Jesus would enter Jerusalem riding on a donkey (Matthew 21:1). Two disciples were sent ahead. Wyclif identifies them with the priests and the seculars, who are sent on towards the 'castle', which is Jerusalem. It is their duty to bear witness against the endowed clergy, the *castellani* who control the castle.[165] He attacks the friars for squabbling about the rights and wrongs of going barefoot. They should have more important priorities in following Christ than debating whether he wore shoes or went barefoot.[166] Wyclif could be scathing in his sermons in his criticism of those who might propose another explanation; these others merely give their own opinions, which does not stand up nearly so well to reason as that of Wyclif,[167] he claims.

Important distinctions were to be made in theory among at least four types of sermon, but the lines of demarcation might be blurred when someone got into the pulpit: liturgical sermons were the bread and butter of the faithful in ordinary parish life; the sermons preached by monks and friars who did not have pastoral charge of the people they were addressing, with all its capacity for causing resentment among parish priests when their people went to listen to the travelling preachers who had come to the parish; university sermons, preached as part of the requirements for the completion of a Theology degree and also on ceremonial and other occasions in the university year; and occasional sermons which could be opportunities for rabble-rousing, or perceived to be so by the authorities, ecclesiastical and secular.

The University Sermon was a genre in its own right. When Nicholas of Hereford was invited to preach the Ascension Day sermon in 1382 there was a controversy involving the Chancellor, so the University was clearly involved; on the other hand, the Mayor would be present, so it was an occasion for the town as well.[168] There was a requirement that preachers who preached at the University Church of St Mary's (the first Sunday in Advent and Septuagesima), including the Bachelors who preached their 'examination' sermons there, should provide a 'true and complete copy' in writing which was to be written out by a registered scribe and then presented to the University's common library.[169]

This takes us firmly back to the academic world, in which both Wyclif's lecturing on the Bible and his preaching on the Bible always remained rooted. In 1372 Wyclif became a Master of Theology and could call himself 'Doctor' in the highest discipline of all, the 'Queen of the Sciences'. Having watched Wyclif incept once, when he became a Master of Arts, we can picture the scene, although now he was moving into a select company of the most senior figures in the University. He was going to be much more important and much more exposed.

Chapter 7

Mixtim theologus: Wyclif and the law

'I have often said that the underlying principles of human law, indeed the very laws of men, are eternal truths more plainly implied in Scripture.'[1]

Wyclif had his theological lectures to give, as Regent Master in Theology, and it is already becoming apparent in what style he delivered them. He was also very soon going to be called in as a consultant by the Government and, before we come to that significant new departure in his career, we need to consider what he had learned about Law, the higher degree subject which most closely rivalled Theology. The question which first brought John Wyclif publicly into politics and controversy was whether the kingdom of England was entitled to hold back payments of taxation due to authorities outside the realm when it needed the money for its own defence.[2] 'Leaving to lawyers what should be said on this point according to canon law, civil Law and English Law,' the only thing to be resolved, suggests Wyclif, is what the law of Christ says about it. The theme of the supremacy of the law of Christ reappears in the writings of his angry old age,[3] and indeed it became one of the themes on which he was most impassioned.

Wyclif became hostile to canon lawyers and reluctant to cite Gratian and the Decretals as he had been doing shortly before. The Pope was now seen as putting his law above that of Christ. This is a notable trajectory because, although he chose Theology not Law for his higher doctoral studies, the two subjects were unavoidably connected. It has been noted that Wyclif makes a number of references to 'law', and that they become particularly thick a little way into his first ventures into writing on the subject of 'dominion'. Wyclif's interest in legal matters continued to grow as work and controversy drew his attention to them. His references to legal sources become much denser in Book II of the *De Civili Dominio*[4] and writings of about 1379, including the *Dialogus*,[5] 'On the Office of a King'[6] and 'On the Power of the Pope',[7] show him still thinking about the technical questions of the law.

Those who have so far looked for Wyclif the lawyer have been looking chiefly for Wyclif's knowledge of Law as it related to contemporary English affairs.[8] They have not asked themselves what academic and practical knowledge of Law he had, where he got it and how he approached, as a Doctor of Theology, the 'interdisciplinary' questions of the relationship of Law and Theology. There were distinct kinds of legal study, some of them appropriate for theologians and some of them less obviously so. The first, the Law of the Gospel or divine law, fell to be considered in the context of Bible study and in systematic Theology too; it is treated, for example, in Aquinas's *Summa Theologiae*. Canon and civil Law were the proper academic study of the lawyers of Oxford. The laws of England (*leges Anglie*) tended to be treated as an 'applied' or 'vocational' study on the academic fringes of Oxford. These all involved the use of some of the same technical vocabulary and raised a number of questions about disciplinary boundaries.

It was of course undeniable that the two subjects, Theology and Law, 'canon' Law especially, were dealing with many of the same themes.[9] *Iustitia* is a term of art for both Theology and Law in the Middle Ages; it can be translated in English as 'righteousness' or as 'justice'. Terminology was important in an age where higher education was much preoccupied with the analysis of terms and their behaviour. When Wyclif says that 'civilly' is not a lawyer's term, *quod civiliter non est terminus iuris*,[10] he is raising a concern for exactitude in the use of vocabulary which all his academic colleagues would understand.

Wyclif says that those lawyers who try to apply their technical knowledge to Theology are hybrids. 'Therefore the canon and civil lawyers are "mixed-up theologians" (*mixtim theologi*). This is not necessarily a bad thing. When lawyers understand Theology, he suggests, they may preach more effectively and build up the Church better than those who are received as Doctors of Theology.[11] 'This comes about in no small part because of the sinfulness of theologians and the fact that the lawyers pay attention to Theology, which is the "life" of their science.'[12]

Being a *mixtim theologus* was not necessarily a good thing either, however. Wyclif does not always use it as a compliment. One '*doctor humanae tradicionis et mixtim theologus*', a disciple of Antichrist, had argued that Luke 22:38 (where the disciples produce two swords at the time of Jesus' arrest), applied only to rule by unbelievers.[13] Wyclif speaks of this mixed-up theologian as formerly a special friend of his, and a defender of catholic truth.[14] But the relationship had evidently gone sour. He had accused Wyclif of setting himself up as an 'austere' and spiritual man.[15] Wyclif's stab at him in return accuses him of having let 'human traditions' corrupt the purity of his theology. Wyclif found himself travelling in the opposite direction, trying to make himself, as a Doctor of Theology, into an acceptable hybrid.

He emphasizes how separate was specialist teaching of the various disciplines in the University. The Professor of each Faculty teaches only the rules or 'laws' of his subject or science, so that, in the Arts course, 'the arithmetician teaches the rules of number; the geometer the rules of "figures"; the astronomer the laws of celestial motion; the natural scientist the laws of natural bodies; and so on'. For law itself, the 'laws' are those of the right conduct of human life, and those are taught by specialists in politics or by the legists.[16]

In theory students did not mix subjects at the advanced level of study for a higher degree. But leading names such as Thomas Brinton appear both as Doctors of Law and as preacher-theologians.[17] And they certainly mixed with one another. In the small academic community of the day there could be no difficulty in finding someone to ask about a puzzling point. Wyclif mentions colleagues reporting to him the opinion that monks could seek return of their property under civil law.[18] Certainly lawyers appear among Wyclif's eventual enemies, and not only on the various committees and councils convened to condemn him. By the end of the fourteenth century the lawyers in Oxford probably outnumbered the theologians in the small community of senior scholars, and their swelling numbers caused resentment when they took up financial support which might have gone to theologians. Wyclif comments on the unsuitability of the King of England's allowing civil and canon lawyers to be maintained by ecclesiastical benefices ('from the patrimony of the Crucified') 'so that they may study such laws'. That kind of financial support should go, he argues to students of Theology. The clergy would be more useful to him and would better promote the good of Church and state.[19] All this perhaps reflects the lively rivalry of the most able scholars in the higher degree Faculties.

Wyclif expressly distinguishes between English law and Roman law.[20] Wyclif's general approach to the question of English law is political as much as technical. He claims that the laws of the realm of England are better than the imperial laws (*Et hinc leges regni Anglie excellent leges imperiales*).[21] Wyclif maintains that it is an advantage that they are not too numerous (*quod leges ille sint pauce*) because too many laws distract people's minds from the law of God.[22] To support assertions of a similar sort 'Therefore in English law (*unde in lege Anglicana*) the rule of inheritance 'conforms better with the law of nature than does the law of Rome''.[23] If English law permitted goods to be taken away from delinquent clergy, that, in Wyclif's opinion, was right because it was in accord with Scripture.[24]

On the showing of the frequency of his citations, Wyclif acquired a good knowledge of Gratian and the Decretals.[25] That does not necessarily imply thorough reading. He could have got to know even quite technical extracts from the set texts the academic lawyers studied, second-hand. *Quod principi placuit, legis habet vigorem*, 'What pleases the ruler has the force of law', is a saw from Justinian, which could travel in extract and quotation in that way.[26] The use of 'cribs' in medieval writing was pervasive. Many of the quotations from Roman poets are standard lines derived from a 'dictionary of quotations' rather than directly from the source-texts, and do not betoken any serious knowledge of the poet in question. Peter Lombard's *Sentences* are, in a sense, a 'crib' to key opinions of the Fathers. Gratian's great legal textbook of the mid-twelfth century[27] fulfilled something of the same function for the lawyers, as did the work of Hostiensis, which was much favoured for quotation by colleagues and immediate precedessors of Wyclif.[28] (Hostiensis is, for example, cited a good deal by Ockham.) Hostiensis's *Summa Aurea* has headings which, to a researching Wyclif looking for authoritative support for his arguments, would have proved hard to resist. For example, Wyclif quotes him 'On the life and honesty of the clergy', *De Vita et Honestate Clericorum* (III).[29] He is there at the tip of Wyclif's pen as he writes *On the Truth of Holy Scripture*.[30] Hostiensis (III) is cited as authority in the definition of 'reputation' (*fama*).[31] Hostiensis teaches that a layman is bound to give a tithe to his 'higher' neighbour (*proximo superiori*), who has a duty to convert the said tenth into a tithe to be given to the Church. Wyclif argues that the cleric who falls from grace is not entitled to the tithe any longer.[32] Canon law does not allow a cleric to be a businessman (*publice procurare*) unless he has a special licence from a bishop, notes Wyclif, citing Hostiensis.[33] The picture which emerges is of a clever eclecticism, an admixture of legal references rather than a solid understanding of the whole conspectus of legal source material and authorities such as a Doctor of Law would be required to master. The uses to which others were putting Hostiensis before Wyclif's time give a fair indication of the method.[34]

Wyclif points out that legal authorities contradict one another, at least the Decretals do.[35] This too was a commonplace, the complaint on which the academic study of Law was partly founded, for it required study to reconcile the contradictions. But it is also an expression of natural exasperation Wyclif could well have heard from acquaintances in the other Faculties, as they struggled to master Law in its branches. Some of the remarks Wyclif makes strongly suggest the prompting of conversations with friends.

But when we take stock of Wyclif's actual reference to the huge questions of the nature and purpose of Law, which underlay the whole discussion for him, and try to get a sense of the nature of the 'mixture' he was looking for, it becomes plain the lawyerly knowledge remained for Wyclif always something to be put at the service of theology. The context of his remarks about the canon and civil lawyers being *mixtim theologi* was his assertion that 'faith' is what theology is all about. Faith is the 'supreme theology' (*summa theologia*). He discusses the rule, expressed in the Decretals, that a bishop has a duty to examine anyone who is to teach or preach the faith to ensure that he is *literatus*, and instructed *in lege domini* ('in the Law of the Lord'), and can explain the authoritative texts of the faith in simple language (*fidei documenta verbis simplicibus*).[36] On this showing, lawyers could make perfectly adequate theologians, but theologians they must be if they are not to distort important truths.

This leads him into a series of areas in which Law and Theology come face to face. Again it is clear that despite his compliments to the *mixtim theologi* Wyclif really wants his readers to think about Law in a theological way, rather than to consider Theology in a lawyerly way. Wyclif's contention is that fundamental law governing right behaviour does not change. The *lex moralis*, such as the ten commandments, 'stands' (*stat*). Human law or civil law, by contrast, 'runs' with whatever is the current view of society. This is the assumption on which Scripture says that 'in the time of Caesar Augustus' there went out a decree (Luke 2:1). Wyclif was primarily interested in the Law of God, which he identifies as Christ's law; this is not necessarily to be found in the books lawyers study. Christ did not write his law for humanity 'on the skins of dead animals', but in 'the inner man remade in his image'.[37]

It is there to be read in Scripture, and the preoccupations of the work Wyclif was doing on the ten commandments and the question of 'dominion' break through in the *De Veritate Sacrae Scripturae* of c. 1378,[38] where from time to time he raises a legal question. For example, he cites Hebrews 7:12. Does this imply, he asks, that any change in the rules governing the priesthood requires a change in the law? There was a *sacerdocii translatio* (transfer of priesthood) in the time of Constantine, and before that the Church of Rome occupied no special position, he suggests. Nor was there an actual decree, changing the law, to make the Bishop of the Church of Rome necessarily a Primate over others. Wyclif is confident that the existing law can be interpreted so as to allow secular authority to intervene – not of course in questions to do with the sacramental aspects of ordination – but in matters of jurisdiction. The Bible sets the precedent. Solomon shows how 'temporal lords' have 'power to rectify the priesthood' (*habent potestatem ad rectificandum sacerdotium*). If priesthood is beneficial 'for the public good' (*ad utilitatem rei publice*), an improved priesthood must be even more for the public good,[39] so the deep intention of the law is respected.

Wyclif's basic ideas on law and rights emerge again and again in his detailed analysis of particular issues arising in his teaching and writing. The *De mandatis divinis* begins with a reference to the definition of *ius* in Isidore's *Etymologies*, which is also used by Gratian. *Ius* (right or law) is a general term related to justice or righteousness. He notes that philosophers, using the term in metaphysics, have introduced a good deal of ambiguity.[40] Wyclif selects various senses of the term for consideration, taking both biblical and classical (Ciceronian) contexts.[41]

Wyclif distinguishes between divine and human, created and uncreated law. The *lex humana* is that which 'ordains' or puts a man in order in relation to goods, fame or fortune (*que ordinat hominem quoad bona naturalia, fame vel fortune*).[42] It is obvious that the Church's many traditions go beyond what is stated in the law of Christ. The question is how far Christians are bound to obey these additional rules. What are the circumstances in which the private regulations of human beings (*ordinaciones hominum*) begin to be laws (*incipient esse leges*)?[43]

'All law which is repugnant to God's law is unlawful, as for example law concerning duels and usury.[44] Many laws are good and holy, and yet their abuse or wrong interpretation, or following them in an erroneous way, is sinful.'[45] Such thoughts take Wyclif into the subject of the relationship between sin and crime,[46] and into other interdisciplinary problems, for here are 'encounters' with the philosophers as well as between theologians and lawyers. 'Secular philosophers say…,' he admits, touching on a discussion about circumstances in which homicide may be lawful.[47]

These indications of the ways in which Wyclif's new qualification in Theology may have spilled over into a fairly detailed knowledge of another highly specialized and advanced area of study in contemporary Oxford are significant. He was laying the ground for preoccupations which were about to become important to the advancement – and the rapid ruination – of his career. As with his study of the Arts, he crossed boundaries and made applications of one thing to another, as he gradually began to see his way to his own point of view. Wyclif was about to take a turning in a direction from which he would never really look back, to move into public life.

> 'There was a greater and more real world awaiting him, than to be found in those bowers of Academus to which youth is apt at first to attribute an exaggerated importance.'[48]

Chapter 8

Consultant to Court and Parliament

Public life

In Wyclif's England power was exercised openly and patronage was the normal route to advancement. Wyclif would have seen nothing amiss in his youth in trying to win himself influential 'friends'. He succeeded rather well, acquiring as his patron John of Gaunt, the Duke of Lancaster, son of the ailing Edward III and in all but name the ruler of England, as his eldest brother, Prince Edward, the Black Prince, was frequently absent abroad waging war. Wyclif had been born into a family which lived on lands which were under the overlordship of John of Gaunt for thirty years until 1372, and this may have helped him gain the great man's notice.[1] Yet he never achieved power himself, even in the microcosm of Oxford. He became a pawn in other people's political games.

> 'The Good Business Man... has a finger on the pulse of the Great World – a distant and rather terrifying region, which it is very necessary to keep in touch with, though it must not be allowed on any account to touch you.'[2]

Thus warns Cornford in the *Microcosmographia*. It is hard to know how politically naïve Wyclif was, how well he understood at the beginning the principle that if, as an academic, he was to have truck with the world outside, he would need to be careful to keep his distance. The likelihood is that he was of a type still to be met with in academe, vain of his own abilities, taking it for granted that his cleverness would open doors for him.

England was still a 'feudal' monarchy, and feudal assumptions and terminology were often adopted in theological imagery; it seems to have been far from clear to those who did so that they reflected only one way of ruling a country and were not fundamental to the structure of the universe. Wyclif himself talks in such language, seemingly hovering between a literal and a figurative understanding of what he is saying. 'The righteous who persevere to the end are the sole heirs of the kingdom, having a perpetual right for them and theirs,' he explains. They are 'free-holders'. There is talk of 'forfeiture' and 'hereditary title' coupled with the technical, theological vocabulary of 'congruent merit'.[3] Argument by analogy was powerful to medieval minds, going far beyond the mere perception of likeness. Wyclif was not the first northern European to take it that feudalism was almost a law of nature. Anselm of Canterbury imports feudal assumptions into the *Cur Deus Homo* ('Why God became man') in much the same way. One of the questions at issue in Wyclif's early debate with his colleague Cunningham (or Kenningham) was the idea that the grant of dominion might be like the grant of a lease in perpetuity. That would mean that on the production of a document the lessee could claim dominion whatever his personal fitness to exercise jurisdiction.[4]

These theoretical abstractions of feudal life were embodied in much pragmatic wheeling and dealing among the politicians. Contemporary English Government was in a stage of constitutional evolution. Certain figures were powerful as much because of accidents of birth and force of personality as because of the holding of particular offices. The committee with most real power in the land was probably the 'continual Council', which included several senior bishops. They included William Courtenay, who appears at intervals throughout Wyclif's life, once in 1367 as Chancellor of Oxford, then as Bishop of London and eventually, from 1381, as Archbishop of Canterbury.

It was important to be in the right place at the right time and to have one's lips to the right ear. Influence then as now was a personal matter. It is not impossible that Wyclif's family was known to John of Gaunt because of the Yorkshire connection, but we have no way of knowing what first caused him to take up the promising young academic and employ him as a political consultant. There were many others he could have chosen, and Wyclif had the disadvantage that he was not a member of a religious order; he was not one of the friars who could gain entry to the world of high politics through becoming confessor to the well-placed or their wives.

Parliament was not yet formally constituted as the national assembly. The 'Method of holding a Parliament' (*Modus Tenendi Parliamentum*) is a fourteenth-century treatise,[5] probably of about 1321.[6] Its author, clearly familiar with contemporary parliamentary processes, also had a manifest wish to modify and develop them; it may be more a piece of propaganda than an objective account of what usually happened.[7] When a *parliamentum* was called in the reign of Edward III (1327–77), as happened forty-eight times in the course of his long reign, the lords spiritual (the bishops) and the lords temporal (the barons) were individually summoned, and with them various officials and royal councillors, representatives (proctors or *procuratores*) on behalf of the clergy, and representatives for the shires, the cities and the boroughs. A Parliament could continue in session after the 'Commons' had gone home, but the Commons were now an essential constituent part of Parliament and could expect to be summoned at the outset. There was a lively tension between the 'elected representatives' and the 'magnates' of the realm, who were summoned by virtue of office or by right of birth. There were other 'constituencies' too, straining for power, notably the 'administrative classes', the civil servants and lawyers and notaries, the 'managers' of affairs, who had been in a strong position in the reign of Edward I (1272–1307). The balance of power among the clergy was also being adjusted. There was pressure to strengthen election of proctors by the archdeaconries and thus to undermine the powerful position of the bishops and the cathedral chapters.

It should not be forgotten that there was a good deal of family overlap between these classes and of movement between them. The barons were the brothers and cousins and uncles and nephews of the lords of the Church. The lords of England in feudal times, the lords spiritual and the lords temporal, could expect to be present in the councils and Parliaments of the realm, for the bishops were landholders too, by virtue of holding the lands of their 'sees' or dioceses. Many bishops had risen from positions as royal clerks; clerks of the Chancery often held prebends in cathedrals, sometimes more than one, and would therefore be in a position to influence the votes which brought clerical representatives to Parliament. We shall see Wyclif confronting assembled magnates, with the seating adjusted to reflect their positions and offices and status.

Alongside official 'Parliaments' were held all sorts of meetings, councils of the powerful in Church and state. A royal council might consist of no more than the king's current intimates. There was still room for considerable variation in the vocabulary used to describe the meetings of Parliament itself. When Wyclif is reported as being present at or even addressing a 'Parliament', it is not always possible to be certain whether the meeting was truly a meeting of Parliament or a council meeting or even some other kind of meeting. [8]

'Councils' of the Church, on the other hand, took place within a very ancient tradition which rested, at least in theory, on quite different assumptions. From the time of the first decision-making gathering recorded in Acts 15, it had been the custom of the Church to make its mind up about matters of discipline, ritual and even faith, by meeting 'in the persons' of the leaders of the local communities so that decisions might be arrived at which would, in theory, carry the consent of all the people of God. It had been acceptable from the early centuries for councils to be convened and ended by secular authority, but the decision-makers who 'agreed' a council's decrees were by convention the leaders of the Church, the bishops, and not the leaders of the state, who were not allowed to participate in the actual decision-making at all. A bishop 'brought his diocese with him', spiritually as well as literally representing it. The assembled bishops were, in principle, supervised by the Holy Spirit, and they were supposed to have arrived at their 'unanimous' decisions by consensus under the Spirit's guidance.

The custom of holding English Church councils had lapsed for a time, but it had been revived at the end of the eleventh century by Lanfranc while he was Archbishop of Canterbury. He also established once and for all the primacy of the See of Canterbury over the two English provinces of Canterbury and York.[9] In reality, politics were as rife in medieval councils of the Church as in those of the state, and some of the meetings described as 'councils' in the story which follows were strange hybrids of different kinds of members and would not for a moment have stood up as the genuine article ecclesiologically if Wyclif had attacked their status from that point of view.

Wyclif had been born in the northern province of York, but his adult and professional life was spent almost entirely in the southern one of Canterbury. There he encountered bishops and archbishops acting in various capacities, as colleagues on a diplomatic mission, as judges in an inquiry into the orthodoxy of his teaching – and also sitting in judgment on him side by side with barons. The Archbishop of Canterbury might appear at a meeting in the capacity of Archbishop of Wyclif's ecclesiastical province, in company with his provincial Bishops or as the Primate of England, and it may have been hard for Wyclif or anyone else to be sure on any given occasion what authority attached to the activities afoot.

Additional uncertainty was introduced by inviting 'academic experts' to some of these official meetings and inquiries. They came in capacities which are not always clear, perhaps as expert witnesses, perhaps as consultants, sometimes with a vote in the decision-making, sometimes not. Such experts were selected with an eye to ensuring that there was a spread of special interests, much as modern Church committees are commonly 'packed' in a similar way, so that decisions reached and proposals made will appear to carry the support of all camps and parties. Representatives of each of the religious orders were likely to be included, and of the constituencies of the lawyers and the theologians, and above all so as to lend the greatest possible air of plausibility to their recommendations as to what was to be done about Wyclif.

At a later time, when the scales had fallen from his eyes and he was no longer thrilled and flattered to be invited to the 'councils' of the great of the land, Wyclif has some robust things to say in the course of his book *On the Church* about the goings-on in Parliament and the arrogance of the higher clergy in particular:

> 'Ignorant bishops and doctors are led into madness. They would try to make a fool believe that he could do as much in the Church as Christ. Thus the Bishop of Rochester said mockingly to me in public in Parliament that he had heard from the Roman Curia in a secretary's letter that my opinions were condemned. That seemed to many to be a rash assertion: first because it verged on defamation of the Roman Curia; secondly because it put a stumbling-block in front of our King and Kingdom; and thirdly because it showed that he and his brothers had been conniving in suspicion.'[10]

The question of the Pope's right to exact taxation

All English land was ultimately royal land. Under the feudal system even the highest and most powerful barons 'held' their land from the king in return for 'service', normally the provision of so many knights to fight in the royal armies for so many days a year. The religious houses were no exception. For these purposes their abbots were barons. Nor were the bishops any different, for the lands of their dioceses were also in the gift of the king. Below the highest came lowlier landholders, who could, up to a point, buy and sell the rights to their holdings – as, in a modest way, Wyclif's family seems to have done.

This royal dominion over English land carried responsibilities. It was deemed to allow the King the right to exact extra payments when the kingdom stood in special need or in danger. The Pope, as the head of the Church, considered he had a right to make exactions too, in the form of the alms Christian people should be only too willing to offer, for this was represented as the Christian continuation of the tithes of the Old Testament. The Pope needed the revenue to pay for his conduct of military campaigns, which were, naturally, 'just' wars. Peter's Pence, the old papal tax on the whole 'people of God' in the nation, had been commuted into a nominal sum administered through the dioceses.[11]

But that was not the only tax the Pope regarded as his due. The clergy were liable to pay a 'subsidy of love' (*subsidia caritativa*), a form of tax on their income; also an annual charge (annates); and, in addition, 'procurations'. The subsidies or tithes were in practice collected by royal authority, and the King took so large a cut – half or three-quarters for the royal exchequer – that the Pope would be lucky to get anything substantial. Popes did not make much effort to enforce their claims to tithes in the mid-fourteenth century, but they returned to the attempt in 1360 and again in 1371. Annates were equally unpopular. These were taxes equivalent to the value of a benefice in the first year of a new incumbent's tenure. The underlying idea was that the Pope was in some sense the original 'provider' to the benefice. John XXII (1316–34) devised a strategy for gathering even more by this route through his Bull *Execrabilis*. This sought to outlaw pluralism, and of course meant that many benefices were suddenly vacated, for pluralism was common, and the Pope could claim the annates as soon as they were given to new incumbents. Annates were denounced in Parliament in the 1370s and in 1376 there was a petition of the Commons against them. Procurations were by comparison a minor irritant. These were exactions to pay for the cost of sending a papal envoy or keeping a resident papal tax-collector in England.

The pronouncements of the Third Lateran Council of 1179 were much concerned with discouraging conspicuous consumption by bishops while making provision for priests serving in parishes to have the necessities of life (*necessaria vitae*) without undue burdens being placed on the laity. One result was the confirmation that the parish priest had a right to the freehold of the parish, with which his bishop could not interfere.[12] This touched on the temporalities a parish priest controlled, in ways which were to be important in the debates Wyclif helped to stimulate. It tilted the balance of control of 'temporalities' still further away from the Church's episcopal hierarchy.

There was, then, a good deal of reason for the English Government to take an interest in the question of payment of any taxes due to the pope. The stated pretext for the exaction of both the internal (royal) and the external (papal) taxes was much the same – that the proposed war was just. The Pope's claims in such circumstances took considerable liberties with the underlying principle, for the money was not to go to the relief of the poor of Christendom at all.

In addition, there was a more recent tax the Pope considered to be due from the English. An embattled King John had ceded his kingdom to the Pope in 1211 in order to bring to an end the interdict (or general excommunication) he had placed on the kingdom, which was encouraging John's subjects to refuse to behave as though they were his subjects at all. John had received the kingdom back in return for a feudal oath of fealty and homage, which made him a subject of the Pope, and a payment of a thousand marks a year to the Holy See.[13] English Governments regularly withheld the payment due, so as to bargain for papal assistance and support before it had to be handed over, but it hung between the Pope and the English King as a potential source of dispute.

Nothing at all was paid by way of papal taxation between 1333 and 1365.[14] On 6 June 1365 Pope Urban V wrote to Edward III to ask for what he considered he was owed. 'Dearest son, you have not paid since 1333,' he chides. He explains that he has held back so long from sending this reminder because he knows England has been involved in the expense of protracted wars. Now there is peace, he is reminding the King of his debt.[15] Edward III referred the pressing papal demands to Parliament, which gave them short shrift.[16]

Arnald Garnier appeared in England in October 1371 as a tax-collector for the Pope. His mission was to get hold of the clerical payments due, so as to enable Pope Gregory XI to pay for sufficient forces to win back church lands in the region of Milan.[17] Deals were done, as was expected, for the Crown was determined not to allow the tax to be taken unless it could take a proportion for itself and make some royal profit out of the exercise. In 1375 Gregory was allowed to collect three-fifths of what he had asked for, but there was an outcry from lay interests in England.

Wyclif met Garnier in person, for Garnier mentions him in 1373 or 1374.[18] The papal taxation question will have affected Wyclif personally. In 1374 Wyclif had been presented to the rectory of Lutterworth in Leicestershire, a lucrative preferment in the royal gift, and an indication of the approval in which Wyclif was then apparently held in high places.[19] We know he was a poor payer of taxes due from his livings in later years. Wyclif had paid only £6 13s 4d by way of the firstfruits from his prebend at Aust (Westbury-on-Trym) and there was a claim outstanding against him for £29 5s 8d more. On 2 May 1377 the fruits of his Caistor prebend were sequestered and he was admonished for non-payment. Robert Wyclif, who may have been his nephew, paid £13 6s 8d on his behalf, but there was still a debt of £32. By 13 January 1378 the prebend had passed to Philip of Thornbury.

John of Gaunt identified Wyclif as a useful advocate of the position of the English Government, which was, naturally enough, that it should not have to pay taxes to the Pope at all. The *Chronicon Angliae*, whose author was Thomas Walsingham of St Albans Abbey, presents Gaunt as a wily politician, 'who was always working out how best to get his own way'.[20] (St Albans Abbey did not like Gaunt.) Gaunt wanted, says Walsingham, to undermine the liberties of the Church and the city of London alike. So he took to him a certain pseudo-theologian (*pseudo-theologus*), or as he might more accurately be called, God-challenger (*theomachus*),[21] who had already spent many years in the schools teaching against the Church. He had invented many novel opinions without foundation, and had misled many simple folk, for they are always avid to hear new ideas.[22] This cannot be correct. For, at the time when John of Gaunt took up with Wyclif, Wyclif had barely graduated in Theology and could not possibly have been misleading people for years (although there are indications that, before Wyclif was chosen to go to Bruges and be a diplomat, he had lectured and even written on the subject of dominion).[23] However, it is not impossible that the two had met and talked, and made the Yorkshire family connection into a personal connection, and a few years later Wyclif seems to have thought Gaunt capable of understanding a theological problem. The story of Gaunt's extraordinary and sustained support for Wyclif does not perhaps need to be accounted for entirely in terms of Gaunt's eye to the political main chance.[24] In 1371 the king himself allowed Wyclif to keep some of the tithes due from Ludgershall, where he was then rector. It would not as a rule have been in the power of the King to give such a dispensation, but the circumstances were unusual. This could well have been a present for services rendered, so perhaps Wyclif had been employed as a consultant to 'Parliament' or the 'continuing' Council. In any case, it seems to show that Wyclif was in good odour with the court at this time.[25]

Wyclif describes in his book *On Civil Dominion* how he had 'heard members of the religious orders which have possessions (*religiosos possessionatos*)[26] in a certain "Parliament" in London' ask to be freed from the obligation to pay taxes to the king.[27] One lord more eloquent than the others had responded with a fable. The story he told was this. He had been at a parliament of fowls, a meeting of birds at which an owl without feathers and shivering begged for the merciful gift of feathers from the others. The bird was then so heaped with feathers by their generosity that he was quite loaded down. Then danger threatened the flock and the birds seized all their feathers back in a great hurry so that they could be ready to defend themselves. 'So it is,' said the speaker, 'that if the nation is threatened all special concessions of freedom from taxation must end and the temporal possessions of the clergy must be seized for the common good.'[28]

English law was inevitably in the forefront of Wyclif's mind as he strove to construct the case the Government had hired him to make and help it resist papal claims to the payment of the overdue taxes owed. Much of the debate about dominion concerned rights over property (*ius ad rem*)[29] and Wyclif testifies to the fact that this was one of the questions discussed in the schools. He refers back to the previous year when William Woodford had been engaged with the question whether members of religious orders could sue for their possessions in the civil courts.[30]

The embassy to Bruges

> 'The Young Man in a Hurry is afflicted with a conscience, which is apt to break out, like measles, in patches. To listen to him, you would think he united the virtues of a Brutus to the passion for lost causes of a Cato; he has not learnt that most of his causes are lost by letting the Cato out of the bag, instead of tying him up firmly and sitting on him, as experienced people do.'[31]

After Whitsun in 1374 a 'council' was called at Westminster by the King. There met state and Church, Prince Edward, the Black Prince and heir apparent to the aging Edward III, and the Archbishop of Canterbury (William Whittlesey), each with his entourage of lords, temporal and spiritual respectively. The seating reflected status and position. Facing the two great princes of the realm, the secular and the ecclesiastical, sat four Masters of Theology; John Uthred, monk of Boldon; John Mardisle, a Franciscan; an Augustinian friar, Thomas Ashburn; and the current provincial of the Dominicans. Flanking them sat civil and canon lawyers.

The Pope's latest Bull was read out. He called himself the 'spiritual lord and head' (*dominus spiritualis et capitalis*) of the kingdom of England. He referred to the occasion when King John had made a gift of the kingdom to the Pope. He stated that he expected the present King to raise a tax throughout the land to provide the Pope with money to overthrow the Florentines.

A debate began, with the clerical 'academic' experts going first. They were divided in their opinions and in their approaches. The question the King put to them was whether the Pope is the lord of the English because he is vicar of Christ. The Archbishop said he was. John Uthred attempted to 'apply' the text in Luke 22:38, which describes how the disciples produced two swords at the time of Jesus' arrest and Jesus said 'it is enough' (*satis est* in the Vulgate Latin translation). It had first been proposed by Pope Gelasius I (492–96) that this 'enough' should be taken literally, that it referred to a duality of powers in the world, Church and state, spiritual and temporal. The image was discussed by a series of medieval commentators from Bernard of Clairvaux in his *On Consideration*, written for Pope Eugenius III in the mid-twelfth century[32] and his friend William of St Thierry[33] to controversial figures of the generations immediately before Wyclif,[34] and it would certainly have been familiar to him.[35] He mentions in the *De ecclesia* the idea that 'within the aforesaid Church are both swords, the corporeal or temporal and the spiritual'.[36]

Mardisle maintained that Christ and his disciples had no worldly dominion, and that when Pope Boniface VIII (1294–1303) had tried to assert such dominion he had come to grief.[37] The Dominican Provincial asked to be excused from answering so hard a question and advised that, when his order faced difficult business (*ardua negotia*), it was the custom of the friars to sing a hymn and invoke the Holy Spirit so that the Spirit might guide them to the truth. When the laity had their turn to speak it was pointed out that, although indeed King John had given the kingdom of England to the Pope, he had done so without their consent.[38]

On 26 July 1374 Wyclif was made a member of a commission which was to meet a papal delegation at Bruges. It was perhaps apparent that these were circumstances in which the skills of a diplomat or perhaps a team of diplomats would be useful, and possibly also that it would be helpful if someone on the team were a highly qualified academic. The commission was to be led by Bishop John Gilbert. There were seven members. No better choice seems to have presented itself among the 'secular' Masters than Wyclif, although the Benedictine academic Uthred of Boldon was there alongside two laymen, John Sheppey and Sir William Burton. As far as we know, this was the only time Wyclif left England.

It is not clear that Wyclif proved an asset to the English negotiators in Bruges. The outcome of the affair was not on the whole to the advantage of the English clergy. The discussions led to no conclusions and, when a second commission was appointed the next year, Wyclif was left off it. The second commission had better success, although there is no way of knowing whether that was because Wyclif was no longer with them.

Yet Wyclif must have worked out his ideas on papal taxation quite fully in connection with an occasion on which it was important for him to 'do well'. There were matters here which he would not necessarily have studied at all fully in the Theology course. It got him engaged with a trail of implications which carried him along to the end of his life. It was to prove an intellectual turning point for him, the most significant in his life.

An account of Wyclif's advice to the Government is to be found in the *Fasciculi Zizanorium* ('Bundle of weeds'). It was that the realm may indeed withhold taxes from the Pope for its own defence. He rests his case on the philosophical argument that there is an inherent power and tendency in all created things to preserve their essential nature, the way they 'ought to be'.[39] The rulers of a state, those exercising dominion within it, have a responsibility under the 'law of conscience' to defend the prosperity of the realm.[40]

The Pope's right to levy taxation, he says, depends on the gift being regarded as alms, a charitable benefaction. It is not a requirement he can 'enforce'.[41] Certain sanctions would be at the Pope's disposal if he *wished* to enforce his claim to take taxes. He could lay an interdict on the Kingdom. But, knowing the exaction to be unjust, God would not take this to have any effect.[42] The theory of dominion that Wyclif is beginning to work out rules that no one who is in the wrong has any lawful power over others.

Rewards

The Bruges mission was to be a turning point in Wyclif's life for another reason. He did not think it unreasonable that he should profit from his venture into public life. Others were being rewarded. Though John Gilbert had led the emissary, as Dominican Bishop of Hereford, his own subsequent career did not suffer as a consequence of its failure.[43] It is possible that Wyclif fancied his chances of appointment to the See of Worcester at this time (vacant from 1373 to 1375), and it was put about later that his disgruntlement with secular and Church authorities alike was partly prompted by his failure to get it. The other three clerics sent to Bruges became bishops almost at once.[44] On the other hand, Wyclif was not alone in being disappointed of what might have seemed reasonable hopes of preferment. Fewer graduates of the universities were obtaining benefices and other fruits of patronage.[45]

In 1373 Gregory IX had promised Wyclif a preferment. In 1375 it was given to someone else. Sir John Thornbury was the priest who obtained the prebend he expected and Wyclif calls him an idiot.[46] An angry and disappointed Wyclif even seems to have claimed that his enemies had gone so far as to denigrate him to the papal *curia* so as to get his benefices taken away, although this may have been in the more heated circumstances of the next few years.[47] Wyclif may have misunderstood the true meaning of the promise he claimed had been broken, which was for him as applicant to bid for the canonry at Lincoln when it became vacant. The processes of appointment to it were fairly mechanical and not necessarily likely to be interfered with by the Pope or anyone else out of pique. Wyclif evidently thought pique was a possibility.

He was bitter. He almost certainly has the matter in mind in his book *On Civil Dominion*, where he points furiously to the way conflict of interest gets in the way of fair conduct. He mocks the *frontosa vel fallax illusio* that a privilege or gift (*gracia*) is what it seems when tomorrow it is taken away. 'Surely the truthfulness of a promise does not depend on the will of a changeable Pope?'[48] Moreover, Wyclif maintains, he had 'paid' for the exercise of patronage in his favour.[49] These are striking thoughts, in view of Wyclif's indignation about simony only a few years later. But at the time he was perhaps outraged at what must have seemed a failure of the world to reward him when he had so recently seemed to be setting out on a distinguished career in public life. Whether the loss of these lucrative advancements was chance or a consequence of Wyclif having caused offence or proved a disappointment, this period seems to have brought about something of a watershed in his attitudes.

He woke up at this point, if he had not done so before, to the corruptness of the world and the way big organizations work. He can be seen in his next writings to be thinking this through. He went very quickly from being a willing 'new boy' in politics, eager to please and hopeful of worldly advancement, to being a dark and brooding commentator and something of a loose cannon. The man on the way up is generally willing to tolerate, in his own interests, things he does not entirely approve of. The able man with no prospects may discover his principles and become a danger to the Establishment. This seems to have been exactly what now happened to Wyclif. If it is a fair assessment, this ties in with the general pattern of 'reactive formation' observable in the emergence of Wyclif's leading ideas.

Wyclif had had a taste of moving in the circles of public life. He may also have been preaching in London as well as Oxford – the fourteenth-century equivalent of writing columns in newspapers. Wyclif was attacking the powerful where they minded most. For it became a campaign, and Wyclif quickly lost sight of the wisdom of protecting his back, or perhaps he was too naïve to see the need. He had had the fair wind of approval from powerful interests in the state. He was about to find himself confronting an angry ecclesiastical 'Establishment' and to discover that the two worlds were not wholly distinct, and that he could not expect politicians to be consistent with their backing or to share the more idealistic aspects of the concerns he was now expressing. The medieval Church behaved as a force in the world. It locked horns with the secular authorities. It made demands. In what followed, the theology and the politics can rarely be separated.

Despite all this Wyclif became a commentator on theological politics, perhaps much as Ockham had, partly in response to the challenge of fellow academics. Once he had begun, he discovered, just as Ockham had done, that the university world of debate on academic questions was not an ivory tower at all, but was taking him into issues of real current practical importance in the world outside the University. Once Wyclif had received flattering invitations to take sides with the state and make public statements, he found himself committed to following through the entailments of what he had first said. This took him a long way and ultimately into personal condemnation and professional disaster.

Part III

The Troubles Begin

Chapter 9

Wyclif becomes notorious

i. The Good Parliament

Wyclif was certainly not leading a low-profile life in the next two years, although his movements and activities cannot be mapped exactly. He was probably lecturing in Oxford and holding disputations on the themes he was now thinking hard about. Things were moving rapidly in public life too. The 'Good Parliament'[1] sat from April to July 1376. The Chamberlain and a financier were accused of corruption and impeached, and a permanent 'continuing' administrative council was appointed to advise the King and remove from his side various unsatisfactory advisers and his mistress.[2] The King was ageing at the end of a long reign and the health of the heir apparent, Edward the Black Prince, was giving cause for concern. Prince Edward died on 8 June 1376. Wyclif refers to this event in a treatise apparently written at the time, 'On the devil of the noonday'.[3] He is writing about the sickness of the realm and the stumbling block to the faithful presented by wealthy clergy who are taking from the poor instead of helping them. He says that the spiritual benefits to be had through the systems of penance and indulgences are really only available to the rich who can afford to pay, so the gifts of grace are being denied to the poor.

In taking this line, Wyclif was enlarging upon his premises in the papal taxation controversy, developing the notion that when the clergy misbehave it is the business of the secular government to redress the wrong, because it affects the spiritual health of the whole community. Not to do so leads to the ruin of the realm for it undermines its very foundations.[4] These are stock ideas, also to be found in the legend of the Fisher King, which is found in the Arthurian cycle. There the king is sick, of a sickness which is spiritual as well as physical, and the whole kingdom suffers, the crops fail, the cattle die. Pointing a moral, Wyclif exclaims that, 'The aforesaid Lord Edward is dead (*Predictus dominus Edwardus mortuus*).'[5]

After the Good Parliament, the *Chronicon Angliae* says, John of Gaunt used his influence. He speedily repudiated and undid what he could of the Good Parliament's new provisions.[6] He 'arranged' for the election of new members of Parliament who would support him (for such elections could easily be influenced by bribery and promises). Only twelve of the members of the Good Parliament survived, the *Chronicon* says, but in fact the number re-elected seems to have been smaller still. The reasons for this are likely to be much more complex than the chronicler suggests, but the fact was that the Parliament of January 1378 contained a higher proportion of supporters of the court than the Good Parliament had done.[7] Feelings ran high, however, especially among the leaders of the argumentative confrontations of the previous year. The subject of the exaction of papal taxation remained highly sensitive.

ii. Wyclif the author

When Wyclif came home from Bruges, and possibly even before he went, he began to lecture and write extensively on property and ownership, developing the ideas he had begun to work out when he was called in to help the Government with its tax problem, but also reaching behind them, trying to understand the fundamentals. The *De dominio divino*, 'On Divine Dominion', was written in 1373–74, perhaps just before.[8] A further set of what had probably begun as lectures circulated, becoming the book we now know as *De civili dominio*, 'On Civil Dominion' (1375–76). He was also working on monographs arising out of his routine commentary on the Bible (on the 'state of innocence' before the Fall and the ten commandments), topics which turned out to be relevant to his developing interests.

Already Wyclif had made himself conspicuous enough to be called to answer to the Church's leaders and to have the state's great men stand shoulder to shoulder with him on the occasion, with the populace breathlessly waiting for serious trouble to erupt. Why? The reasons are ecclesiological as much as political and we need now to look more closely at what Wyclif was teaching and writing which was causing all this trouble.

A long history of controversy about the idea of the Church, and in particular the relationship between Church and state, lay behind the debates of Wyclif's time. The remarkable thing is how long it took him to get to grips with questions which had seemed to Augustine of Hippo and many of those who came after him the obvious place to start. Perhaps one reason he was slow to move into the mainstream of that long history of debate[9] was that the most acrimonious battles of the late medieval Church were about power and the abuse of power, which led into the classic questions down different avenues.

So Wyclif began with the idea of 'dominion'. This preoccupation, which was shared by others of Wyclif's generation, had probably been prompted by the work of Richard FitzRalph. FitzRalph had been a Fellow of Balliol before 1325, after which he resigned his Fellowship so that he could study Theology. During the period 1325–29, when he left for Paris, he is known to have given the usual required lecture-commentary on the *Sentences* of Peter Lombard. Most of his subsequent life was spent climbing the ladder of ecclesiastical preferment, culminating in the archbishopric of Armagh in Ireland (1346–60). In this real world of ecclesiastical politics his interests turned to questions of power and control, which we can see interesting Wyclif more and more from the point in his life when he had his first encounter with the realities of politics.

A strong doctrine of God was the natural starting point for all theologians trained – as all theologians then were – in the 'systematic' approach of the *Sentences*. FitzRalph seems to have been particularly drawn to questions about divine omnipotence. He argued that God can always choose to do directly what he normally does through intermediate causes. In other words, God never hands power over to his creatures and washes his hands of the matter. The medieval theology of miracles is based on exactly this supposition that, although God created the world to run according to the laws of nature, he can always intervene and interrupt the natural order. Normally oak trees grow from acorns, but should God wish to place a full-grown oak tree in the middle of a field, he can do so at any time. The only limitation FitzRalph allows is that God cannot act in a way which goes against his own nature. This raised a number of interesting questions which were just the thing for formal debate in the schools and an excellent way to educate student theologians. Could God have made things better than they are? Could he remit mortal sin even if the sinner did not repent? Could God inspire a prophet to say things which will never come to pass?[10] This had a direct relevance to the running of the Church, for it was central to FitzRalph's argument that the Holy Spirit gave 'power' to the clergy only up to a point. He could always act directly (by 'grace'). He could always take back the power if it was abused.

FitzRalph's ideas were not born solely of his own independent reflections. Giles of Rome (d. 1316) had set out an extreme theory, against which all this was a reaction. His contention was that the only just lordship is that which is derived from the Church, and that God had given the Church of Rome a universal dominion over temporal things. The question what are the practical circumstances in which a Pope might interfere in temporal affairs is not at all the same question as whether a Pope's authority overrides temporal authority as a matter of general principle.[11] Giles of Rome drew a distinction between power over temporal things considered as temporal and temporal things which relate to the spiritual welfare of the faithful. Over the first he thought the Pope had only a higher and primatial dominion (*dominium superius et primatum*). Over the second, he believed the Pope had an immediate and executive dominion (*dominium immediatum et executorium*).[12]

Dominium is not a common Vulgate term. It occurs only in 1 Maccabees 11:8 and one other apocryphal passage (Tobias 8:24). However, the verb *dominare* occurs a good deal in the Vulgate, and again and again God is called *Dominus*. In Matthew 20:25 and Mark 10:42, there is a reminder that while the gentiles are 'ruled' (*dominantur*) by their princes, among Christians the rulers are to behave as though they were their people's servants. The comparative lack of concern with the matter in the Bible had not meant that there had been no discussion of dominion. Whether the Devil had dominion over fallen humanity or any Devil's 'rights' became a point of active dispute for a while at the end of the eleventh and the beginning of the twelfth century.[13] Some theologians had argued that, at the fall, Adam and Eve became vassals of Satan and he therefore had some rights which must be respected in any attempt to rescue them.[14] This particular question had not entirely faded even in the thirteenth century. *Dominium* is quite a frequent term in the influential, thirteenth-century Franciscan author Bonaventure, and he uses it in that context. For example, he speaks of the deceit of the Devil 'in usurping the dominion of the first man'.[15] But by then the area of anxiety had moved elsewhere, and the 'dominion debate' of Wyclif's day was concentrated on the rights and wrongs of human not satanic 'dominion'.

Bernard of Clairvaux's language of dominion provides a closer twelfth-century forerunner of FitzRalph's line of argument, and also that of Wyclif, for he uses it in the context of a discourse about the balancing of lordship and service. He speaks of a priestly gift of ministry (*ministerium*), not lordship (*dominium*). He emphasizes that the bishop who is considering what his own ministry of oversight should involve should concentrate on developing a sense of duty and service and responsibility, and not think of himself as exercising dominion.[16] Those things and persons over which a priest may be said to have 'lordship' should be regarded rather as being in his 'care' or 'cure'.[17] The only area in which dominion is really appropriate in Bernard's view is that of *self*-rule, that is, self-discipline.[18] A bishop should certainly be in control of himself. Modern sexual abuse scandals show that the problem of the unworthy minister has not gone away.

The great shift of preoccupation after the end of the twelfth century, which made a different set of worries about the nature and exercise of dominion important to Wyclif and his contemporaries, had come about largely as a consequence of the founding of the orders of friars, particularly the Franciscans, for whom a life of poverty was a definitive part of the attempt to live the apostolic life in imitation of Christ. This implication was recognized quite early. Already at the beginning of the thirteenth century, in the time of Robert Grosseteste (c. 1175–1253), the issues were lining up with a new emphasis. For although the Franciscans, above all others, saw poverty and simplicity of life as their calling, as soon as they began to be offered gifts by the pious, they ran into difficulties. So we find Grosseteste discussing the giving of a temporal good in such a way that it passes into another's dominion, and suggesting that this is a matter of handing over rather than giving,[19] and so not an outright gift, which might be unacceptable.

There are often contextual reasons in society and politics why a theological issue suddenly becomes topical. Book VII of FitzRalph's *De Pauperie Salvatoris* ('On the poverty of the Saviour') of 1355–56 included direct criticism of the ecclesiastical state of affairs in Ireland. English experience chimed with Irish experience, and there was indeed a list of complaints which had been put forward by the clergy of the province of Canterbury in 1356.[20] Clergy were turning actively to pastoral work and were finding the friars in their way, preaching literally 'on their territory'. FitzRalph did a good deal of preaching in Oxford and London and received encouraging support for his ideas from the Dean of St Paul's (Richard Kilvington) and the Bishop of London (Michael Northburgh), both old Oxford friends. The friars resident in the London houses of Franciscans and Dominicans, a powerful group, reacted angrily. FitzRalph preached a sermon before Pope Clement VI in 1350 in which he begged the Pope to rescind the privileges the friars enjoyed.[21] His argument was that the work of the friars, coming into parishes to preach, was disruptive of the proper pastoral work of the parish priest, who should be hearing his people's confessions himself and doing his own preaching. There followed a century of preoccupation with pastoral issues in theological debate.[22] The threat the friars posed to the parish system was different in some respects from that presented by the 'popular preachers' who aroused the ire of ecclesiastical authority at the end of Wyclif's life.

These particular questions were just emerging when FitzRalph was 'invited' to write about his views, and this probably really rather half-hearted commission led directly to the writing of 'On the poverty of the Saviour',[23] which is accordingly dedicated to Innocent VI. It purports to be a report of an inquiry commissioned by Clement VI (1349–50) into the implications of the poverty debates which had been running with some heat in mendicant circles and outside them for a century. FitzRalph confronts outright the question which lay for many at the heart of the 'poverty debate'. How could those who claimed to seek to live the apostolic life justify the conspicuous consumption of their wealthy lifestyles when Jesus was poor and his life was simple? Here Western Christendom's brightest minds were locked in a paradox. On the face of it Christ's teaching clearly encourages his followers to embrace poverty. The apostolic life was that of a wanderer, preaching the Gospel in trust that the Lord would provide for the bodily needs of his missionaries. But on all sides the religious orders and the clergy held property, and some religious houses and higher prelates were conspicuous for their wealth. They were not going to give up this comfortable style of life lightly, just because someone had written a book reminding them of the way Jesus wanted his disciples to live. Power as well as wealth was involved. But an opulent lifestyle seemed more scandalous when it came to the mendicants, especially the Franciscans, whose special calling was to poverty. FitzRalph says that he has tried to get to the root of the matter (*investigare radices*).[24]

'Let us enter this fog, then,' says FitzRalph invitingly.[25] Let us distinguish property-holding (*proprietas*) and lordship (*dominium*).[26] We must not confuse lordship over something and the right to use it.[27] The thrust of FitzRalph's argument is that the 'lordship' apparently enjoyed by human beings is a mere loan from God. It is really only the right to use things, and on conditions. God can take his loan back if the conditions on which he makes it are not fulfilled, for does his omnipotence not retain the power to do directly what he normally does through an intermediary?[28] Man may have authority over things but the power really remains God's own.[29] When he sinned, Adam lost the lordship he was given in Genesis 1:28, although some restoration took place with the death of Christ.[30] There is a discussion of the right of rule over others and what it can legitimately involve in a 'state of innocence' and in a 'state of sin'.

FitzRalph died in 1360, so he could take no active part in steering the continuation of the debate he began. In Oxford his book divided the religious orders.[31] The *possessionati*, the monastic orders which had possessions, tended to favour him; the mendicants, who were supposed to be dedicated to poverty, tended not to.[32] 'On the Life of the Gospel' (*De Vita Evangelica*) of the 1370s, written by Geoffrey Hardeby, an Augustinian friar, observes in Chapter 6 that there is a conflict between the idea that rightful dominion can be lost by sinning and the doctrine that an unworthy minister retains his priestly powers.[33] Wyclif was well aware of FitzRalph's work and refers to it.[34]

Wyclif's 'On Divine Dominion' (*De dominio divino*) revived in Oxford debate some of the points FitzRalph had made in the *De Pauperie*. Oxford was hot with the topic, to judge from William Woodford's response in his 'Defence againt the man of Armagh' in about 1375.[35] Disputation was for grown-ups too, especially the *quodlibets* on any topic. Wyclif begins from much the same strong doctrine of God as FitzRalph, an exploration of what follows from God's nature, as any theologian trained upon the *Sentences* would be likely to do. God's will and foreknowledge are utterly reliable elements in the universe, and any description of creation must take that as given.

He had probably made a beginning on this work, perhaps in lectures, before he was chosen to go to Bruges. Unless he was to back down altogether – which was never his way – Wyclif's pioneering ecclesiology was now going to require him to work out in this wider context the implications of the claims he had so boldly made on behalf of the English Government when it had invited him to be its theological 'consultant'. He had devised arguments which would support the wish of the English Government to avoid paying its overdue tax bill from Rome. He had daringly extended his ideas to encompass the assertion that secular authority was allowed to take possession of Church property if the Church misbehaved itself. He maintained[36] that in certain circumstances, since kings can grant temporalities, kings may remove temporal possessions from ecclesiastical persons if they regularly misuse them. This is allowed 'medicinally' so as to discourage sin.[37]

There are enormous questions here, for Wyclif seems to be disregarding a difference in kind between the two jurisdictions, temporal and spiritual, which had been painfully worked out during the Investiture Contest of the late eleventh and early twelfth centuries, when Church and state had battled out their respective roles in the choosing, appointment and consecration of bishops.[38] Wyclif began to sketch a view of the equality of lay and ordained. Wyclif's principle at this stage is that erring clergy are merely the 'sinful brothers' of their non-ordained fellow-members of the human race.[39] Ecclesiastics, even Popes, he says, are subject to lay courts. This thrust against a dividing line which had been drawn in and after the Investiture Contest with great difficulty and expense. The principle is that erring clergy are merely our sinful brothers.[40] He thus moves from criticism of corrupt contemporary practices to a radical reconstruction of the fundamentals of ecclesiology, and only gradually perhaps did the scale of the claims he was making and their implications become clear to him or anyone else.

'On Divine Dominion', the first of Wyclif's series of books on dominion,[41] opens with a grand statement of his methodology and also of his purpose, a kind of self-imposed '*accessus*' (or formal introduction of the kind academic lecturers regularly provided when they began to study a new 'set book' with their students). He provides an opening statement about the way he proposes to deal with the use of sources. The Bible is his principal authority. 'I lean in the order of proceeding on the reasons and the sense of Scripture, to which I have professed a special obedience in [my] religion. For I know that the mode of speaking of Scripture is both grammatically and rhetorically most proper; that it is most subtle in its easiness, rightness and solidity logically and metaphysically; and that it is most fruitful in its truth and consistency and its usefulness in proving.'[42] In the *De civili dominio*, his next book, Wyclif takes all this further, because he was intent on showing that his theory was a general theory, which would fit civil dominion as well as clerical. It was essential that it should if it was to be serviceable in justifying the interference of secular authorities in ecclesiastical affairs.

This adventurous journey threw Wyclif further back still into the basics. Justification for Wyclif seems to require more than faith. The Latin *iustus* can be translated 'righteous' and also 'just'. Nor is it simply a question of the way a person appears in the sight of God. 'The Christian, and especially the theologian (*theologus*), ought to die virtuous,' that is, to behave in accordance with God's design for the universe. Wyclif's doctrine of man takes virtue to be at least partly a matter of behaviour. Wyclif's fundamental premise[43] is that only those in a state of grace, the virtuous, can legitimately exercise dominion over others, or over things. Accordingly, he defines dominion as the habit of a rational nature, by virtue of which that nature is said to be set over that which serves it.[44]

He explores the argument that a righteous person has an automatic lordship over all things in the natural world.[45] He supports this proposition with an argument from the Truth, Christ himself, who says in the Gospel (Matthew 6:33), 'Seek first the kingdom of God and all these things shall be added unto you.' He coaxes the scriptural quotation into a syllogism. Every righteous person has the use of the whole created world. No righteous person makes use of that over which he does not have lordship. So every righteous person has lordship over the whole created world.

He is then able to continue from his initial premises that the righteous man has the legitimate 'use' of the whole material world to the corollary that God does not bestow that right unconditionally, indefinitely or outright. 'God does not give this dominion except for the duration of the righteousness of the righteous man.' It is a conditional gift. Yet it is, within its terms, an unreserved gift. 'Just as it would be out of keeping with (*repugnat*) the magnificence of the King of England to give to someone in great need a mere atom (*atomum*), so it would be out of keeping with the magnificent generosity of the King of Kings' to give to so needy a member of his 'household' what Scripture calls 'dung' and 'dust', unless as mere accompaniments to a more 'complete' gift. Otherwise he would be recompensing his hard-working servant only in part and incompletely.[46]

The same passage contains a summary of Wyclif's doctrine of the operation of grace in this area of control of possessions. He seems to be saying that a gift of grace is *also* a reward which has been earned or merited. What God has given can be taken away by no one except by the recipient's own act, certainly not without God's making some compensatory gift. For example, if a righteous man's coat is stolen and he goes on loving the thief, grace is 'added' to him as a reward for his virtue. The greater the grace informing the human exercise of dominion, the more closely it resembles the divine dominion. This is why Augustine says, paradoxically, that temporal things are possessed the more truly if they are not prized. Thus those who steal away the temporal things of a righteous man positively strengthen his title to them.[47] The love of temporal things takes away from the love of God and therefore diminishes a person's state of grace, and weakens his right of possession.

God compensates the righteous man with something better, when something is taken from him, by recognizing his 'merit'. If a person perseveres in the grace of patience in suffering, his suffering is meritorious.[48] Furthermore, to the human being who 'deserves' it, God does not give a merely created good but also the uncreated Good; for the gift of grace is the gift of the Holy Spirit himself. Wyclif intends this to be a demonstrative or 'necessary' argument for it is marked with the familiar markers of reference to points established earlier from first principles. The conclusion is reached that 'it is not possible for a man to receive this gift unless he has with it the whole world'.[49]

Good reputation follows from the gift of grace. Those over whom dominion is exercised know then that it is legitimate, that God has granted dominion to that creature, and that this presupposes in turn that the creature is in a state of grace. For someone who is not in a state of grace to pretend to exercise dominion is hypocrisy. It is 'infamous' because it involves a pretence not only that the dominion is being exercised justly but that he who exercises it is also just, 'while actually he is unjust'.[50] It will be easy to object that this theory is right only with reference to the state of innocence.[51] A perennial difficulty of a strong Christian doctrine of sin is that sin must be taken to breach the connection Wyclif describes. His answer is that, through the passion of Christ, remission of sins brings about a restoration of dominion. So now in the time of grace the righteous man has full dominion over everything.

It is not clear that, at this stage of his thinking, Wyclif saw the implications which leap to the eye of anyone familiar with the debates of the Reformation period. This is an example of his setting off on a road which led a long way further than he seems to have been aware. Wyclif seems to be quite happy to believe that there is a divine requirement of positive virtue linked to deeds, acts, works. That does not mean that he is insensitive to the complexities of the way grace may work within an individual to produce good deeds as the consequences of its presence. No reader of Augustine could be unaware how far that debate had already gone, and Wyclif was certainly a reader of Augustine. But he evidently does not see the sharp distinction between justification by faith and justification by works which was to come into view with Luther.

Among the 'markers' of Reformation thought are the strong emphasis on the sufficiency of the 'work' of Christ and the uselessness of human effort; and on faith in Christ as the sole 'justifier' in the sight of God. There are hints of both in Wyclif, but neither is fully developed.[52] It is not easy to say how far Wyclif's Christology went. He speaks more often of the Word in Scripture than of the Word made flesh. He envisages a 'saving teaching' rather than an act of faith which saves.[53] 'Christ gave a saving teaching for the individual and the people, for this time and the future'[54] is still his argument late in his life.

Wyclif was saying all this in the context of an active Oxford debate. William Woodford gave lectures in 1377 to which part of the *De civili dominio*[55] seems to be an attempt at a reply. Wyclif may be referring to Woodford when he says, 'And truly I have often turned over in my mind what moved that master and colleague of the order of St Benedict among all the important persons of Oxford to tackle that matter so preposterously and in such a singular manner.'[56] Wyclif feels it obligatory to reply. 'And truly I am obliged, the more so because I learned many notable truths with this doctor in the various degrees and scholarly acts.' Wyclif was certainly speaking of Woodford in other passages.[57] He speaks of William Woodford's defence of the clergy's right to property.[58] He argues against, 'in the way he has, fully and subtly,'[59] as he puts it.

John de Acley was a monk of Durham and listed by his order among the 'Fellows' (*socii*) at Oxford for 1373–76, though he may well have been at Oxford in earlier years when he was not so senior, and there is evidence that he was there from time to time in the years leading up to Wyclif's death. The provincial Chapter of the Benedictines, or Black Monks, entrusted to him the responsibility of undertaking formal responses to counter Wyclif's teaching. In which year this happened is not certain. Chapters were held in 1372 and 1381, and probably in 1375 and 1378. The letter and introductory rubric which describe this commission suggest too that it was no small thing that was being asked, for to enter into controversy might be to stir it up further; and members of the king's council, it was said, had forbidden John de Acley from involving himself in any activity which might tend in that direction.[60] Here is another indication that Wyclif was not alone in causing alarm in high places in Church and state by debating such matters.

That debate was about to change its character as it was deliberately taken outside the university world and made the subject of high ecclesiastical disapproval. What happened to Wyclif was not at all unusual. A Franciscan friar who had preached on the poverty of the primitive Church had been made to recant at St Mary's. Pope Gregory XI sent out a number of letters all over Europe with warnings that this teaching or that was heretical.[61] It was only realistic to be nervous on the subject. But the result for Wyclif went much further than for most academic authors who fell foul of influential ecclesiastical politicians. Wyclif was saying things which chimed with what FitzRalph had said, which contributed to debates which were going on elsewhere in Europe as well as in Oxford. He was giving voice to ideas which were provoking controversy in France and Italy.

There is one more aspect we must touch on before we come to the process of attack and condemnation Wyclif was about to face, for it is a reminder that most of what happened to him took place in the already contentious world of academe. It is apparent here and there that he could be hurt, that he was bewildered to discover the difference between the friendship of fellow-students and colleagues and the superficial amity which vanished at once when two Masters fell into opposition. 'I was recently greeted by a certain Doctor, whom I had believed to be my special friend.' He acknowledges a duty to do as Scripture says and suffer personal injuries (*personales iniurias*) with patience. But he obstinately sees it as his duty to 'remove stumbling blocks', despite his sense of betrayal by his now hostile colleagues.[62] His was the inbred Oxford world, the world in which, to borrow from Cornford's *Microcosmographia* about Cambridge in 1908, 'the men who get things done are the men who walk up and down the King's Parade, from 2 to 4, every day of their lives'.[63] Colleagues of Wyclif, more adventurous travellers of the international dimension in which the religious orders moved, were more aware that this 'bush telegraph' was spreading such debates a long way. Although Wyclif did not know it yet, the discomfort of being cut dead in the street by a former fellow-student was less important to his future career than the way it all looked in the wider arena of Europe.

Chapter 10

Calling Wyclif to account

'The priests, and then after them the archbishop, took the matter in hand, depriving him of his benefice which he had in Oxford; but being somewhat befriended and supported by the king (Edward III) he continued and bare up against the malice of the friars, and of the archbishop, until about 1377.'[1]

Fist-waving at St Paul's

On 3 February 1377 the convocation of the province of Canterbury met at St Paul's Cathedral. A deputation of lay barons came to present the demands of the King to the assembled leaders of the Church. Robert Ashton, who had already been speaking in Parliament on the subject of papal taxation, asked the Church for financial help in dealing with the Pope's demands. Over the next few days controversy mounted over the old, vexed questions of the balance of power between Church and state. On 5 February William Courtenay, then Bishop of London, read out to the convocation a list of articles embodying the grievances of the clergy on various points of conflict between ecclesiastical and secular jurisdiction.[2] There were meetings of the bishops on their own on 9 and 11 February and of the whole of convocation, bishops and priests, on 13 February. On 16 February the 'lower house' of the clergy suggested that the Church should refuse to make a grant until the Members of Parliament had agreed to make one on behalf of themselves as the laity. The surviving evidence as to what was going on in Parliament during this time is less detailed, but it is clear that no grant had been made by 16 February. A series of cases was afoot raising specific questions about these issues of jurisdiction. They were not merely academic but grittily real.

Wyclif became the focus of an exciting episode during this convocation, to which Foxe gives full dramatic value, taking his details from the *Chronicon Angliae*, a source heavily prejudiced against Wyclif.

> 'Through the favour and support of the Duke of Lancaster and Lord Henry Percy, he was protected long against the violence and cruelty of his enemies; but at last the bishops, still urging and inciting their archbishop, Simon Sudbury, who had already deprived him, and afterwards prohibited him,[3] obtained by process and order of citation to have him brought before them.'[4] 'The duke [John of Gaunt] having intelligence that Wyclif was to appear before the bishops' brought together four masters of divinity to side with him [Wyclif], one from each of the orders of friars. On the day Wyclif was to appear, 19 February, 'he went accompanied with the four friars, and the duke of Lancaster, and lord Henry Percy, lord marshal of England.'

This scenario sets the royal friend and patron of Wyclif and his 'side' squarely against the ecclesiastical authorities.[5] 'A great concourse of people was gathered to hear what should be said and done',[6] probably motivated in this instance at least as much by their dislike of the plans of John of Gaunt and Percy and Thomas of Woodstock to enlarge the jurisdiction of the Marshal in the city of London,[7] as by interest in the theological questions at issue.

'Such was the throng of the multitude,' says Foxe, 'that the lords (notwithstanding all the authority of the high marshal) with great difficulty could get through. The Bishop of London seeing the stir that the Lord Marshal kept in the church among the people, speaking to the Lord Percy, said, "That if he had known before what authority he would have assumed in the church, he would have stopped him from coming there." At which words the Duke, not a little angered, answered, "That he would keep such authority there, whether the Bishop like it or not".'[8]

Eventually everyone was assembled in the Lady Chapel of St Paul's, 'where the dukes and barons were sitting with the archbishops and other bishops'.[9]

'John Wycliffe, according to the custom, stood before them, to learn what should be laid to his charge.' The meeting broke up in confusion almost at once, when Lord Percy invited Wyclif to sit down and the Bishop of London responded angrily. ' "Neither was it fitting," said he, "that he, who was cited before his ordinary, should sit during the time of his answer." '[10] It seems there was no presenting of points to Wyclif so that he could answer, only the altercation at the end of which an incensed Gaunt finally said that he would have the Bishop of London, William Courtenay, dragged out of the church by his hair.

A riot ensued, which the citizens of London gladly joined in, and the story breaks up in some confusion from 20 February.[11] The crowd of interested Londoners present had had a good show, and the name of Wyclif was lodged in their memories.

The citizens of London could take an inconvenient interest in affairs of Church and state, and they liked to be taken seriously. The merchants and tradespeople of London were organized in guilds whose basic structure was exactly the same as that of the academic *universitas*. There were large and small 'mysteries', five or six being particularly powerful, the vintners, fishmongers, grocers, mercers and goldsmiths and perhaps the skinners, providing from their membership most of the mayors and aldermen. There were civic courts whose jurisdiction was jealously protected. There were privileges granted and renewed by the kings of England.[12] A dynamic was at work, the dynamic of an independent citizenry with a strong conviction of belonging to a 'body'.

The citizenry would appear in rowdy crowds when something was afoot in which they had an interest. This was a not uncommon phenomenon in the Middle Ages. Crowds would sometimes gather for academic disputations and especially where the ecclesiastical authorities were rumoured to be moving to condemn someone for his opinions. It was partly for this reason that there was so much fear among ecclesiastical leaders that the faithful could be led astray by what to the modern eye appear to be arguments too obscure and complex for ordinary people to understand. Whether or not the populace fully undertood the theological issue, they loved a rebel and could easily turn him into a demagogue. The burgesses in Parliament were the more fearsome because they were of this bourgeoisie.

Sometimes it was a rabble which presented itself. However, on the accession of the ten-year-old Richard II in 1377 – heir to the throne after the death of his father, the Black Prince – the Londoners sent an embassy 'of the leading citizens' (*de valentioribus civibus*) to Kingston upon Thames, where Richard was at that time with his mother Joan, 'to recommend the city and its citizens to him'. There was, inevitably with such a young heir, a question whether power, and indeed the succession, might be snatched from him by ambitious barons. John Philpot, 'citizen of London', made a speech offering recognition by the citizens of London exclusively to the new King in return for a settlement of their dispute with John of Gaunt over who ruled London.[13]

Scheming for Wyclif's downfall

With hindsight, it is easy to see that some of Wyclif's ideas had explosive potential, but Wyclif did not know yet how explosive. In any case, it would be misleading to suggest that he was planning to be a 'dissident'. His judgment may well have been undermined by disappointment and resentment about the failure to reward him for his service to the Government at Bruges; he was, perhaps, in a devil-may-care mood as a lecturer, employing the skills in charming an audience to which some testify, so as to shock the students – always a temptation for an academic. But the driving force of his writing and lecturing at this stage was probably chiefly the sheer interest of developing his ideas in the current climate.

But this was a time and a climate when the expression of politically sensitive opinions could provoke a negative response. Others might plan to build their own careers on the wreckage of the career of an outspoken lecturer lashing out against powerful persons who had failed to exercise their patronage in his favour as he believed he had had reason to expect. Rome was informed that Wyclif was speaking out of turn in Oxford. The Pope said to the Archbishop of Canterbury and the Bishop of London that he had got his information from 'many credible persons'. Wyclif had his own ideas about who they were.[14]

Wyclif had a particularly energetic enemy who understood the politics of the Rome as well as those of the university. Adam Easton, a Benedictine monk we have already met in the guise of a keen bibliophile, formerly studied and taught in Oxford as a theologian, and had been Prior of Gloucester (now Worcester) College. The Black Monks made good use of his skills when they needed to maintain their position against the bids for power made by their rivals, the friars. For example, he had been called back to his house in Norwich to argue against the friars in East Anglia.[15] Now, in the mid-1370s, he was currently with the papal *curia*-in-exile at Avignon. He had gone there in the late 1360s in the entourage of the English Benedictine, now Cardinal and Archbishop of Canterbury, Simon Langham.[16]

With a book of his own under way, and more than likely with an eye to the advantage of being seen to take a firm line over Wyclif's challenge to papal taxation, he wrote to the Abbot of Westminster – seeking further information about the teaching of Wyclif – and began to press at the papal court for sanctions against him. His letter arrived at Westminster Abbey in November 1376. It asked the Abbot to obtain for the writer a copy of the sayings (*dicta*) of a certain John Wyclif, who is said to be speaking against the Benedictines at Oxford; a copy of his disputations 'against the Church' and a copy of his book on royal power, the *De potestate regali*.[17] *Dicta* can mean written as well as spoken 'sayings', and would also include *reportationes*, the notes taken by students at lectures.

Probably before the Great Schism began in 1378 (for he does not mention it), Easton had completed his own book the 'Defence of Ecclesiastical Power' (*Defensorium Ecclesiasticae Potestatis*), and presented it to the Pope. It was the fruit of twenty years' labour, he says. The Pope rewarded him in 1381 by making him Cardinal Priest of St Cecilia, but that may have been for other services rendered. There are refutations of Wyclif in it, mostly confined to Book I of the *De civili dominio*, which seems to have been based on lectures Wyclif was giving in Oxford about 1375. This suggests a date for the *Defensorium* close to the time of the Bulls the Pope sent out in 1377 condemning Wyclif, a period when the Wyclif affair could have been much under discussion at the papal court. Easton knew of the later books of the *De civili dominio*, but he deals with them differently, rather as though he was adding notes on them as the debate developed.[18]

Easton's *Defensorium* takes the form of a dialogue between king and bishop (the bishop's side naturally being Easton's own). It is an enormous work, in which he set out to cover all the ground encompassed by past authorities and masters on lordship and related subjects. It is intended to impress, bodying forth in its scale his own personal ambitions. The reader and potential patron is to come away with the idea that Easton is expert, loyal, assiduous, an ideal papal servant and one deserving of advancement. From about halfway through Wyclif is quoted a great deal, in a way which makes it plain that Easton had read, and read very thoroughly, at least Book I of Wyclif's book 'On Civil Dominion'.[19]

'On Civil Dominion' was itself continuing to develop at this time. There is ample precedent in the Middle Ages for the publishing of a book only for the author to discover that there is a rush of comment and challenge. The Middle Ages had its own forms of pamphlet warfare. 'Publishing' need involve no more than circulating a few copies, perhaps merely sending one off to a patron, so it was no great matter for an author to put out revised versions if he had second thoughts. He then wrote a further book or books in response, and tacked the later writing on to the first edition so that modern readers now have a book which is not the completed single work it seems, but was really written in episodes and afterthoughts. The lectures which Wyclif gave in 1375 and 1376, on which Book I of the *De civili dominio* was based, stirred up dispute and generated criticism and Book II, written perhaps in 1376–77, bears the marks of the author feeling the need to respond to the points which had been raised. In fact Book II of the *De civili dominio* may have been prompted by the lectures given by William Woodford in 1377, while Wyclif himself was probably still lecturing on the subject of dominion in a rival series. *De civili dominio* II.xiv may even have circulated separately from the rest of Book II.[20]

Quotations, opinions (*sententiae*), 'sayings' (*dicta*), alleged to be reprehensible opinions of Wyclif, were apparently being sent to the Curia from more than one direction while all this was going on. Characteristically, Walsingham's account gets ahead of itself, so that he accuses Wyclif of teachings he had probably not articulated as early as 1377. He may be more reliable when he says that 'about fifty conclusions' of Wyclif's were sent to Rome to be put before Pope Gregory, from which thirteen were selected for papal condemnation.[21] His delation to Rome seems to have involved a huddle of scandalized correspondence between the Benedictine brothers of Oxford, and it seems likely that Easton was not the only critic actively campaigning to have Wyclif's teaching condemned. Wyclif mentions that Brinton had told him of the condemnation of his errors, for Brinton had been sent a copy of the list by his 'brothers', with annotations.[22] The Bishop of Rochester said to him in public in Parliament that his conclusions were to be condemned, as had been testified to him in a formal document he had been sent by the Curia. And it seemed to many that this was an indiscreet assertion, first because it tended to defame the Roman Curia and secondly because it put a stumbling block in the way of our King and this Kingdom, and thirdly because it showed that the Bishop and his brothers were plotting together in suspicion.

Wyclif shows understandable signs in the *De civili dominio* of what could seem paranoia if it had not been so fully justified. It is here that he begs for 'kindly listeners' and not 'sinister reporters', people who will set the truth free and not be concerned with personalities.[23] Wyclif thought he knew who had 'reported' him. Wyclif was very much afraid that he was being misreported to the Roman Curia, and said so in a *Sermon*.[24] He spoke darkly of 'boys' who had betrayed him.[25] These could perhaps have been pupils scandalized by remarks he had made in lectures, but recently he had been lecturing to Theology students who were not boys but grown men. He was left with lingering resentment over what had been said about him.

In a *Sermon* on the Epistle for Palm Sunday, possibly preached in 1378 or a year soon after, but in any case, while he was filled with resentment about this 'tale-telling', Wyclif refers to one *tolstanus*, possibly a corruption for Toledanus, which would mean someone who had studied at the University of Toledo. Robert Waldby would fit that description. He was an Augustinian friar who was to have a successful ecclesiastical career, becoming Archbishop of Dublin and Archbishop of York before his death in 1397. If it was he, Wyclif was insulting him in terms which could scarcely fail to alienate someone who carried a certain clout. 'The aforesaid Toledan and his pups [...] are said to have reported all the way to the Roman Curia but too idiotically, for neither they not the Curia understand two words.' 'For a certain catholic doctor' has been misrepresenting what he had said. The 'chattering pups' had reported what he had said incorrectly, and so they were left with a conclusion they did not know how to construe and which was such as might be condemned as heretical.[26] There is an evident frustration here at being, as Wyclif sees it, misunderstood and misrepresented. He goes on to suggest that this kind of 'lying comment' has the potential to destroy the University and even catholic truth.[27] But again, we should not lose sight of Wyclif's sensitivity to slights.

Determinationes

> 'You think (do you not) that you have only to state a reasonable case, and people must listen to reason and act upon it at once.'[28]

> 'Are you not aware that conviction has never yet been produced by an appeal to reason, which only makes people uncomfortable?'[29]

There was nothing Wyclif could do but argue back or fall silent and Wyclif was not one for falling silent. Nicholas Radcliffe of St Albans called him *fortissimus pugilis*.[30] He was about to learn that he could not hope to defend himself successfully by modest and reasonable argument, still less by furious protestations. Wyclif publicly protested his innocent intentions. He has never intended to be anything but a faithful Christian. If he has failed in this through ignorance (*ex ignorantia*) or for any other reasons, now he retracts and humbly submits himself to correction by Holy Mother Church.[31] He continues with a step by step consideration of the opinions which have been condemned.

> 'I was in favour of the proposal until I hear Mr. –'s arguments in support of it.'[32]

> 'Once start a comma and the whole pack will be off, full cry, especially if they have had a literary training.'[33]

There was one thing the academic world of Wyclif's day understood very well and that was how to 'determine' disputed questions. The trick of it was that they remained debatable: a 'determination' was final for the afternoon in question. A Benedictine notebook[34] copied by a Worcester monk in the 1360s preserves more than a hundred questions, which may well have been someone's list of those actually debated in the schools or proposed for debate. They are on topics known to have been favourites for the purpose, such as future contingents, but some of them are novel.

Perhaps it was partly in the lingering hope of establishing that he had been unfairly condemned, that Wyclif engaged in public disputations[35] in Oxford with two Benedictines, William Binham (Vryngham) and Uthred of Boldon. It is harder to separate 'disputation' from 'dispute' when it comes to this kind of exchange.

In the debate with William Binham in 1377–78[36] Wyclif makes particular reference to the Oxford context; the 'determining' had gone on after the Feast of St Thomas, 7 July, when the long vacation began and the students set off for their homes, and that had been in breach of the oath which a Doctor had to take to observe the praiseworthy custom of the University.[37] There seems to have been some underlying rivalry about patronage. Wyclif complains in his *Determinacio*[38] of the arguments of William Binham that his opponent had defamed him to the Curia not only with the purpose of having him deprived of his benefices, but so that he himself might win the goodwill of Rome.[39] Wyclif identifies himself as the King's 'special' (*peculiaris*) clerical apologist (*Regis clericus*) and it is in that capacity that he 'puts on the habit' of a responder and defender and persuader of the view that the King may justly rule the kingdom of England and refuse to pay tribute to the Roman Pontiff.[40] Uthred was perhaps also presenting himself as 'the Pope's man'. Uthred was sufficiently returned to favour to be sent to Avignon in 1373 to put the English position on subsidies and provisions. He made a speech in London in 1374 defending the papal claim.

The two 'determinations' of Wyclif on the subject of relations between state and Church survive.[41] There is a question why Wyclif should choose to 'determine' these particular questions at this point – probably between 1374 and 1377 – if they had to be retrieved piecemeal from Uthred's work. Could there have been a live debate?[42] Binham's and Uthred's works against which these *Determinaciones* were written have probably not survived, but then they may originally have been no more than live contributions to the live disputations.[43]

Wyclif's reply to Uthred begins with that elaborate pretence of ironical courtesy familiar in academic debate. 'My most reverend doctor and special Master Dom Uthred, among other lovely truths which he has drawn out of Scripture and disseminated according to his custom for the instruction of the school of Oxford',[44] has said things which Wyclif feels moved to argue against. Uthred had raised three points to which Wyclif replies: priestly rule is better than lay rule; the priesthood is not subject to the judgment of lay power; priests cannot be deprived of the right to tithes or oblations and no one should teach that they can.[45]

Wyclif's *Declarationes* evince the passion on the subject of getting anyone to listen to what he was really saying, which became ever more marked as the condemnations continued during the next few years. Wyclif was still unequivocal that it had never been his intention to be unorthodox. 'First, I protest publicly, as I have often done elsewhere, that I propose and wish with all my heart, with the help of God's grace, to be a wholehearted Christian (*integer Christianus*) and, as long as breath remains in me, to put forward and defend the law of Christ as well as I can.'[46] He offered to submit himself humbly to the correction of the Church if he was found to have been wrong in anything he had said. His *Declarationes* to this effect evince an expectation which has again and again proved naïve in academic and ecclesiastical witch-hunts: that, if the accused explains himself clearly, his opponents, once they understand properly what he is trying to say, will cease to pursue him as a heretic.

The Papal Bulls of 1377

In late May 1377 Pope Gregory XI issued Bulls against Wyclif, directed to every power in England which might be able to call him to account. Three were sent to leading figures in the Church, Sudbury, the Archbishop of Canterbury, and Courtenay, the Bishop of London. The first of these three Bulls contrasted the vigilance in defence of the faith of earlier generations of English prelates with the present negligence in doing anything about Wyclif; it pointed to lamentable similarities between his teaching and that of Marsilius of Padua and John of Jandun.

It is not at all certain that Marsilius of Padua was an influence on Wyclif,[47] or that he had read his *Defender of the Peace*. Adam Easton had (quoting and referring to it closely in his *Defensorium*),[48] and it may be he who made the link which led to the mention of Marsilius in the Bulls of 1377 and sowed in Italian minds the idea that Wyclif was an English Marsilius. Marsilius's *Defender of the Peace* had been published in the 1320s. It deals, in Dictio II especially, with the question of the rival jurisdictions of Church and state. Among his themes was the idea that Christ's own life of poverty and submission to secular authority must be the example now for his Church, with the state having authority to keep the Church's excesses in check. In a similar spirit, Dante had seen in Joachim of Fiore a true prophet pointing away from the institutional and structural, the hierarchical and juridical, and towards a simple humble attempt to imitate the life of Christ; and the reverberations of their thoughts are almost certainly to be heard in what Wyclif says.

Marsilius was also hostile to what he saw as the excesses to which papal claims of plenitude of power had now come. He challenged the very idea of a papal primacy. Only Christ was head of the Church. The Church was not under a human but a divine authority. The ordained ministry as a whole must cease to regard itself as possessing the powers it was now claiming. Marsilius argued that the priesthood had a merely spiritual role and ought not to regard itself as better and higher than the ordinary faithful. The Donation of Constantine, which Marsilius saw as genuine but a downward step, had encouraged the Church to get above itself in its claims to superiority over the secular authority. Peter had been the chief of the apostles as an individual, but no inference was to be drawn that Christ intended a succession. Each bishop was equally a successor of the apostles so long as he lived the apostolic life. The most important implication of these similarities with things Wyclif was saying, or was later to say, is the reminder how pervasively all this was 'in the air'.

The prelatical pair in charge of the southern province (or 'at least one of them') were instructed to conduct a secret enquiry into Wyclif's teaching and, if they found that he had indeed been the author of certain doctrines which had been attributed to him, they were to imprison him and extract a confession, sending the offending writings secretly to Rome, while keeping Wyclif under lock and key. Wyclif's own Bishop, Buckingham, the Bishop of Lincoln, does not seem to have been sent a Bull specially addressed to him, though Wyclif was technically his priest. He had asked Wyclif some awkward questions in the past, but those had been about his sources of income and his benefices.[49]

Having (presumably) sent this off, the Pope bethought himself of a postscript. He realized that if Wyclif got to hear about this he might hide. He therefore sent instructions that, in that event, Wyclif should be cited to appear before the Pope within three months and posters should be put up everywhere he might be, especially in Oxford, to ensure that he knew of the citation. There was a further afterthought, resulting in a third Bull. Scholars were to be found of reliable opinions and sufficient expertise to explain to the King, his court and councillors that the propositions which were attributed to Wyclif were heretical and a danger to any of the faithful who were brought to share them. All this chasing-up seems to have been ineffective. After the text of the Pope's letter copied into the *Chronicon* of Walsingham it is suggested that the Bishops the Pope had instructed to proceed against Wyclif were slow and faithless in obeying his commands. 'How carelessly they fulfilled his commands it is better to be silent about than to say.'[50]

One Bull was sent to the King himself. In it the Pope recognized that no attempt to silence Wyclif could hope to be successful without the support of the King and the secular Government. He therefore solicits that support.

The last Bull went to the Chancellor of the University of Oxford. The Pope was displeased that the scholars had allowed false teaching to go on among them. Unless the University suppressed the teaching of a perverse doctrine, and moreover seized Wyclif and handed him over to the Archbishop of Canterbury and the Bishop of London, along with any other scholars whose opinions he had infected, the University would lose its privileges. It was the obvious threat for a Pope to make, since some of the privileges were papal gifts. But it created an additional problem for the University. Oxford was not at all sure whether it should be seen to receive this Bull at all, not because it necessarily wished to defend or protect Wyclif, but because it did not wish to acknowledge that the Pope had the right to send the University instructions. Wyclif had his friends there too, and even his enemies might see him as 'one of them' when it came to any challenge from the outside world. Yet it is not difficult to establish that it was jealous Oxford colleagues who had delated Wyclif to Rome in the first place.

Nineteen opinions

It was not in the end patient reading of Wyclif's ideas in context, but the listing of shocking opinions in the form of alleged *dicta*, which formed the basis for his condemnation.[51] Nineteen opinions were condemned by the Pope in this first salvo against Wyclif.[52] The method of condemnation of selected erroneous opinions was nothing new. It had been used in the case of Peter Abelard in the first half of the twelfth century. It was used several times in universities in the thirteenth century when the newly obtained philosophical writings of Aristotle seemed to be leading academics to question fundamentals of the faith. It had the advantage of narrowing the matters in issue to a manageable compass, and enabling those who had to form a judgment to give their reasons.

Could Easton have been the compiler? There were others in the papal entourage who had a strong interest in these matters, notably some lawyers, including John of Legnano.[53] The Pope naturally did not do the work himself and it would make sense of Easton's letter to Westminster if the sequence of events had gone something like this. Easton expressed concerns about anti-papal talk in England, as a means of ingratiating himself with the Curia. He was asked for more detail. He wrote to Westminster, as we saw, asking for information against Wyclif to be sent out to him in Rome. He was invited to draw up a list of the points he found particularly dangerous. More than half of the points the Bull condemns appear in the *Defensorium*.[54]

The summary of Wyclif's offending ideas which is provided in the nineteen condemned theses runs roughly as follows (with some paraphrasing):

It is not for human beings to decide who has political dominion. It is for God. Even God cannot grant a civil dominion which can be exercised forever by the heirs of the original grantee, for the legitimacy of the exercise of the dominion depends upon the state of grace of whoever purports to exercise it. Human authorities cannot grant a 'civil right of inheritance' forever by giving a charter. A man in a state of grace, and who is therefore justified in the sight of God, possesses all God's gifts. Human beings can hand on dominion only by way of entrusting a 'stewardship' of things. Authority in the Church may lose dominion too if it falls from a state of grace. In that circumstance temporal lords may lawfully remove dominion from ecclesiastical authorities, and to do so is meritorious in them. It is for the temporal lords to investigate whether this is the situation, and if they find it is, it becomes their duty to seize the temporalities of the Church. It is not for the Pope to pronounce anyone fit or unfit to exercise dominion of his own volition. Excommunication is something a person does to himself. If it is formally pronounced, it is not binding except on someone who has already excommunicated himself by falling from grace. Power deriving from Christ or the apostolic power he gave his disciples should not be exercised by excommunicating those subordinate to it, especially for refusing temporal payments. On the contrary, the followers of Christ have no power to exact temporal payments by such censures. There is no absolute power from God which is exercised by the Church which can loose or bind the sinner independently of his own conformity or otherwise to the law of Christ. Any priest validly ordained has power to administer any of the sacraments and so any priest can absolve any contrite person. Kings are allowed to deprive ecclesiastical authorities of their temporalities if they misuse them. Whoever endowed the temporalities, it is lawful to take them away in proportion to the fall from grace. It is lawful for a subject to rebuke or even arraign an ecclesiastic, even the Pope.[55]

Oxford's official handling of its Papal Bull

> 'What is the reputation of the whole cabinet, great Captain and all, put together, compared with that of Oxford, built up (as it is) in the lapse of centuries?'

'Now is it not hard that because a Minister chooses deliberately to change his opinion, that Oxford must suddenly in a few days change too?'[56]

'A few days before Christmas the Lord Pope sent a Bull to the University of Oxford.' The text of the Papal Bull is given in Walsingham's *Chronicon*, with his censorious comments. He criticized the University for allowing erroneous opinions to be broadcast within it, specifically those of John Wyclif. The then Proctors had so far degenerated from the standards of their predecessors that, on hearing that a Papal Bull was on its way, they deliberated for some time as to whether they should receive or reject it. 'O University of Oxford, how grave a falling-away have you been responsible for, from the high point of your wisdom and knowledge,' laments Walsingham.[57]

The Bull is addressed to the Chancellor, as the Pope's 'Son' and to the University as an entity within the diocese of Lincoln. The Pope reminds the University that it has its privileges by his concession and he reminds it that those privileges are intended to allow the University to teach Scripture and defend orthodox faith and that, unless it does, souls will be imperilled. John Wyclif, Rector of the church of Lutterworth, 'a professor of the Sacred Page' and '(would he were not), Master of Errors', has put forth false teachings which threaten to subvert 'the condition of the whole Church and even that of the secular polity', and a comparison is made with the work of Marsilius of Padua and John of Jandun. The Bull calls for Wyclif to be arrested and sent under safe custody to the Archbishop of Canterbury and the Bishop of London, and anyone else he has infected with his opinions.

The question remained what Oxford was going to do 'officially' about its errant Doctor of Theology. Oxford continued to be unsure whether it should be seen to 'receive' this Bull, embarrassing though Wyclif was, and much as he appeared to be damaging the University's reputation, for fear of the loss of autonomy if it submitted to outside interference. Was it going to close ranks to protect him or close ranks against him? And how was it going to decide? Wyclif had his friends there too, and even his enemies might see him as 'one of them' when it came to any challenge from the outside world. These were questions which had more to do with politics than the pursuit of the truth, and the University was justifiably nervous that this affair would open a chink for outside interference which could widen into a crack.

The preliminary questions about who had a right to tell whom what to do when it came to the University's affairs had not been resolved. King, Parliament, Pope, University, all had much to play for when it came to the question who had jurisdiction in a matter such as this, when a scholar of the University was being accused of heresy. They were concerned not only about which of them could call such a scholar to account and discipline him if he was found to be at fault, but also which authority could give instructions to any of the others. Although it did not involve quite so many disputatious parties, the diplomatic mission to Bruges had been concerned at bottom with similar alarms over questions of conflicting jurisdiction. It was a type of problem utterly familiar to the medieval world.

Oxford's response to the letters of the Pope announced that 'the friends of the aforesaid Master John Wyclif and Wyclif himself had consulted in the Congregation of the Regents and the Non-Regents', and it was their view that they should not imprison 'a man of the King of England' (*hominem Regis Angliae* – a feudal view of the relationship between the English King and his subjects) on the orders of a Pope. That would be to allow the Pope royal powers in the kingdom of England. The alleged view of Wyclif in the Bull had been submitted to the Masters of Theology for their individual consideration. They all gave their views to the Chancellor.[58] He expressed their consensus when he said that, although the Masters were not prepared to impugn the truth of the articles condemned, they recognized that they might be offensive to the ears of the pious.

The subtle blending of considerations of truth and considerations of the politics of the real world manifested in Oxford's reply was already the usual academic way six hundred years ago. The decision neither condemned nor approved of Wyclif, and the Regent Masters regretted that it was beyond their power to act as the Pope wished, when their duty to the King of England went against it. So the University formulated its response to the Bull in an equivocal manner entirely in keeping with the combination of political sophistication and pusillanimity characteristic of the academic mind.

Wyclif indignantly and characteristically said that what was true should not be suppressed merely to avoid causing offence. It was delicately suggested that Wyclif should be invited to put up with being confined in the Black Hall in Oxford so that the Pope might be appeased and there need be no threat of removal of the University's privileges. Wyclif was indignant about that suggestion too, and angry about the sentence of imprisonment. He said it was contrary to the law of the King.[59]

Wyclif was let out of prison (the Vice-Chancellor taking his place), but things were changed. He was now a figure conspicuous for being controversial. Decisions had to be made about how he was going to continue and in what capacity.

Tonworth was not long to remain Chancellor. There was a complaint that a group of monk-scholars of the University had insulted some of the royal household, who happened to be in Oxford on royal business. They had fired arrows at the windows and 'chanted a certain song in English attacking the royal honour'. The next morning one of the offended knights arose and took his complaint to the King. On 22 March the Chancellor and the Proctors were summoned before the Bishop of St David's, Chancellor of England. The Vice-Chancellor could not be present because he was in prison in place of Wyclif. The Chancellor of England asked the Chancellor of the University why he did not punish the scholars. The Chancellor answered that he feared to act 'irregularly', that is, against the University's rules. The Chancellor of England said to the Chancellor of the University that *lèse-majesté* could not be allowed and, if the University could not keep proper discipline so as to prevent that kind of thing, the state would have to take over and override the privileges of the University. The King, he asserted, 'can remove the University and you from Oxford'. Minded to object that there could be no royal authority to remove him, because he was a subject of the Pope as well as of the King, he thought better of it and resigned in order that the privileges of the University might not be put at risk.[60]

As it turned out, Wyclif did not need to despair at once of the continuing approval of the Government. Oxford seems to have been willing to please the politicians by electing as Chancellor the John Gilbert, Bishop of Hereford, who had led the embassy to Bruges. It was startling to choose a serving Bishop, and he had quarrelled with the University in 1366 and gone to Paris to get his degree. It is not even certain that he actually did the job of Chancellor in person, and he was not Chancellor for long. Nevertheless, the unusual choice at this juncture was bound to send a signal about the Government's concern that Wyclif's future position should not be untenable.

What the Government did about the Bulls of 1377

Oxford's response was not the only one called for. The Pope's challenge to the Government came at a particularly difficult time. The Bulls went out from Rome in May 1377. In June the King of England died. His eldest son had died the previous year. The heir presumptive, his grandson Richard, was only ten. A power struggle was inevitable among his elders. His mother Joan, Edward's widow, and John of Gaunt, his uncle and Wyclif's patron, were obvious contenders for the exercise of the real power in the realm. Everyone could see that the fate of Wyclif, the way the authorities were going to respond to the bulls, would depend upon the future position of John of Gaunt, who had publicly made himself Wyclif's protector. In Parliament, Peter de la Mare was Speaker again, and he had been John of Gaunt's adversary in the period of the

Good Parliament.[61] There was now a 'continual Council' and there were efforts to ensure that it made it more difficult for John of Gaunt to get his own way.[62]

Moreover, there is a possibility that Wyclif was invited to speak to Parliament in his own defence. The manuscript known as the *Fasciculi Zizaniorum* includes a 'little book' (*Libellus*) which certainly suggests in its title that he put it before Parliament.[63] In the *Fasciculi Zizaniorum* the *Libellus* is followed directly by Wyclif's *Responsio*.[64] 'There is some question...,' Wyclif begins, impersonally, 'whether the Kingdom of England may lawfully prevent the treasure of the realm from going to foreigners in the event that it required for its own defence.'[65]

The problem in establishing what happened is that the Parliament of the autumn of 1377 had not yet considered the papal condemnation and, if Wyclif appeared before it to defend himself, he would have been seeking to fend off an attack which Parliament had not yet taken note of. And there is no mention of the episode in the *Rolls of Parliament* and nothing in the *Libellus* itself decisively identifies it as a document presented to Parliament or a record of Wyclif's address to Parliament.[66] This *Libellus* may just conceivably record an actual speech, but in the circumstances it seems more likely that this 'giving to the Parliament' was done by means of the handing out of the text in the form of a pamphlet, and that the date remains uncertain, or that it was in fact presented not to Parliament but to the King's Council. The text may represent Wyclif's defence of his position on the nineteen propositions the Pope had accused him of wrongly holding, noted by someone who heard him. Or it could, as the *Historia Anglicana* hints, have been made not to Parliament at all, but to the Bishops who summoned him before them when they were assembled at Lambeth in March 1378.[67] The magnates who sat in Parliament but were also churchmen would have needed to go carefully.[68]

The issues touched on in the *Libellus* are familiar, the ones which had now become the staple of the controversy surrounding Wyclif: whether God gave civil dominion to man and his heirs in perpetuity; whether the Pope enjoys an enduring political dominion in the world; what is the status of documents carrying a merely human authority; whether those not in a state of grace can legitimately control property or exercise dominion.[69] Wyclif maintains that in certain circumstances kings may remove temporal good and lands from clergy who habitually abuse their powers; that since kings can grant temporalities they can remove them; that this is allowed as a medicine to prevent sinning.[70] Wyclif's theme in this work is that the Pope cannot have power over the goods of the Church as a Lord, but only as a governor, administrator and procurer of the needs of the poor. He supported the Government in the view that it was lawful to withhold taxes due to Rome if England needed the money more for its own defence. Of course it is harmful to impoverish the kingdom and to impose a great burden on it. The opening question of the *Responsio* is precisely whether the kingdom of England can, when it badly needs the money for its own defence, legitimately hold back the treasure of the realm and not allow it to leave English shores, even if the Pope threatens penalties and points to the duty of obedience to himself.[71]

Wyclif advanced three arguments. The first was that every natural body has a God-given right to protect or defend itself, and the kingdom of England was such a body. The second was that the Gospel allowed the Pope to accept money only when it was a gift of alms. There was no duty of almsgiving in time of need. The Gospel would allow the Pope to use the money for the relief of the poor anyway, and in such circumstances England itself was to be considered 'poor'. The third argument concerned the operation of the law.[72] These would appear to be admirable arguments from the Government's point of view and hardly views they would wish to silence. So why did the thoughts in the *Responsio* elicit an attempt to gag Wyclif? For this is the episode where one of the manuscripts says, at the end, that 'silence' was imposed on Wyclif concerning these matters by the Lord King and the King's council.[73]

What the Church did about the Bulls of 1377: the summons to Lambeth

Before 27 March 1378 Wyclif was summoned to appear in the Archbishop's chapel at Lambeth before a tribunal of Bishops.[74] The charges were that Wyclif had maintained the nineteen propositions condemned in the Papal Bulls of 1377. He went as he was bidden, although he claims to have been considerably alarmed. He had, after all, only recently been let out of prison in Oxford.[75] He conjures with the idea that Archbishop Sudbury was off to Rome to arrange for him to be killed, and he says he was afraid to go to Lambeth.[76] He could be in no doubt that he was facing something more than mere condemnation of his opinions.

The Government tried to interfere in the Church's process, possibly at the instigation of John of Gaunt, who was currently keeping an unusually low personal profile amidst the buffetings of the winds of change at court. On the first day of the Lambeth meeting Sir Lewis Clifford presented himself as an emissary, ostensibly from Joan, the Black Prince's widow and now the Queen Mother, since King Richard was still too young to be plausibly supposed to be authorizing such things. Clifford requested that the meeting would not pass formal sentence on Wyclif. This apparently had an extraordinary effect on the hitherto fierce, would-be clerical defenders of the faith. As the chronicler

Walsingham put it, 'Men who had vowed not to submit to the princes and peers of the realm until they had punished the chief heretic for his excesses were struck with fear when they saw Sir Lewis Clifford.'[77] The assembly addressed itself to its task in a chastened mood.

It is possible that the meeting place was chosen in the hope that a repetition of the public embarrassment of the St Paul's episode could be avoided, but the attempt to avoid another 'St Paul's episode' was thwarted by the people of London, or the 'rabble' of the people, as one chronicler puts it. 'I do not call them the citizens of London, but the lowest of that body,' he says. They broke in to support Wyclif, who, the chroniclers suggest, had the favour and love of the Londoners.[78] The *Chronicon* offers a lively description of the rioting of the people of London when Wyclif was tried at Lambeth. They 'impudently presumed to enter the chapel', and they said their say and they impeded the business of the meeting.[79]

Wyclif had evidently been thinking hard about how to get himself out of trouble without compromising his integrity. His defence shows that he had drawn back as far as he felt able in conscience to do from the positions which had caused offence.[80] Wyclif's confidence that he could 'win over' his enemies by responding this way at Lambeth is the more surprising because he was used to the adversarial world of the university disputation. Yet on the face of it he succeeded, in the short term at least. The *Eulogium* says that he 'proved before the Archbishop of Canterbury and the Bishop of London that those conclusions were true'.[81] The decision of the Lambeth meeting was that Wyclif was to cease to say these things in the schools or in sermons, because they could present a stumbling block to the laity.[82] This was the end of direct attempts to confront Wyclif at meetings. Henceforth his ideas were to be tried and condemned in his absence.

In the midst of all this, in 1378, Pope Gregory XI died. The Great Schism followed when would-be successor Clement VII set up a rival curia to that of his enemy, the other would-be Pope Urban VI, at Avignon. It is sometimes suggested that this took the heat off Wyclif for a time; more probably it took the heat out of English anti-papalism, for the French Pope Gregory XI had been associated with the resentment about papal taxation and he was in any case French. Urban was reassuringly Italian. Clement now had the backing of France, but England set its face so resoundingly against him that it would not even allow his emissaries to argue his case before Parliament and those Cardinals who had supported Clement had their English benefices confiscated by the Parliament which met in Gloucester in 1378.[83]

Sanctuary

There was to be one more episode in which Wyclif was asked to serve as a consultant by a Government evidently uneasy about him, but still regarding him as a convenient expert. Surprisingly, Wyclif was willing to oblige.

In principle all churches could be regarded as places of sanctuary. Westminster Abbey was among those select, consecrated places which had a charter giving them a special right of sanctuary. Two knights, Robert Hauley and John Shakell, were at the centre of the affair.[84] Shakell had taken a prisoner-of-war while serving with the Black Prince in Spain in 1367. The prisoner had left his son in his place while he went home to raise the required ransom. No ransom was forthcoming. John of Gaunt had a claim by marriage to be 'King of Castile'. In that capacity, in 1378, he demanded that the young man be released. The two knights said they would not let him go until they had the ransom. They were put in the Tower of London. It was when they escaped that the breach of sanctuary occurred. They ran for refuge into the Abbey, pursued by the Constable of the Tower and fifty armed men. The pursuers forced their way in, right into the choir, where Mass was being said. Shakell escaped them. They killed Hauley there in the choir, together with his servant and one of the monks who got in the way. Hauley was buried in the south transept as a martyr and the Abbey was closed for worship for four months. Even the sittings of Parliament were suspended. Shakell gave up his prisoner, but he did get his ransom and a hundred marks a year for life.[85]

In the period of public shock after this episode the Archbishop of Canterbury brought before Parliament the question what 'sanctuary' now meant. If the servants of the state felt free to behave in this way in a church and invade a consecrated building, especially one which enjoyed the protection of a charter confirming it as a sanctuary, and shed blood in a holy place, questions of jurisdiction were surely being raised? The public dismay and fear that some of society's most basic protections were under threat is perhaps comparable with the anxieties which began to surface as civil liberties were eroded in the name of the 'war on terrorism'of the first decade of the twenty-first century.

Wyclif and some other clerics made depositions before Parliament at Gloucester in October or November 1378 on the limitations of sanctuary. Wyclif also wrote a probably 'commissioned' piece to justify royal invasion of sanctuary at Westminster Abbey. This may have been the last thing he did for the Government as an adviser. Part of his submission became *De ecclesia* Chapters 7–16, so it is possible to make an accurate guess at his arguments; and Chapter 7 may represent his actual speech. He begins by asserting that he is acting in the public interest: 'We have come together at the command of the

Lord King to say what seems to us to be true in the matter laid before us' and he lists the interests he has in mind: the honour of God, the well-being of the Church, the stability of the realm. He assembles Old Testament precedents. He cites the excuse of danger to the realm. He says, in a manner reminiscent of the arguments of US President George W. Bush and UK Prime Minister Tony Blair, when they took the USA and Britain into war in Iraq in 2003, that it was no good waiting until the danger to the realm had happened.[86]

He asserts that the Law of God did not intend sanctuary to be used to protect criminals;[87] one cannot break the law and then expect the law's protection.[88] He refers to the claim that Westminster Abbey has a special privilege which allows it to give sanctuary to all, which might include even criminals. Such a special right of sanctuary cannot go beyond the express intention of the granter of the privilege. The Prince, as granter of the charter in question, could not in any case have had power to grant a 'right' which verged on injury to God, the destruction of his kingdom and the undermining of its laws.[89] For what could be more injurious to God than to make his house a den of thieves?

Chapter 11

Oxford's final condemnation

i. Academic freedom?

> 'Professors complained bitterly when [the then vice-chancellor-designate of the University of Oxford] declared that anyone who criticised the intellectual fitness of his colleagues for government funding would be "summarily fired". Unrepentant, Hood responded that his "unequivocal support" for academic freedom didn't apply to those "who choose arbitrarily and gratuitously to disparage their colleagues". That message couldn't be tolerated at Oxford, where disparagement is served alongside the sherry.'[1]

This kind of thing could not be tolerated when Wyclif did it either; it was about to turn him into an 'outsider' in his own university. Among those who threw themselves into the controversy now swirling around Wyclif was Master William Barton a fellow-'secular'. He had 'energetically' (*strenue*) 'determined against Master Wyclif' in the schools (*determinavit contra magistrum Johannem Wycclyff*).[2] Wyclif was frequently involved in such encounters in his work.[3] Topics were under discussion from at least the 1360s[4] which were to reach heights of controversy with the witch-hunting of Wyclif, and Wyclif himself had not been idle in keeping them at a pitch of excitement. So the mention of their former encounter may merely indicate that Wyclif and Barton had formerly had a lively debate, or that some formal disputation had been particularly memorable when Barton held that Wyclif was in error. But it may betoken real personal animosity. Perhaps Barton got the worst of it when they were face to face as equals, and the malice commonplace in academic life is visible once more in his determination to get his revenge.

The rotation of the senior offices of the University meant that sooner or later one of Wyclif's opponents might find himself in a position of power. Barton was Chancellor from 1379. Perhaps he simply seized his moment to settle old scores. Claiming that Wyclif was threatening the faith of the faithful and the reputation of the University, Barton got the support of the Faculty of Theology and the Faculty of Canon Law to proceed against Wyclif. He sent out a 'mandate', 'to all those called sons of the University and to whom our present mandate shall come'. He greets them and requires their total obedience. 'It has come to my ears, not without considerable displeasure,' he says, that certain heretics, bent on rending the garment of the Church, heretics already solemnly condemned by the Church, are at it again, with new claims. 'And they are publicly "dogmatizing" within the University and outside it. The accusation of dogmatizing could embrace preaching as well as formal teaching within the schools.

There had not been systematic 'official' attempts to condemn the actual ideas taught in the schools of Oxford since 1315, although several scholars had been criticized and the whole regular process of disputation and determination routinely condemned one set of opinions in declaring another correct. This new episode was to raise a number of questions both of principle and of politics. For this was perceived inside the University to be a very different matter from the University's responding to external attempts to have the opinions of a member of the University condemned. While that might get scholars closing ranks, and presenting a united front and a clever temporizing reply, this internal attack by one scholar, currently Chancellor, upon the views of another, formerly his equal opponent in academic debate, needed to be dressed in at least an appearance of authoritativeness. So he called together well-known experts in Theology and Law, so that they could form a collective view. It is this committee or working party which was to condemn Wyclif's teachings on these points as *erroneas*, not merely the Chancellor.[5]

Academic freedom to pursue the truth

There are 'scholars' in Philip Pullman's fictional other-worldly Oxford.[6] Lyra his heroine grows up with a sense that 'scholars' are different from other people, knowledgeable, expert, willing to answer questions and explain things for the love of clarifying the truth. These are personal characteristics, but they are also in a sense institutional. For most of the centuries of its continuance, the culture which began in the ancient Middle East, Egypt, Greece and the Roman Empire was sustained by individuals without the protection and the discipline of an institutional framework. Since the end of the twelfth century such a framework has been provided by universities. The 'freedom' of the individual academic may depend in practice on the 'autonomy' of the university in which he or she works. Wyclif was, perhaps inadvertently, testing the relationship of the scholar's task or purpose to that of the University itself. Was Wyclif, teaching as an academic in the University of Oxford, free to say anything lawful in the pursuit of the Truth he made into a personified 'character' in his *Trialogus*, and would the University protect his freedom to do so? If it chose to regard what he was saying as unacceptable, what could it do about it?

At the heart of the expectations of both medieval and modern academic 'speech' is an assumption that scholars will be in pursuit of the truth in whatever they say. The medieval world has an embedded assumption that 'the truth' is Christian orthodoxy. To depart from it is to be deemed to be driven by the Devil. Modern concerns tend to be voiced about different reasons for suppression of the truth, especially the danger that the funder of a piece of university research – for example, a biotech or pharmaceutical company – may try to suppress the results if it does not like them. We have just seen Wyclif make exactly that claim. In the Middle Ages, as now, there were academics who would say it is right to give false opinions for a 'good end'. Some *moderni doctores*, says Wyclif reprovingly, 'approving a lie and saying that such truths of Scripture are not to be stated because they trouble the Church,' are in fact the Church's enemies in their arrogance.[7] But the individual who claims truth for views the 'authorities' dislike courts trouble. Wyclif had been doing that as he 'wrote up' and published his lectures and responded to the challenges of others.

Wyclif even seems to have acknowledged something close to a whistleblower's duty. He says that if 'modern churchmen' did not sin by being too self-effacing to speak, the Church would not be so much under the tyranny of the Devil,[8] which naturally he considers to be driving the remarks of others, not his own. The modern assumption has been that the protection of personal academic freedom and institutional autonomy for universities is 'in the public interest'. The public interest has been defined in terms of the value of protecting the independence of research and expert opinion, so that governments can be challenged and policy-formation restrained by objective and disinterested research and analysis. That has been seen to be a useful protection against the arbitrary or ill-considered exercise of the power of the state. Alarm bells ring when politicians are seen to attempt to suborn the academics and undermine their independence by making the funding of their research dependent on their arriving at conclusions acceptable to the Government of the day.

Academic freedom under the protection of the institution has never been identical with a freedom for an academic to do what he or she pleases 'in the University's name', and the question of 'not bringing the University into disrepute' was a lively one long before it became routine to include it in modern contracts of employment for academics. William Barton, as Chancellor of Oxford, said Wyclif had in no small way damaged the University's reputation because he was perceived to have said what he had in its name.[9] Nor was it acceptable in the Middle Ages to criticize the University itself. Johannes, an Austin friar, was disciplined in 1358 because he called the University 'a gymnasium [school] of heretics'. In 1360 he retracted, along with others who had criticized the University.[10]

In any case, there were established rules allowing the safe discussion of disputed questions, in a context where no one need be led astray by hearing the 'wrong' view aired. There was a range of permitted opinion but not a complete freedom for individuals to say anything they liked without submitting it to the public testing of the formal disputation. Medieval academic speech of the kind that involved the expression of an opinion or a judgment characteristically took the form of the setting forth of a 'question' (*quaestio*) or opinion or judgment (*conclusio*), for formal public debate. There were institutional safeguards when this happened within the University. Disputations which formed part of the training and degree-course requirements were presided over and 'determined' by a Master in his teaching capacity. The disputations which survive from the course of Wyclif's professional career and which took place outside, or additionally to, the routine training of students in disputation skills, still had built-in protections, those of being held in public and under the aegis of the University. Several examples have cropped up in this story and we have not seen the last of them yet; everywhere in the background of the controversy of the last years of Wyclif's life is the possibility that it will throw up a question for 'determination' by the familiar method of formal disputation. So clearly was it recognized that this provided a safe forum for the 'testing' of dangerous ideas that, as the repeated condemnations of Wyclif and anyone teaching 'his' ideas went on, it was accepted that it might have to be possible for them to be mentioned in teaching so that lecturers could explain why they were banned.

It is only too clear that the 'independence' of the expertise it was bringing in was not much in the minds of the Government when it brought in Wyclif as an academic expert. We have already seen Wyclif acting as an academic consultant to Government, and how he had recently been invited to 'advise' once more, in the expectation that he would uphold the propriety of a dramatic breach of the sanctuary of Westminster Abbey. Wyclif himself did not consider – or did not acknowledge – that there might be a perceived conflict of interest arising from his debt to his patron, John of Gaunt, and his extreme current need for heavyweight approval. There were claims about public interest in this episode.

John Wyclif began his speech to Parliament – or at least the version of it he gives in his *On the Church* – by asserting that he is acting independently and in the public interest: 'We have come together at the command of the Lord King to say what seems to us to be true in the matter laid before us.' He lists the 'public' interests he has in mind: the honour of God, the benefit of the Church and also the stability of the realm. He assembles Old Testament precedents so as to underline the importance of this principle of danger to the realm. He said that it was no good waiting until the danger to the realm had happened.[11] Wyclif also appealed to the 'real-world' context in which politicians like to operate, claiming that the Law of God did not intend sanctuary to be used to protect criminals;[12] one cannot break the law and then expect the law's protection.[13]

This then was the context of very large questions, implicit and explicit, in which the final push of officialdom against Wyclif was about to take place. It is an irony that the issue should have been a new one, not one of the questions on which he had already made himself unpopular.

ii. What was Eucharistic orthodoxy?

The author of the *Eulogium*, like other chroniclers, did not hesitate to include a little academic theology when it assisted the story.[14] He says that in 1381 Wyclif had 'determined at Oxford that the sacrament of the Eucharist is bread, citing Berengar'. In this Wyclif went against what 'all the learned men of the first millennium after Christ believed about the sacrament, during the period when the book of Revelation says that Satan was bound'. 'But all the Regent Masters of Theology in Oxford determined against that doctrine, especially the Master of the Friars Minor.'[15]

It is curious that it was his teaching on the Eucharist that proved so especially dangerous to Wyclif, for on the face of it this had little to do with the threatening reconstruction of the presumptions of political and social life to which his ideas about dominion had been leading. He had of course reached a stage of 'demonization', where almost any opinion he put forward was likely to be challenged as dangerous merely because he said it. The controversy about Holy Communion appeared to turn on what actually happened when a priest holding the bread or the wine, in the context of a celebration of the Eucharist, repeated the words of Jesus at the Last Supper and said, 'This is my body' or 'This is my blood'. The formulation of the doctrine of transubstantiation in the late eleventh and twelfth centuries had tried to established it as orthodoxy that, while the outward appearance of bread and wine did not change, the substance became the actual body and blood of Christ. Barton singled out for disapproval two positions on the Eucharist, first that the substance of the bread and wine remain substantively and not merely in appearance after the consecration alongside the body and blood of Christ ('consubstantiation'); and 'more execrable', that the body and blood of Christ are present not 'essentially' (*essentialiter*) or 'substantially' (*substantialiter*) or even 'bodily' (*corporaliter*) but merely symbolically (*figurative seu tropice*). These views are said to have endangered the catholic faith, threatened the devotion of the people and in no small measure damaged the good name of the University. He gathered in support of this claim all the traditional arguments of the 'hammer of heretics'. (Old heresies are being revived; heresy divides the Church and ill-intentioned persons are bent on 'rending the tunic' of its unity.) Moreover, he alleged, the teaching of heretical falsehoods is spreading beyond the University. It was the Chancellor's declared opinion that such things must not continued to be said in the University without correction being issued by its authorities.

The *Eulogium* seems to be correct in saying that Wyclif began to take up a controversial position of his own on the Eucharist only some time between 1379[16] and 1381,[17] and at any rate, towards the end of his life.[18] The *Fasciculi Zizaniorum* agrees that Wyclif began to 'determine' on the doctrine of transubstantiation as late as the summer of 1381.[19] That presents some difficulties, since the process of condemnation in which Barton is about to play his part as Chancellor must be dated at the very beginning of that summer. Barton would have left office as Chancellor on 30 May 1381 and Wyclif was defending himself on 10 May. Perhaps the date is a slip for MCCCLXXX, and there is indeed an alteration in the manuscript at that point.[20]

Wyclif himself confirms that it was only late in life that he began to dissent from the doctrine of transubstantiation.[21] The question is what happened to the bread and wine when the priest said the words of Jesus at the Last Supper, 'this is my Body and this is my Blood'. Were they symbolically or literally the flesh and blood of the incarnate Christ? In the eleventh century the grammarian Berengar said that any literal understanding of what happened would go against the laws of nature and logic,[22] and he had generated such a debate that for a time almost every theologian was contributing his pamphlet 'on the sacrament of the altar'. In the climate of a new kind of study of Grammar and Logic, it was possible to put the question in a new, crisp Aristotelian way. In the

Categories Aristotle distinguishes substance and accident. The accidents of a substance may change without its becoming a different substance. The proposal which eventually took root and grew into the doctrine of 'transubstantiation' was that the bread was changed not in its accidents but in its substance when a priest said the words of consecration. It continued to look and smell and taste like bread. But it was now truly the actual body of Christ, the very flesh which had lived on earth. It took until the late twelfth century for the technical term 'transubstantiation' to emerge, but once adopted it became fundamental to the theology of the Eucharist in succeeding medieval centuries.

Wyclif says that it took him a considerable time to understand why there was a problem. He describes in a very technical sermon on John 6:56 his long struggle to grasp from the teaching of the friars what they understood by transubstantiation.[23] 'The whole difficulty consists in the "what-it-isness" of that consecrated bread (host), and so I have striven for many years, consulting the friars, monks and others of the "private religion" to understand what they say the "host" is in its nature. And in the end they said to me that the host is nothing.'[24] Wyclif was clearly still attracted by the intellectual challenge of these questions which probably have much more to do with the Physics studied in the Arts course than with Christology and ecclesiology. Wyclif knew about Berengar, and mentions him a number of times.[25]

Thomas Bradwardine (Archbishop of Canterbury 1348–49) had been there before him. Bradwardine was drawn to questions which were fundamentally mathematical, questions of quantity and motion and the way forms arise and change and the nature of the infinite. For some centuries people are known to have asked awkward common-sense questions, such as where the substance of the bread 'went'; how the whole of Christ's body could be contained in a wafer; or conversely, how all the wafers consecrated over the centuries were not much greater in quantity than the real body of Christ; or how Christ's body could be 'all there' in one place, parish after parish, when a number of Eucharists were celebrated all at the same time; or what happened when a crumb fell to the ground and a mouse ate it. (Was there some salvific effect upon the mouse?)[26]

William of Ockham had tried a logician's approach in conjunction with the approach of a physicist. He suggested that, when the bread 'became' the body of Christ, all the parts of that body could be 'there' without being 'extended' in space at all. There was no need to be puzzled that the 'true body' was not an ordinary bodily size. (And this did trouble the faithful. One woman was reported as saying that she did not see how the consecrated host could be the true body of Christ because it had no arms and legs.) Moreover, it did not seem to Ockham that there was any logical reason why the substance of the bread should not still in some sense persist after the change if the divine substance was now present. The long-standing discussion of tenses we met in the Arts course was brought to bear. Something which is could be made by God 'not-to-be' in the future, although it would still 'be there' at the time when it was, for all times are present to God.[27] These arguments of Ockham proved highly contentious and were quite widely challenged,[28] so that it is more than likely that Wyclif had encountered them in the debates of the schools.[29] As soon as he grasped the full implication of the doctrine of transubstantiation Wyclif objected to it, 'and perhaps there are many, Christians in name, who are worse than the pagans' in believing this,[30] not least because Wyclif found it outrageous that 'they base' this 'not on authority nor on reason but upon Innocent III, that is, upon the mere decrees of the Fourth Lateran Council of 1215' – and a thousand years of 'lying testimony'.[31] The doctrine of transubstantiation cannot be founded on Scripture, he insists.[32]

iii. Barton's committee decides

Barton's committee of two monks, four friars, four seculars and two Doctors of Law included among the seculars the future Chancellor, Robert Rygge, who was to be thrown disastrously into the midst of the Wyclif problem while he was in office – at which point it all, both the politics and the theology, seems to have appeared much less clear-cut to him. Among them were other names which are to be encountered elsewhere in this story: Abbot Henricus Croupe [Henry Crump]; a monk of Ramsey Abbey, Johannes Wellys; the Dominicans Johannes Chesham, William Bruscombe and Johannes Wolverton; for the Augustinians, Johannes Schypton; of the Franciscans, Johannes Tyssington; the Carmelite Johannes Loueye. John Landreyn was one of the most senior of the secular Masters. There were two canon lawyers: Johannes Moubray (*utroque iure doctor*) and Johannes Gascoyne (*doctor in decretis*).[33] Wyclif comments on this committee in his *De blasphemia*. 'The Devil has invented a new art… deficient in arguments… but in order to make it more colourful (*coloracius*) he has brought together six or seven who are jealous of the truth into a conclave and they make the truth which displeases them into a heresy. They have signed their testimony to this effect.'[34]

A certain pattern of conduct can 'take an academic committee over', even in the modern world, and make it think collectively in ways its individual members would never countenance in reaching conclusions in their own teaching or research. Barton's committee smelt Wyclif's coming exclusion. So they looked for ways to please the ecclesiastical authorities at the same time. 'A certain recently-qualified doctor, called John Wyclif... has for a few years been sowing the seeds of error in the lovely field of your Province of Canterbury', they write to the Archbishop.[35] They unanimously condemned Wyclif's alleged teachings, alleging that in teaching contrary to the Church he rends the garment of Christ. This teaching has gone on inside the University and outside it. The Chancellor gives orders that if anyone at all publicly accepts, teaches or defends these opinions, in the schools or outside them within the University,[36] he shall be imprisoned, shall not be allowed to carry out any scholastic acts and shall be excommunicated (with reversal of the excommunication reserved to the Chancellor himself and his successors). Anyone who even listens to such teaching shall also be excommunicated.[37] To this he affixed his seal.[38] The authority of the Chancellor is insisted upon, with a nod to the unanimous consent of a named list of *Magistri*.[39]

The University's public condemnation was sent to Sudbury, Archbishop of Canterbury, in the expectation that he would attach to it an additional authority, albeit one which opened the question of the vigilance of the University's protection of its own autonomy; it is preserved in his register.[40]

10 May 1381

Promulgations were generally read out in the public schools or at a sermon, to ensure that as many as possible got to hear of them. The Chancellor's decree was published in the school of the Augustinians while Wyclif was actually teaching the condemned ideas.[41] The opinions, not the man, had been condemned, but everyone knew who was really being attacked. Wyclif undoubtedly took it personally. Not only would he not recant or submit himself to the Chancellor as his 'ordinary'; on 10 May he repeated his assertions in public debate, where he 'determined' the questions. He 'began to make a certain confession' – in the sense of public assertion – 'in which was contained all the former error, but in which he set out his ideas more secretly under a veil of words'. And 'just like the persistent heretic he was, he refuted all the learned men of the second millennium on the subject of the sacrament of the altar.'[42] Wyclif asserts in the *Confessio de sacramento altaris*[43] – a published version of the response which he made in Oxford on that same day, 10 May 1381 – that he believes and always has believed that the same body of Christ which was born of the Virgin and died on the Cross and lay buried for three days and was resurrected and ascended after forty days and sits eternally at the right hand of God, is substantively or truly and really the sacramental bread after consecration. The proof is that Christ himself says so. He merely wants to be more exact about what that means.

Wyclif once more showed that he was no strategist. He made the classic academic mistake of overcomplicating the argument, making it more subtle than was wise; for, as others had learned before him, refined distinctions were likely to prove an irresistible temptation to his enemies, who would with little effort be able to discover unsoundness in them. He also made once more the tactical error of going on the attack himself in the face of a witch-hunt. Those who framed the doctrine of transubstantiation were, he claims, infidels, men who, having set their hands to the plough, looked back. Their conception that 'an accident can be the body of Christ' is 'mean'. Christ's words, 'This is my body' were a shortened form of the technical expression, 'This accident without substance signifies my body.'[44] His third polemical tactic was to summarize his own position while pointing to the undesirable consequences if his opponents (whom he categorizes as *secta*, a sect) were right.[45]

He found himself being answered by Tissington and Winterton, whose responses survive in the form of Tissington's 'Confession' and Winterton's 'Absolution'.[46] Here we are inside one of those very conversations with the friars Wyclif claimed he had, but made formal and turned into public disputation. Once more it is possible to glimpse the way comment and debate moved in and out of the technical categories of the set-piece 'scholastic acts'. Tissington begins from the premiss that Holy Mother Church is accustomed to approve those learned men who take the faith to be simple and who strive to defend its simplicity of faith.[47] God hides mysteries from the wise and prudent.[48] Tissington is not above some academic obscurantism himself. There is a discussion of verbs, adverbs, nouns, as used in Eucharistic debate.[49] He sneers at the philosopher who cannot grasp – or does not wish to grasp – how an omnipotent God can make a body of any sort of 'quantity'.[50]

Ironically (for was Wyclif not accusing his opponents of exactly this losing touch with the essential simplicity of things?) he groups Wyclif with Berengar and his 'accomplices' and that 'mad old heretic' Peter Abelard and his modern disciples. Tissington indicates that he too was familiar with the debate of the late eleventh century on these matters: Lanfranc and Wimund are also names he knows.[51] He himself prefers to define the Eucharist as it was understood by Ignatius, Dionysius, Ambrose, Augustine and other respectable Fathers of the first millenium. Tissington accuses Wyclif of proposing a doctrine dating merely from authorities of more recent times – with a side-swipe at the notion that teaching after the loosing of Satan is likely to be unreliable.[52] Anselm, Richard of St Victor, Hugh of St Victor and others, including Peter Lombard, were as shining in their lives as in their teaching. Later lived Grosseteste, in comparison with whom the most modern scholars are like moons in eclipse by his sun. All these Wyclif is sweeping aside in his wilful blindness.[53] 'From these testimonies of the saints it is obvious what the Eucharist is, for the body and blood of Christ are nowhere in the sacrament unless they are under the form of bread or wine, and this is by the power of the words of consecration, by which the bread and wine are changed,' cries Tissington. He insists that, once the words are said, the bread and wine are indeed the body and blood of Christ.[54] This is implied in the separate consecration of bread and wine, making them respectively quite specifically the body or the blood of Christ.[55] He claims that while Wyclif's view has been found among the laity since much earlier times, the Church has *always* held the doctrine of transubstantiation, although he concedes that it was formally stated only in 1052.[56]

Winterton, an Augustinian friar, is the author of the parallel text with the title *Absolution*.[57] Winterton proposes a similar assemblage of authorities to Tissington and he makes similar allegations that Wyclif is wifully obscurantist. 'But, as it is reported of this doctor, he calls every mode of speech of Holy Scripture literal and truth according to its outward sense and its grammatical sound.'[58]

He sets out thirty objections to what he understood Wyclif to be teaching. His own 'fundamental position' is that the same actual body of Christ which was born of the Virgin and suffered on the Cross is truly and really the consecrated bread of the host which the faithful see in the priest's hands. He knows that Wyclif is disparaging about the opinions of modern scholars, from Book IV of Peter Lombard's *Sentences* to 'as it were, all the doctors who came after him who are accepted as authentic in the schools and in the Church,' so Winterton offers him older authorities.[59]

Wyclif refused to stop teaching the condemned opinions.[60] He appealed. The normal and proper route would have been to appeal to the Congregation of Regent Masters and then to the whole Convocation, which would have included the Non-Regent Masters not currently teaching. But Wyclif, perhaps nervous that he could not hope to succeed against his colleagues, appealed to the King instead,[61] and John of Gaunt came to Oxford in person to discuss the matter. He seems to have advised or ordered Wyclif to accept the sentence. There were elements of seeming mediation and considerable diplomacy in Gaunt's handling of this. Can Gaunt have considered that he himself knew as well as anyone else what the true doctrine of the Eucharist was and would he have been prepared to argue the point with academics?[62] Apparently Wyclif explained the theological problems to him, presumably in English or French, and the two of them arrived at a compromise. There are indications in the *Trialogus* that John of Gaunt may have coaxed Wyclif to modify at least his words and to refrain from using the words 'substance of material bread and wine' outside the schools. Wyclif speaks of a 'pact' or agreement.[63] But it should be noted that he thought it sufficiently consistent with their agreement to explain this, using the forbidden terminology, in a treatise which was probably intended for a more general readership than his fellow-scholars.

It is not impossible that the Duke had something to do with Wyclif's subsequent retreat from Oxford in the immediate heat of the controversy. If this, too, was his advice, it again indicates his goodwill and his political and diplomatic skills.

iv. The Peasants' Revolt

The finality of Wyclif's withdrawal from Oxford may also have been made unavoidable by the Peasants' Revolt, an episode as much social and economic in its causes as theological, but with a strong association with religious dissent. A case can precariously be built for placing Wyclif in the chain of causation of the Peasants' Revolt.[64] Although it was probably not Wyclif's work, yet his name became associated with it. John Ball, one of its leaders, had been travelling England teaching those who would listen to him to defy authority. The *Chronicon* says he had been doing so for more than twenty years and knew very well what would please a popular audience, for example, mocking the higher clergy and saying that the people did not need to pay tithes. The chronicles say he taught John Wyclif's ideas too.[65] Even if he did so in a confused form, and without Wyclif's personal authority for what he was doing, he had only to mention Wyclif's name for Wyclif to get some of the blame in the minds of the authorities of Church and state. Both Walsingham and Knighton say that Ball was a disciple of Wyclif's for some time before the revolt.[66] William of Rymington, who wrote his *XLV Conclusiones* between the Peasants' Revolt and the autumn of 1383, puts the unrest down to Wyclif's teaching.[67] (Wyclif replied in 1383 to these conclusions, which he describes as 'monkish arguments' (*ad argucias monachales*).[68]

The chronicler Walsingham, who has Ball addressing huge gatherings of 2,000 people, attributes to him the couplet:

Whanne Adam dalfe and Eve span,
Who was thanne a gentil man?[69]

Knighton describes how John Ball was executed in 1381 and cut into four pieces, which were sent off in different directions to be displayed *pour encourager les autres*.[70] The *Fasciculi Zizaniorum*[71] depicts the arrested and condemned Ball being given two days' stay of execution so that the Archbishop of Canterbury could encourage him to confess, although Sudbury had been killed in the revolt, so it is not clear this can have happened. There is a purported confession, linking him to Wyclif, recorded by Netter. This alleged that Ball had been a disciple of Wyclif for two years and had imbibed his heresies from him directly. It described the formation of a group with the purpose of going round England to spread these ideas further. It named names: Nicholas Hereford, John Aston, Laurence Bedeman, Master of Arts.[72] We shall hear of some of these again.

A confession was said to have been made by Jack Straw, another leader of the revolt. The text of this purported confession, given by eager Walsingham, admits that at the time the revolutionaries got to Blackheath (part of modern London) their plan 'was to put to death all the soldiers, then to kill the king, and then to wipe from the face of the earth all categories of cleric and monk'.[73]

In February 1382 the Oxford mendicants sent a letter on behalf of the four orders to John of Gaunt, the Duke of Lancaster, accusing Nicholas Hereford and his accomplices. It expressed their resentment that the friars had been accused by various 'false doctors' of the Wyclif persuasion of having had a hand in the revolt. It was being said that they had impoverished the people by exactions, encouraged them to be lazy workers through their own example of idleness, and failed to discharge their duties as confessors, which could have prevented the disturbances.[74] The letter suggested that the real author of the uprising had been Wyclif.

Part IV

Coping with Failure

Chapter 12

Wyclif in retreat

> 'Throughout my life there is… a thread of militancy, which is not to be confused with quarrelsomeness. I have been involved in many controversies, most of which I have neither sought nor avoided, but none of them have been about incidental matters which I could easily have ignored; they have been about a great cause in which I believe.'[1]

> 'Fight, fight, you can fight to the death. Lord knows, there are fools enough on the other side ready and waiting to fight you back… . Christ, isn't there somewhere a solitary sentient human being humble enough and clear enough to stand up and say… let's stop!'[2]

The anticlerical William Thorpe[3] was arrested on 7 April 1407 in Shrewsbury, where he had been preaching, and was imprisoned by the Bishop of London for disseminating Wycliffite doctrines. He was 'examined' in August by Thomas Arundel, no friend of the friends of Wyclif and since 1399 Archbishop of Canterbury and Chancellor of England. Thorpe described to his inquisitors the impression he had had as a young man when he met popular preachers. He says that his mother and father 'spent much money in various places' on his education, 'in entent to have me a priest of God'. But when he came to years of discretion he found he had no wish to be a priest and there were many family rows until he agreed to go and talk to some who had the reputation of being wise priests. He was attracted by the lives he saw them to be living, but he also saw bad examples. It was, he explained, Nicholas Hereford and John Purvey and Robert Bowland and Philip Repington who taught him to distinguish the true vocation to ministry from that which was unworthy. The Archbishop said, 'these men of whom you speak now were fools and heretics'. Thorpe replied that they might be so in the eyes of this world but not, he believed, in the eyes of God. He described a time when Wyclif 'was held by many men to be the greatest clerk that they knew living upon earth', that he was 'innocent in his living', and 'therefore men of great learning and others were much drawn to him and communed often with him'. But the Archbishop warned him that 'that lore you call truth is open slander against Holy Church as Holy Church proves'.[4]

Thorpe had been close, then, to some of those who were involved in the events which sent Lollardy out into the world as a movement with Wyclif's name attached. He allows us to glimpse the rosy glow with which his name became surrounded within a generation, the sense a number of the leaders of Lollardy had of being his 'followers'. There are, however, significant questions about the real relationship of Lollardy to Wyclif himself. There was certainly by now a growing body of wandering preachers, more or less clear about the genuine ideas of Wyclif, broadly anti-establishment, some reputed to be on the lunatic fringe in their extreme preaching of an 'apostolic life'.[5] We are approaching one of the greatest puzzles of our story, how Wyclif became involved with these preachers and their project – if indeed he did.

Those who wish to become legends do well to retreat a little from the scenes of their active engagement. That is not to suggest that Wyclif had it in mind to become a myth, but he did now withdraw from the Oxford scene, possibly on John of Gaunt's advice, and we hear no more of Wyclif as an academic in Oxford.[6] It does not seem that the long-standing amicable relationship between Wyclif and his patron was soured. His view of John of Gaunt about 1383 is to be found in a treatise 'On the Seven Gifts of the Holy Spirit' in which he mentions an attempt to assassinate Gaunt. This is put down by Wyclif to the anger of the friars that he was unwilling to punish faithful priests, among whom Wyclif certainly included himself.[7]

Simony, apostasy, blasphemy

A group of writings begun at the very end of Wyclif's time in Oxford make it clear that he was in no mood to go quietly. As Wyclif's anger and sense of embattlement mounted, he began to write more and more wildly on 'simony', 'apostasy' and 'blasphemy', as he understood these subjects. *De simonia, De apostasia, De blasphemia*, are diatribes. He consciously linked the themes of this trilogy, with the assertion that the vices are really all one vice, just as the virtues are all one virtue.[8] He describes the three as 'modes of heresy'. Simony is a sin against the Holy Spirit; apostasy a sin against the Father; and blasphemy a sin against the Son.[9]

The first treatise, probably of early 1380, deals with the matter of unworthy ministry in the Church, which remained close to the heart of Wyclif's concerns. What is the simoniac doing when he 'buys' his office? Simony is defined by Wyclif as an inordinate act of the will,[10] which seeks to exchange what is spiritual for what is temporal. The simoniac is committing the sin against the Holy Spirit (Matthew 12:32), for he is trying to buy grace, and what he does therefore destroys peace and order.[11] Wyclif discusses, only to reject it, the definition of simony to be found in the Decretals, in an example of Wyclif's being severe with the lawyers and pointing them to the law of the Gospel. In the Decretals it is argued that the 'purchase' of holy office is not simony if what is 'bought' is merely the temporalities which go with the pastoral and sacramental duties, the 'spiritualities'.[12] Wyclif says this is rubbish. A priest who accepts more than he strictly needs for the spiritual edification of the people, and who does not receive it with the people's blessing, must be regarded as a simoniac.[13] So must someone who accepts an appointment from impure motives or when he is incapable of discharging the duties which go with the position.[14]

Wyclif's own earlier hunger for preferment was, it seems, no longer so keen. Wyclif is now censorious about patronage, though not against it in principle, distinguishing between a 'proper' and an 'improper' exercise of patronage. It is allowable for someone in a position of influence to 'move' a patron to give a benefice to an appropriate recipient.[15] On the other hand, an otherwise fit recipient makes himself unfit if he makes an effort to obtain the preferment.[16] And, forgetting his own efforts not many years before and his own fury when Rome failed to deliver the preferment he thought he had been promised only a few years earlier, he now says it is not allowable to go to Rome to seek a living,[17] because that would evince an excessive and disorderly 'will' to gain preferment.[18]

Nor does he overtly consider in these arguments the position he had himself been in while he was taking the income from Lutterworth and not discharging his pastoral duties there; indeed he was probably still in that position, while he was writing the *De simonia*. In the *De veritate sacrae scripturae* he had contended that, if the clergy were poor, there would be fewer abuses.[19] He asks whether he is a traitor for arguing in this way? No.[20] Underlying the whole problem, he now says, is the practice of endowment, the giving of property to monks and friars and priests. He examines disapprovingly the way the Pope, the Bishops, the religious orders and temporal lords behave over property. From this, simony flows. For, once the Church began to lay claim to property, it was lost; no longer could it 'freely give' what it had freely received and it was enmeshed in wars and theft.

This startling shift of attitude on patronage is an excellent example of the pattern of development of Wyclif's thinking. It is characteristic of him to 'find' the principle, identifying and occupying the high moral ground as events drive him upon it, rather than seeing it afar from the beginning and heading towards it.

De apostasia is probably a work of late 1380.[21] 'What is religion?' asks Wyclif. This must be clear before it can be easy to say whether someone has apostatized from it. First, it is obedience to the law of Christ (*observancia legis Christi*). 'God gave a complete rule [of life] in the law of Scripture' (*Deus dedit regulam completam religionis in lege scripture*).[22] Wyclif furnishes scriptural examples, such as the Ethiopian eunuch of Acts 8:27–40, in order to show that the rule of life does not depend on the Petrine office or derive from it.[23] True religion is that which was observed by Christ and the apostles; and it should be defined, in accordance with James 1:27, as 'religion that is pure and undefiled before God and the Father', which is 'to visit orphans and widows in their affliction and to keep oneself untainted from the world'.[24] But there is another sense in which the term is wont to be used. That is when it refers to the members of religious order who are distinguished from the rest of the people of God by setting up new sects with bodily rites.[25]

The *De apostasia* continues the theme of the interconnectedness of the vices and heresies. Wyclif thinks apostasy to be serious sin, which involves turning away from God, rather than necessarily an abandonment of faith altogether, and embraces blasphemy (the sin against the Son) and simony (the sin against the Holy Ghost). 'It is not possible for anyone to fall into mortal sin, unless he is an apostate and by consequence a blasphemer and a simoniac.'[26] Simple ordinary Christian life is better than private religion. Private religion involves adding rites and ceremonies. Departing from those is not apostasy, for they are not true religion at all, and not necessary to salvation. Indeed it is possible to apostatize by adhering to a private religion, as much as by leaving the true religion.[27]

By the time he wrote the *De blasphemia*, probably between mid-1380 and 1381, Wyclif was very upset. The language is extreme, the text a *cri de coeur*. 'If only our country was not led astray by satraps since the death of Pope Urban VI.'[28] Wyclif writes of a 'maniacal sect' rubbing out the greater part of the Gospel as though it were false. This sect is in Oxford, he insists. Indeed, it has the University in its hands.[29]

He identifies three 'blasphemies'. The first is the belief in a hidden power (*potestas abscondita*) of the Pope, and that is a blasphemy because really the Pope has no special powers more than any other priest.[30] Wyclif adds that taking vows as monks and friars do is a blasphemy under this head. The second blasphemy is the claim that the Pope has a secret wisdom which enables him to rule the Church in a way no other mortal can do.[31] The third blasphemy is the falsehood that the Pope's exercise of power proceeds from a wish to defend the law of Christ.[32] The *De blasphemia* includes a tirade which shows how heated Wyclif was becoming on the subject of the Eucharist, comparing the 'carnal' Church, all appearance and no reality, to the doctrine which claimed that there could be accident without substance in the consecrated host – a blasphemy because such a thing would be an obscenity in the natural world.[33] These three books are indicators of an extreme state of mind, a distress which was heavily influencing Wyclif's sense of proportion, exacerbating the effects upon his equilibrium of the public condemnation of his views about the Eucharist. John Hus later paid him an undeserved compliment, when he claimed that 'there are three kinds of heresy according to the most famous doctors, simony, blasphemy and apostasy',[34] for the grouping of this trio seems to be special to Wyclif and not a commonplace at all.

Lutterworth

Wyclif retired to his parish at Lutterworth in Leicestershire to lick his wounds, consider his position and revise his writings. He expresses his feelings quite openly and at some length. He is bitter. He writes angrily about the envious Oxford characters at the meeting which had condemned him – envious of the truth, he says, but it seems a good deal more personal an envy to him – who declared anything heretical which they did not like and put their signatures to it to add colour to their condemnation.[35] 'A certain colleague (*socius*) whom I suppose to be jealous of the truth, inveighs a great deal against opinions which he conceives me to have expressed.'[36] The disciples of Antichrist, when they lack reasons, make up arguments in which there is not a spark of colour; for example, 'God exists, and so the consequence I wish follows.'[37]

De fratribus ad scholares, if it is authentic, preserves a wistful passage of description of Oxford which suggests that Wyclif was missing it. 'For I was there at the University of Oxford, which is appropriately known as the Lord's Vineyard, founded by the holy Fathers,' he says with a hint of longing, describing how Oxford is well situated, watered with springs and rivers, surrounded by fields and pastures and undulating countryside, with its woods and shady places, a most fitting place to be God's house and a gateway to heaven. 'And here have come in our own time the mendicants, ravening wolves dressed as sheep.'[38]

Wyclif found no rest at Lutterworth and perhaps he did not really seek it. There was in every sense too much unfinished business, both positive and negative. He was full of anger and resentment. His language breaks into violence in sermon after sermon. It is hard to escape the impression that he had more enemies than close friends, that he made enemies of some admirers and some who set out to be his friends. Adam Stockton, who first made a copy of Wyclif's *determinatio* with admiration of the 'venerable doctor' (c. 1379–80), was later calling him 'execrable seducer'.[39]

His own enmities were fierce. Wyclif had referred to the Benedictine apologist John Wells as 'a certain Black Dog'; he speaks of him as capering about in his arguments like a monkey when he finds that barking like a dog gets him nowhere.[40] Purvey is described as barking against Wyclif's opponents and commending those who agreed with him.[41] The animal epithets flew and a certain Carmelite, [42] preaching publicly, had called Wyclif a fox,[43] although this at least had a respectable theological pedigree in the traditional interpretation of the 'little foxes' of the Song of Songs as heretics.[44]

The battle with Wells exemplifies the spirit of disputatious Oxford and a petty territoriality and tendency to bear grudges which are still to be found in academic life. For thirteen years Wells was in charge of Gloucester College (now Worcester College), the Benedictine *studium*, and he evidently took far from kindly to Wyclif's attacks on the religious orders. His yellow face, the colour of gall, appears again and again when there is an official attack on Wyclif which he can support, including the Blackfriars Council of 1382. 'The appearance of his face shows what he was like,' says a satirical poet of the time.[45]

Allowance probably has to be made for the state of Wyclif's health. For, very soon after he retreated to Lutterworth, he seems to have had a stroke or something like it. It cannot have been easy for him to develop a sense of perspective, cut off from the life of Oxford and its self-defining squabbles. He claims that friends are pressing him, 'friends of the truth' if not necessarily friends of his own, to make out a case against the friars in reliance upon the authority of Scripture.[46] Yet these were 'friends' in a limited sense. Even the young John Purvey seems to have been too much of an admirer to have been able to shake Wyclif out of his darker moods with a little friendly teasing. Knighton says he was Wyclif's table companion (*commensalis*) as long as Wyclif lived.[47] He does not seem to have been a man with a circle of close friends and confidants of his own age with whom he could share his bewilderment. He did not have secretaries maintaining an 'official' correspondence, for he never attained the kind of office which would justify it.

Conversely Wyclif had, or perceived himself to have, a number of enemies with a personal interest in doing him down. Wyclif defends himself against particular accusers.[48] This was by no means necessarily paranoia. Reflecting on the attack made upon him by John Wells, Wyclif complains that a disputation would have been a more appropriate forum for at least the initial discussion of reforming ideas. 'And truly I have often revolved in my mind what prompted that colleague and Benedictine among all the leading figures of Oxford to launch so singular and preposterous an assault. I call it preposterous because it seems to many wise men that it would have been a good idea to discuss this subject in an academic context before preaching about it from the rooftops.'[49]

Revising his writings

At the beginning of his *Retractationes*, a book Wyclif would certainly have had opportunities to read, Augustine of Hippo explains what he has tried to do in this review of his own work, which he made at the end of his life. He has reconsidered his writings with a critical eye and has crossed out, as with a censor's pen, the things which now offend him. He has looked for mistakes (*errata*) and for things he ought not to have said and for things which now displease him.[50] It is not easy to be as clear what Wyclif was trying to do in his comparable period of stocktaking at Lutterworth: leave a legacy, make a 'comeback' or provide a body of reference material and exhortation for a future 'movement' which would carry forward his ideas and keep them alive. These are important questions if there is to be clarity about Wyclif's true place in the 'Lollard' movement which was emerging.

Oxford's elderly dons may still be seen in its libraries today, eagerly pursuing their researches into their eighties and nineties. Wyclif's Oxford was different in that its energies chiefly went into debate. The stocktaking of an ageing scholar could amount to little more than it did in Wyclif's case – a reworking of his sermons, some revision of earlier writings and some pamphleteering on matters of unfinished business – rather than a drawing together of a life's work into a definitive statement. The fact has to be faced that Wyclif, prolific though he was, left not one single work which stands as a monument to his thought. He was no Augustine, to be copied and kept in every library. The words in which his ideas are preserved in his writings are no longer read. The ideas his writings contained were among a number of contemporary tributaries to a stream and then to the river of Reformation.

Wyclif always seems to have been reluctant to 'waste' the effort he put into his lectures, and there are plentiful indications that he worked them up into some of the writings we now have in treatise form. Such material could be reused in a variety of different forms and for different purposes. We do not know Wyclif's ultimate intentions for particular works. *De religione privata* II, 'Concerning private religion', for example, has some claim to be a sermon,[51] a very late sermon, but it has chapters and also a claim to be a treatise. Was Wyclif polishing it up to be something other than a sermon? Or is this a sermon in process of being made out of a book?

'On civil servitude and secular dominion',[52] allows us to glimpse Wyclif at work in the course of these late revisions. Much of the text is close to 'On Civil Dominion' (for example, where Wyclif discusses slavery and servitude)[53] and the first part may date from the mid-1370s when he was evidently thinking about this subject in that way. He explores ideas also to be found in Augustine – for instance the question whether the dominion of one person over another is a consequence of the fallen state of mankind.[54] The treatise proceeds at a measured pace to the end of Chapter iv when it is as though Wyclif took up his pen with a cry of fury to write the last sentence: 'All clergy and especially those four sects ought to embrace poverty!'[55] From that point the treatise continues as a diatribe against the Pope and the friars with all the obsessive preoccupations of the very end of Wyclif's life. There is no careful reworking of the earlier part, merely these two additional chapters. It is impossible even to guess whether he was so blind to the contrast, to his own change of mood and style, that he was not aware of this abrupt transition or whether he meant to come back to the text and work over it as a whole making adjustments and unifying his arguments.

De fide catholica, 'On the catholic faith' (in some manuscripts called *De ecclesia*, 'On the Church'), seems to be an abbreviation of Wyclif's big book on the Church, with some additional themes, written perhaps about 1383.[56] It must be fairly late, because he mentions his *Trialogus*, the last serious attempt to draw his ideas together in a form which would be comprehensible to the general reader.[57] It is notable that he has still not tackled the major difficulty of the Reformation, that a doctrine of *sola Scriptura* (Scripture alone) requires fresh thinking about ecclesiology, though it was already controversial. Nor has he resolved what must have been a real difficulty, the question whether to revise the *De ecclesia* itself or write something new.

Another illustration of the difficulty of 'fixing' Wyclif's 'definitive version' is 'On the composition of man', *De compositione hominis*, of about 1372. The question is what Wyclif intended to do with this at the end of his life, as he sat revising his writings.[58] If he returned to this piece, did he make the connection?

Did he look from place to place in his evolving writings on dominion and related subjects – as he had penned them in the course of several years – and think about ensuring that the arguments harmonized? We simply do not know.

Any unity or polish Wyclif might have achieved is fragmented by his repetitive explosions of anger as he begins book after book and is distracted by his sense of injustice and his indignation into diatribes against his enemies and particularly the 'sects' of the religious orders. 'On the Lord's Prayer', *De oracione dominica*,[59] shows Wyclif puzzlingly attacking 'modern heretics' who, he says, impugn the Creed and the Lord's Prayer. They prove to be the familiar crowd of his by now rather generalized enemies, for his discussion of the petitions of the Lord's Prayer is interrupted by the usual furious asides. In the *De salutacione angelica*,[60] Wyclif discusses the 'Hail Mary' and its meaning and grumbles about the 'addition' made by papal authority in joining together two passages from Luke (Luke 1:28 and Luke 2:43) to make the salutation 'flavoursome'.[61]

This raises the further question how, mechanically speaking, Wyclif actually composed at Lutterworth when he was no longer working within the familiar academic framework of lecturing and preaching, with students hired to take notes, and the lecturer writing up the results into treatises. Some degree of physical incapacity may have affected his ability to write. In such circumstances the comments of an amanuensis may carry great weight, and an uncritical and admiring secretary could fail to check habits of expression which now show up as major faults. There was no publisher's editor to stop him from self-indulgence or insist on rigorous revision.

The final condemnation and burning of Wycliff's books in Oxford in 1410[62] destroyed important early manuscript evidence of the state of Wyclif's revisions at the time of his death, and what might have been gleaned about his intentions concerning 'final versions'. Many works survive only in copies carried off to Prague by Hussite supporters.

New writings

A considerable number of little choleric works came from Wyclif's pen during these last few years in Lutterworth. Like his revisions to earlier works, these were not the products of an intellectual maturity but of a disappointed old age. They lack any coherence but that lent by his obsessive anger. This was not the saintly old age of hagiographical convention but a raging against the dying of the light, and against anything else which came in his way. He took the criticism of his ideas extremely personally. His sense of frustration about the difficulty of getting his name cleared burns throughout his last writings. He disliked being misquoted. 'But what troubles me more, my dearest friends, with whom I had often discussed God's meaning, report the opinion I have offered either wrongly or imperfectly.' 'I have never said that all the laws of men are wicked.'[63]

One other possible reason has been alleged for Wyclif's writing these late short works: that he was trying to meet the needs of 'his' poor preachers.[64] The problem is that there is no evidence whatsoever that Wyclif was encouraging and guiding a body of preachers who had no theological education and might need summaries from Wyclif (in Latin) to assist them. Nor are these works of a kind which could provide useful reference books or preceptive manuals. They may simply be the kind of thing to be expected from a 'cornered' rebel. John Hus wrote like that while he was at Constance awaiting his own fate, 'Today I finished a small treatise about "the body of Christ" and yesterday another "about matrimony"; have them copied', he asks his correspondent. 'Some Polish knights visited me, but no Czechs, unless one that came with them,' he adds disconsolately.[65]

As we penetrate further into the period when Wyclif was baffled and embattled, up against authority, we increasingly feel the need for a body of correspondence such as other medieval authors have left. Wyclif was not in general a person – such as Peter of Blois[66] or John of Salisbury[67] – to whom people wrote for advice either personal or scholarly, although there are a few examples of 'letters' he wrote in response to questions people had sent him. There are occasional glimpse of matters of human interest. In one such reply he tells the enquirer he may choose as he wishes among the various conditions of this life (*status viatoris*), which Christ instituted, that is, priesthood, being a soldier or being a labourer; and he may choose (depending on his choice in the first group), between marriage and celibacy. The most highly desirable state is to be a celibate priest, as Christ himself was. But Wyclif admits that other conditions of life suit some people better. Everyone should study the Bible carefully (*sedule*) in the language in which he understands it best.[68] This is formal advice, if it is advice at all, not a concerned letter to personal friend. In 'Eight beautiful questions' (*De octo questionibus pulcris*)[69] the 'questions' are more impersonal still. There are one or two letters written in pursuit of a resolution of his difficulties. A letter to William Courtenay, Archbishop of Canterbury, strikes an uneasy balance between being an overture towards reconciliation and a statement of familiar positions.[70]

Wyclif's theory of Scripture

There were no great books from Wyclif in this period, either as a result of revision of earlier work or by way of new compositions. It is clear, however, that he was giving thought in this last period of his life to the theories about the Bible and the importance of reliance on the Gospel, which he had rough-hewn in his early debates with John Cunningham.

Wyclif used 'Gospel' (*Evangelium*) with something of the double meaning the term carries in modern English, for in Wyclif's day, too, the term could be used equivocally even in Latin. It referred of course to the four Gospels. It could be extended to embrace the Epistles, which were read alongside the Gospel in Church and which, says Wyclif, are of equal authority with the Gospel and are themselves the Gospel, because they were 'dictated' by the same Spirit.[71]

Wyclif's contemporaries could even refer to the whole of Scripture as 'the Gospel'.[72] Wyclif did not think this was inappropriate, but he strongly objected to the extension of 'Gospel' to include any content of a sermon which might be added by a friar to the scriptural text on which he was ostensibly preaching. He reproved 'modern priests who accept preferment only for money and whose conversation is full of lies, for example that any truth useful to the people' is Gospel.[73]

Those who claim that the Bible is nothing more than the manuscripts it is written in sometimes comment that these can have copying mistakes. It is not suggested that the scribes are inspired and cannot err. But this does not undermine the claim that Scripture is true. 'Holy Scripture is more than its copies,' Wyclif points out.[74]

A new book on Scripture: the Opus Evangelicum

One of Wyclif's new works of this last period, the *Opus Evangelicum* or 'Gospel Work', is something of an oddity in terms of its structure. He died working on it, as all its manuscripts note.[75] It contains no hint that Wyclif was breaking new ground or thinking out a theory of exegesis. These are still his familiar stamping grounds. He suggests that, important though it is that the whole Gospel would bring its benefits through the annual round of readings, three passages repay special attention. These are Matthew 5:7; Matthew 23:5, John 13:17.[76] He takes the first of these, citing Chrysostom at length in support, as evidence of the significance Jesus himself attached to preaching to the multitude of ordinary people.[77] The long stretches of patristic quotations are not Wyclif's usual style, and it is not impossible that we can see here the marks of the assistance of Horne or Purvey. For John Horne as well as Purvey is reported to have been Wyclif's curate at Lutterworth.[78]

His opening theme develops the ideals he now attaches to the preacher's art, the cultivation of a personal virtue and the choice of 'Gospel' words which come as from the mountain from which Jesus preached his sermon on the Mount.[79] The first part of the treatise is a hymn to holiness, as portrayed by Christ himself in the Beatitudes, but closely woven with Wyclif's arguments against his favourite abuses and culminating, ironically enough in the light of his own behaviour, with a discussion of the imperative to love one's enemies.[80]

When he arrives in Book III at his second key passage, Matthew 23:5, and the subject of Antichrist (*De Antichristo*), he promises to be briefer, for his treatment of the first passage has filled two books. He begins with a very lengthy extract from Chrysostom, as an introduction to his analysis of the historical evolution of priesthood.[81] He does not reach his third proposed passage, the one from John. This work-in-progress survives alongside other pieces on this part of Matthew's Gospel on which Wyclif seems to have been working.[82]

The drift of this last book on Scripture seems clear. There are no automatic, special, divine preferences for any particular class of Christian, priest or monk or friar; it is personal virtue which counts. The Bible is not reserved for the educated or the ordained. The Bible is for all the people of God.

Wyclif shared with almost all his contemporaries a straightforward acceptance of a divine inspiration which literally dictated the words of Scripture to its human authors. Nor was he disturbed by the questions which were to loom with the Reformation and Renaissance, concerning the relationship of the authority of Jerome's Vulgate translation to that of the text in its original languages of Greek and Hebrew in which God had 'dictated' it. This immensely important question for the Bible translator does not seem to have struck Wyclif at all. He took it for granted that God spoke the words which he read on the page without giving much thought to the fact that the Vulgate is itself a translation. Yet some of his contemporaries saw that the answer might have implications for the question of translation into the vernacular. About 1401, the Oxford academic Richard Ullerston raised the important question of what is the difference between Jerome's rendering of the Greek and Hebrew into Latin and translation from Latin into 'other, inferior, languages'.[83] This is, he notes, such a burning topic that 'two doctors' are spending almost all their time in lectures upon it – in itself an interesting indicator of the degree to which a particular issue could take over the syllabus when a lecturer became interested in it.[84]

Wyclif's attempts at popular theology

The general sympathies of the movement with which Wyclif's name was now being linked, and his own stated view that the Church embraces all kinds of people, takes us next to the question whether he was trying to popularize his ideas in his late writings, and if so, how well he succeeded.

Wyclif's *Dialogus* or 'Mirror of the Church Militant' of 1379[85] had apparently been intended to have a popular appeal, and Wyclif explains there his thinking about the kind of thing the general reader will find attractive and palatable. He tempts the reader by promising variety; for, he says, sameness is the mother of weariness and a beautiful 'alternation' gives delight.[86] He decides to write in Latin, because he thinks that will give him a wider range of expression and it seems to others – with whom he implies he has discussed it – that a collection of 'sentences' put together for the faithful will have a more general appeal if it is in Latin.[87] This breadth of appeal is important because it will make the text more illuminating (*plus illustrat*).[88] If he really thought writing in Latin was a better way to reach the mass of ordinary people, that has implications for the whole vernacular 'project'. But it can also be read as an indication that 'more general' may have meant the general run of students rather than the whole mass of ordinary people. This is a difficult question, and not only in relation to Wyclif's own last years. Among the Wycliffite and Lollard sermons which survive in English are some which suggest that English could be a perfectly acceptable vehicle for the discussion of the opinions of learned authorities.[89] But even if that was the case, a reference to, for example, Origen, assumes that the listener will have some idea who Origen was and some way of judging whether he thought as the preacher alleges he did.

There are touching divergences between what Wyclif recognized as good practice and what he himself did. He wrote the book as a dialogue between Truth and Falsehood, though from Chapter 4 onwards Truth (*Veritas*) is simply Wyclif, Wyclif embattled and emphasizing that his motives are pure and he is ready to suffer persecution to defend the truth. Wyclif-*Veritas* gets all the best lines and most of the space.

The result is an untidy construction, unified only by its dialogue form. Wyclif divides the Church Militant into three orders in a conventional enough way: clergy, temporal lords, the common people.[90] Falsehood (*Mendacium*) says that, although Christ preached poverty, he did not really mean it to be an enduring law.[91]

In the *Trialogus* too, Wyclif seems to have chosen the dialogue form in the belief that people would enjoy it and find the work more readable, adopting the character of Phronesis (Wisdom) for himself and Pseustis (Liar) for his opponent. The obvious link between the titles makes it probable that he was consciously following the ground rules of the genre he had set out in the *Dialogus*. In the *Trialogus* he is much briefer about his reasons for choosing the dialogue form, saying in his prologue only that it pleases many.[92]

The *Trialogus* is perhaps the nearest Wyclif really came to writing a textbook of systematic theology, covering: God; the world; vices and virtues and the Saviour; 'signs' (sacramentology). Clear and simple though his presentation is in comparison with the dense and often confused style of his earlier academic writings, it is still impossible for him to get away from the patterns of the disputation and a lifetime's adversarial habits. This is not a Socratic conversation but a debate between opponents.

It was also perhaps difficult for him to achieve a realistic understanding of the level of basic theological knowledge his congregations – or whatever general readership he had in mind – were likely to have. His difficulty becomes ours. Wyclif begins the discussion of penance in the *Trialogus*[93] by distinguishing its three 'parts', contrition of heart, confession of the mouth and doing something to make satisfaction, and allowing his interlocutor, Alithia, to say it is hard to comment on what kind of thing penance is, since its three parts are of different kinds. It is important not to think of them as 'parts' in a quantitative sense, says Alithia. What matters is the relationship of the three within the whole. We are back in the world of the *logica vetus* in the Arts course.

Wyclif, in the person of Phronesis, goes on to pick up the question whether this last 'part' is necessary, and once more we are in academe. One should rely on Johannis de Deo, who disagrees with many opinions in his gloss on the Decretals and says that in his view the Church should content itself with the first two, 'as I have explained on many occasions,' he says.[94] His objection to *doing* penance is that it is a 'new tradition', a 'human institution' and simply not necessary to salvation. He also dislikes the fact that it tends to make penance a matter of money. Wyclif is not always so well disposed to this canonist, and this example of the use of a relatively recent modern 'authority' is a reminder how strong was the academic habit of taking quotations out of their contexts and applying them to the immediate purpose.

So the *Dialogus* and the *Trialogus* are a good deal more simple than anything Wyclif had managed before, but they are still a long way from the level of a popular theology which was likely to speak directly to the ordinary believer.

Campaigning issues

This takes us conveniently into what may be called the 'campaigning issues' of Wyclif's last years, where the general picture is of a reforming zeal still largely fixed at the stage of rebelling against things as they are.

It is an important question whether Wyclif's increasing insistence in these last years on looking for a biblical basis before approving of anything was motivated by a genuine feel for the primacy of Scripture or by the need for ammunition to use against claims he disliked as coming from his inveterate enemies. In either case, the result was the same. He was adding his voice to a mounting cry which was to become a shout during the sixteenth-century Reformation. Nevertheless, Wyclif's reasons for saying what he did were not necessarily the same as those of the sixteenth-century reformers. A Bible-based Christianity which disowns all forms of institutional, ecclesiastical authority as mere 'human inventions' was for Wyclif a means of putting the noses of the mendicants out of joint. An 'inclusive' view of the Church which allows no special status to priests and members of the religious orders presented a challenge to Pope and bishops and to the mendicants. So Wyclif is against what he calls 'private religion', by which he meant by now any assertion of special rights and privileges for any class of Christian. There is a case for saying that the views he was pressing were favoured not primarily because they were perceived as positively good or better in their own right, but in reaction against abuses. This is a big claim to make, as we come to Wyclif's death. Let us leave it here for now and consider it more fully in conclusion, where the beginnings of Lollardy can form part of the context.

The death of Wyclif

On St Thomas's Day, 1384, that

> '…organ of the Devil, enemy of the Church, confusion of the common people, idol of heretics, mirror of hypocrites, instigator of schisms, sower of hatred, inventor of lies, John Wyclif, was suddenly struck down by the judgment of God and felt a paralysis invade every part of his body.'[95]

Thus one of the chroniclers describes the death of Wyclif, in what must still have been only late middle age. It was only ten years or so since he had graduated in Theology. Another account, recording his death and his burial at Lutterworth, notes that his body was later exhumed (in 1428) and his bones burned.[96] This was probably not Wyclif's first stroke. There is evidence he had had one earlier, which John Horne his curate said, left him paralyzed for the last two years of his life. Horne swore an oath in 1441 that Wyclif had had a stroke on 28 December 1384 and died on 31 December.[97]

Wyclif mentions himself as ill in 'On frivolous citations and other ambushes of Antichrist', saying: 'and here speaks someone weak and "crippled" who has been cited to appear before that court'.[98] Wyclif could just have been speaking of a broken ankle or arthritis. There is another reference to his illness and the summons to Rome in his 'On civil servitude and secular dominion'. There Wyclif declares it unreasonable of the Pope to expect someone incapacitated by weakness or illness to travel so far.[99] He considered himself too ill to go, but he wrote to the Pope to declare himself willing to amend his opinions if he has been in error, and he says he would have come in person if it had been within his power.[100] There was, naturally, an undertow of comment about the issues running beneath the surface of this claim to be too ill to engage with them. He puts a spin on the whole affair. His argument in 'On frivolous citations' is analogous with his much earlier line of argument about papal taxation. The Pope has no authority to 'cite' royal subjects without the King's consent. In any case, there is no scriptural warrant for citation and, if there is no valid basis for temporal lords to insist on it either, it can only come from Satan.[101]

A very late letter to the Bishop of Lincoln, John of Buckingham, calls on him to insist that the friars state their own position on the transubstantiation question; and if it proves to be heretical, he asks the Bishop to condemn them. Wyclif writes as the 'humble servant of Christ' and the devout obedientary of his Bishop.[102] There are problems with this evidence and its dating.[103] This may all have happened some years earlier, before Wyclif left Oxford for good. But if it is really to be dated to these last years, and set in the context of Wyclif's alleged letter to the Pope of 1384, there would be a case for saying that at the very end Wyclif sought some sort of reconciliation. The letter insists that the Pope must be obedient to the Gospel, but it also has Wyclif making a provisional apology. 'If I am wrong in what I have said above I am willing to be corrected, accepting death if necessary.' He adds the pious hope that the Pope may be saved from 'malicious advice' and the reflection that it is well known that a man's enemies are likely to be among his household familiars.[104] It is possible to argue that a repentant Wyclif, too ill to argue, gave in at last and recanted, even if only in these equivocal terms.

The alternative and more plausible view, since it fits better with everything we know about his character and habits of mind, is that Wyclif did not die quietly, but was still productive to the sudden end of his life, writing the embittered, repetitive, obsessive pieces we have been discussing. But the possibility that he took stock of his spiritual state cannot be discounted altogether. In a medieval theological writer as prolific as Wyclif there are likely to be reflections on death and the life to come, both personal and general, both conventional and particular. 'I trust in the mercy of God that when this brief life is over I shall have my reward from God abundantly for this legitimate struggle,'[105] he cries from a burdened heart in the *Trialogus*. 'Reward' theory and talk of 'merit' remind us that Wyclif was not a man of the Reformation, but in most respects an utterly typical medieval figure of his time.

Wyclif's spirituality was not, as far as the evidence allows us to guess at it, of any notable profundity. There are no indications of the conventional sensitivities of late medieval mysticism, no hint of Wyclif giving an ear to the inward voice of the Spirit. There is no Boethius here, thinking out in his final imprisonment a theory or a theology of the meaning of life. Wyclif explains in a conventional enough way that there are three kinds of prayer identified in the Bible, of the mind, the voice and the way life is lived.[106] But he is not trying to teach the reader how to pray. His concern is to disabuse his readers of the teaching on prayer he says the 'sects' put about. Christians should not rely on the prayers of others to win for them 'time off' their appointed period in purgatory.[107] Nor should they approve of the selling of prayers by the sects to be used vicariously in the same way.[108] In a treatise on the 'seven gifts of the Holy Spirit'[109] he is once more both conventional and polemical. By their deeds the sects uphold the opposite of the seven gifts of the Spirit.

'The threefold bond of love',[110] seems to have begun life as a sermon. In it Wyclif discusses the three kinds of human love: between parent and child, between husband and wife, between the faithful Christian and his neighbour. The first is an image of the Father's love; the second of the love of Christ (for the Church or for the soul said the traditional exegesis of the Song of Songs, in which the Bridegroom is Christ); the third is in the image of the Holy Spirit. Yet this sermon, too, drifts inexorably in the direction of the sects and their wrongdoings.

Wyclif's idea of heaven was also unremarkable, at least in his earlier years, when he was interested in it in connection with his lecturing duties on the Bible. Paradise is described in the *De statu innocentiae* as a place which was well-suited to the needs of human beings, and he comments that the 'art of the Supreme Maker' knew well how to design it so that it received the influence of the heavens in the most advantageous way possible. There was exercise there which did not tire the body and there was neither hunger nor thirst but only a moderate appetite.[111]

At the end of his life he seems to have set before himself an ideal of universal unity and unanimity, which had become clearer to him in recent years. It remained hopelessly entangled in the painfulness to Wyclif of many features of contemporary politics. There will be no peace until, in every sense, the schism ends, not merely the conflict between the Pope and the anti-Pope,[112] but the division between clergy and laity. That will happen when the clergy are of one mind in humbly following Christ, and do not despoil the poor, but take care of them and cease to seek their own advantage.[113] The conflict currently taking place within the once-more-divided papacy involved Clement VII and Urban VI and it had gone as far as exhortations to murder.[114] The 'Despenser Crusade' was the project of one of the English Bishops, whose scheme was to invade France through Flanders so as to weaken the support available to Urban VI, the Pope favoured by the Count of Flanders. The scheme was well advanced in preparation by March 1381, with plenty of indulgences available from Urban VI to support it, but the Peasants' Revolt caused an interruption and by the autumn of 1381 the French themselves were invading Flanders. The expedition from England eventually left in April 1383 and it was a failure.[115] This was the conflict whose peaceful resolution Wyclif was seeking at the time when his own death was imminent, not an eternal peace. Eternal peace was not, it seems, uppermost in his mind.

Wyclif's preoccupation with Antichrist in these last years is of a similarly 'mixed' character. It fits with an interest in eschatology which might naturally be sharper in the mind of a man contemplating his end, and an unsatisfactory end at that.[116] *De vaticinacione*,[117] is an apocalyptic piece preoccupied with Antichrist. In it Wyclif refers to Merlin and to Hildegard of Bingen (though in fact to a forged, alleged work of hers, the *Revelatio Hildegardis de fratribus mendicantium*).[118] The suggestion that the Pope is Antichrist had been abroad since the beginning of the thirteenth century or fractionally earlier; it is a theme already found among the followers of Joachim of Fiore, and developed by Peter Olivi in his Lecture on the Apocalypse.[119] Antichrist talk lingered in the air, as commentators expounded the book of Revelation and the fashion for calculating the 'ages of the world' came and went, sometimes with careful arithmetic about the number of years Satan had been bound, and whether he was now 'loose' (Revelation 20:7). In the *De solutione Sathanem* Wyclif was contributing to a lively contemporary debate about the way the 'thousand years' of the binding of Satan, to which the book of Revelation refers, was to be interpreted. Satan was to be released at the end of that time. There was disagreement among the authorities as to whether it was a figurative thousand (so Satan had been 'loose' in the period of the persecution of the early Christians) or literally a thousand and then the question was when the binding had happened and at what date it concluded. Was it at the death of Christ, which would have Satan on the loose again in 1033, or when Constantine became the first Christian Emperor in the fourteenth century, which might have meant he was loosed only in or close to Wyclif's lifetime. The one thing which seemed clear to Wyclif in his last, maddened years, was that Satan was loose at last and occupied the office of the Pope.[120] The subject continued to be of interest into the sixteenth century. John Bale wrote about it to Matthew Parker, Archbishop of Canterbury.[121]

This is a bleak and terrible scene in which to take leave of the stricken Wyclif as he suffered his final stroke, but there is no saintly deathbed scene, no reconciliation; there are no edifying words of wisdom to report. We have to turn from him as he fell, angry and despairing.

Chapter 13

Distilling Wyclif

i. Inward grace and outward order

a. What is the Church?

It is time to try to pull together the essentials of what Wyclif had been saying and to set these in the context into which they were now beginning to be incorporated. For it is clear that he was making a contribution to something which was afoot quite independently of his efforts, and sometimes despite them.

Wyclif's thought had its tensions. His doctrine of the Church and his theory of the state were at first interdependent, to the point where his idea of the Church was framed largely over against his idea of the state. That is because the main political problem of the day was the power relationship between the two kinds of authority, and in particular which should have control over the other and in what areas this jurisdiction should operate. The papal taxation affair had been a case in point. This was far from being a new problem, but it was not easy to make it go away because examples kept arising, locally, nationally and internationally, of conflicts of interest in matters of land and money. This constant irritation must partly account for the continuing vigorous interest of both 'authorities' in what Wyclif and others were saying and for the mounting persecution.

But, later, Wyclif began to think through an ecclesiology for which this first scuffle had merely raised a set of presenting questions. He began from the perfectly conventional view that there is no salvation or remission of sins outside the Church.[1] He became interested in the much profounder question of the relationship of the direct leading of the Holy Spirit and order.

The surviving version of Wyclif's intended major work 'On the Church', the *De ecclesia*, is in a confused state.[2] It contains indications that it was written in 1378–79, but Wyclif apparently did not get it into a final order. Chapter 23, which contains a discussion of indulgences and the treasury of merits, and the question whether a pope can have authority to distribute the surplus merits of the saints, has Pope Gregory XI still living, although he died in March 1378.[3] In Chapter 2, Urban VI is already Pope, although his papacy did not begin until 8 April 1378 and lasted until 15 October 1389.

This was a Pope of whom to begin with Wyclif approved, as did many in England. He was an Italian and not a Frenchman and that altered the pattern of resentments for a time. In Chapter 2 he is writing 'Blessed be the Lord of our Mother [the Church], who provides in these days a Catholic Head, a man of the Gospel, Urban VI,' who he sees as 'putting right the Church of our time', so that it may live in conformity with the law of Christ.[4] In Chapter 13 the Schism has begun, for Wyclif is writing of the 'schism which now pullulates between the two pretend-monks'.[5] This places that part of the work after September–October 1378. In the middle of the book is a long, more or less self-contained treatment of Wyclif's views on the question of sanctuary. Chapter 7 is probably a version of the speech he made to Parliament in November 1378, and the succeeding chapters up to Chapter 16 contain his development of the theme and its implications. The reason for this muddle may be that Wyclif died in the middle of revising the book,[6] or perhaps while he had scarcely tackled the redrafting it needed. If so, there may be changes and additions which were made after the initial period of composition in 1378–79.

The general shape of his ecclesiology is echoed in John Hus's *Tractus de Ecclesia*, a book which shows a considerable debt to Wyclif,[7] but puts together the framework more tidily. In this present world Hus finds the word 'Church' being used in at least three senses. The first is simply to refer to a building, for example 'the church' in a particular village. So long as this is not confused with the local community of the faithful, that usage raises no particular difficulties, though in the sixteenth century the role of the 'gathered congregation' and its relation to the universal Church was to become a matter of heated debate.

The second meaning takes the Church to include the priesthood alone. There were theologians and canonists who would separate the clergy from the 'laity' by reason of their 'ordination', and even went so far as to regard the clergy alone as forming the Church.[8] On this model, the laity are merely the object of priestly ministry rather than a constitutive part of the *laos* or people of God.[9] Wyclif decided in favour of a concept of the *laos* or people of God as a whole, which included both the clergy and the laity. 'Everyman' can receive the gift of grace. It does not come only with ordination.

The third sense of 'Church' that Hus identifies includes all people who can be said to be 'under the rule of Christ'.[10] Here Hus makes a distinction between those who are predestined to heaven – some in the Church triumphant (heaven) some in the Church militant (earth), some in the Church dormient (purgatory) – and those 'foreknown' by God to be among the damned.

Predestination

We must pause here for the sake of clarity and sketch the debate on predestination, for it exemplifies very well the degree to which Wyclif was a 'responder' rather than an 'instigator', and how readily his arguments ran away down the familiar tracks of contemporary scholastic debate, for this question of the foreseeability of the future was of course in the old Arts course.[11] We find Wyclif in the *De ecclesia* discussing the familiar question whether the Church includes the Old Testament 'saints'.[12] The question is the one about the continuity of the Church in time. Wyclif approaches it as a logician. The conclusion is denied because the antecedent is true and the consequence is false. Was there a Church before the Incarnation? If not and if it is true that there is no salvation outside the Church, none of the Old Testament figures can be saved, on the 'supposition of the schools' that only what is in the present time exists.[13] Wyclif makes a distinction between the mystical 'catholic Church' which was from the beginning of the world and which has been in existence continually throught the generations of its members, to the end of the world; and the particular Church.[14]

The live debates of the day were thus, as ever, an important stimulant to Wyclif. Some of the issues as they looked to contemporaries had been set out by Wyclif in his debate with Ralph Strode, logician and lawyer in early 1379,[15] and we have here a useful example of the way the framing of questions was conditioned by the education of the day. In *The City of God*, Augustine explains that some of the citizens of heaven have already lived, some are living now and some have yet to be born, but they are all united in Christ and form a single 'city' of the Church.[16] His fourteenth-century successors agree that Church can be described as a 'body of the predestinate made up of those who have already lived and of those who are yet to be born' (*universitas predestinatorum qui fuerunt vel erunt*). But for them this is not at all a simple matter. It leads naturally into the area of the logic course which dealt with future contingents. 'Here I put an opinion concerning future necessity, namely that no creature can resist God's ordinance.'[17] By now, partly under the influence of the mathematical studies of the fourteenth century, the question had reformulated itself so as to encourage scholars to think of time as a succession of instants. This emphasis is also reflected in the discussion. 'In this way,' it is suggested, 'the succession is perpetual, even though it is new in some "parts"'.[18]

If the Church is the body of the predestined, the distinction between those 'foreknown' and those 'predestined' is important. Augustine had become an extreme predestinationist; yet he held that, if God 'predestined' some for hell, that would make him the author of evil. He was firm against such 'double predestination'. God foreknows what will happen to those who are not predestined, but he is not the cause of their damnation. Wyclif discusses all this against the background of Augustine. He was not a forerunner of Calvin, for Calvin had no difficulty with double predestination. Calvin held both that God predestined to hell as well as to heaven and that the 'saved' know that they are saved. Wyclif would accept neither premiss.

Grace is a mystery and its own master. The institutional and sacramental acts of the Church do not 'automatically' classify people as saved or not saved by any 'effect' they have. Wyclif was 'with Augustine' in another of his key presumptions, which was that the true Church was invisible, even to its members. It was Augustine's conviction, and it grew firmer as he grew older, that the predestinate do not know who they are. It was obvious to Augustine that not all the baptized could be known to be of the City of God. (Wyclif permitted himself the triumphant observation that the Pope cannot know he is among the elect and so it cannot be certain that any given claimant to the papacy is actually a member of the Church at all.) The conviction that the Church is invisible or 'spiritual' had a sound patristic pedigree, then. But less respectable figures in more recent times had been emphasizing the invisibility of the truly spiritual Church. One of the themes of the followers of Joachim of Fiore, who had been condemned as a heretic for his Trinitarian theology by the Fourth Lateran Council, was the notion that the Church is invisible and spiritual. He looked to the 'new spiritual men' of the forthcoming Third Age of spiritual renewal.[19] There is of course a visible Church, the institutional framework of the community in which the sacraments are administered. Augustine believed that God had chosen to leave the visible community of those calling themselves Christians in a 'mixed' state, wheat and tares growing together until harvest. Wyclif's spiritual true Church is not mixed. It does not contain any of the reprobate.[20] It is the Church of those in a state of grace. It will be apparent that these basics were capable of being stated by a great and long-standing authority like Augustine and were not in essence Wycliffite.

b. The doctrine of ministry

The 'doctrine of ministry' in its theoretical aspects had evolved a considerable distance by Wyclif's time. The 'orders' to which it was possible to be 'ordained' had grown from the New Testament two (deacon and presbyter or bishop) to three, so as to form an ascending series of steps up which it was possible to climb, from deacon to priest to bishop. These 'ordained ministers' now formed a class of 'clergy'. By now Wyclif wanted to do away with the whole run of subordinate 'orders' (or non-orders) of the tonsured, acolytes and subdeacons and so on. These orders below the rank of deacon had multiplied in the medieval Church. (They entitled the holder to benefit of clergy but did not require him to be celibate. So Wyclif's contemporary, the poet William Langland, could call himself a *clericus*, although he says he was a married man.)[21]

'On the degrees of the clergy of the Church' (*De gradibus cleri ecclesie*), written probably towards the end of 1382 when Wyclif was back in parish life, discusses the question how many orders of ordained minister there are or ought to be. A 'certain secular, honestly zealous for the truth of the Christian faith' it mentions may have been John Purvey.[22] Whoever he was, he asked pressingly what was required on the part of the person ordaining in order that he might duly ordain a priest or a deacon, and he wanted to know whether other orders were legitimate. This 'urgent question' originating with some *perversus magister* was designed so that Wyclif would not be able to answer it without putting himself in a difficult position one way or another.

Wyclif begins[23] by considering whether ordination is of divine or human origin. His view is that all ministerial authority comes from God, and that God does not necessarily give more or less power to clergy in a hierarchical sequence. Those ordained to the priesthood were deemed to have been entrusted with functions specific to their orders. Both priests and bishops could consecrate the bread and wine at the Eucharist and declare absolution to repentant sinners. Only bishops could ordain priests. It is plain that there are concerns here which go far beyond the shepherding metaphors of 1379, where Wyclif was chiefly considering what was best for his sheep. Nevertheless, despite its preoccupation with power, this was a 'pastoral' not a 'sacerdotal' controversy. The term *ecclesiasticus* rather than the word *sacerdos* flows from Wyclif's contemptuous pen when he wishes to be particularly cutting. At issue was mainly the fitness of ordained ministers to take care of their 'sheep' and the relation of the sheep to their shepherds. Contemporary satire mocks 'prelates' for their theological ignorance and the easy way they can be bought, not for claiming to repeat the unique sacrifice of Christ. 'Few are "baptised" by studying in the theological schools but they are bought for cash or a word,' says a contemporary satirical poem:

Scolis theologicis pauci baptizati
Sed prece vel pretio vel penna sublimiti.[24]

Wyclif is no longer in favour of bishops. He thinks that the only orders of ministry ought to be those of priest and deacon, since, although the vocabulary of the New Testament is hard to interpret, it does seem to be consistent in referring to only two orders, deacons and presbyter-bishops. Wyclif lays down the important principle that a distinction of duties or office does not necessarily require a difference of order. 'For as far as the power of the order is concerned all priests are equal in power.'[25] The simple priest has as much 'plenitude of power' as the pope. 'According to Jerome, bishop and priest were once the same,'[26] and Wyclif believes that was the way God wanted it to be. The underlying principle of equality of powers he identifies – and minimal powers at that – is important to his late theology of ministry. 'It would seem to be in harmony with the Gospel to take away all superfluous domination.'[27]

Once more Wyclif was discussing something which was being debated by others at the time. Woodford's first question in his *Responsiones contra Wiclevum et Lollardos* is how many 'orders' (*ordines*) there are in this earthly life and which of them is most perfect. The debate ran beyond the question how many 'orders' of the 'ordained' God had intended there to be, to the religious 'orders'. He begins with a philosopher's reminder that 'order' has a wide range of meaning. The supreme perfection of order is that of the Trinity itself. 'But perhaps you are really asking how many orders of different conditions of life and religious orders there are in the world?'[28] Woodford identifies many. His answer to the question which is the most perfect is to group together, as a collective 'order' of the greatest perfection of life, priests and those in 'private religion'. One of the groups forming part of such 'order' is that of the friars.

Woodford envisages order and sub-order arranged in such a way that he himself can say that he is of the order of creatures, and within that the order of Christians, and within that of the order of the ordained ministry (made up, as he details it, of priest, deacon and subdeacon), and he himself, finally, is of the order of Friars Minor.[29] The next question is who 'made' this order? Both ordinary and private religion are of God.[30] Woodford's argument in support of this is that any good thing made by man is made by God rather than man. So even if Francis was the founder, the order is more of God than of Francis. There is no perfect rule but that of Christ. He is claiming that this rule of his order is not really a human invention.[31]

Wyclif asks in his last treatises whether Christ approved more religions than the one 'religion pure and undefiled' referred to by James (James 1:27).[32] Woodford's response is that the religion of which James speaks is included (*includitur*) in the 'religion' of Augustine, Benedict and Francis. And so it is false to state that a Franciscan or Dominican is in some way in secession from the religion the blessed James spoke of.[33] If it is all one order, say some, it is reasonable to ask why the friars appear to be outside the order of the Church in general, in that they are not subject to the visitation of bishops and the law of the King. Woodford protests that the friars are ready to do service to the King and obey him in all that their order allows. And they are no different from other religious in having special papal exemptions. Their own internal discipline is so strict that they need none of that laxer visitation they would get from bishops.[34]

c. *The papacy*

The view that the Pope 'seems to be the abbot and patron of all those private orders'[35] was a conviction which grew on Wyclif in his angry last years; it led him to scrutinize very closely the Pope's claim to special status, which had not troubled him at the outset of his Government-directed researches into the papal right to take taxation from the kingdom of England. Although Wyclif never formally rejected the papacy, he did everything he could in his last arguments to diminish it. He eventually concluded that the Pope cannot claim apostolic warrant for any supremacy. He points out that there is no biblical warrant for the title of 'Pope'.[36] For the Pope is the special case whose office tests all the ground rules of Wyclif's doctrine of ministry. If he is not the legitimate holder of the powers he exercises, disobedience is justified, as it is always justified, he says, when 'novel traditions' are imposed which are not founded on the law of God.[37]

It is important not to lose sight here of the chain of medieval events which had led to the aggrandizement of papal claims to plenitude of power and to the establishment of what was in reality by now a papal 'monarchy'. Pope Gregory VII (d. 1085) had made a remarkably successful bid to insist that ecclesiastical power is supreme over secular power. The simultaneous discontents prompted by the Investiture Contest (as a result of the the creeping tendency of kings and emperors to intrude into the sacramental and ecclesiastical part of the appointing and making of bishops, so that they could keep better control of the temporalities of the Sees which lay under their stewardship) reached an uneasy truce with the Concordat of Worms in 1122; it was more or less settled that the state was to confine itself to the 'temporalities' and the Church to the 'spiritualities'.[38]

A decade or two later, Bernard of Clairvaux set out in the five volumes of his *On Consideration* a theory of papal plenitude of power.[39] He did this for the benefit of Pope Eugenius III, who had once been one of his own monks and was now struggling to establish his new priorities while floundering in a flood of appeals to the papal law courts which were taking up far too much of his time. The book articulated and consolidated the radical shifts in the balance of power between Church and state of the previous generation.

The balance of power within the Church was altered too, for the bishops meeting in council were no longer the equal partners in the running of the Church which they had been in the first centuries, but were being treated as the 'subjects' of a primatial papal monarchy. The 'conciliar' movement of Wyclif's own time had a hard and ultimately unsuccessful struggle to shift that balance back again. Papal infallibility was not to achieve the status of a dogma until the nineteenth century, and then it was claimed only in strictly limited circumstances, but the notion was beginning to hang in the air that a Pope could never be wrong.[40]

Wyclif asks what God has ordained about the way in which hierarchy should be set up and operate in the institutional running of the Church. His argument that the Christ alone is head of the Church, which is there in Hus's ecclesiology too,[41] should not make ears prick up too sharply. This was not a new and challenging idea. Christ is described as *caput ecclesiae* in the Vulgate translation (Ephesians 5:23). It was to be found in the mouths of the friars as well, for in itself it was a neutral and obviously scriptural statement. Bonaventure says in the *Collationes in Hexaemeron* that 'Christ has the supreme position as Head of the Church.'[42] The headship of Christ was not in itself incompatible for Wyclif with the existence of a human primacy in the Church. Christ gave the primacy to Peter because it was Peter who loved him most. To Peter and Peter alone he gave the 'keys'. But where did that primacy go after Peter? It is not necessarily associated with the bishopric of Rome, Wyclif argues. The true successor of Peter is the man who resembles him in his love of Christ. And, in any case, Peter's primacy was nothing to do with the exercise of jurisdiction, most particularly not with temporal jurisdiction.

Antichrist's appearance in writings about the papacy was not only occurring in Wyclif's writings. Wyclif gives eleven indicators that the Pope is to be regarded as Antichrist,[43] which are also to be found in the notebook of Adam Stockton,[44] an Augustinian friar at Cambridge and *lector* about 1375. Stockton has a note: *in quadam sua determinacione* which strongly suggests a context of formal disputation in the background of this list. Wyclif's own Antichrist is in many respects simply the Pope gone astray. He is a liar; he leads the people into temptation; he loves wealth and worldly power; he invents new laws without biblical foundation; he promotes the interests of worldly men; instead of preaching the Gospel as Christ commanded, he sits on a throne in a palace; he strives for temporal dominion in contrast with Christ who forbade his disciples to wield the sword; he uses money extracted from the poor to pay his mercenary army; he excommunicates those who resist his tyranny; he claims to be everyone's judge although Christ was submissive to the judgment of others; Christ was God made man but the Pope behaves like a man made God; Christ forbade simony but the Pope practises it. It behoves popes and bishops and all prelates to live in imitation of Christ, in poverty, but the Pope as Wyclif depicts him here does not.

This extreme position was in several respects a test of the implications in Wyclif's mind of going wrong about grace and allowing the institutional, and particularly the power structures, to get out of balance with it. And once more we see Wyclif's clearly articulated principles emerging only under the pressure of events and as a reaction to them. He did not begin by disapproving of the papacy, for did he not hope for papal patronage himself in youth and middle age? In 'On the power of the Pope', *De potestate pape*, in autumn 1379, which mentions the 'recent' election of Pope Clement VII, he seems to have moved from approval of Urban VI to calling him a *pseudomonachus*.[45]

d. An inclusive Church and the private religions

> 'The world, leaving and forsaking God's spiritual world and doctrine, was altogether led and blinded with outward ceremonies and human traditions. In these was all the hope of obtaining salvation fully fixed, so that scarcely anything else was taught in the churches.'[46]

From the vantage point of the sixteenth century, Foxe thus emphasizes the importance of the resistance to 'human traditions' in Wyclif's 'reforms'. Obedience to the Pope is not necessary for salvation, he was to claim in the *De blasphemia*, and if this were understood the reign of Antichrist would be ended. All that is needful is to love Christ purely and keep his law.[47]

One of the chroniclers[48] describes what, if it did in fact take place, must have been one of Wyclif's last 'determinations' in the University. The *Eulogium* says Wyclif insisted that the only religion which is 'deserving' before God is that 'common religion' which is spoken of by the apostle as 'religion which is pure and immaculate' (James 1:27). All other 'private religions', said Wyclif, are superstitious, irrelevant to salvation, and established by human beings as new inventions. These new inventions and human 'traditions' and rites are objectionable because they impose a burden on the faithful which resembles that of Judaism; it is an unnecessary burden. In the *De fide catholica*, a digest of Wyclif's ecclesiology (evidently written at the end of his life because he mentions the *Trialogus*), he sets out very simple necessities.[49] It is a 'necessity of faith' to love Christ, the bridegroom, and his bride, the Church.[50]

Wyclif defines 'the religion of Christ' as 'simply that which Christ expressly instituted', without any later admixture of human ceremony.[51] The pure Christian religion is more perfect than the private.[52] Wyclif was not hostile to all the friars as individuals. Unless he intends an irony, he was able to speak in the *De apostasia* of 'my very dear sons among the mendicants who are not apostates'.[53] 'Private religions' became inseparable in Wyclif's mind from the imposing of additional requirements upon those who would be saved. *De quattuor sectis novellis*, really a treatise on the three theological virtues (1 Corinthians 13:13), is also urgent about the shocking 'novelty' of the sects.[54]

There was a literature about 'precept and dispensation' in which Bernard of Clairvaux and others had discussed what was in fact necessary to salvation by way of the keeping of rules.[55] Wyclif may well have read at least Bernard on the subject, and it seems that he did believe some rule-keeping was expected. He speaks of 'Antichrists' who turn aside from God's commandments.[56] We saw him earlier accepting the idea of merit and not resisting the expectation that Christians might earn their salvation. But he disliked any suggestion that actions could be 'effective' for salvation.

The 'common' Christian religion is simpler, more necessary, more authoritative, 'and therefore it is more perfect,' he insists. Private religion is more difficult, more demanding and less focussed, so it is less perfect. Matthew's Gospel (11:30) promises that Christ's yoke is sweet and his burden light.[57] And 'common' religion is for everyone.[58]

Wycliff regarded 'private religions' as 'sects' because they cut themselves off from the commonality and lay claim to superiority over them on the basis of a purely human assessment of what is required to please God.[59] Several of Wyclif's sermons, apparently preached in reply to the attacks of the Benedictine John Wells,[60] discuss the subject of 'private religion'. Those expanding private religion are the Devil's procurers and leaders-astray of their neighbours.[61] The ordinary 'common' religion, by contrast, is about rational keeping of the ten commandments and anyone can do that. There is no need to be ordained or tonsured.[62]

At the front of Wyclif's firing line remained the friars, with other religious orders at their shoulders. In the 'Description of a friar' (*Descriptio fratris*) the whole work is a definition of the enemy. The friar is a 'false brother', the Devil incarnate, intent on sowing discord in the Church on earth.[63] His venom, which embraces friars and monks everywhere, is directed in particular at the four 'sects' in England.[64] Antichrist is the leader of an army with two 'arms', the right arm of religious orders which have possessions and the left arm of the mendicants, and they are all mere hired soldiers, fighting for pay, when they should be members of the Christian army through their profession.[65]

Both Wyclif's preoccupations about the friars and the debate about orders drive him further towards a theology of ministry in which, because special claims are disallowed, ordinary people may exercise a ministry traditionally reserved to the clergy. Heaven says that 'everyone predestined' for heaven is a priest in this life and does not need the sacraments celebrated by the priests of the Church.[66] He underlines what seems to him the lack of scriptural warrant for the contemporary hierarchical structures. 'I do not remember any mention of the Pope and cardinals, monks, canons and friars in Scripture,' he says.[67]

This kind of thing could very easily have led to Wyclif's rejecting the conventions of ordination and ceasing to call himself a priest. He did not do so; as far as we know he did not even consider it. The sixteenth-century reformers faced a similar dilemma, to which some responded by abandoning ordained ministry and some by accommodating it within a 'reformed' ecclesiology. The indignation Wyclif expresses has its echoes in the debate of the Council of Florence early in the fifteenth century, and in the protests of Luther about the way the systems of penance and indulgences operated to keep the faithful in bondage to ecclesiastical authorities

In the absence of any evidence that Wyclif put real effort at any time in his own pastoral ministry into easing the lot of widows and orphans, this should probably be taken to be a rhetorical embracing of the poor, the ordinary, the whole people of God, over against those who make claims to be their superiors in the eyes of God, and not for its own sake. Wyclif's inclusion of all the people of God (the predestinate) in the saving community of the Church[68] was a logical entailment of his earlier arguments and not necessarily an indication that Wyclif really cared about the common people. 'On the Devil of the Noonday', *De daemonio meridiano*,[69] which can be dated to 1376 because of its references to the death of the Black Prince in that year, gives an early indication that Wyclif may have been genuinely concerned about the plight of the poor. But more important are the indications that he wanted the Church to be seen as inclusive.

e. Charism and order

'A recently qualified so-called professor' [Wyclif][70] has been teaching that the priests of Christ ought to minister humbly to the Church and that they ought to live a life of poverty. He says that it is especially important that Christ's priests should live in imitation of Christ and his apostles. This is not an obligation which alters with the changing climate of the times, nor can it be dispensed from by papal authority.

It is hard for the modern reader to see at first sight what can possibly be wrong with this, how Wyclif can have been condemned for saying such things. But behind this apparently straightforward call to the imitation of Christ stands an ancient ecclesiological question. A wild-haired charismatic figure, or even quite a tidy and well-behaved one, could 'preach the Gospel' stirringly to the people of a locality. Jesus had sent out his disciples to do exactly that. But that was when the Gospel message was simple and no institutional Church had taken upon itself the responsibility of vigilance about exactly what the faithful were taught. The apostles had the teaching of Jesus echoing in their ears. The early Church soon faced a number of situations in which individuals claiming to be inspired directly by the Holy Spirit undermined the 'order' which was emerging in the nascent pastoral structures of the young Church and taught a 'faith' it did not recognize. After those first centuries it was insisted that those who *taught* the faith must also *maintain* the faith and hand it on in its essentials the same from generation to generation.[71] It was this same dilemma over what to do about those who claimed a direct gift of grace, and who said they were acting on the special intervention of the Holy Spirit, which led to the 'domestication' and ultimately the 'institutionalization' of the Holy Spirit in theological thinking, so that the Spirit was regarded as acting within and through the Church's structures. That is the context in which a bishop still calls on the Holy Spirit to grant a gift of grace for a specific purpose, when ordaining or confirming someone.

The phenomenon of the 'new spiritual men' whose coming was foretold by Joachim of Fiore at the end of the twelfth century, was posing a similar 'charismatic' challenge to the patterns and assumptions of the institutional medieval Church.[72] Richard FitzRalph had complained about the proliferation of preachers who were entering parishes without the permission of the local bishop or priest. 'On Friars' lies' (*De mendaciis fratrum*) is a very brief late work of Wyclif.[73] The subject is the friars' claim that no one should preach without a special licence from the Bishop.[74] Where is the evidence that St Paul got a licence from St Peter, he mocks? Paul was preaching before he ever set eyes on Peter. The popular wandering preachers of Wyclif's day were doing nothing essentially new in the history of the Church, but they prompted concern when they appeared to be out of control. There were also questions about the level of theological knowledge of preachers who were self-appointed.

Wyclif takes it that ordination is required for the normal proper exercise of priestly ministry.[75] He is conventional, even Augustinian, in asserting that the people may profit even from the work of a wicked priest since grace can use any channel.[76] But he also argues that only he who lives according to Christ's law can absolve from sin or 'bind' the sinner by refusing to absolve him.[77] Wyclif had already asked in the *De civili dominio* whether the power to bind and loose, which was the ministerial power most obviously based on Christ's commission (Matthew 16:19), was an absolute power which is conferred with ordination or is dependent on the good behaviour or 'worthiness' of the priest.

This draws a fine line. It deems it to be the grace of God which acts and not the priest himself.[78] No one receives absolution unless God deems him worthy. That is true, Wyclif insists, even if he is absolved by the Pope. The Church's ministers should instruct the faithful so that they will become worthy of absolution. That is their task, not the exercise of personal powers to bind and loose. Wyclif maintains that no mere vicar of Christ, no priest, can do more than announce to the Church whom God (re)habilitates[79] or restores.[80] Excommunication will not be effective automatically, *simpliciter*, just because a bishop or even the Pope says so, but only if the person excommunicated has in fact offended God. A *maledictio* cannot bind in the sight of God (*quoad deum*) if God is not in truth offended.[81] The reality is that people excommunicate themselves.[82]

It follows, in Wyclif's view, that pious lay people must separate themselves from a wicked priest and have nothing to do with him, that the people of God have power to choose priests and may reject those who are unworthy.[83] He points out, insisting that he means no offence, for he is merely quoting canon law, that even the Pope may be accused by the laity.[84] Debate about the question whether a legitimately appointed ruler might lose the right to exercise the authority entrusted to him was nothing new.[85] But the question as it struck Wyclif was perhaps first sharply focused by Henry of Ghent late in 1288, when he proposed that a ruler's actions should be judged in the context of the 'order' within which they are appointed to be exercised, the constitution and structure and purpose of the body or kingdom over which he rules. Henry suggested that absolute power could be used validly even though sinfully, but that a power which is 'ordained', in other words given for a purpose and within an 'order' of things, cannot be used validly if an attempt is made to use it outside the order in question. Even God cannot act outside the 'order' in which all his acts are just.[86]

These ideas made the relationship between the soul and God all-important. The clergy (and only the best of them) become instruments and channels of God's operations. They get no special or automatic powers. Yet this did not, for Wyclif, logically entail the removal of the whole structure of an ordained ministry. The tension he perceived lay between 'inwardness' and 'outwardness'.

If the fundamental ideas sketched in this chapter represent the essence of Wyclif's mature thought and its internal tensions, they can be mapped only loosely onto the patterns of argument of the Lollards. The emphasis on the popular front was naturally upon the more superficial and easily grasped aspects of all this, in particular popular resentment of wealthy and idle senior clerics. Such simplified notions could be taken out of Wyclif's writings by anyone with the energy to do so, but many of them appear to have been abroad quite independently of him, in the calls of John Ball and his like. It would be a much more uphill task[87] to show that the subtler theologizing of Wyclif was able to command the same eager assent from the whole *laos* as it did from some university students.

We must now consider the question of Wyclif's contribution to the popular dissemination of such theories in English, for unless people could understand his teaching, its potential influence was limited.

ii. Popular and vernacular

a. The Englishing of the Bible

Wyclif's was the first generation for whom English was sometimes the language of choice for doing serious business. As English grew into a mature language, it was replacing Norman French for use in Government, but it had remained the vernacular of the ordinary population after the Norman Conquest. Wyclif was a decade older than Chaucer and they had some of the same friends. Chaucer found English the natural vehicle for the telling of the 'Canterbury Tales'; just as Wyclif and the popular preachers who became associated with him increasingly found it to be for preaching.

There is no evidence at all that Wyclif personally wrote anything in English or took any active steps to ensure that others translated what he had written in Latin. There is a fair degree of certainty about the authorship of most of the Latin writings which survive attached to his name. No such confidence is possible in the case of any English writing. So following Wyclif himself into the vernacular is not at all an easy matter.

Nevertheless, *Of mynistrys in the churche*,[88] someone's English version of Wyclif's 'On Matthew 24'[89] gives a picture of the way arguments could be presented to ordinary people in their own language in such a way as to give them a sense of being close to Scripture and learning directly from it.[90] The author wants the English speakers he is writing for to be conscious that what they hear read in church is not the whole text of this Gospel but only a passage from it. 'This Gospel (Matthew 24) tells much wisdom, that is hid to many men; and specially for this cause, that it is not all read in church.' He explains why he thinks it is profitable for people to have access to this in their own language, 'since it is of equal authority with other Gospels of Christ… some men would say it in their mother language as best they can'.[91] This is a particularly important text because it should be in everyone's mind that the end is nigh: 'It is said oftentimes before how Christ loveth to specify coming of the day of doom; but he tells of perils before.'[92] The 'not knowing when the end is to come' is profitable, just like 'knowing that there will be signs beforehand'.

Stories can be well told in any language and it was precisely the friars' discovery of how well they went down with an audience that had encouraged their drift into overuse of illustrative material, going well beyond the biblical. The English Wycliffite sermons resist that temptation in favour of story-building on Scripture. 'Christ says that then, the men who are in Judaea will flee to the hills,' etc.[93] 'These words of Christ are misty, but they are very good and full of wit and counsel to whoever can understand them.' The 'understanding' proposed is a figurative one. It is that 'these men who are in Judaea were priests (*prestus*) of Christ's Church, for Judaea is confession and these priests should principally confess Jesus Christ in word and in life. These priests should "flee to the hills" so as to find the example of holy priests of earlier times who lived poorly on alms, and especially the high hill that is Jesus Christ', for Jesus lived in poverty although on the highest 'hill'.[94] 'The second part of the Church is secular lords.' Their task is to defend the poor. 'The third part of the Church is said to be in the field, for labourers commonly make the third part of the Church.'[95]

The opportunity is taken to drop in one or two of the more easily grasped regular themes of anti-establishment thinking, for example to complain that false priests and pope 'believe in ceremonies as if they were the law of Christ',[96] and there is no hesitation in attacking the papacy. 'And we suppose that Antichrist… shall be Pope of Rome.' The Pope is linked with the 'new orders',[97] and both are 'called by Christ pseudo-prophets'. It is not difficult to demonstrate that the pope is Antichrist, if that is desired. 'It seems that this Pope is moste prowd in herte of alle men on earth, for wordly lordship and his pride go together.'[98] The Pope is anxious to be called by names which elevate his status but this is contrary to Christ's teaching that 'if he seek thus his own glory, his glory is nothing but falsehood and hypocrisy'. These outright criticisms of the highest in the Church ought to be very striking for this was lion-baiting by mice. It was courageous. It was also well-judged to ensure that the ideas lodged in people's minds as they heard them again and again.

Glossing the Bible for ordinary people, and vernacular Bible study

There is no doubt that Wyclif approved in principle of teaching and preaching in English. He speaks of the 'satraps and pharisees' who say that no one should preach or interpret in English in case English exegesis should win respect.[99] Approving is one thing, however, and doing is another. It is far from certain that Wyclif translated a single word of the Bible into English as a contribution to the endeavour which produced the first versions, and there is scant evidence in the authentic writings of the last years that he was thinking along these lines at all.[100]

John Purvey's real long-term importance may lie in the effort he put into the creation of an English translation of the Bible, though the links in the chain of evidence are frail. It is very late (1720) when it was suggested that Purvey was to be credited with much of the work on the English translation.[101] John Purvey seems to be the author of a vast commentary on the Apocalypse,[102] completed between 1385 and 1389, of which some copies mention his imprisonment in 1390, so he became an active practising exegete in his own right. It used to be thought that the General Prologue to the first English Bible[103] was at least partly his work; but it now seems beyond question that this, like the translation itself, was a team effort and that it involved the assembling and coordination of a great deal of scholarly labour, of a kind which required academic knowledge and recourse to reference books likely to be available only in Oxford or in the home libraries of religious houses. Whoever formed this editorial team, it was working over a longish period, between the death of Wyclif in 1384 and 1396, the date of the first surviving manuscript.[104]

The Prologue describes a series of stages involving 'much travail, with divers fellows and helpers,[105] to gather many old Bibles and other doctors and common glosses, and to make one Latin Bible some deal true; and then to study it anew, the text with the gloss and other doctors as he might get, and especially Lire on the Old Testament, that helped full much in this work; the third time to counsel with old grammarians and old divines of hard words and hard sentences, how they might be best understood and translated; the fourth time to translate as he could to the sentence, and to have many good fellows and cunning at the correcting of the translation.'[106] The *Prologue* to the Lollard Bible does indeed rely a good deal on the *Postill* of Nicholas of Lyre which gives the literal interpretation, and it associates him with Richard FitzRalph, although FitzRalph is admitted to make room for both literal and figurative interpretations, giving 'many goode groundis to vndirstonde holy scripture to the letter, and goostly vndirstonding also'.[107]

Indications of scholarly input are evident in the way this introduction chooses its themes. For example, there is a discussion of the important question of which books count as scriptural. 'Fyue and twenty bookis of the old testament ben bookis of feith, and fulli bookis of holy writ.' A list follows.[108] Then there is a classification of the books of the Bible by genre. 'The old testament is departed in to thre parties, in to moral comaundementis, iudicials, and cerimonyals.' The moral commandments 'bynden ever'. The 'judicials' (the Law of Moses) are no longer binding on Christian men, because when Christ was made man he 'ordeyned law of mercy and of charite'. Ceremonials ceased to be a matter of obligation when Christ died ('ceessiden outrily, as to obligacioun, in the tyme of Cristis deth'). They are positively harmful to those who continue to observe them, because they imply that Christ is not yet come and did not die for mankind and that is heresy.[109]

The Wycliffite translation was by any standards a success. More than 250 manuscripts survive, more than for any other medieval English text, and others were confiscated on episcopal orders.[110]

Translating was a topic in the air in Oxford in the last years of the fourteenth century and the beginning of the fifteenth, possibly because of the challenge the compiling of this English translation had presented. About 1401 or shortly after Richard Ullerston, William Butler and Thomas Palmer[111] all wrote on the subject, concentrating on translation into English from Latin, for translation from Greek and Hebrew was not then at issue, nor was the other burning sixteenth-century question, whether the Vulgate would still 'do' as a translation or was too full of inaccuracies and needed to be replaced.

There was an awareness that making a translation into English at all might be controversial. Ullerston in particular did not see this as necessarily a matter for polemic. There are pros and cons and he sets them out quite calmly. In the process he raises a number of the issues which were to become contentious in the next century or so, once the effect of the attempt to close down the whole discussion in Arundel's *Constitutions* of 1407 had faded. There is the danger of encouraging the uneducated (*rustici*) to teach things they do not understand.[112] Richard Ullerston thought it acceptable and right for each to teach or 'serve Christ' according to his capacity and his place in the scheme of things. A husband could teach his wife, a parent a child.[113] William Butler's treatise[114] takes this emphasis on preserving good order much further.

That worried the ecclesiastical authorities. 'Christ gave the Gospel to the clergy and the learned,' asserts Henry Knighton the chronicler. He complains that John Wyclif has made it available to lay people and those not strong enough to understand it, feeding them the Word on demand as the moment required.[115] This has cast pearls before swine; it has opened up the possibility of lay men and women[116] acquiring knowledge which they are not equipped to handle and turning the Bible into a joke.[117] These were not new arguments. This was all part of an ecclesiology which confined membership of the Church to the clergy. And there are numerous precedents from the earliest Christian times for the idea that only those fitted by intellect, education or piety should be allowed into the innermost secrets of the Christian religion.

Thomas Palmer, writing about 1407, includes reflections on the difficulty of achieving a translation which will give the literal sense, when *translatio* means both putting the Latin words into another language (the modern English meaning of 'translation'), and giving them in a 'transferred sense' in the original language, and thus perhaps in a figurative sense, which would be more naturally described in modern English as interpretation or paraphrase. The translator should be conscious that the meaning of the same Latin words may be different in different passages and he may not know what sense is right for a given context. Nor is it sufficient to concentrate on the literal sense, for even that depends on the context and the intention of the author and not everyone agrees what that is.[118]

Beyond the provision of a vernacular translation lay the whole business of Bible study for people who could now hear the text read to them in English and some of whom would be able to read it themselves. For an academic, Bible study meant formal 'glossing'. For house groups of ordinary people reading the Bible together, it might mean something quite different, for they would have neither the habits nor the resources of Latin academic biblical scholarship.

A fairly comprehensive set of glosses was provided to the Wycliffite Bible. This work was probably also carried by a collaborative effort and also in Oxford (with complaints that the friars kept many useful reference books shut away in their own libraries, although one example, the *Opus Arduum*, was written in prison, its author claims, so reference books cannot have been essential). This part of the 'project' did not result in a coordinated and finished 'gloss'. The glosses do not amount to an English *Glossa ordinaria*, for they are not standardized.[119] They derive mainly from Lyre and the Latin *Glossa ordinaria*.[120] The 'Englishing' did however include the provision of some study aids. The concordance which survives in British Library, MS Royal 17 Bi, is prefaced by the helpful explanation that, 'if a man have mynde oonly of oon word or two of sum long text of the newe law and hath forgetyn all the remnaunt, or ellis if he can seie bi herte such an hool text but he hath forgeten in what stede [place] it is written', the concordance will give him the rest of the passage or the location.[121]

In some collections of Wycliffite sermons there are indications that the compiler intended to provide other preachers with a study aid as well as actual texts for sermons. Advice on how to expand what is to be said on particular topics and where more material can be found is included, and also discussions on how to sway an audience and awaken it from torpor.[122]

There was the attraction of danger and excitement and sheer challenge too, for ordinary people drawn to sermons by the idea that they might attempt a little Bible study for themselves. They were also tempted to 'do Theology' independently. Knighton records congregations setting up a mocking chant of 'Trewe prechours, false prechours!'[123]

b. Latin or English for preaching to the people?

The best-tried method of interpreting the Bible for ordinary people was of course preaching, and preaching in English was one of the most controversial things the dissidents did. The twelfth-century Peter of Blois, excusing himself for ceasing to preach, includes as one of his reasons the difficulty of having to preach to the English when French is his native language. He describes how, when Joseph found himself in Egypt among people who did not speak his language, he sometimes used an interpreter (Genesis 42:23).[124] The question of a choice of language for preaching had not grown less pressing in the intervening centuries, even though the English vernacular was growing into a much better vehicle of sophisticated communication. Among the 'Lollard sermons' in English is preserved a scrap of Robert Grosseteste[125] which affords a glimpse of the method of explanation a preacher might use when he was preaching to an English-speaking congregation well before Wyclif's time, for Grosseteste was an author whose work he admired and could have chosen to imitate.[126] Galatians 5:24 was a particularly useful text for preachers because it allowed them to concentrate on a favourite theme for sermons, exhorting the congregation to the cultivation of the virtues and the defeat of the vices. The Latin of the Vulgate is read out. Then it is translated into English: 'They that are of Christ, of Christ's children, have crucified their flesh with vices and desires.' There follows an explanation of the key terms. 'The flesh here may be understood [to be] the bodily substance of a man, with the deeds of his members. Vices are evil customs, with their deeds. Desires are lusts, which move people against reason.' Then the implications are spelt out. 'These three it behoves, according to the apostle, to fasten to the Cross, for those who are Christ's array for themselves first a Cross in their minds... On this Cross of love, the flesh is crucified' when the flesh, vices and desires are crucified. This is figurative interpretation, but it is also moralizing and practical and easy for the ordinary Christian to grasp.

Wyclif had some comments to make on the subject of the appropriate language for preaching in a treatise probably written about the time he was collecting together his sermons. In 'A Mirror for Secular Lords', the *Speculum secularium dominorum*, he says even-handedly that there is a place for Latin and a place for the vernacular and things can often be said in either language. Secular lords, the subject of his treatise, need to have the faith taught to them in their own language because they are expected, just as much as clerics, to obey the law of Christ in all things. Those heretics should not be listened to who say that lay people have no obligation to know the law of God, but that it is sufficient for them to be aware of the things priests and prelates tell them. The rule should be to teach in whatever language the listener or reader understands best. Christ and his disciples used the language their listeners knew most familiarly.[127]

A surviving collection of sermons from the early fifteenth century, with a Benedictine origin, conveys in a lively way the relative simplicity of the style in which, and the level at which, inherently complex issues could be addressed in sermons, even sermons addressed to the clergy. There could be some games-playing here. The preacher breaks into English every few words, as if embarrassed to 'find the words' in Latin. Preaching about the ship of state, he cites the now lost *De institutione ad Trajanum*, a pseudo-classical work which is 'cited' by John of Salisbury (but is almost certainly an invention of his own). The well-conducted ship of state must have three parts, merchants, craftsmen and labourers. The preacher goes on to set out the various parts of this ship and their relation to one another. It used to be a strong and beautiful ship. The forecastle was the clergy, and its covering was perfection and holiness. Aft was the baronial class, notable for their strength and hardihood. The bowels of the ship, the community, was laden with a great cargo of riches. And so the fable unfolds and the congregation is invited to compare this desirable state of things with the condition of the ship now.

> 'Tho topcastel huius navis sunt sancti quiescentes in hoc regno quorum almis neuritis et precibus sepius salvamur a periculis et habemus victoriam de inimicis. Ista fuit olim pulcra navis et fortis. Antecastellum clerus was

> pavysid wt perfeccion et helines.[128] In the hyndcastel the baronie was pigt a stondard of bodile mygt and hardiness. Corpus navis, communitas, was ful frawt magna copia diviciarum. Quando nostra navis was ful taclid, the thre castelles full apparailid wt stremores and pavys, hit was a faire vessel to loke opoun.'[129]

What can be credited to Wyclif? The corpus of 294 sermons now known as the 'English Wycliffite sermons'[130] remain puzzling, for they were clearly put together as a collection and that involved some organization and collaboration, and yet their authorship remains unclear.[131] The English Wycliffite sermons are not Wyclif's own sermons, though they show some resemblance to his general lines of thought.[132] Even where a direct comparison can be drawn between one of Wyclif's Latin sermons and an 'English Wycliffite sermon' on the same Gospel or epistle, it is far from clear that the English preacher relied on Wyclif's Latin model. A sermon on 2 Corinthians 11:19 (*Libenter suffertis insipientes*) for Sexagesima Sunday contains extra material in the English version to add to some common exegetical ground of a fairly routine kind.[133] Another, for Septuagesima, on 2 Corinthians 9:24 (*Nescitis quo ii qui in stadio*) bears no relation at all to Wyclif's surviving sermon on the same text.[134]

The English Wycliffite sermons themselves convey the tone and expectations of a simplified teaching in English, which was evidently effective in pleasing an audience. 'This Gospel tells how our love should be stretched out to all men, both to friends and enemies, for all men are our neighbours. And thus says Christ through Matthew, "You have heard that it was said to men of former times (to olde men), you shall love your friend and you shall hate your enemy. But certainly I say to you, love your enemies, do good to them that hate you, and pray for those who pursue you and challenge you falsely". And this thing should you do, "to be sons of your Father which is in heaven".'[135] It was felt appropriate to drop in round criticism of the friars, as Wyclif himself would not have hesitated to do. 'And here teach these new Orders a new cast of the Devil, that English men must fight first with enemies of other lands, for else they would first fight with us.'[136]

Wyclif was an experienced public speaker but mainly in the University. There is no evidence that he considered that his more political or polemical remarks, or even his more academically technical ones, were unsuitable for use with a popular audience. There seems to have been no absolute separation between the two, for vernacular sermons were designed on the same system as those in Latin. In 1363 the General Chapter of the English Benedictines stipulated that, when their monks were sent to Oxford to learn to preach, they should be required to master preaching in Latin as well as in the vernacular.[137]

Undoubtedly some of those we now have in Latin were originally given in English. Medieval sermons given in the vernacular were sometimes preserved only in Latin.

There is also the question of the limitations of English as a vehicle for the greater obscurities of the Latin academic debates. Wyclif comments that, since the same thought can be expressed in different languages (*cum racio sit ante linguam*),[138] the choice of language ought not to affect the communication of the point. But of course it does.

c. *Wyclif the popular preacher?*

If Wyclif was not, as far as can be seen, personally involved in the vernacular Bible project, or the author of any surviving English sermons, this does not mean that he was not a keen preacher to the populace, at least in theory. But here, too, it is hard to be quite clear about his attitudes and achievements. The preaching of sermons, on the evidence of surviving examples, could spill over into mention of topics of current concern and where they were given in Latin to an academic Congregation there would even be room for mischievous asides criticising other academics and challenging their opinions. We have already glanced at examples of the level of technical abstruseness he allowed himself in a sermon. The 'Forty Sermons' (*Sermones quadraginta*) of 1357–59 show that Wyclif went on preaching actively in Oxford after his formal obligation to preach as part of the requirements for his degree had been discharged. The phrase *fraternitas vestra*[139] is likely to suggest that his congregations were from the University or at least clerical, and only in the University would a Congregation of clerics be likely. Much of Wyclif's teaching and writing from this point was of this kind.

Nevertheless, Wyclif was evidently known as a preacher outside Oxford.[140] There were practical differences in urban and rural preaching, in the scale of the influence and the numbers who were likely to be able to hear a given sermon and the speed with which the rumour of the exciting things which had been said could spread. Wyclif complains in the *Trialogus* of the 'poor priests' being chased in the dioceses of London and Lincoln.[141] 'It was Christ's wish,' says Wyclif, that when his disciples were fully instructed, they should not shut themselves up in buildings but go out into the wide world and preach the Gospel for the good of the Church.[142] Knighton's *Chronicon* implies that Wyclif, as early as 1378, had the support of Londoners (*favore et diligentia Londoniensium*), and that he spread his teachings in the metropolis (*spreto suo metropolitano praecepto*).[143]

But there were deeper questions to be asked than whether Wyclif's idea of a 'popular' sermon was distinct from his idea of an academic one, and whether he actually got much practice outside Oxford and his own parish. There are questions about his methods and his effectiveness in communicating with his listeners, for these were active concerns of other preachers. At the end of the twelfth century, in one of the first of the new manuals on how to preach a sermon, Alan of Lille explains how important it is for a preacher to watch his audience and gauge reaction to what he is saying. 'Nothing dries up faster than a tear,' he comments, counselling the preacher to stop as soon as he observes that he has moved his listeners to weeping.[144] When Alexander Neckham or Nequam preached in Oxford in the late twelfth century, he too considered his audience. People do not like to be made to feel uncomfortable. They say, in effect, 'Do not put before us gloomy things from sacred history but give us something sweet.'[145] He preached to clergy assembled in synod and to monks in monasteries and to the townspeople of Oxford, who he reminds (in Latin, or at any rate the sermon is preserved in Latin) of their good fortune in having an academic community in their midst to teach them about Scripture and the Christian faith (*viros litteratissimos qui vos diligenter informarent*). The people of Oxford cannot pretend to say that they are like the children who asked for bread and no one broke it and gave it to them (Lamentations 4:4). There are many who break this bread and give it to the people of Oxford.[146]

Compare a sermon of Wyclif's, a Palm Sunday sermon, possibly given in 1378. 'The idiot ought to learn the rules which govern contradiction.' 'He should not be declaring his ignorance in the schools.' 'And… he calls to witness the whole school of children and women and their like, who do not know how to avoid the most elementary contradiction.'[147] And 'there is now no lay person with a knowledge of languages' but wastes his time with scholastic exercises. 'This offender has introduced the art of lying into virtuous Oxford.'[148] Whether this was a sermon given in the University or not, it cannot be said to have at its heart the concerns Neckham expresses. Wyclif treats the sermon as a platform for polemic. He berates his audience. He speaks offensively of those who are not professional academics to an audience of just such persons.

It may well be that in his day congregations who flocked to hear sermons because they were dangerous and exciting looked for this kind of thing and found it thrilling rather than insulting. Nevertheless, he promised something quite different in his last years, when he put together the collection of sermons of which this forms part.

One set of sermons stands a little apart. The 'Forty Sermons', which survive largely unrevised in the Latin – though they may well have been preached in

English[149] – were given on a number of datable occasions, largely between February 1376 and September 1379.[150] It is often not at all easy to guess the date of delivery of individual examples or how much change Wyclif made in the course of his revising, although it is striking that he allowed to stand many passages which now appear angry digressions.

When Wyclif drew his own sermons together[151] he may have been fully aware that he had made what would turn out to be his last retreat to parish life after Oxford's final condemnation. He was taking stock of the motivation and methodology of his preaching through a lifetime. In his preface, he says that he has assembled his sermons 'so that the thoughts of God should be clearer and his useless servant [Wyclif] more readily excused'. 'Because I am at leisure from scholarly pursuits and for the building-up of the Church at the end of my life, it seems to me good to collect my simple sermons for the people.'[152] Preaching of the Word is the Church's best nourishment, he says in his 'Mirror for Secular Lords', probably of 1380 or 1381.[153] But that is not the impression the reader of the sermons is left with. They evince, as might be expected, different preoccupations – on the one hand, those of his University life and times of controversy, on the other, those of the village priest with a simple pastoral duty towards the people in his cure, but often jumbled together in ways which must have been extremely confusing to his listeners, if he really delivered the sermons in the form in which they survive.

'No one ought to presume in this life that he is saved.'[154] This takes the listener, whether he knows it or not, and Wyclif certainly knew it, into the heart of a debate which had been heated since the days of Augustine of Hippo. But it is also a simple idea which the ordinary faithful could understand and were bound to be interested in. He allows himself an aside, the point of which only those with an Arts degree (who had studied conditional futurity) would see. 'It should be noted that it is appropriate for this to be put in different ways because of the range of opinions among the faithful about future necessity.'[155] He refers the interested inquirer to his *Trialogus*.[156] There the reader again discovers that he has to master technicalities. In this book for the general reader Wyclif discusses the distinction between God's predestination of his chosen ones to heaven and his mere 'foreknowledge' that those he did not 'choose' would go to hell.[157]

Whether or not Wyclif had the common touch, whether he genuinely cared to ensure that his sermons were effective for the spiritual edification of ordinary people, is important if it is seriously to be maintained that he set in train a great popular movement. The truth seems to be that others, before and after Wyclif as among his contemporaries, were better equipped to put the essence of the ideas involved simply and in a way ordinary people could understand.

It was justly said by one of the chroniclers that Wyclif made no allowances for the less sophisticated understanding of the laity when he preached to them. 'He did not mix in asides to make things easier for their ears but taught them plainly and nakedly.'[158] The division between academic and popular writing[159] is obvious to modern readers, but it was a conception still forming in Wyclif's day and, even when he says he consciously set out to make it, there is no evidence that he got very far. But it is fairly clear why the laity, nobles as well as commoners, flocked to hear more. 'They freely listened,' says the *Chronicon*, 'to these *perversa*, especially what concerned the Church and ecclesiastical persons.'[160] The principal attraction may indeed have been the delicious thrill of hearing great institutions and important persons publicly criticized.

d. The minds of the laity and the popular campaign

Can we get inside the minds of the laity who were being reached by all these efforts of Wyclif and the Lollards? John of Northampton, Mayor of London in 1381,[161] was rumoured to be sympathetic to ideas with a Wycliffite colour. Walsingham the chronicler says he was inspired by Wyclif and followed him in actions 'in censure of the prelates',[162] and there is evidence that he tried to carry out a purge of immoral behaviour in London.[163] This does not mean that he controlled opinion in the city. We noted the barefoot procession which went through London on 30 May 1382 to 'publish' the findings of the 1381 Blackfriars Council and John Cunningham, Wyclif's old academic adversary, preached a sermon. Knighton, reporting this, records the presence at the sermon of 'a venerable knight' called Cornelius Cloyne, one of the gentry on a visit to London. This knight had had strong Wycliffite sympathies. He thought bread was bread. But, when he went to Mass on 31 May and saw the consecrated host broken, he believed he saw the name of Christ written upon it in letters of blood and raw flesh. The conversion he experienced was evidently reported to the friar who was celebrating the Mass and the next day the friar preached a sermon in which he told the story and 'at the end of the sermon the same knight, who was present, told in his own words (*narravit oratenus*) what he had seen, publicly and openly for the strengthening of our faith'. He promised to fight to the death if necessary in defence of the doctrine of transubstantiation.[164] There is a glimpse here of the fluidity of popular opinion and the use by each 'side' of the theatrical opportunities provided by processions and celebrations, as well as by sermons, to work upon it. Individuals would have their own half-formed ideas about complex theological matters and those could often be changed quite easily by a vivid illustration or an argument, and perhaps changed back again equally readily. It is not recorded whether Cornelius Cloyne had second thoughts when he next went to hear a sermon preached by a 'Wycliffite' sympathizer. The ebb and flow of mass opinion was made up of such individual views excited by the behaviour patterns of crowd psychology.

Two 'confessions' in English on the Eucharist were copied into his Chronicle by Henry Knighton, the second of them embracing a form of 'consubstantiation', in which it is argued that, just as it is heresy to believe that Christ was a spirit without a body, so it is heresy to believe that the consecrated host in the Eucharistic sacrament is God's body and not also bread. The first confession, he indicates, was made before the Blackfriars Council convened by the Archbishop Courtenay in 1382 and the second confession was made before the Dons of Oxford in the same year.[165]

Whether or not these come from Wyclif's pen (and it is improbable), they constitute an attempt to put into English and into forms which might strike echoes in the thoughts of an ordinary English listener, the abstruse matters with which Wyclif had been engaged and which were bringing official condemnation irrevocably down on his head in that year.[166] When the priest has said, 'This is my body,' the faithful will not see the consecrated bread actually looking like a body 'in mannes figure', the figure of a man. But the believer should be able to do as a believer is encouraged to do with any image, and that is to 'set his thought on him whose image it is' and devoutly worship not the thing he sees but that of which it is an image. There is also an early hint of the Reformation doctrine of 'worthy receiving', the belief that the participation of the faithful has a part to play in what 'happens' in the Mass, for Knighton says that the worshipful receiver 'receives God spiritually more medefully than the priest who sings the mass in lesser charity'. Wyclif himself thought that 'worthy receiving' was important.[167] These examples are helpful as hints of the way in which theologically technical and difficult ideas could be simplified for ordinary people.[168] But they are also reminders how difficult it was. Some theological topics would always lie beyond the technical competence of ordinary believers.

Satire and social comment

'I smell a loller in the wind,' quod he.
'How! Good men,' quod our hoste, 'herkneth me;'
Abydeth, for goddess digne passioun,
For we shal han a predicacioun;

> *This loller heer wil prechen us som-what.'*
> *'Nay, by my fader soule! That shal be nat,'*
> *Seyde the Shipman; 'heer he shal nat preche,*
> *He shal no gospel glosen heer ne teche.*
> *We leve alle in the grete god,' quod he,*
> *'He wolde sowen som difficultee,*
> *Or springen cokkel in our clen corn;*
> *And therfor, hoste, I warn thee biforn,*
> *My joly body shal a tale telle...*
> *But it shal nat ben of philosophye,*
> *No physices, no termes queinte of lawe;*
> *Ther is but litel Latin in my mawe.'*[169]

Chaucer could make jokes like this, confident that they would be appreciated by his vernacular readership, among whom were sophisticates who could appreciate a theological reference. Chaucer's (and Wyclif's) contemporary William Langland also had some sneaking sympathy with Wyclif and the Lollards.[170] Langland's *Piers Plowman* ends with a beginning. Conscience decides to begin on a pilgrimage and walk through the world.[171] That was what the Lollards saw themselves as doing, and the satirists watched them with a crisp sense of the challenge they presented to respectable expectations. This was a world in which political and social satire could help to spin the plot.[172]

A rumoured threat to good order may become a self-fulfilling prophecy. Wyclif had been so insistent for so long and so loudly that it was legitimate for the state authorities of England to involve themselves in certain aspects of ecclesiastical affairs[173] that his ideas were almost bound to become associated in the minds of the authorities, ecclesiastical and lay, with the danger of destabilizing society. Equally predictably, he was taken to be encouraging those popular preachers who were, quite independently of him, inciting ordinary people to rise up against various perceived abuses.[174] Thomas Brinton, who has already appeared several times in these pages, was among those who thought Wyclif and the popular preachers posed no uncommon threat to the stability of the realm. Sermons of Thomas Brinton link England's bad fortune in battle, crop failures, pestilence and general decay of conduct in public life with her departure from the straight and narrow way of true belief.

The themes Wyclif had developed, from the period when the Government brought him in as an adviser on the payment of papal taxation were as much political as theological. King Henry IV[175] expressed concern over the political dangers of allowing unregulated preaching.[176] Yet in 1399 there were moves towards a disendowment scheme in the Commons; for, if indeed the state could take the temporal possessions of the clergy, a hard-up Government might find itself in profit. The truth was that Lollard teachings had an appeal to perfectly respectable circles in Government. Parliaments could be anticlerical. Ullerston set out to provide a sensible assessment of the issues in his 'Proposals' for Church reform.[177] Wyclif could have been a hero to the Establishment in his own time.

Recent theories have allowed Wyclif a role as a conscious instigator of reform but suggested that he tried to stir up the gentry rather than the common people to lead the changes he wanted to see. There was a middle category, the articulate bourgeoisie. Clerks and clerics still had a monopoly of the 'learned professions' and a near-monopoly of literacy, although that was breaking down in Wyclif's day with the advent of a literate middle class, Chaucer's audience among them.[178] It is possible to assemble a convincing enough list of the 'long-established, trusted and experienced royal servants, who were influential members of the royal household administration, men at the very centre of government', who were not ill-disposed to Wyclif or to Lollard ideas.[179] The Blackfriars accusation that the troublemakers were to be found among the magnates as well as among ordinary people, is plausible.[180] But the drive, the hunger for reform, was not likely to be deriving its energy from a quarter where a cooler self-interest was involved. For the secular government and its scions chiefly wanted to rebalance the powers of Church and state in favour of the secular arm.

Conclusion:

The legend and the reality

No work in English which can be attributed with certainty to Wyclif survives; nor is there any evidence that he actively got the work of translating the Bible into English under way or was even directly involved in it. Not a single 'great book', or any book of lasting importance, bears his name. We can point to no quotation so memorable that it echoes down the years. He was not the only one among his contemporaries putting forward the particular arguments which came to be associated with his name and the only 'English freedom' he certainly fought for was the refusal to pay taxation decades overdue to the papacy from the kingdom of England; even there he was acting as one of a diplomatic mission and not as a solitary hero. It is not at all easy to say in the end what Wyclif's achievement was.

It is much easier to say what Wyclif's *reputation* became. 'The English [works of Wyclif] are precious for the history of our language, interesting as the first appeal of the Reformation to the people of England, and not without intrinsic value.'[1] When the historian Walter W. Shirley wrote thus in 1865, in the preliminaries to his attempt to catalogue Wyclif's writings, it was not yet accepted that no such works are known to survive, though he admits that 'they are mentioned in no catalogue earlier than Bale' – in the sixteenth century – and that they 'never… refer themselves to other works of their author'.[2]

Rudolf Buddensieg, a Dresden schoolmaster, spent his holidays for twenty years in editing Wyclif's polemical works so that the English-speaking world should be able to read them in their original Latin. It was Buddensieg who explored the repositories in 'Upper-Lusatia, Bohemia, Moravia and Lower-Austria' and discovered the whereabouts of many of the manuscripts now known of Wyclif's writings, including a set carried off to Sweden by the Moravians during the seventeenth century.[3] Buddensieg describes the foundation of the Wyclif Society by the energetic F.J. Furnivall and his helpers in March 1882. Their adoption of a scheme of publishing Wyclif's writings, adumbrated earlier in the century on the occasion of W.W. Shirley's earlier attempt to list the extant writings of Wyclif in preparation for a scheme for the Oxford University Press to publish a selection from his works, was a great relief to him,[4] for he says that he could not persuade the delegates of the Oxford University Press to undertake the project. He had captured the interest of the English enthusiasts by writing a letter to the magazine *Academy* in September 1881.[5]

The notions of national 'identity' which inspired Wyclif's nineteenth-century German editor belong to another age. For Buddensieg, John Wyclif is 'the great reformer, in whom the characteristics of the Christian and the Englishman meet and combine in almost equal fulness, as they do in Luther Christianity and Germanity'.[6] All this reflects a nineteenth-century pattern of scholarly enthusiasms, which had their value; without them we should not have the long series of editions of texts and publications of learned societies on which much modern scholarship still depends. Within a few years, Buddensieg published his *John Wiclif, Patriot and Reformer* (London, 1884), enlarging upon his theme. 'England owes to him her Bible, her present language, the reformation of the Church, her religious, and to a very large degree, her political liberty,'[7] and he finds it 'painful' that 'his most important works should have been until now allowed to lie buried in manuscript'[8] without its apparently occurring to him that the lack of early printed editions might be an indication of the uncertainty of their actual importance.

The legend Buddensieg unquestioningly trusted was largely manufactured in the sixteenth century, although John Hus and others at Prague and Constance had given it a push in the early fifiteenth century. The Hus correspondence preserves the opinion that 'since the birth of Christ no heretic, except Wyclif, has written more dangerously against the Church' than Hus,[9] which gives Wyclif a certain prominence. Hus busied himself with the 45 articles of Wyclif which were under consideration by the Council.[10]

With a sharp and often bitter pen, the edgy John Bale (1495–1563), a convert to Reformation ideas and full of the zeal of the convert, compiled a mordant account of the 'Wycliffite Martyrs', *A Brief Chronicle concerning the Examination and Death of Sir John Oldcastle* (London, 1544), and a list of English writers. It is he who famously calls Wyclif *stella matutina*, 'Morning Star of the Reformation'. The Protestant apologist John Foxe (1516–87) put Wyclif first in his own list of 'martyrs' in his first Latin version of 1554 (despite the fact that Wyclif was never actually martyred), claiming for him the distinction of being the author in whose time the persecution of the witnesses to the truth first began.[11] In the English version of the *Acts and Monuments* of 1563 Foxe draws on John Bale in his 'Morning Star' passage.[12]

Foxe had a wide influence. The *Book of Martyrs* was approved by the English bishops and went through four editions before Foxe's death. It led future generations to polarize the events and the context of Wyclif's story into a tale of good and bad, white and black, and to credit him personally with much that, as we have seen, was going on among his contemporaries in any case: 'There were not a few by whom it pleased the Lord to work against the bishop of Rome, and to weaken the pernicious superstition of the friars; but our countryman was specially raised up to detect more fully and amply the poison of the Pope's doctrine, and the false religion set up by the friars.'[13] And: 'After he had a long time professed divinity in the University of Oxford, and perceiving the true doctrine of Christ's Gospel to be defiled with the inventions of bishops, orders of monks, and dark errors, and after long deliberating with himself, with many secret signs, and bewailing the general ignorance of the world, could no longer bear it, he at last determined to remedy such things as he saw to be out of the way.'[14]

The problems Wyclif sought to check, Foxe suggests, stemmed from a neglect of those fundamental topics of Christian theology in which the theologians of his own day were particularly interested: 'As to faith, – consolation, – the end and use of law, – the office of Christ – our impotency and weakness, – the Holy Ghost, – the greatness and strength of sin, – true works, – grace, and free justification by faith, – the liberty of a Christian man; of all these things wherein consists the sum of our professions, there was no mention, and scarcely a word spoken.'[15] Yet these are the priorities of the Reformation of the sixteenth century, and several of them were not really Wyclif's own preoccupations at all.

One of the most difficult tasks is to trace the unfolding in Wyclif's own mind of those notions which truly led onward towards the Reformation and those which look backwards rather, into the long-running battle of the earlier Middle Ages between the interests of the ecclesiastical authorities and those of the articulate ordinary Christian with a grievance about the way the institutional Church is behaving. Foxe puts into Wyclif's mind a degree of foresight and planning he did not really demonstrate. He gives him a purposeful campaign, although we have seen that he tended to react to events, often with bewilderment: 'From these beginnings the way was opened to greater matters, so that at length he came to touch the matters of the sacraments, and other abuses of the church. Touching these things this holy man took great pains, protesting openly in the schools, that it was his chief and principal purpose to call back the church from her idolatry to some better amendment, especially in the matter of the sacrament of the body and blood of Christ.'[16]

Wyclif and the international scene

It is sometimes suggested that the popular heresies of mainland Europe had left England largely untouched in the earlier Middle Ages. There had been no visible 'Waldensian' movement in England. If that is correct, it is necessary to try to explain why the movement linked with Wyclif's name took off in England as it did, and when it did, and proved to be England's first serious encounter with a popular anti-establishment heretical movement.[17] It is more probable, however, that there was already fertile ground, dark mutterings of popular resentment of clerical excesses, in England as everywhere else. Chaucer's humour is pitched to a well-filled gallery. It would take little orchestration to wake the mutterings to a shout. Wyclif's growing notoriety made his name useful to the ringleaders of discontent and it is not hard to envisage him being dragged into their 'camp' by association, whether he chose to be or not.

It is also sometimes suggested that there was an unusual combination of the 'academic' and the popular elements in the Wycliffite phenomenon. Throughout the history of heresy up to this point, there had been a tendency for the Church's apologists to tell the tale, a near-monopoly of academic commentators giving an account of the opinions they disapproved of. This enabled those arguing against a school of thought on behalf of the Church to define them as opponents of the truth, classify them with earlier rebels, and accuse them of putting stumbling blocks before the faithful. The 'wrong opinions' are stated in the categories and terms of the orthodoxy from which they are alleged to depart. Wyclif had been more capable than the leaders of popular anti-establishment heresy in the twelfth century of putting his views into the public domain in his own words, and complaining if he was misrepresented in the ensuing official condemnations. He was one of the most highly educated of dissidents. 'I did not say that!' 'I did not mean that!' we hear him cry. But as we have seen, that did not necessarily make him more inclined or better able to bridge the gulf of technical difficulty which lay between the professional theologian and the popular asker of simple but awkward questions.

The academic world has always been international, and in the Middle Ages it was partly co-terminous with the equally international ecclesiastical world. We saw in the Roman machinations of Adam Easton that it was easy for an academic or ecclesiastical politician to make trouble for someone in a far country. 'The whole body of monks and begging friars were set into a rage and madness, and, even as hornets with their sharp stings, assailed him on every side,'[18] says Foxe, and that is true to the extent that the friars could easily make sure that Wyclif's reputation was damaged throughout Europe. They had heard so much about Wyclif in Prague,[19] that the Council of Constance in 1415 commented particularly on the efforts of the academy there to suppress this line of teaching. The assiduousness with which academic interest in Prague had set about acquiring copies of Wyclif's works is well-attested, and without it we should be very short of copies of his writings, and some would have been lost. The interest it all aroused in England is easily explained within this international dimension.

Wyclif is unusual among the notable of medieval academe in spending almost all his working life in England and never lecturing in Paris or elsewhere in Europe, or even travelling there except for his one brief period with the diplomatic emissaries to Bruges. Wyclif's personal appearances in actual disputations and debates were unusually confined to a narrow Oxford circle. These were wrestling matches in which the participants tumbled out of the ring and went on fighting by way of their writings and their reputations before the European 'audience' of talent-spotters and fellow-debaters. Wyclif as a professional scholar knew very well how it was all supposed to work, and one of the puzzles the evidence does not allow us finally to resolve is why he could not *make* it work; become one of the travelling circus of international debaters; get his chances in the entourage of one of the prelates on missions; win patronage in ecclesiastical high places; and make his mark as an international figure to be reckoned with.

The strength of a 'movement' originating in the teaching and writing of an academic of international reputation would most naturally lie in the written word. Henry Knighton comments that the talk of Lollards had a family resemblance. It was as though they had all been to the same school and been taught by the same schoolmaster.[20] There seems to be no evidence that the writings Wyclif was so anxiously revising at Lutterworth ever formed a corpus to which Lollards would turn in future for reference. This is not entirely to be explained by the burning of the books in Oxford in 1410. Wyclif seems to have been read in Bohemia more than in England in the early fifteenth century. Several letters in John Hus's correspondence speak with regret of the burning.[21] In a letter to Peter of Mladoňovice on 29 June 1415, facing his own condemnation, Hus says, 'Choose from the few of Wyclif's works whatever pleases you.'[22]

The lack of a real personal intellectual legacy for Wyclif may be connected with this failure to work the system to his advantage as the ambitious academic he undoubtedly was in his early years. Wyclif emerges from his life-story as a dissenter despite himself,[23] rather than as a man of vision, truly a star lighting the way for others. Augustine of Hippo left his name upon a legion of medieval writings which were not his own. A good many (now anonymous) authors of later ages wanted to claim his authorship for work which they wanted to be taken seriously, so manuscripts containing all sorts of writings contain surprising attributions.[24] There is no real equivalent for Wyclif, although some works which are probably not authentic Wyclif appear in the collections which contain his own undubitable work, and with titles enticingly resonant with his preoccupations.[25]

Those of Wyclif's ideas which had chimed with the thinking of ordinary people who were 'angry with the system' were not new. They simply joined a river of similar ideas which was already flowing strongly, and had been doing so in Europe for at least two centuries. There is no evidence that it was Wyclif who stimulated Englishmen's enthusiasm for them; it seems that popular preachers were already disseminating them in the years when he was becoming infamous and the object of disapproving notice by the authorities. In other words, his name was linked with something which was already happening.

If he did not really 'start anything', did he crystallize anything, give it definitive statement? Again it is hard to show that he did, because of the lack of important books and even any significant remarks to be quoted in a conclusion such as this. In the international world of exchange of academic ideas he was apparently merely a contributor to scholarly debate who got entangled in some heated ecclesiastical politics, and that is how we should rate him if he had not notoriously been condemned and if Foxe and Bale had not set about making him a hero.

The greatest lack, for the biographer who would rebuild Wyclif's reputation in terms which reflect the surviving evidence, remains the absence of a legacy of important and influential writings. There were copies of Easton's work in monastic libraries – but not of Wyclif's. Netter's *Doctrinale* became an early printed book,[26] but almost nothing of Wyclif's was rushed into print in the sixteenth century. Wyclif's *Trialogus*, at best a late minor work in which he tried to present some of his ideas in a popular form, was published at Worms in 1525, 'now that the sun is shining again, driving back the darkness and thickest mists inimical to light',[27] as its additional prologue says. But there was no attempt to publish the rest of his *oeuvre* in the sixteenth century, even though this was an age in which the important books of antiquity and the Middle Ages were coming off the new presses of Europe in a torrent. John Bale made a list of titles of Wyclif's works which he had found in manuscript,[28] but even with this as a starting point the trail of the early printed material in

England is thin. Item after item in Thomson's modern review has only the Wyclif Society editions of the nineteenth and early twentieth century.[29] *Wycliffes Wicket* (London, 1546), and again (London 1548), expounded by W. Tyndall and I. Frythe, was a snippet of Wyclif's arguments on the Eucharist. J. Wycliffe, *The Dore of Holy Scripture* appeared in London in 1540. *The true copye of a prolog written about two c yeres paste by Iohn Wycliffe* (London, 1550) prints the Prologue to the Wycliffite Bible, which was not Wyclif's work at all, 'the originall whereof is founde written in an olde English Bible betwixt the olde Testament and the Newe', which we are assured is attributed to him. 'He did florish in Oxford longe while,' explains the publishe, adding that he was protected under Edward III but not under Richard II. Verses follow, faithfully depicting the mythical reformer.

'Yet dyd thys good man never alter his stile
But wrote mani volumes whils he was alive
To extinguish errour, and truth to revive.'

Oxford's equivocal verdict

All this requires us to ask why Wyclif's name suggested itself so forcefully to the story-makers who elevated him to Morning Star status. Part of the answer lies in the way the academic world worked. The durability of the trouble which surrounded him is quite exceptional, for the small, fierce scandals which eddied about the figures of the more exciting academics of the Middle Ages usually died away quite quickly, rather as did the cult of the more ordinary saints.[30] The question is why an academic no more outrageous and opinionated and daring than others, whom the Church sought to put in their place from time to time in the Middle Ages, should have had so large an apparent impact; the answers take us beyond his actual personal achievement and require consideration of factors which were not under Wyclif's control. For, as it was pointed out in the correspondence of John Hus, a writer does not become a heretic merely because he has 'written heresy in his books'. Augustine did that, and many others, including Peter Lombard in his *Sentences* and Thomas Aquinas. 'For in their pronouncements they scholastically posited heresies.'[31] Even Arundel accepted that unorthodox opinions have to be discussed in order to be refuted.

What eventually became the Hussite movement also had its lively stimulus in an academic context as the notorious ideas of Wyclif circulated in the University of Prague at the instigation of those who had picked them up from

Oxford and brought them home.[32] Similarly, Wyclif's reputation had become a thing to be conjured with by his own University of Oxford. On 5 October 1406 a letter was issued with the seal of Congregation. It praised Wyclif as without an equal in the University in Logic, Philosophy, Morals, and Speculation. The letter, in an exercise of spin of which a modern university Press Office might be proud, claimed Wyclif had never been convicted of heresy.[33]

And the topics which engaged Wyclif did not go away. Richard Ullerston's writings indicate the steadiness of the continuing interest in Oxford in the themes Wyclif had helped to bring to prominence. He gave a course of lectures at Queen's College in 1404 in which, he says, he touched on the subject of the duty of an able-bodied member of a religious order to do honest manual work.[34] He wrote a 'Defence of ecclesiastical endowments' (*Defensorium Dotacionis Ecclesie*), which emerged after the condemnation of William Sawtry and of which he sent a presentation copy to the Archbishop of Canterbury.[35]

Did Wyclif start a movement?

Some of the chroniclers, anxious to make the story gripping, depict an expanding movement winning converts, producing publications and appealing to all classes. Knighton's image is of a 'growing population of believers in that doctrine' which multiplied like sprouting seeds.[36] The *Eulogium* gives a similar picture of a group spreading rapidly on the basis of great popular appeal. 'The disciples (*discipuli*) of this John [Wyclif] gave their energies to learning how to preach. They went throughout England preaching the teaching of this master of theirs, and they corrupted the [people's] faith in the sacrament of the Eucharist and devotion to the Church and religion, not only that of ordinary people and the laity but also the nobility and the learned... They also wrote famous books in English against the friars and they wrote down their errors in English.'[37] The *Fasciculi Zizaniorum* speaks of 'adherents'.[38] Thomas Netter has Wyclif as a 'preceptor' of the Lollards.[39]

Wyclif had of course *discipuli* in the sense of 'pupils' during his teaching years, but none of them can now be identified as having formed a loyal attachment to him as a scholar or as a leader of reform. It is not apparent that he had 'disciples' in this other sense. In the absence of any close-up of Wyclif's relationship with John Purvey – if Purvey was indeed his table companion at Lutterworth – or any way of knowing whether others came to see him in exile at Lutterworth, it is impossible to reconstruct a picture of possible conversations in which a sick and depressed Wyclif may have encouraged these younger followers to do what he himself could no longer do but still wished to see in train. The reality for Wyclif at the end may have been a very lonely life, not the energetic organizing hinted at by some commentators.

Some of the sources speak of these so-called 'followers' forming a movement, a *secta Wyclyf* or something like it. One of the most influential describes Wyclif as a Master in Oxford 'holding publicly in his determinations and disputations erroneous and heretical conclusions' to the detriment of the University's reputation.[40] There hung about with him, the story continues, some pupils of his wickedness, also living in Oxford, who wore long russet robes and went about spreading these errors among the people and preaching them publicly in sermons.[41] John Ball under examination affirmed that he was of the *doctrina* as well as of the *secta* of Wyclif and that he had joined in a Wycliffite conspiracy with others of like mind (*qui conspiraverant quondam confoederationem*). Wyclif admits that he is aware that there are many 'heretics' in his own 'private sect', but only with heavy irony.[42] *Secta* was for Wyclif, a term of abuse designed to cause the maximum offence among those who themselves used *secta* as a term of opprobrium for the religious orders.[43] It was others who were eager to make that label stick.

The other indication that Wyclif did not deliberately start a 'movement' is that the existence of a self-conscious 'group of Wycliffites' or even of 'Lollards' in Wyclif's lifetime or soon after it is also hard to establish. Knighton speaks of Wyclif's 'heretical disciples and accomplices' and imputes to then a sufficient sense of 'belonging' to get them claiming that they would rather go to prison or be burned than forswear their beliefs. But he points out that, when these threats really presented themselves, they recanted quickly enough,[44] and they did not rush to the aid of their 'members'. There was a sense of 'fellowship' and common cause but it does not seem to have operated at this practical level. In the correspondence of John Hus is an exchange with Richard Wyche, whom we earlier observed retracting his heretical opinions. Wyche writes (in a letter dated 'written in London on the Nativity of the Glorious Virgin', September 8, 1410), in support of Hus and his allies, 'for the distance of the lands cannot separate those whom the love of Christ has effectually united'.[45] Hus calls Wyche 'a fellow-worker of master John Wyclif in the labours of the Gospel'.[46]

We must now review the known names which were associated with Wyclif or with Lollardy at this early stage, for in these particular examples the lack of attachment to any organized group emerges clearly. Knighton, writing within a few years of the events, has a good deal to say about John Purvey.[47] He describes him as a chaplain, of simple mien, unassuming and hard-working and assiduous in winning people's hearts, with a face older than his years.[48] It is upon Knighton's authority that the story rests that Purvey was Wyclif's companion at Lutterworth in the last years. John Purvey (1353?–1428?)[49] was probably a young man still. He seems to have been ordained only in 1377–78. There is no evidence that he was a student at Oxford or a pupil of Wyclif in the ordinary way.[50] His precise role at Lutterworth, the nature of his relationship with Wyclif, the capacity in which he served him in these last years (secretary, curate, friend?) and how he was chosen for the role, or persuaded Wyclif to accept his company and support, remain as obscure as the question whether he was there at all. But if he was at Lutterworth, as Wyclif's table companion, he must have lived in some intimacy with Wyclif at Lutterworth at the end of his life.

If that is correct, it is to Purvey that we might look for someone possessing the youthful energy and idealism to motivate a movement and conceive of new schemes. But here again no clear strong line emerges, and no 'structure' or organizational 'identity' for the movement is to be found in his work or suggested activities. He became, or perhaps already was, one of the wandering preachers who were causing offence in ecclesiastical high places and in 1387 the Bishop of Worcester forbade him to 'itinerate' in his diocese, so by then his name had come to some prominence. His writings were shortly after included among those allowed to be seized. In 1390 he was put in prison. But he was not made of heroic material and no organized support for him appeared. By 1401 he had had enough and he found he did not want to follow William Sawtry to burning as a martyr. He recanted,[51] and perhaps became a rather lukewarm Lollard, for William Thorpe's evidence in his account of his own trial of 1407 is that by that time John Purvey 'shows himself neither hot nor cold'.[52] This is a pattern which is visible in the lives of other leading names. Knighton describes John Aston, in the period when the witch-hunt inspired by William Courtenay, Archbishop of Canterbury, was actively seeking out those who might be *sectatores* of Wyclif. Aston is said to have been a persuasive conversationalist and popularizer, 'boldly putting the opinions of his master Wyclif as forcefully as he could "upon the table" for simple minds with the aim of seducing them'. Indeed he had no shame in adding to Wyclif's teachings and wherever in the kingdom he preached he sowed tares with the wheat. Knighton accuses Aston of demonizing those who do not agree with him. He praised his own preachers and called all others 'false preachers'.[53] Aston, Knighton reports, preached a sermon in Leicester one Palm Sunday (possibly in 1381), in which he advanced various controversial opinions. No one should excommunicate another except to save his soul; any sentence of excommunication with the purpose of preventing people from hearing the Word of God is of Antichrist; there will never be true peace in the realm until the clergy are deprived of their temporal possessions; the 'sects' which are really so recent as to have been founded 'only yesterday' should not claim to be 'more perfect'; members of religious orders ought to work for their livings not beg; the bread remains after the consecration in the Eucharist. Aston is also recorded as preaching in Gloucester on 24 February 1382 and on the Despenser crusade.[54] Knighton says that Aston never taught the doctrine of 'consubstantiation' (that the material bread remains in the consecrated host), and gives his reason, 'for [I] wote wele that the mater and the speculation thereof passes in heyte myn understondyng.'[55] There is also a Latin record of Aston's views in the *Fasciculi Zizaniorum*.[56] He, too, proved unwilling to be a martyr for something not clearly identifiable as a 'cause' or for fellow-sympathizers with whom he had no strong bond.

Repington and Hereford would be prime candidates for Wyclif's 'sending' because of their prominence in the Blackfriars episode. Knighton's most significant omission from the list of Wycliffite sympathisers is Philip Repington, his fellow-canon in the Augustinian house at Leicester and soon to be his Abbot. This is the more conspicuous because Knighton has a good deal to say about Nicholas Hereford, who is said to have taken up with Wyclif and his views in 1381–82. As a Bachelor of Theology he had been 'very humble' and 'kindly' and he was well thought of by everyone till then – but on his inception as a Master, when he was 'made a doctor' in the summer of 1382, he gave his first public lecture, held up Wyclif and his teaching with admiration, and declared his intention of pressing for the acceptance of Wyclif's views on the Eucharist.[57] The Chancellor was also approached with the warning that Hereford's teaching smacked of heresy. The *Fasciculi Zizaniorum* preserves the account of the ways in which Hereford 'favoured Wyclif's opinions at every point' and said he could 'find no fault in anything Wyclif said'.[58] But Hereford was in effect 'run out of town'.

Richard Wyche claimed that he had never meant to say anything which was not underpinned by Scripture and if he has done so he retracts. Knighton gives a description of William Smith, who, he says was deformed and had been spurned by a woman and took up extreme asceticism as a reaction,[59] not, he implies, out of principle. A cloudiness hangs over the scene, with nothing definable for anyone to 'belong' to, the passing enthusiasm of certain individuals for a range of ideas, many of which were commonplaces of dissidence for centuries before Wyclif.

College loyalties and the opportunity college life afforded for people to pass on ideas may have been a far stronger bond here than anything offered by way of loyalty to Wyclif personally. Wyclif's time at Merton could have made him a talking point in the College as his name emerged into the limelight and then into notoriety. William James, Fellow of Merton in 1376, continued to be resident in Oxford until 1411. He was a notably loyal 'Wycliffite', whose arrest was ordered in 1394, with another Fellow of Merton known as Gamylgay. An order for Gamylgay's arrest was renewed in 1395, and with him yet more Fellows of Merton, Richard Whelpington and Thomas Lucas. The three of them were put in prison in Anglesey. Meanwhile James was pursued and caught up with in Bristol and he too was put in prison.[60] These condemnations did not necessarily end careers, any more than they did for Repington in the long term. The Merton colleagues were allowed back into Oxford life in due course and in James's case the Warden of Merton threw a party to welcome him back.[61] Lucas proved loyal to the movement like James. He was reported as late as 1416 still 'counselling and abetting', assisting the revolutionary Oldcastle in putting about Lollard opinions.[62] Another Mertonian again was Robert Lychlade, expelled from Oxford in the same 1390s period of 'purging', but restored on the King's orders in 1399. He provides an important link with the Czech dissidents. He offered hospitality for two of them at Kemerton while they copied the *De ecclesia* of Wyclif and on this visit they also went to Braybrooke to copy the *De veritate sacrae scripturae* and make corrections to it. They are reported as having taken a 'relic' from Wyclif's tomb at Lutterworth too.[63]

It is, then, possible to string names together, but they do not form an identifiable conscious 'movement', let alone a movement made up of preachers brought together, trained and sent out by Wyclif. The clinching evidence that Wyclif was not busy 'sending out' the preachers who were undoubtedly actively at work must be that he says nothing about it.[64] He did not write to them or for them, providing no surviving manuals or instructions. It was others who were busy linking his name with what was going on. Knighton the chronicler depicts John Ball the revolutionary of the Peasants' Revolt as Wyclif's John the Baptist 'preparing his ways before him' (Matthew 3:3).[65]

Wyclif apparently did nothing so purposeful as to collect and send out disciples, although preaching certainly went on in his name. That is the distinction which it is crucially important to bear in mind.

The Lollard label

When a famous leader of popular religious opinion or of reform, or the founder of an order, dies, there is a precarious moment when those who have been 'followers' must take over if the thing is to continue. The death of Francis of Assisi had been the most notable medieval occasion when a question had arisen about the way the 'Franciscans' were to carry on. The division between those who saw a need to institutionalize and those who thought the followers of Francis should go on with a simple imitation of Christ, as they conceived the *vita apostolica*, had led into the long-running 'poverty debate' to which Wyclif had himself become a contributor. In his ability to win a 'following' with personal loyalty to himself, Wyclif was not a Francis or a Dominic; nor was he a Luther, a Calvin, a Wesley. He had not got as far as any of them towards the creation of an entity which could be expected to bear his name. It has been suggested that the mendicants were afraid that the Lollards were going to form a new preaching order which would rival their own.[66] But Wyclif made no attempt to do as Francis and Dominic and others had done in their own day, which was to win papal recognition for a movement or an order.

The 'movement' linked with his name was to become known as Lollardy, which was of course a term of opprobrium; it was not to bear Wyclif's name, although his name was to remain associated with it. The term 'Lollard' was already in use when Knighton wrote his account and he links it with 'Wycliffite' (*Wyclyuyani seu Lolardi*).[67] John Gower, also writing about 1390, uses the word as a term of disapproval in the Prologue to his *Confessio Amantis*, and again later in the text.[68]

It is a term apparently of Middle Dutch origin (*lollaerd* meaning someone muttering or gabbling prayers). It was used disrespectfully of the religious enthusiast and, Latinized to *lollardus*, it was employed as a scornful epithet against the Beguines and Beghards in the early fourteenth century. These 'lay religious'[69] must have come readily to mind at the sight of lay people talking theology. The Latin *lolium* (weeds or tares) was naturally associated with it, so that Chaucer could jest:

> *'I smelle a loller in the wynde,' quod he …*
> *He wolde sowen som difficultee,*
> *Or springen cokkel in our clene corn'.*[70]

When eventually Lollards adopted the term to describe themselves and wished to emphasize more positive connotations, there was ready to hand the Middle English 'loll', to enable them to link themselves with Christ hanging (lolling) on the Cross.[71] But, labelled or not, Wyclif and Lollard were easily lumped together as enemy or even as Antichrist.[72] The truth of the matter is probably that the link was made by adversaries and by Lollards themselves, wishing to borrow Wyclif's name, and not by Wyclif.

Envoi

Those sixteenth-century adulators who made Wyclif what he was not did him no favours. The real Wyclif was an able academic, not untypical of his times in the subjects which interested him and the lines he took in his teaching and writing. He had some interesting ideas. He was capable of developing them, of working out their implications over time. He was probably a good teacher and a provocative preacher when he had an academic audience, although he was less successful when it came to making a permanent record of his thoughts and discoveries in a form which future readers would find useful. He was not an effective politician or a subtle strategist and he was knocked completely off course by the misfortune of becoming the *bête noire* of others more ambitious, more ruthless and more politically astute than he. Some of the consequences were his own fault, for he would answer back in unnecessarily strong language; but, then, he felt cornered and betrayed at the time. History gains rather than loses when it becomes possible to treat a hero as a complex and fallible human being, with all the dimensions which enrich as much as they challenge the earlier, simpler pictures of the man who was hero and villain.

End notes

Preface

1. Montagu Burrows, *Wiclif's place in history: Three Lectures Delivered before the University of Oxford in 1881* (London, W. Isbister, 1882), pp. 6–7.
2. *CivDom I*, pp. xviii–xix.
3. For a collection, see the Bollandist *Bibliotheca Hagiographica Latina* (Brussels, 1899–1901), 2 vols., and *Supplementum*, ed. H. Fros (Brussels, 1896), which gives a survey of more than 9,000 texts.
4. On this phrase and its use, see *John Foxe at home and abroad*, ed. David Loades (Aldershot, 2005), p. 142; see also the Conclusion.
5. *PW*, I, p. v.
6. Carol Shields, *Mary Swann* (London, 1990), p.83.

Chapter 1

1. *FascZiz*, pp. 12, 14, 19, 67, 456; and *Workman, II*, p. 121.
2. *VSS, I*, pp. 360 and 363. For a translation of the *De veritate scripturae*, see *John Wyclif on the Truth of Holy Scripture*, tr. Ian Christopher Levy (Kalamazoo, 2001).
3. *VSS, I*, p. 366; *CivDom IV*, p. 538.
4. *VSS, I*, p. 366.
5. *FascZiz*, p. xlv, n.3; *Workman, I*, p. 51.
6. *Workman, I*, pp. 45–46. I am indebted to Workman for much of the detail about Wyclif's family. His researches in this area have not yet been comprehensively revisited.
7. *Wyclif, Political ideas and practice: papers by Michael Wilks*, ed. Anne Hudson (Oxbow, 2000), p. 1.
8. G.H. Martin and J.R.L. Highfield, *A History of Merton College*, Oxford (Oxford, 1997), p. 100.
9. *On the family and the early years*, see Workman, I, pp. 37–47.
10. *Workman I*, p. 53; MunAcad, p. 346 (1459) when the 'bryngers to' and the 'fetchers from' were paid 5d per boy per day.
11. *Workman, I, pp. 57 and 83.*
12. *OxHist I*, pp. 156–58.
13. *De ecclesia*, p. 15.
14. *OxHist II*, p. 1.
15. Robert Holcot, quoted in *Smalley, English Friars*, p. 199 (translation slightly amended).
16. John of Salisbury, *Historia Pontificalis*, ed. M. Chibnall, Oxford Medieval Texts (Oxford, 1986), is John's memoirs.

17. *Peter Abelard, Historia Calamitatum*, ed. J. Monfrin (Paris, 1967), pp. 68–69.
18. *John of Salisbury, Metalogicon*, ed. J.B. Hall, CCCM, 98 (1991), p. 70–73.
19. *John of Hauteville, Architrenius*, ed. P.G. Schmitt (Munich, 1974), pp. 161–77.
20. *Speculum Stultorum, Anglo-Saxon Satirical Poets and Epigrammatists of the Twelfth Century*, ed. T. Wright, RS 59a (1872), p. 63.
21. *PL 163*, pp. 759–70; H.E. Salter, *Medieval Oxford, OHS, 100* (1936), p. 29; and *OxHist I*, pp. 5–6.
22. *OxHist I*, p. 6.
23. Leff, p. 77; cf. *OxHist I*, p. 8.
24. *Nequam* (Oxford, 1984).
25. *OxHist I*, p. 37; and see BioReg, I, p. xvi.
26. *Snappe's Formulary*, ed. H.E. Salter, *OHS*, 80 (1924), p. 318.
27. Philip Pullman, *Northern Lights* (London, 1996).
28. *OxHist I*, pp. 47–48.
29. Compare Gaines Post, 'Parisian Masters as a Corporation,' *Speculum, 9* (1934), pp. 421–45, p. 424 and pp. 437–38 on attempts to excommunicate the University of Paris.
30. J.I.M. Stewart, *Full Term* (London, 1978), p. 9.
31. For example, Romans 12:4–8.
32. Matthew 5:29.
33. John M. Fletcher, 'The Teaching and Study of Arts at Oxford,1400–1520' (DPhil thesis, Oxford, 1961) p. 203.
34. *On Grosseteste*, see R.W. Southern, *Robert Grosseteste, the growth of an English Mind in medieval Europe* (Oxford, 1992).
35. P. Kibre, Scholarly privileges in the Middle Ages, *Medieval Academy of America, 72* (London, 1961), p. 274.
36. Specifically the Court of the Common Bench.
37. J.I.M. Stewart, p. 9.
38. Foxe, II, p. 48.
39. Roger Bacon, *Opera inedita*, ed. J.S. Brewer, RS 15 (1859), p.
40. The custom of requiring members of the university to dress distinctively in public lapsed in Oxford and Cambridge only at the end of the twentieth century, when it still led to attacks on undergraduates.
41. *Collectanea, I*, pp. 15–16.
42. *Medieval Archives of the University of Oxford*, ed. H.E. Salter, *OHS, 70* (1920), p. 143.
43. *OxHist I*, pp. 146–47.
44. *Planctus Universitatis, a dialogue between the university and a scholar*, from Bodleian Library MS Bodl. 859, is probably of about the time when Wyclif was entering the university, c. 1356–57. Henry Furneaux, 'Poems relating to the riot between town and gown on St Scholastica's Day (February 10, 1354/5) and two following days', *Collectanea, III*, pp. 163–87.
45. Salter, pp. 158–60.
46. Salter, p. 143.
47. *OxHist I*, p. 149.
48. MunAcad, p. 8.
49. J. Hatcher, *Plague, Population and the English Economy 1348–1530* (London and Basingstoke, 1977), pp. 21–25. *OxHist II*, p. 31.
50. *Workman, I*, p. 83.
51. *Workman I*, p. 84.
52. *OxHist I*, p. 658.
53. *OxHist II*, pp. 31–32.
54. For a list from 1458, see *OxHist II*, p. 156.

55. Chauncer, *The Prologue, ll.* 165–67
56. Chaucer, *The Prologue, ll.* 208–11
57. Although Uthred, one of Wyclif's sparring partners, is mentioned, the invective is generalized. The 'author' of the poem, Tryvytlam, accuses his enemies of heresy and schism and of blasphemy. Henry Furneaux, 'Tryvytlam de laude Universitatis Oxonie', *Collectanea, III*, pp. 188–210.
58. *Snappe's Formulary*, ed. H.E. Salter, *OHS, 80* (1924), pp. 308–11 (1366), p. 309.
59. Cornford, p. 95.
60. William J. Courtenay, *Schools and scholars in fourteenth-century England* (Princeton, 1987) discusses some of the local religious houses. For examples of the beginning of the trend away from offering infants and towards older entry, see *Guibert of Nogent, De Vita Sua*, ed. G. Bourgin (Paris, 1906).
61. II Timothy 3:6.
62. Wendy Scase, *Piers Plowman and the New Anticlericalism* (Cambridge, 1989), p. 15.
63. See Penn R. Szittya, *The Antifraternal Tradition in Medieval Literature* (Princeton, 1986), p. 18. William of St Amour mentions them along with the False Preachers.
64. W.A. Pantin, 'The English Black Monks', *Camden Society*, Third Series, 47 (1933), pp. 83ff.
65. *Benedictines in Oxford*, ed. Henry Wansbrough and Anthony Marett-Crosby (London, 1997).
66. M.W. Sheenan, 'The Religious Orders, 1220–1370', *OxHist I*, pp. 193–224, p. 194.
67. Brinton, p. x.
68. Brinton, p. x.
69. Brinton, p. xii.
70. The Hospitallers of St John were also keen landlords. Emden, Hall, p. 54.
71. *Augustine of Hippo and his monastic rule*, ed. G. Lawless (Oxford, 1987).
72. Sheenan, pp. 193–224, p. 194.
73. *OxHist I,* p.194.
74. F. Roth, *The English Austin Friars 1249–1538* (New York, 1966), pp. 320–21.
75. *OxHist I,* pp. 195–96.
76. *OxHist I,* p. 196.
77. Sheenan, p. 195.
78. Little, p. 22.
79. William A. Hinnebusch, *The early English Friars Preachers* (Rome, 1961), pp. 264–65.
80. See Chapter 3: John Wyclif, Regent Master.
81. *OxHist I*, p. 196.
82. Southern.
83. Hinnebusch, pp. 265–66 and Roger Bacon, *Opera inedita,* p. LV, 399, as translated and adapted by Little, p. 42.
84. Little, pp. 42–43.
85. Two short treatises against begging friars, p. 30, and see Little, p. 43.
86. Little, p. 42 sets out the evidence for this calculation in a footnote.
87. Little, p. 45.
88. Little, pp. 45ff., p. 50.
89. Ronald Millar, *The Masters*, play based on C.P. Snow, *The Masters* (London, 1964), p. 296.
90. *SA*, pp. 78–81, 110–11.
91. Emden, Hall, p. 3; and SA, pp. 226–27.
92. *OxHist I,* p. 374.
93. Emden, Hall, p. 31; and SA, pp. 226–27.
94. Emden, Hall, p. 42.

95. Emden, Hall, p. 43.
96. Leff, p. 148.
97. *OxHist I*, p. 369.
98. *SA*, pp. 233ff.
99. Unless he is a new graduate about to 'incept' (see Index for inception).
100. *SA*, p. 82.
101. *SA*, pp. 60–61, 82, 107.
102. *Glosam obscuriorem textu*, Geoffrey of Auxerre, *Libellus*, PL 609B.
103. *OxHist II*, p. 595. See too A.B. Cobban, *English University Life in the Middle Ages* (London, 1999).
104. *OxHist II*, p. 595.
105. Emden, Hall, p. 35.
106. Emden, Hall, p. 35.
107. Ps.-Boethius, *De disciplina scolarium*, ed. O. Weijers (Leiden, 1976).
108. *OxHist II*, p. 500. That is twelve pence in the old English system of coinage, where there were twelve pence to a shilling and twenty shillings to a pound.
109. In the same period payments for graces (dispensing from the requirements) range from 6s 8d to 20s. A 'grace' in both Oxford and Cambridge is a legislative act of the university which makes or dispenses from regulations.
110. *OxHist II*, p. 500–01.
111. *OxHist II*, p. 502.
112. *OxHist II*, p. 502.

Chapter 2

1. *OxHist II*, p. 499.
2. *SA*, p. 28.
3. C.P. Snow, *The Two Cultures and the Scientific Revolution* (Cambridge, 1959).
4. Genesis 2:20.
5. *De statu innocencie*, Thomson No. 27, pp. 495–99; mid-1376.
6. *CCSL*, 144, p. 471
7. *CCCM*, 24, p. 2040.
8. Robert Kilwardby, *De Ortu Scientiarum*, Chapters 46–62, ed. Albert G. Judy (London/Toronto, 1976), pp. 146–213.
9. *CivDom I*, pp. xviii–xix
10. R.W. Hunt, 'Oxford grammar masters in the Middle Ages', *Oxford Studies presented to Daniel Callus, OHS*, NS, xvi (1964), 163–93.
11. R.W. Hunt, 'Oxford grammar masters in the Middle Ages', *Oxford Studies presented to Daniel Callus, OHS*, NS, xvi (1964), 163–93. p. 186; and cf. *SA*, p. 170. p. 218.
12. *SA*, pp. 20–21.
13. J. J. Murphy, *Medieval Rhetoric: a select bibliography* (2nd edition, Toronto, 1982).
14. For example,Thomson 386, *Litera parva ad quondam socium*, late 1381; *Opera Minora*, pp. 10–11.
15. *Religious Lyrics of the XIVth century*, ed. Carleton Brown (Oxford, 1924).
16. Priscian, *Institutes*, ed. H. Keil, *Grammatici Latini* (Leipzig, 1855–58), vols. 2–3; and Donatus, ed. H. Keil, *Grammatici Latini* (Leipzig, 1864), vol. 4.
17. William of Sherwood's *Treatise on Syncategorematic Words*, tr. N. Kretzmann (Minneapolis, 1968); see, too, William of Sherwood, *Syncategoremata*, ed. J. Reginald O'Donnell, *Mediaeval Studies*, iii (1941); cf. *OxHist I*, p. 409.

18. *William of Sherwood's Treatise on Syncategorematic Words*, tr. N. Kretzmann (Minneapolis, 1968), p. 23.
19. *VSS* 1.14, 54; *VSS* 1.215, 28, 107, 189.
20. *VSS* III, vol. I, p. 54.
21. *OxHist I*, p. 408.
22. *Logica Mod.*, vol. II.i, p. 379; *OxHist I*, p. 408.
23. *Logica Mod.*, vol. II.ii, p. 379; *OxHist I*, p. 408.
24. *Logica Mod.*, vol. II.ii, p. 417–447.
25. For example, Roger Bacon's *Sumule dialectices*; and see *OxHist I*, p. 413.
26. He never completed his project of turning all of Aristotle and Plato into Latin because he was executed, caught up in the heated political circumstances of the time. On Boethius, see Henry Chadwick, *Boethius* (Oxford, 1981) and M.T. Gibson, *Boethius: his life, thought and influence* (Oxford, 1981).
27. On Berengar, see J. de Montclos, *Lanfranc et Bérengar, SSLov,* 37 (Louvain, 1969). On the controversy which concerned Wyclif, *see* Chapter 12.
28. *PL* 64; and *see Porphyry on Aristotle, Categories*, tr. Steven K. Strange (Duckworth, London, 1992).
29. *OxHist I*, p. 413 on treatises influenced by Kilwardby.
30. Thomson, no. 11, dated 1368–69.
31. *See* summary in A. Kenny, 'The realism of the De Universalibus', *Wyclif in his times*, ed. A.Kenny (Oxford, 1986), pp. 23–25; and see *Commentary on the Posterior Analytics*, ed. P. Rossi (Florence, 1981).
32. *De actibus anime, Miscellanea Philosophica*, I, p. 106.
33. Chaucer, ll. 4427–32
34. Thomas Bradwardine, *De Causa Dei*, ed. H. Savile (London, 1618); and see Gordon Leff, *Bradwardine and the Pelagians* (Cambridge, 1957).
35. *Posterior Analytics*, 71b, ed. H. Tredennick (Loeb, 1970); *Aristoteles Latinus*, IV, 1–4, ed. L. Minio-Paluello (Paris, 1968).
36. John of Salisbury, *Metalogicon*, IV.6, CCCM, 98, p. 145.
37. *Logica Mod.*, II.i, p. 15.
38. *OxHist I*, p. 404.
39. Robert Grosseteste, *Commentary on the Posterior Analytics*, ed. P. Rossi (Florence, 1981).
40. *Tractatus de universalibus*, ed. Ivan J. Mueller (Oxford, 1985), pp. 59, 107, 363, 373. Gonville and Caius, Cambridge, MS 337, f.45b; S. Harrison Thomson, *Writings of Robert Grosseteste* (Cambridge, 1940), pp. 84–85.
41. Genesis 2:20.
42. 'Supposition' as a word used in the schools to describe this branch of logic is of uncertain origin. *Logica Mod.*, II.i, p. 157 discusses possible sources.
43. P.V. Spade, *The medieval liar: a catalogue of the insolubilia literature* (Toronto, 1975); and see *Franciscan Studies*, 30 (1973).
44. Amos 7:14.
45. J.P. Torrell, *Théorie de la prophétie et philosophie de la connaissance aux environs de 1230, SSLov*, 40 (1977).
46. Beryl Smalley, 'Wyclif's Postilla on the Old Testament and his Principium', *Oxford Studies presented to Daniel Callus, OHS*, NS, xvi (1964), pp. 253–96, p. 261.
47. Thomson no. 5; Oxford, MS Magdalen College, 38.
48. *OxHist I*, pp. 621–23; and see William of Ockham, *De predestinatione* ed. Boehner, p. 69 and *Expositio Aurea*, on *Perihermeneias*, I.ix.15.
49. *OxHist I*, p. 624.
50. *OxHist I*, p. 624.
51. *OxHist I*, pp. 607f.

52. Roger Swyneshead, *Obligationes*, ed. Paul V. Spade, *AHDLMA*, 44 (1977), pp. 243–85.
53. Ps.-Boethius, *De disciplina scolarium*, ed. O. Weijers (Leiden, 1976).
54. *OxHist I*, pp. 408–09, citing MS Exeter College, MS 28, f.59rb.
55. J.I. Catto, 'Wyclif and Wycliffism at Oxford 1356–1430'; *OxHist II*, pp. 175–263, p. 176.
56. *OxHist I*, p. 409.
57. Thomson, no. 1.
58. *Logica*, vol. I, p. 1.
59. Peter Abelard, *Historia Calamitatum*, ed. J. Monfrin (Paris, 1967), pp. 68–69.
60. *Logica*, vol. I, p. 8.
61. *Logica*, vol. I, p. 69.
62. *Logica*, vol. I, pp. 72–74.
63. Thomson, no. 2.
64. *Logica*, vol. I, pp. 75.
65. J. Cousin, *Recherches sur Quintilian* (Paris, 1975), pp. 1–38.
66. Discussed in Boethius, *De Topicis Differentiis*, tr. E. Stump (2nd edition, Ithaca, Cornell, 1988).
67. Boethius, *Arithmetica*, ed. G. Friedlein (Leipzig, 1887).
68. Thomas Bradwardine, *Tractatus de Proportionibus*, ed. and tr. H.Lamar Crosby (Madison, Wisconsin, 1955).
69. *OxHist I*, p. 628.
70. *OxHist II*, p. 184.
71. *De statu innocentiae*, p. 477.
72. *De statu innocentiae*, p. 477.
73. Thomson, no. 12, c. 1368, a text which survives unusually for Wyclif in fourteen manuscripts. See Thomson, p. 25, on the possible connection between this piece and Wyclif's debate with Cunningham.
74. *SA*, pp. 234–35.
75. Thomson, no. 6, unedited.
76. *De materia et forma*, Thomson, no. 20, dated by Thomson as late as 1370–72 and after the *Summa de ente*.
77. Johannes Blund, *De Anima*, ed. D.A. Callus and R.W. Hunt (London, 1970), pp. ix–x.
78. Ignatius Brady, 'Background to the condemnation of 1270: Master William of Baglione, OFM', *Franciscan Studies*, 30 (1970), pp. 5–48.
79. Robert Kilwardby, *De Ortu Scientiarum*, ed. Albert G. Judy (London/Toronto, 1976), p. xii.
80. Leff, p. 142 and p. 271.
81. *Tractatus de universalibus*, ed. Ivan J. Mueller (Oxford, 1985), p. 213.
82. *Tractatus de universalibus*, ed. Ivan J. Mueller (Oxford, 1985), p. 109.
83. *Tractatus de universalibus*, ed. Ivan J. Mueller (Oxford, 1985), p. 109.
84. Grosseteste's *Commentary on Aristotle's 'Physics'*, ed. Richard C. Dales (Colorado, 1963).
85. *ManDiv*, p. 2
86. *De actibus anime, Miscellanea Philosophica*, I, pp. 1–127; Thomson, no. 4, c. 1365.
87. *De actibus anime, Miscellanea Philosophica*, I, p. 1.
88. *De insolubilibus*, Thomson, no. 5.
89. Thomson, p. 9 n.2, suggests that the marginalia in the copy of this treatise in MS Merton College, p. 308, could possibly be Wyclif's own.
90. *De actibus anime, Miscellanea Philosophica*, I, pp. 2, 12, 14, 38, 46, 53, 116, 121.
91. For example, *30 libro declaratam, De actibus anime, Miscellanea Philosophica*, I, p. 38.

92. *De actibus anime, Miscellanea Philosophica*, I, pp. 30–31.
93. ManDiv, 4, pp. 31–32.
94. G.H. Martin and J.R.L. Highfield, *A History of Merton College* (Oxford, 1997), p. 101.
95. *SA*, pp. 234–35.
96. On the arts curriculum see also J.A. Weisheipl, 'Curriculum of the Faculty of Arts at Oxford in the early fourteenth century', *Mediaeval Studies*, 26 (1964), 143–185; and Weisheipl, J.A., 'Developments in the Arts Curriculum at Oxford in the early fourteenth century', *Mediaeval Studies*, 28 (1966), 151–175.
97. *Logica*, I, p. 1.
98. *Logica*, III, p. 145.
99. *Prologue to Logica, Logica*, III, p. 144.
100. *Logica*, III, p.145.

Chapter 3

1. Leff, pp. 149–77; *OxHist I*, p. 372.
2. *SA*, pp. 28–29; and *MunAcad*, p. 433.
3. *SA*, pp. 233ff.
4. Little, p. 48; *MunAcad*, p. 393.
5. Little, p. 48.
6. Oxford, Bodleian Library, MS Digby 55. See *OxHist I*, p. 411 on its contents.
7. Quoted *OxHist I*, p. 411.
8. *SA*, p. 28.
9. Little, pp. 51.
10. E.M.Doyle, 'William Woodford, OFM (c. 1330–c. 1400). His Life and Works Together with a Study and Edition of His *Responsiones contra Wiclevum et Lollardos*', *Franciscan Studies*, 43 (1983), pp. 17–187, p. 27.
11. Oxford, Bodleian Library, MS Bodley 703, f.49ra.
12. *Opera Minora*, pp. 431–53; Thomson no. 389, date uncertain.
13. *Opera Minora*, pp. 431. Cf. Bernard of Clairvaux, *De Consideratione*, III, xv, *Opera Omnia*, ed. J. Leclercq and H.M. Rochais (Rome, 1963), p. 441.
14. *Opera Minora*, pp. 432.
15. *Opera Minora*, pp. 432.
16. *Opera Minora*, pp. 434.
17. Cornford, p. 100.
18. *Collectanea*, III, p. 121.
19. *SA*, p. 129.
20. *OxHist I*, p. 45.
21. *OxHist I*, p. 39.
22. *OxHist I*, p. 72.
23. *Snappe's Formulary*, ed. H.E. Salter, *OHS*, 80 (1924), pp. 86–89.
24. *OxHist I*, p. 34ff.
25. *OxHist I*, p. 71.
26. *OxHist I*, 73.
27. *SA*, pp. 285–86, c. 1470.
28. A.B. Emden, 'Northerners and Southerners in the organisation of the University to 1509, *Oxford Studies presented to Daniel Callus*, *OHS*, xvi (1964), pp. 1–30.
29. Leff, p. 99, gives a list of thirteenth-century fights.
30. Examples are attested in 1314, 1319, 1334, 1385, 1388, 1389, but there were

undoubtedly others. The episodes of 1385, 1388, 1389 may even have reflected the divisions there were in the University by then over Wyclif and his alleged 'followers'.

31. *OxHist I*, pp. 84–85.
32. *SA*, p. 86, p. 108.
33. *SA*, p. 107, of 1231.
34. *OxHist I*, p. 42.
35. *OxHist I*, p. 55ff.
36. *OxHist I*, p. 57.
37. *OxHist I*, p. 61.
38. *SA*, pp. 156, 179, 293.
39. *OxHist I*, p. 52.
40. *SA*, p. 86.
41. Unless he is a new graduate about to 'incept'.
42. *SA*, p. 82.
43. *SA*, p. xlii.
44. *OxHist I*, p. 54.
45. *SA*, p. xli and xlii.
46. *Collectanea*, III, p. 140.
47. See Chapter 11.
48. *FascZiz*, p. 113.
49. Ps.-Boethius, *De disciplina scolarium*, ed. O. Weijers (Leiden, 1976), pp. 123ff.
50. Before 1350, among the *iuramenta* or oaths required to be sworn, *SA*, p. 19.
51. *Brinton*, I, pp. xi–xii, p. 134.
52. R.L. Poole, 'Henry Symeonis', *EHR*, 27 (1912), pp. 515–57; *SA*, p. 20.
53. Bygott, J., *Lincolnshire*, The County Books Series (London, 1952), p. 190f.
54. Gerald of Wales, *Topographia Hibernica*, ed. J.S. Brewer, *RS*, xxi, 8 vols. (1867), vol. 5, pp. 3–204; *De Rebus a se Gestis*, vol. I (1861), pp. 72–73; *OxHist I*, p. 38.
55. Parkes, *Books*, pp. 407–83; and *SA*, pp. 235–66; et al. Parkes's analysis provides the foundation for what follows in this section.
56. Chaucer, *Prologue*, ll. 285–86, 290–96.
57. Parkes, *Books*, pp. 411–12.
58. *Brinton*, I, p. xi.
59. Little, p. 60.
60. A 'Decretal' is a papal decree or epistle that determines a particular point of doctrine or ecclesiastical law. Collectively, 'the Decretals' came to form part of canon law and the term as Wyclif and his contemporaries use it normally refers to the additional collection which was added up to Pope Gregory IX after Gratian's *Decretum* collection had come into use as a textbook from about 1140. See *Corpus Iuris Canonici*, ed. A. Friedberg (Leipzig, 1879), 2 vols.
61. J.R. Magrath, *The Queen's College* (Oxford, 1921), p. 126.
62. *SA*, p. 216, of 1412, refers to a university library and a librarian and his salary.
63. *OxHist II*, p. 2; and Parkes, Books, pp. 470–71.
64. Parkes, *Books*, pp. 466–67.
65. Parkes, *Books*, p. 407; *SA*, p. 46.
66. *Collectanea*, I, ed. C.R.L. Fletcher, *OHS*, 5 (1885), pp. 59–70.
67. *OxHist II*, p. 423.
68. Parkes, *Books*, pp. 423–30.
69. Parkes, *Books*, p. 413 and p. 419.
70. Parkes, *Books*, p. 422.
71. Parkes, *Books*, p. 418.
72. Parkes, *Books*, p. 448.

73. *OxHist II*, pp. 431ff.
74. Little, p. 55; and *Bullarium Romanum*, I, p. 251.
75. MS Canonic Misc. 75, f.80b, quoted in G. Little, p. 56.
76. Little, p. 56.
77. Parkes, *Books*, pp. 410–11.
78. Parkes, *Books*, p. 419.
79. Parkes, *Books*, p. 409.
80. R.W. Hunt, 'The medieval inventories of Clare College Library', *Transactions of the Cambridge Bibliographical Society*, 1 (1950), p. 125.
81. *SA*, pp. 167–68.
82. *DomDiv*, pp. 64, 69.
83. For example, *DomDiv*, p. 147, quoting *De Concordia* I.2, S.II, pp. 248.6–7.
84. *DomDiv*, pp. 115, 195, quoting *Hexaemeron*, pp. 42, 198; *Dicta*, p. 213; *Dicta* pp. 236, 237, 238, 249 and p. 247ff.
85. A.J. Minnis, *Medieval Theory of Authorship* (Aldershot, 1988).
86. Grosseteste's *Commentary on the Posterior Analytics*, ed. P. Rossi (Florence, 1971), p. 93.
87. One of the first surviving examples, from mid-twelfth-century Paris, is Simon of Tournai, *Disputationes*, ed. J. Warichez, SSLov, 12 (1932).
88. Cf. *OxHist I*, p. 625.
89. *Luthers Werke* (Weimar, 1932), vol. 39II, p. 6.
90. *Luthers Werke* (Weimar, 1932), vol. 39II, p. 206.
91. *VSS*, I.14.54, I.215,28,107,189 CHECK.
92. Adam Usk, *Chronicon*, ed. and tr. E.M. Thomson (London, 1876, 2nd edition, London, 1904), pp. 46–47; and *OxHist II*, p. 211.
93. *De officio regis*, pp. 98 and 129ff., S.H. Thomson, 'Three unprinted *opuscula* of John Wyclif', *Speculum*, 3 (1928), pp. 248–53, p. 253. And see *OxHist II*, p. 210.
94. This is discussed by Thomson with reference to the various early writings which derive from Wyclif's teaching period in the arts. For example, Thomson, pp. 21–22.
95. *Reportatio* was the medieval university practice of taking notes in lectures at the lecturer's instigation, so as to create a record for the lecturer's future use.
96. R.W. Southern, *Robert Grosseteste: the growth of an English Mind in medieval Europe* (Oxford, 1986, 2nd edition, 1992), p. 73 on the *Dicta* and the way they were compiled from Grosseteste's notes.
97. *CivDom I*, p. 267.
98. *CivDom I*, p. 267.
99. *OxHist II*, p. 8.
100. Thomson, nos. 1ff.
101. Thomson, nos. 4, 5. Possibly compiled late 1373 or after (Mueller, p. xxxii); J.A. Robson, *Wyclif and the Oxford Schools* (Cambridge, 1961), p. xi.
102. Pantin, *Halls*, pp. 31–100, p. 35.
103. Pantin, *Halls*, pp. 31–100, pp. 86–89.
104. A.B. Cobban, 'Colleges and halls 1380–1500', *OxHist II*, pp. 581–634, p. 585.
105. James McConica, 'The rise of the undergraduate college', *The History of the University of Oxford*, vol. III, *The Collegiate University*, ed. James McConica (Oxford, 1986), pp. 1–69, p. 2.
106. Pantin, *Halls*, p. 34.
107. Anthony and Thomas Bek, who were later to be Bishops of Durham and St David's respectively. Pantin, *Halls*, p. 33. Pantin gives several more examples of rich students who rented a house for themselves.

108. Bernard William Henderson, *Merton College* (Routledge, repr. 1998), p. 38.
109. G.H. Martin and J.R.L. Highfield, *A History of Merton College, Oxford* (Oxford, 1997), p. 1.
110. A.B. Emden, 'Northerners and Southerners in the organisation of the University to 1509', *Oxford Studies presented to Daniel Callus*, *OHS*, NS, xvi (1964), 1–30.
111. Richard of Bury, Bishop of Durham, early fourteenth century *Philobiblon*, ed. and tr. E.C. Thomas (London, 1888), Chapter 9, pp. 212–13.
112. G.H. Martin and J.R.L. Highfield, *A History of Merton College, Oxford* (Oxford, 1997), p. 100.
113. Parkes, *Books*, p. 421; M. Powicke, *The Medieval Books of Merton* (Oxford, 1931); and MS. Bodley 752.
114. G.H. Martin and J.R.L. Highfield, *A History of Merton College, Oxford* (Oxford, 1997), p. 99.
115. J.A. Robson, *Wyclif and the Oxford Schools* (Cambridge, 1961), p. 11.
116. H.W.C. Davis, *A History of Balliol College*, revised Davis and R.W. Hunt (Oxford, 1963) pp. 6–29.
117. Pantin, *Halls*, pp. 92–93.
118. John Jones, *Balliol College, a history* (2nd edition, Oxford, 1997), p. 25.
119. J.A. Robson, *Wyclif and the Oxford School* (Cambridge, 1961), pp. 10–14.
120. *Oxford Balliol Deeds*, ed. H.E. Salter, *OHS*, 64 (Oxford, 1913); John Jones, *Balliol College, a history* (2nd edition, Oxford, 1997), p. 26.

Chapter 4

1. Anthony Trollope, *Barchester Towers* (Oxford, 1953), pp. 186ff.
2. Chaucer, *Prologue*, ll. 479–84, 509–10, 512.
3. Chaucer, *Prologue*, ll. 527–28.
4. *Ad simplices sacerdotes*, p. 7. Thomson, no. 416, mid-1370s.
5. *De officio pastorali,* Thomson, no. 53.
6. *De officio pastorali*, p. 31
7. *De gradibus cleri ecclesie*, Thomson no. 394.
8. John Jones, *Balliol College: A History* (2nd edition, Oxford, 1997), p. 15; and see F. de Paravicini, *The Early History of Balliol College* (1891), p. 168.
9. Margaret Harvey, 'English views on the reforms to be undertaken in the General Councils (1400–18) with special reference to the proposals made by Richard Ullerston' (DPhil thesis, Oxford, 1963), pp. 2ff.
10. Margaret Harvey, 'English views on the reforms to be undertaken in the General Councils (1400–18) with special reference to the proposals made by Richard Ullerston' (DPhil thesis, Oxford, 1963), p. 115; and see E.F. Jacob, 'On the promotion of English university clerks during the later Middle Ages', *JEH*, 1 (1950), pp. 172–86; also E.F. Jacob, 'Petitions for benefices from English Universities in the Great Schism', *TRHS*, Fourth Series, 27 (1945), pp. 41–59.
11. Joseph H. Dahmus, 'Wyclif was a negligent pluralist', *Speculum*, 28 (1953), pp. 378–81.
12. Also Workman, II, pp. 263–66 lists the many benefices.
13. *CivDom* I, pp. 387–88, and *CivDom* III, p. 334.

Chapter 5

1. Cornford, p. 93.
2. This is puzzling if Wyclif was appointed Warden (or head) of Canterbury College in this year.
3. Magrath, p. 112, n. 310.
4. Magrath, p. 112.
5. Magrath, p. 113.
6. Magrath, p. 115.
7. Magrath, p. 116.
8. Margaret Harvey, *English views on the reforms to be undertaken in the General Councils (1400–18) with special reference to the proposals made by Richard Ullerston* (Oxford DPhil thesis, 1963), pp. 7–8.
9. Ronald Millar, *The Masters*, a play based on C.P. Snow, *The Masters* (London, 1964), p. 280.
10. J.R. Magrath, *The Queen's College* (Oxford, 1921), pp. 105–07.

Chapter 6

1. Cornford, p. 93.
2. Henry Harclay who died in 1317, had been Chancellor. John Lutterel succeeded him as Chancellor, soon after he had incepted as a master. Richard Campshall was still a fellow of Merton in 1305 and completed his lectures on the *Sentences* by 1316–17; and see *OxHist II*, p. 9; and *OxHist II*, p. 187.
3. *OxHist II*, pp. 373–406.
4. See *Logica*, vol. III, Chapter 10.
5. *John Wyclif, Tractatus de Universalibus*, ed. Ivan J. Mueller (Oxford, 1985), p. xxxvi.
6. Mueller, p. xxiii; *FascZiz*, pp. 471 and 473.
7. *OxHist I*, p. 614.
8. *The Register of Congregation 1448–63*, ed. W.A. Pantin and W.T. Mitchell, *OHS*, 22 (1972), 60; also *OxHist I*, p. 369.
9. *OxHist I*, p.370.
10. A.B. Emden, 'Northerners and Southerners in the organisation of the University in 1509', *Callus Studies*, 4; *OxHist I*, p. 371 n.4; and see *SA*, p. lxxvi and pp. 64–65.
11. *SA*, p. 142, pp. XXVI–XXIX, p. 156, p. 179.
12. *SA*, p. 156.
13. *SA*, p. 127.
14. See *SA*, p. 200 and p. 378; and John M. Fletcher, 'The Teaching and Study of Arts at Oxford, 1400–1520' (DPhil thesis, Oxford, 1961), pp. 113–14 .
15. E.M. Doyle, 'William Woodford, OFM (c.1330–c.1400). His Life and Works Together with a Study and Edition of His *Responsiones contra Wiclevum et Lollardos*', *Franciscan Studies*, 43 (1983), pp. 17–187.
16. Little, p. 81; cf. London, British Library, MS Royal 7.B.III, f.46r.
17. London, British Library, MS Royal 7.B.III, f.46r. Woodford wrote Seventy Questions on the sacrament of the Eucharist, *FascZiz*, p. 517.
18. *FascZiz*, p. 517.

19. E.M.Doyle, 'William Woodford, OFM (c.1330–c.1400). His Life and Works Together with a Study and Edition of His *Responsiones contra Wiclevum et Lollardos*', *Franciscan Studies*, 43 (1983), pp. 17–187, p. 28.
20. *FascZiz*, pp. lv, 3 and 86.
21. Each side claimed the earthquake was an omen in its favour.
22. On Uthred, see D.H.Farmer, 'New light on Uthred of Boldon,' *Benedictines in Oxford*, ed. Henry Wansbrough and Anthony Marett-Crosby, (London, 1997), pp. 116–132.
23. *Opera Minora*, p. 405.
24. This unique manuscript in which Thomas Netter collected texts connected with Wyclif and the Lollards remains an immensely important source.
25. *FascZiz*, p. 241; cf. *OxHist I*, p. 643, for a list of known Oxford theologians, some of them scarcely studied as yet.
26. William of Remington, a Cistercian from Sawley, was Chancellor of Oxford in 1372–73 when Wyclif became doctor of divinity. Bodleian MS 158 contains his *Dialogue between a catholic and a heretic*.
27. Cornford, p. 103.
28. Cornford, p. 105.
29. W.A. Pantin, *Canterbury College, Oxford*, vol. IV, *OHS*, NS, 30 (1935); and H.S. Cronin, 'John Wycliffe, the Reformer, and Canterbury Hall, Oxford', TRHS, Third Series, VIII (1914), pp. 55–76.
30. W.A. Pantin, *Canterbury College, Oxford*, vol. IV, *OHS*, NS, 30 (1935), p. 17.
31. W.A. Pantin, *Canterbury College, Oxford*, vol. IV, *OHS*, NS, 30 (1935), p. 17.
32. *OxHist II*, p. 187 and p. 592.
33. See Little, p. 81.
34. *FascZiz*, p. 517.
35. *FascZiz*, p. 517.
36. There was a new statute requiring that a lecturer must lecture on the *Sentences* of Peter Lombard before he was allowed to lecture on the Bible 'biblically', that is, exegetically. The Dominicans complained that that was absurd. Lecturing on the *Sentences* was more difficult, they said, and should be reserved for those who had already demonstrated their competence in biblical exegesis and not treated as introductory material.
37. H. Rashdall, 'The friars preacher of the University', *Collectanea*, II, pp. 195–273, pp. 201–03.
38. H. Rashdall, 'The friars preacher of the University', *Collectanea*, II, pp. 195–273, pp. 203–04.
39. H. Rashdall, 'The friars preacher of the University', *Collectanea*, II, pp. 195–273.
40. *Medieval Archives of the University of Oxford*, vol. I, ed. H.E. Salter, *OHS*, 70 (Oxford, 1920), pp. 204–05.
41. Before about 1359 only Oxford, Cambridge and Paris offered degrees in Theology. A. Cobban, *English University Life in the Middle Ages* (UCL, London, 1999), p. 166.
42. *SA*, pp. cx–cxi and p. 51.
43. *OxHist I*, p. 608ff.
44. Little, p. 46.
45. See M. Colish, Peter Lombard (Leiden, 1994) and *Medieval Commentaries on the Sentences of Peter Lombard*, ed. G.R. Evans (Leiden, 2002), vol. I.
46. Peter Lombard, *Sententie* (Spicilegium Bonaventurianum, 1971), 2 vols., I, p. 4.
47. Walter of St Victor, 'Le contra quatuor labyrinthos Franciae de Gauthier de Saint-Victor', ed. P. Glorieux, *Archives d'histoire doctrinale et littéraire du môyen age*, 19 (1952), pp. 187–335. Walter was of the second generation of the Victorine canons who are

first to be met with in the Paris of Peter Abelard from the beginning of the twelfth century.

48. Walter of St Victor, '*Le Contra quatuor labyrinthos Franciae* de Gauthier de Saint-Victor', ed. P. Glorieux, *Archives d'histoire doctrinale et littéraire du môyen age*, 19 (1952), pp. 187–335, p. 201.

49. M. Reeves, *The Influence of Prophecy in the Later Middle Ages* (Oxford, 1969).

50. N. Tanner, *Decrees of the Ecumenical Councils*, Lateran IV, 2 (Georgetown, 1990), vol. 1, p. 231.

51. Emily Allen Hope, Writings ascribed to Richard Rolle, Hermit of Hampole and materials for his biography, Modern Language Association of America and (New York, 1927), p. 177; cf. Richard Rolle, *Emendatio vitae and orationes ad honorum nominis Ihesu*, ed. Nicholas Watson (Toronto, 1995), Richard Rolle died in 1349, perhaps during the Black Death.

52. *OxHist I*, pp. 642–43.

53. *OxHist II*, p. 5.

54. J.I. Catto, 'Wyclif and Wycliffism at Oxford 1356–1430', *OxHist II*, pp. 175–263, p. 179.

55. William of Ockham, *In Librum Primum Sententiarum Ordinatio*, ed. G. Gál and S. Brown, *Opera Theologica*, I (Bonaventure, New York, 1967)

56. In his remarks on *Sentences*, Book I, Distinction 4, Question 1 and following

57. *OxHist I*, p. 618.

58. *OxHist I*, p. 619.

59. *OxHist I*, p. 618. Walter Burley, 'De puritate artis logicae tractatus longior', ed. P. Boehner (New York, 1955).

60. *OxHist I*, p. 618.

61. *De benedicta incarnatione*, Thomson, no. 22.

62. Some of the earliest manuscripts of Peter Lombard's *Sentences* preserve three treatises which belong with Book III: on the Incarnation, on the Eucharist and on marriage. Discussed and edited in *Sententiae in IV Libris Distinctae*, Spicilegium Bonaventurianum, vol. II, pp. 53*–87*.

63. *Tractatus De benedicta incarnatione*, ed. Edward Harris, Wyclif Society (London, 1886), I, p. 3.

64. *De benedicta incarnatione*, I, p. 3.

65. *De benedicta incarnatione*, I, p. 11.

66. *De benedicta incarnatione*, I, p. 12.

67. *De benedicta incarnatione*, p. 1.

68. Hurley, 'Scriptura sola: Wyclif and his Critics', *Traditio*, 16 (1960), pp. 275–352, and Kantik Ghosh, *The Wycliffite Heresy: authority and the interpretation of texts*, Cambridge Studies in Medieval Literature, 45 (Cambridge, 2002).

69. *Theologia* tended to be reserved for the topics which overlapped with those of classical philosophy. See G.R. Evans, *Old Arts and New Theology* (Oxford, 1983).

70. *VSS*, I, pp. 20–21.

71. *VSS*, I, p. 2.

72. *VSS*, I, p. 2 and p. 35.

73. *VSS*, I, p. 2 and p. 36.

74. B. Smalley, *The Study of the Bible in the Middle Ages* (3rd edition, Oxford, 1983), remains the classic study.

75. J.P. Torrell, *Théorie de la prophétie et philosophie de la connaissance aux environs de 1230: la contribution de Hugues de Saint-Cher, SSLov*, 40 (Louvain, 1977).

76. Robert Grosseteste, *Expositio in Epistolam Sancti Pauli ad Galatas*, 6:9, ed. James McEvoy and Laura Rizzerio, *CCCM*, 130 (1995), p. 87.

77. For example, Bonaventure, Sermo 16.13, *Sermones dominicales*, ed. J.G. Bougerol, *Bibliotheca Franciscana Scholastica Medii Aevi*, 27 (1977).
78. B. Smalley, 'John Wyclif's Postilla super totam bibliam', *Bodleian Library Record*, iv (1953), and 'Wyclif's Postilla on the Old Testament and his Principium, *Oxford Studies presented to Daniel Callus*, *OHS*, NS, xvi (1964), pp. 253–96, and G.A. Benrath, *Wyclifs Bibelkommentar* (Berlin, 1966). See also St John's College, Oxford, MS 171 and Magdalen College, MSS Lat. 55 and 117. For a full list see Thomson, nos. 301–371.
79. Thomson, nos. 301–71.
80. *VSS*, I, p. 22 and pp. 20–21.
81. Beryl Smalley, 'Wyclif's Postilla on the Old Testament and his Principium', *Oxford Studies presented to Daniel Callus, OHS*, NS, xvi (1964), pp. 253–96, p. 253, St John's College, MSS 171, Magdalen College lat 55 and 117.
82. Beryl Smalley, 'Wyclif's Postilla on the Old Testament and his Principium', *Oxford Studies presented to Daniel Callus, OHS*, NS, xvi (1964), pp. 253–96, p. 254.
83. Beryl Smalley, 'Wyclif's Postilla on the Old Testament and his Principium', *Oxford Studies presented to Daniel Callus, OHS*, NS, xvi (1964), pp. 253–96, p. 254–5.
84. See the distinction drawn between the 'perfection and sufficiency of Scripture as God's law' and the 'perfection and sufficiency of God's moral law, of the evangelical law of charity,' by Hurley, 'Scriptura sola: Wyclif and his Critics', *Traditio*, 16 (1960), p. 350.
85. G.A. Benrath, *Wyclifs Bibelkommentar* (Berlin, 1966), pp. 339–41.
86. *VSS*, I, p. 2 and p. 29.
87. *VSS*, I, p. 2 and p. 35.
88. On Psalm 135:17ff., G.A. Benrath, *Wyclifs Bibelkommentar* (Berlin, 1966), pp. 337–38.
89. Gregory the Great, *Moralia*, XVI.60, CCSL 143A.
90. But see Kantik Ghosh, *The Wycliffite Heresy: authority and the interpretation of texts*, Cambridge Studies in Medieval Literature, 45 (Cambridge, 2002), p. 1, and see Ian Levy, *John Wyclif: Scriptural logic, Real Presence, and the Parameters of Orthodoxy* (Milwaukee, 2003).
91. Beryl Smalley, 'The Gospels in the Paris Schools in the late twelfth and early thirteenth centuries, II', *Franciscan Studies*, 40 (1980), pp. 298–369, 366–69.
92. 'Il commento di Cola di Rienzo alla Monarchia di Dante', ed. P.G. Ricci, *Studia Medievalia*, Third Series, 6ii (1965), pp. 679–708, p. 705
93. '*Novo sensu sacram adulterare Scripturam:* Clement VI and the Political use of the Bible', *The Bible in the Medieval World*, ed. K. Walsh and D.Wood, *Studies in Church History Subsidia*, 4 (Oxford, 1985), pp. 237–49.
94. *De apostasia*, p. 49.
95. G. Owst, *Literature and Pulpit in Medieval England* (second edition, Oxford, 1961), p. 59. This, with variations, is a standard mnemonic, also used by Nicholas of Lyre.
96. It has been suggested that that *De Veritate Sacrae Scripturae* shows Wyclif moving away from defending the literal truth of Scripture throughout, *OxHist II*, p. 209
97. *VSS*, I, pp. 2–3.
98. *VSS*, I, p. 55.
99. *VSS*, I, p.2 and p. 20.
100. *VSS*, I, p.2 and p. 20.
101. *VSS*, I, p. 1
102. Beryl Smalley, 'Use of the "Spiritual" Senses of Scripture in Persuasion and Argument by Christian Scholars in the Middle Ages', *RTAM*, 52 (1985), pp. 44–63, p. 49.
103. G.A. Benrath, *Wyclifs Bibelkommentar* (Berlin, 1966), pp. 362–63.
104. *VSS*, I, p.2 and p. 27.

105. *VSS*, I, p.2 and p. 21. Wyclif attributes this image to Gregory the Great, but it does not occur where he indicated. Gregory discusses fruits and leaves in his introductory Letter to Leander at the beginning of his *Moralia in Job, CCSL*, 143, p. 7.
106. *VSS*, I, p.2 and p. 23.
107. *VSS*, I, p.2 and p. 23
108. *VSS*, I, p.1 and p. 15.
109. *VSS*, I, p.1 and p. 40.
110. *VSS*, I, p.1 and p. 5.
111. *VSS*, I, p. 16.
112. *VSS*, pp. 17–18.
113. A.J. Minnis, '"Authorial intention" and "literal sense" in the exegetical theories of Richard Fitzralph and John Wyclif', *Proceedings of the Royal Irish Academy*, lxxv, C (1975), p. 4.
114. *FascZiz*, pp. 8–9.
115. *FascZiz*, p. 4ff., gives the debate with Cunningham, and see *OxHist II*, pp. 195–96. Thomson, p. 228, speculates about the place of the extant materials in the full story of this exchange.
116. That does not survive but it is referred to in the Ingressus of Cunningham which is printed in *FascZiz*, pp. 4–13.
117. The controversies with Cunningham concerned a series of topics beyond this central one of the truth of Scripture. Nevertheless, John Cunningham begins the first of his tracts against Wyclif by declaring two purposes. The first is to summarize persuasively his 'determination' against Wyclif. The second is to take the discussion a little further in one area in particular: how the authority of Scripture is to be established. In other words, how do we know it is true? *FascZiz*, pp. 453–76 and 477–80.
118. *FascZiz*, p. 18.
119. *FascZiz*, p. 15.
120. *De apostasia*, p. 49
121. *FascZiz*, pp. 453–54.
122. *FascZiz*, pp. 454.
123. *FascZiz*, pp. 474.
124. *VSS*, I, Introduction, p. VIII.
125. *VSS*, I, Introduction, p. XXI.
126. *VSS*, I, p.i and pp. 1–2.
127. *VSS*, I, p.i and p. 2
128. *Foxe*, II, p. 48.
129. *Foxe*, II, p. 48.
130. *De quatuor sectis novellis*, p. 261.
131. Preface, *Sermones*, I, p. IV.
132. *Opus Evangelicum*, II.35.
133. *Opus Evangelicum*, II.31.
134. *Melius sit operari et predicari populo viva voce quam multiplicare tot codices.* Sermon xxxii, Sermones, vol. III, p. 265.
135. *PL* 210.
136. *PL* 205.
137. *OxHist I*, p. 603.
138. *OxHist I*, p. 604.
139. *Brinton*, Sermons 17, 85, 100, 101, 105, 107, 108.
140. *Brinton*, vol. II, p. 466.
141. T. Plassmann, 'Bartholomaeus Anglicus, De proprietatibus rerum', Archivum Fratrum Historicum, xii (1919), p. 106.

142. G. Owst, *Literature and Pulpit in Medieval England* (second edition, Oxford, 1961), pp. 24–26.
143. Smalley, *English Friars*, pp. 133–202.
144. G. Owst, *Literature and Pulpit in Medieval England* (second edition, Oxford, 1961), pp. 29–30.
145. Beryl Smalley, *English Friars*, p. 79.
146. Waleys, pp. 327–403.
147. Waleys, p. 329.
148. Waleys, pp. 341–42.
149. Waleys, p. 343.
150. Waleys, p. 345–46.
151. Waleys, p. 368.
152. Waleys, pp. 373–74.
153. Frances Yates, *The Art of Memory* (London, 1969) discusses the history of all this.
154. Smalley, *English Friars*, p. 82.
155. *Sermones*, 4.31, vol. IV, pp. 265–66; Thomson, no. 265.
156. *Sermones* 4.31, pp. 265.
157. *Tractatus de officio pastorali*, p. 35.
158. *OxHist I*, p. 604.
159. *De speculum laicorum*, ed. J.Th. Welter (Paris, 1914), p. 1.
160. *Medieval Archives of the University of Oxford*, vol. I, ed. H.E. Salter, *OHS*, 70 (Oxford, 1920), Items 113, 114, 115, p. 203. Item 119, Inspeximus of the University's privileges, 20 July 1378. Cf. Item 140, Inspeximus of 20 Nov 1399.
161. *Brinton*, cited in Horner, p. 202; and see *Brinton*, vol. I, pp. 47, 216 and vol. II, pp. 245, 318,390.
162. R.M. Haines, *The Church and Politics in fourteenth-century England: the career of Adam Orleton, c.1275–1345* (Cambridge 1978), pp. 164–65.
163. *OxHist I*, p. 604.
164. *OxHist I*, p. 604. See,too, *Chronicon*, 116 and *Anonimalle Chronicle*, p. 103.
165. *Sermones*, I, p. 2.
166. *Sermones*, I, p. 24.
167. *Sermones*, I, p. 8.
168. S. Forde, 'Nicholas Hereford's Ascension Day sermon', *Mediaeval Studies*, 51 (1989), pp. 205–241, p. 210. See, too, *OxHist I*, pp. 602–05
169. *SA*, p. 244.

Chapter 7

1. Wyclif Sermon xxxii, *Sermones* III, p. 263, given at Whitsun, Thomson, no. 207.
2. *FascZiz*, p. 258.
3. *Opera Minora*, pp. 74–91; Thomson no. 409, p. 88.
4. *CivDom II*, Thomson, nos. 28, 29, 30; 1375–76.
5. Thomson, no. 408.
6. *De officio regis*, Thomson, no. 33.
7. *De potestate pape*, Thomson, no. 34.
8. F.W. Maitland, 'Wyclif on English and Roman Law', *he Collected Papers of Frederic William Maitland*, ed. H.A.L. Fisher, 3 vols., (Cambridge, 1911), III, pp. 50–53; and see Edith C. Tatnall, 'John Wyclif and the *Ecclesia Anglicana*', *JEH*, 209 (1969), pp. 19–43, pp. 24ff.

9. See my *Law and Theology in the Middle Ages* (London, 2002).
10. *Opera Minora*, p. 415.
11. *VSS*, vol. II, p. 235.
12. *VSS*, vol. II, p. 235.
13. *VSS*, vii, vol. I, pp. 153–54
14. *VSS*, xiv, vol. I, p. 345.
15. *VSS*, xiv, vol. I, pp. 345–75, esp. 345–46.
16. *ManDiv*, 4, p. 32.
17. *Brinton*, vol. I, pp. xi–xii.
18. *Opera Minora*, p. 415.
19. *De officio regis*, Chapter X, p. 237
20. *CivDom* IV, p. 454.
21. *De officio regis*, p. 56.
22. *De officio regis*, p. 56.
23. *CivDom* I, p. xxxv and p. 254ff.
24. *Unde illi qui inficiunt leges Anglicana de aufferendo bona ab ecclesiastico delinquente, quod non possunt esse sine mortali execute, nimis presumunt; cum non repugnant sed consonat Scripture sacre nullum clericum civiliter dominari, CivDom* I, p. xlii and p. 351.
25. See Thomson p. 50 on *CivDom*, where 'a new emphasis' on law is noted. 'His citations from Gratian, the *Decretales* and later canonists such as Hostiensis are sufficient both in number and in precision, beginning at cap. xl of liber I and running throughout the rest of the treatise, to reflect a substantial exposure to the standard texts.'
26. Justinian, *Institutes*, ed. P. Krueger (Berlin, 1869), Inst.1.2.6; see *De iuramento Arnaldi*, ed. Gotthard V. Lechler, *Johann Wyclif und die Vorgeschichte der Reformation*, II (Leipzig, 1873), pp. 573–79.
27. *Dialogus*, p. 47, l. 31, cites the *Decretum Gratiani*, Canon 3a, q.7a, *Si quis in gravibus*.
28. Hostiensis, *Summa Aurea* (Lyons, 1588).
29. *VSS*, xxiv, vol. II, p. 250
30. *VSS*, xi, vol. I, p. 54; *VSS*, xiv, vol. I, p. 332.
31. *VSS*, xxiv, vol. II, p. 246; and cf. *De potestate pape*, pp. 252–53 on Papal Decretals contradicting themselves.
32. *VSS*, xxv, vol. III, pp. 3–4
33. *VSS*, xxvii, vol. III, p. 83.
34. Brian Tierney, *Foundations of the Conciliar Theory* (2nd edition, Leiden, 1998), pp. 136–42. Tierney's account finds no significant Wyclif contribution.
35. *De potestate pape*, pp. 252–53; *Decretum Gratiani*, Pars I, Dist. XXIII.i.
36. *Corpus Iuris Canonici*, ed. A. Friedberg (Leipzig, 1879), 2 vols., I, c.1, Dist. xxiii, *Qui episcopus*; *VSS*, vol. I, p. 234.
37. *ManDiv*, 6, p. 46, cf. Jeremiah 31:33 and Hebrews 10:16.
38. The wealth of the Church impedes the spread of the Gospel, he comments; for example, *VSS*, xxxi, vol. III, p. 264.
39. *VSS*, xxxi, vol. III, p. 235.
40. *ManDiv*, 1, p. 1.
41. *ManDiv*, 3, p. 16.
42. *ManDiv*, 4, p. 32.
43. *ManDiv*, 4, p. 32.
44. *Opera Minora*, pp. 201–57, p. 201.
45. *CivDom* I, p. xlii and p. 351.
46. *ManDiv*, 5, pp. 34–35.

47. *CivDom* I, p. ix and pp. 62–63.
48. Benjamin Disraeli, *Conyngsby*, V, ii (London, 1927), pp. 273–74.

Chapter 8

1. Workman, I, p. 36.
2. Cornford, p. 99.
3. *CivDom* I, ix, pp. 62–63.
4. *Libellus, FascZiz*, p. 245ff; *ManDiv*, III, p. 19.
5. Edited in M.V. Clark, *Medieval Representation and Consent. A study of early parliaments in England and Ireland with special reference to the Modus Tenendi Parliamentum* (1936), pp. 374–84.
6. J.S. Roskill, 'A consideration of certain aspects and problems of the English Modus tenendi parliamentum,' *Bulletin of the John Rylands Library*, 50 (1968), pp. 411–42.
7. May McKisack, *The fourteenth century* (Oxford, 1959), pp. 182–207.
8. Dahmus, *Prosecution*, p. 70 and Richard Rex, pp. 29–30 on questions about Wyclif's attendance at a great council and (presumably not) the meeting of Parliament.
9. See H.E.J. Cowdrey, *Lanfranc, scholar, monk and archbishop* (Oxford, 2003).
10. Wyclif, *De ecclesia*, XV, p. 354.
11. May McKisack, *The fourteenth century* (Oxford, 1959), p. 283–93
12. *Decrees of the Ecumenical Councils*, ed. Norman P. Tanner (Georgetown, 1990), 2 vols., I, pp. 231–33, pp. 211–17.
13. Austin Lane Poole, *Domesday Book to Magna Carta* (Oxford, 1955), p. 457.
14. May McKisack, *The fourteenth century* (Oxford, 1959), pp. 283–93.
15. J. Loserth, 'The beginnings of Wyclif's activity in ecclesiastical politics', *EHR*, 11 (1896), pp. 319–328, p. 319.
16. May McKisack, *The fourteenth century* (Oxford, 1959), pp. 283–93.
17. May McKisack, *The fourteenth century* (Oxford, 1959), p. 285.
18. Thomson, p. 250.
19. Dahmus, *Prosecution,* p. 3, n.6.
20. Roger Dymmok, *Liber contra xii errores et hereses Lollardum,* ed. H.S. Cronin (London, 1922), pp. xlvii–liv.
21. A seventh-century Latinized Greek term, an example of Wyclif's taste for obscure words.
22. See *Chronicon*, p. xxi for the revisions which moderate the account in the latter text so as to avoid its becoming a stumbling block (*offendiculum*); *Chronicon*, p. 115.
23. Thomson, p. 40, says Book II (5 chapters) and Book III (6 chapters) are probably unfinished.
24. Michael Hanrahan, 'Defamation as a political contest during the reign of Richard II', *Medium Aevum*, 62 (2003), pp. 259–276.
25. Holmes, p. 168.
26. That is, the monastic orders as distinct from the mendicants.
27. On the date of this, perhaps 1376, see *FascZiz*, p. XXXI and *Historia Anglorum,* p. 314.
28. *CivDom* II, p. 7.
29. *Libellus, FascZiz*, p. 247.
30. *Opera Minora*, p. 416.
31. Cornford, p. 96.
32. Bernard of Clairvaux, *De Consideratione IV.7, Opera Omnia*, III, p. 454.

33. *PL* 15.1994; and see Baldwin of Ford, Sermo 18.91; *Sermones*, ed. David M. Bell, *CCCM* 99 (1991), p. 287.
34. Dante and Marsilius of Padua are among the later medieval authors who explore this theme.
35. Horner, p. 195, and see *Eulogium*, III, p. 338, on the theme of the two swords.
36. *De ecclesia*, I, p. 13.
37. The bull *Unam Sanctam* of 1302 was a statement of the supremacy of the spiritual power.
38. *Eulogium,* III, pp. 337–38 describes the seating of the magnates, and see J. Loserth, 'The beginnings of Wyclif's activity in ecclesiastical politics', *EHR*, 11 (1896), pp. 319–328, pp. 326–27.
39. *FascZiz*, p. 258.
40. *FascZiz*, p. 260.
41. *FascZiz*, p. 259.
42. *FascZiz*, p. 265.
43. In 1378 John Gilbert became Chancellor of Oxford. He was a surprising choice, because he was a friar and because he had quarrelled with the university in 1366. He lasted only a year. He was replaced by the former proctor, Dr Robert Aylesham, who had been proctor under Tonworth.
44. Holmes, p. 175.
45. G.F. Lytle, 'Patronage patterns and Oxford colleges c.1300–c.1530', *The University in Society*, ed. L. Stone (Princeton, NJ, 1975), 2 vols.
46. *CivDom* III, p. 334.
47. For Wyclif against Binham's arguments, see *Opera Minora*, p. 425, Thomson, No. 382.
48. *CivDom* I, p. 388.
49. *CivDom* I, pp. 387–88.

Chapter 9

1. May McKisack, *The fourteenth century* (Oxford, 1959), pp. 384–419.
2. Joseph Dahmus, 'John Wyclif and the English Government', *Speculum*, 35 (1960), pp. 51–68, p. 545.
3. *De demonio meridiano, PL*, II, pp. 417–25; Thomson, no. 300.
4. *PW*, II, p. 422.
5. *PW*, II, p. 418.
6. Holmes, pp. 166–98; cf. Joseph Dahmus, 'John Wyclif and the English Government', *Speculum*, 35 (1960), pp. 51–68, pp. 54–55.
7. Holmes, p. 184.
8. Thomson, nos. 23, 24, 25. Thomson links it with Wyclif's awareness of FitzRalph's work and with William Woodford.
9. *Wyclif, Political ideas and practice: papers by Michael Wilks*, ed. Anne Hudson (Oxbow, 2000), and Stephen E. Lahey, *Philosophy and Politics in the Thought of John Wyclif* (Cambridge, 2003).
10. Gordon Leff, 'Richard FitzRalph's *Commentary on the Sentences*', *Bulletin of the John Rylands Library*, 45 (1963), pp. 390–422.
11. For the debates of the period immediately before Wyclif, and the chief protagonists, see W.E. McCready, 'Papalists and anti-Papalists: Aspects of the Church/State Controversy in the Later Middle Ages,' *Viator,* 6 (1975), pp. 241–273.

12. Aegidius Romanus, *De ecclesiastica potestate*, 3.7, ed. R. Scholz (Weimar, 1929), p. 181.
13. See C.W. Marx, *The Devil's rights and the redemption in the literature of medieval England* (Rochester, New York, 1995).
14. P. Abelard, Commentary on Romans, *CCCM*, XI, pp. 115–16.
15. For example, Bonaventure, *Sermones dominicales*, ed. J. G. Bougerol, *Biblioteca Franciscana Scholastica Medii Aevi*, 27 (1977), 21.xii.
16. Bernard of Clairvaux, *De Consideratione*, II, pp. ix–x; *Opera Omnia*, vol. III, pp. 416–1
17. Bernard of Clairvaux, *De Consideratione*, III, p. i; Opera Omnia, vol. III, p. 432.
18. Bernard of Clairvaux, *De Consideratione*, V.11; *Opera Omnia*, vol. III, p. 475.
19. On Galatians 6:9, line 232. Robert Grosseteste, *Expositio in Epistolam Sancti Pauli ad Galatas*, 6:9, ed. James McEvoy and Laura Rizzerio, CCCM, 130 (1995), p. 166.
20. *OxHist II*, pp. 181–82.
21. *OxHist II*, p. 181.
22. *OxHist II*, pp. 175–263.
23. *OxHist II*, pp. 175–263.
24. FitzRalph, p. 273.
25. FitzRalph, p. 278.
26. FitzRalph, pp. 280–81.
27. FitzRalph, p. 273.
28. FitzRalph, p. 315.
29. FitzRalph, p. 338.
30. FitzRalph, p. 352.
31. *OxHist II*, pp. 182–83, lists some of the polemical writings for and against roughly the Wycliffite and the FitzRalph positions respectively.
32. *OxHist II*, p.185.
33. Bodleian Library, MS Digby 113, fols, 1–117v, ff. 20v–21r.
34. *CivDom* I, p. 65.
35. 'Defensorium contra Armachanum pro mendicitate Christi', *OxHist II*, pp. 181–82.
36. Wyclif's *Libellus* is dated by Thomson in early 1378, Thomson, no. 400.
37. *Libellus*, *FascZiz*, pp. 254–55.
38. B. Tierney, *The Crisis of Church and State*, 1050–1300 (Englewood Cliffs, New Jersey, 1964).
39. *Libellus*, *FascZiz*, p. 256.
40. *Libellus*, *FascZiz*, p. 256.
41. Thomson's hypothesis, p. 40; and see Thomson, nos. 23–25 (1373–74) on the notion that this may have begun as the opening section of Wyclif's intended *Summa Theologie*.
42. *DomDiv*, pp. 1–2.
43. Wyclif explains that dominion is a *habitus* not a mere power, that it is not a right, that it is founded in grace, belongs to rational natures only, is not eternal and can be lost by sin. *DomDiv*, pp. 4ff.
44. See *DomDiv* i, p. 2, pp. 35, 281, 388ff., on the relation of dominion to possession; pp. 5, 281, 300, 389, 408–413, 468–476, on the relation of dominion to use; pp. 17, 201–05, 279, on the relation of dominion to propriety.
45. *CivDom* I, p. 47.
46. *CivDom* I, p. 49.
47. *CivDom* I, p. 60.
48. *CivDom* I, p. 61.
49. *CivDom* I, p. 49.

50. *CivDom* I, p. 53.
51. Wyclif had been writing on the state of innocence in which Adam and Eve had been before the fall in the *De mandatis divinis* and *De statu innocencie*.
52. *De ordinatione fratrum*, p. 88; and *De religionis vanis monachorum*, Thomson, no. 434 (1382–84).
53. The distinction between 'faith' as 'knowledge' of the content of Christian belief and the 'justifying faith' which Luther made central to the sixteenth-century Reformation was still being discussed in the debates of the 1530s at Wittenberg. Cf. Mark 3:11–12 and Luke 4:41. So 'The Christian faith was nothing then [in Wyclif's day], but that every man should know that Christ once suffered, that is to say, that all men should know and understand that which the devils themselves once knew,' cries Foxe.
54. *De fundacione sectorum*, p. 26; *Purgatorium Sectae Christi*, p. 298.
55. *CivDom* III, pp. xviii–xix, pp. 351ff.
56. *CivDom* II, p. 1.
57. See *CivDom* III, p. 351.
58. *CivDom* III, pp. 351 and 358.
59. *CivDom* III, p. 351.
60. W.A. Pantin, 'A Benedictine Opponent of John Wyclif', *EHR*, 43 (1928), pp. 73–77.
61. Dahmus, *Prosecution*, p.73.
62. *VSS*, vol. I, p. 345.
63. Cornford, p.109.

Chapter 10

1. *Foxe*, p. 49.
2. Lambeth Palace Library, Register of Sudbury, fol.33v.
3. The most severe disciplinary penalties which could be imposed on a priest were deposition and prohibition. His 'orders' were regarded as indelible, so he did not cease to be a priest. He could, however, he prevented from exercising his ministry.
4. *Foxe*, p. 49.
5. *Foxe*, p. 49.
6. *Foxe*, p. 49; Holmes, p. 189.
7. R. Bird, *The turbulent London of Richard II* (London, 1949), p. 25.
8. *Foxe*, p. 49.
9. *Foxe*, p. 49.
10. *Foxe*, p. 49. The Bishop was his 'ordinary', to whom he owed canonical obedience as a priest within the order of the Church.
11. *Chronicon*, pp. 119–21; and see J.H. Dahmus, *William Courtenay* (Pennsylvania, 1966), Chapters 3 and 4; and on the riot, see Bird, *The turbulent London of Richard II* (London, 1949), p. 25.
12. R. Bird, *The turbulent London of Richard II* (London, 1949), Chapter 1, pp. 1 and 15–16.
13. *Chronicon*, pp. 146–47.
14. For example, *De ecclesia*, p. 354, Thomas *Brinton*, Bishop of Rochester.
15. *OxHist II*, p. 180.
16. *OxHist II*, pp. 180–81.
17. W.A. Pantin, *Documents illustrating the Activities of the General and Provincial Chapters of the English Black Monks*, 1215–1540, Camden Society, Third Series, 54 (1937), iii, pp. 76–77.

18. Margaret Harvey, 'Adam Easton and the Condemnation of John Wyclif, 1377', *EHR*, 118 (1998), pp. 321–334.
19. MS Vat. Lat.4116, discussed in Margaret Harvey, 'Adam Easton and the condemnation of John Wyclif, 1377', *EHR*, 118 (1998), pp. 321–34, p. 323.
20. Margaret Harvey, 'Adam Easton and the condemnation of John Wyclif, 1377', *EHR*, 118 (1998), pp. 321–34, p. 325.
21. Margaret Harvey, 'Adam Easton and the condemnation of John Wyclif, 1377', *EHR*, 118 (1998), pp. 321–34, p. 323; *Chronicon*, pp. 395–96; and cf. *HistAng*, pp. 324–25.
22. *De ecclesia*, p. 354.
23. *CivDom* I, p. 267.
24. *Sermones*, ed. J. Loserth, vol. III, p. 189.
25. *Chronicon*, II, pp. 173–81, p. 184, talks of 'boys' carrying the gossip to Rome.
26. *Sermones*, III, p. 189.
27. *Sermones*, III, p. 189.
28. Cornford, p. 93.
29. Cornford, p. 94.
30. *OxHist II*, p. 206.
31. *FascZiz*, p. 245.
32. Cornford, p. 106.
33. Cornford, p. 108.
34. Worcester Cathedral MS F.6.5; and see S.L. Forte, 'A Study of some Oxford Schoolmen of the middle of the fourteenth century, with special reference to Worcester Cathedral MS F.6.5' (Oxford BLit. thesis, 1947).
35. Thomson distinguishes several groups of these, p. 227.
36. *OxHist II*, p. 206. In 'Binham' are speeches of seven lords *in quodam concilio*. Thomson suggests that this was a fictional council. *Opera Minora*, pp. 425–29, Thomson, no. 382.
37. *Opera Minora*, p. 415.
38. Thomson item 378–84 on *Determinacio* literature and the relationship and dating of the various pieces, mostly in the mid-late 1370s
39. And also that he had actively sought papal acceptance of the clergy's acquiring property, *Determinatio* in *Opera Minora*, p. 425, but see Thomson items 382, 383 on this work, or rather these works.
40. *Opera Minora*, p. 422.
41. *Opera Minora*, pp. 405–14 and 415–30. Thomson 381 and 382, dated by Thomson in 1377–78.
42. See Chapter 3 for the malicious misuse of *reportatio* in such situations. *CivDom* I, I.37, p. 267.
43. Thomson, p. 41.
44. *OxHist II*, p. 203 note 93; *Opera Minora*, pp. 405–14, responding to Uthred's unpublished remarks, Durham Cathedral MS, A.IV/33. fols. 69–99v. On Uthred's career, see further *OxHist II*, pp. 184–85.
45. Holmes, pp. 169ff.
46. *Chronicon*, pp. 184–91; *HistAng*, pp. 356–64.
47. Wyclif may have got the idea of an 'ecclesiae pars' from Marsilius, Civ Dom I, p. 267.
48. Margaret Harvey, 'Adam Easton and the condemnation of John Wyclif', *EHR*, 118 (1998), pp. 321–34, p. 326.
49. Dahmus, *William Courtenay* (Pennsylvania, 1966), p. 45.
50. *Chronicon*, p. 183; cf. *HistAng*, I, p. 356.

51. Margaret Harvey, 'Adam Easton and the condemnation of John Wyclif', *EHR*, 118 (1998), pp. 321–34, p. 329.
52. Margaret Harvey, 'Adam Easton and the condemnation of John Wyclif', *EHR*, 118 (1998), pp. 321–34, pp. 331–34, with full annotation.
53. A lawyer whose career at Bologna dates from 1350 and who had supported the papalist side. He had an interest in the theology as well as the legal aspects of the questions under discussion. His *De Somnio* pretends to be a dream Legnano had had in 1372. Legnano leaned towards a Ps-Dionysian theory in which the organizing principle of power in the world is that of a celestial hierarchy, with temporal power flowing from spiritual power. Legnano was the leader of a delegation from Bologna to support the Pope in 1377. See Margaret Harvey, 'Adam Easton and the condemnation of John Wyclif', *EHR*, 118 (1998), pp. 321–34, p. 330; J.P. McCall, 'The writings of John of Legnano with a List of Manuscripts', *Traditio*, xxiii (1967), pp. 415–37.
54. Margaret Harvey, 'Adam Easton and the condemnation of John Wyclif', *EHR*, 118 (1998), pp. 321–34, p. 327.
55. For the sources of these propositions in *CivDom*, see Dahmus, *Prosecution*, p. 51, note 7.
56. Letter to Jemima Newton, 4 March 1829, John Henry Newman, *Letters and Diaries*, ed. Ian Ker and Thomas Gornal (Oxford, 1979), II, p. 127.
57. *Chronicon*, pp. 173–75; cf. *HistAng*, pp. 344–46.
58. Dahmus, *Prosecution*, p. 53.
59. *De apostasia*, ed. M.H. Dziewicki, Wyclif Society (London, 1889), p. 9.
60. *Eulogium*, III, pp. 348–49.
61. On all this see Dahmus, *Prosecution*, pp. 55ff.
62. N.B Lewis, 'The "Continual Council" in the early years of Richard II, 1377–80', *EHR*, 41 (1926), pp. 246–51, p. 250.
63. *FascZiz*, pp. 245–57. On all this see Dahmus, *Prosecution*, pp. 56–57, and Workman, I, p. 311. *Responsio ad quesita regis et concilii de questione utrum licet thesaurum retinere*. *FascZiz*, pp. 258–71 and see Thomson, nos. 398 and 199, which he places in November 1377 and early 1378 and links the latter with the *Protestacio* or *Declaraciones* of the same period. Also Thomson, no. 400. See, too, Rex, p. 28, note 12.
64. *FascZiz*, pp. 258–71.
65. Tr. Joseph Dahmus, 'John Wyclif and the English Government', *Speculum*, 35 (1960), pp. 51–68, pp. 57–58.
66. Dahmus, *Prosecution*, p. 57.
67. *HistAng*, pp. 357–63.
68. *FascZiz*, p. 258; *PW*, I.xlii, lvi, lxxv–vi.
69. *Libellus*, *FascZiz*, p. 257.
70. *Libellus*, *FascZiz*, p. 255.
71. *FascZiz*, p. 258. Wyclif examines elsewhere Arnaldus's pretensions to legitimacy in taking the taxes in terms of the claim he made to be doing nothing harmful to the realm of England (*damnosum regni*). *De iuramento Arnaldi*, ed. G. Lechler, *Johann von Wyclif und die Vorgeschichte der Reformation*, II (Leipzig, 1873), pp 575–79. Thomson, no. 397.
72. Dahmus, *Prosecution*, pp. 59–60.
73. MS Oxford, Bodleian Library, e Musaeo 86, has the reference to the gag at the end. Joseph Dahmus, 'John Wyclif and the English Government', *Speculum*, 35 (1960), pp. 51–68, p. 57; and *FascZiz*. pp. 258–71. Dahmus, *Prosecution*, pp. 58–61, discusses this gagging and concludes in favour of its probability.
74. Thomson, nos. 398 and 399 on documents relating to this.
75. *OxHist II*, p. 208.
76. *VSS*, I, p. 374.

77. *Chronicon*, p. 183; *HistAng*, I, pp. 356, 363, 397; Joseph Dahmus, 'John Wyclif and the English Government', *Speculum*, 35 (1960), pp. 51–68, p. 55, p. 68.
78. *Chronicon*, p. 189, *HistAng*, I, p. 362.
79. *Chronicon*, p. 183; *HistAng*, I, p. 356
80. *Chronicon*, p. 190; and *HistAng*, I, p. 363; cf. Dahmus, *Prosecution*, p. 69.
81. *Eulogium*, III, p. 348; cf. Dahmus, *Prosecution*, p. 70, who observes that Oxford had also accepted that his ideas might well be true if they were better put.
82. *Chronicon*, p. 190; *HistAng*, I, p. 363; Eulogium, III.348.
83. Walter Ullmann, *The Origins of the Great Schism* (London, 1948), Chapter 7.
84. Wyclif's sole known summoning before Parliament was this appearance before the House of Commons later in 1378 to defend a breach of sanctuary by emissaries of the king, which had been committed at Westminster. See Rex, p. 31, for the question which assembly he actually went to. *De ecclesia* Chapter 7 appears to be the opinion of Wyclif put before Parliament at the king's command. See *De ecclesia*, p. ix.
85. J. Charles Cox, *The Sanctuaries and Sanctuary Seekers of Mediaeval England* (London, 1911), pp. 51–53.
86. *De ecclesia*, p. 145.
87. *De ecclesia*, p. 147.
88. *De ecclesia*, p. 149.
89. *De ecclesia*, pp. 148–49.

Chapter 11

1. David L. Kirp, 'Management 101 at the "New Oxford"', *International Higher Education*, 35 (2004), p. 12.
2. *FascZiz*, p. 318.
3. In the list of Masters who disputed or determined against Wyclif are mentioned a monk of Durham and a monk of St. Albans, *FascZiz*, p. 241.
4. See *OxHist II*, p. 184 for an unpublished notebook describing topics in the air in the 1360s in Oxford, now Worcester Cathedral MS F.65; and the Oxford BLitt thesis on this by S.L. Forte, 1947. See too, W. Scase, *Piers Plowman and the new Anticlericalism* (Cambridge 1989).
5. *FascZiz*, pp. 110–13.
6. Phillip Pullman, *Northern Lights* (London, 1996).
7. *De ecclesia*, p. 159.
8. *Opera Minora*, pp. 196–97.
9. *FascZiz*, p. 111; cf. *FascZiz*, pp. 108–09.
10. See MunAcad, vol. 1, pp. 189–90, 207–12, 220–24, for the Proctors' book recording this and giving a picture of the disciplinary process.
11. *De ecclesia*, p. 145.
12. *De ecclesia*, p. 147.
13. *De ecclesia*, p. 149.
14. Probably written after the events it describes here, since it mentions the dispersing of Wyclif's ashes in 1428.
15. On Lollard doctrine on this point, see Hudson, *Reformation*, pp. 105, 108, 111, 115.
16. M.D. Matthew, 'The date of Wyclif's attack on transubstantiation', *EHR*, 5 (1890), pp. 328–30.
17. *FascZiz*, p. 104.

18. Compare *De simonia*, pp. 39 and 69 on the Eucharist.
19. *FascZiz*, p. 104
20. *FascZiz*, pp. vii–viii.
21. *De eucharistia*, p. 52. Wyclif may have begun to teach on the Eucharist as early as 1377, but it was probably not until near the end of his teaching career that he took the subject up, Maurice Keen, *Wyclif in his times*, p. 4.
22. J. de Montclos, Lanfranc et Bérengar, SSLov, 37 (1971).
23. *Sermones*, II, p. 454.
24. *Sermones*, II, p. 454.
25. References to Berengar occur, for example, in *FascZiz*, p. 114, p. 128 and p. 130, in Wyclif's defence. *The Confession* of Master John Tyssington, Friars Minor, mentions Berengar, *FascZiz*, p. 155. Also Thomas Wynterton, Augustinian and Wyclif's Oxford contemporary, *FascZiz*, p. 224, who says the condemnation of Berengar is not to be taken literally.
26. See Anne Hudson, 'The Mouse in the Pyx: Popular heresy and the Eucharist', *Trivium*, 26 (1991), 40–53.
27. *OxHist I*, p. 628ff; cf. William of Ockham, *Quaestiones in Librum Quartum Sententiarum Reportatio*, Book IV, Q.VI, ed. R. Wood and G. Gál (New York, 1984).
28. *OxHist I*, p. 630.
29. Thomson, p. 48; *De ente*, ed. M.H. Dziewicki, Wyclif Society (London, 1909). Book II, Tractate 6 (*De Annihilatione*), last three chapters.
30. *De eucharistia*, p. 3 and p. 26.
31. *Sermones* II, p. 454.
32. *De eucharistia*, p. 3.
33. *FascZiz*, p. 113.
34. *De blasphemia*, p. 89. The vote was divided and it would be useful to know which way Rygge voted.
35. Wilkins, *Concilia*, III, p. 171.
36. *FascZiz*, pp. 112–13
37. In order to know what one must not listen to, one would have to have learned it carefully off by heart, *FascZiz*, p. 112.
38. *FascZiz*, pp. 110–13 and Wilkins, *Concilia*, III, pp. 171–72.
39. *FascZiz*, pp. 112–13.
40. *FascZiz*, pp. 110–13.
41. *FascZiz*, p. 113.
42. Wyclif refuted in this new version all the teaching of the masters of the second millennium on the subject of the sacrament of the altar, except Berengar, *FascZiz*, p. 114.
43. *FascZiz*, pp. 115–32.
44. *FascZiz*, pp. 115–32, pp. 119–20.
45. *FascZiz*, pp. 115–32, p. 125.
46. *OxHist II*, p. 214.
47. *FascZiz*, p. 132.
48. *FascZiz*, p. 133.
49. *FascZiz*, pp. 169–71.
50. *FascZiz*, p. 195.
51. *FascZiz*, p. 156.
52. *FascZiz*, p. 134.
53. *FascZiz*, p. 135.
54. *Confessio*, *FascZiz*, p. 139.
55. *Confessio, FascZiz*, p. 143.
56. *FascZiz*, pp. 145 and 155.

57. *FascZiz*, pp. 181–238.
58. *FascZiz*, p. 183 and p. 195.
59. *FascZiz*, p. 187.
60. *OxHist II*, pp. 213–14 on this, and see Dahmus, *Prosecution*, pp. 133–34.
61. *FascZiz*, p. 114.
62. For some pointers on this question of the theological capacities of John of Gaunt, see William J. Courtenay, *Schools and scholars in fourteenth-century England* (Princeton, 1987), pp. 356–80 on the rise of a literature of the courts in the late 1370s in England. The debate about the existence of a court culture may be found in Gervase Matthew, *The Court of Richard II* (London, 1968), Richard Green, *Poets and Princepleasers. Literature and the English Court in the Late Middle Ages* (Toronto, 1980) and *English court culture in the Later Middle Ages*, ed. V.J. Scattergood and J.W. Sherborne (London, 1983).
63. *Trialogus*, p. 375.
64. In *FascZiz*, pp. 273–74; and see Hudson, *Reformation*, pp. 168ff.
65. *Chronicon*, p. 321; *HistAng*, II.32; and Dahmus, *Prosecution*, pp. 82–83.
66. *Chronicon*, pp. 320–22 and *HistAng* II.32–33.
67. MS Bodley 158; Hudson, *Reformation*, p. 68.
68. *Opera Minora*, pp. 201–05; Thomson, no. 384.
69. *Chronicon*, p. 321.
70. Knighton, pp. 240–41.
71. *FascZiz*, pp. 273–74.
72. *FascZiz*, pp. 273–74.
73. *Chronicon*, p. 309, and *HistAng*, II.10. On the revolt, see Steven Justice, *Writing and rebellion: England in 1381* (Berkeley, University of California Press, 1994).
74. *FascZiz*, pp. 292–95.

Chapter 12

1. Hans Küng, *My struggle for freedom*, tr. John Bowden (London/New York, 2002), p. 1.
2. [Lewis Eliot] in Ronald Millar, *The Affair*, play based on C.P. Snow, *The Masters* (London, 1964), p. 119.
3. See Chapter 1.
4. Hudson, *Selections from English Wycliffite Writings*, Item 4, pp. 29–33.
5. *OxHist II*, p. 214 n.314.
6. He may just possibly have been brought back to appear before the Provincial Synod in Oxford in November 1382, at which the remnant which had held out after Blackfriars finally submitted. The evidence that he did so is slight. See Dahmus, *Prosecution*, pp. 136–37.
7. *De septem donis spiritus sancti*, in *PW*, vol. I, p. 227. Thomson, no. 50, late 1383.
8. *De simonia*, p. 1.
9. *De simonia*, p. 1.
10. *De simonia*, p. 2.
11. *De simonia*, p. 2.
12. *De simonia*, p. 14; Corpus Iuris Canonici, I. 360 (c.11, C.1, q.1); and Corpus Iuris Canonici, I. 360 (c.7, C.1, q.3).
13. *De simonia*, p. 16.
14. *De simonia*, p. 17.
15. *De simonia*, p. 19.
16. *De simonia*, p. 20.

17. *Dubitatur an liceat adire curiam Romanam pro beneficiis ecclesiasticis acquirendis, et videtur quod non.*
18. *De simonia*, p. 23.
19. *Tunc enim clerici viverent Cristo conformius, nec forent tantum maculati cum fastu seculi nec negociis secularibus implicat*, *VSS*, xxxi, III, p. 238.
20. *VSS*, xxxi, III, p. 239.
21. *De apostasia*, late 1380, Thomson no. 36
22. *De apostasia*, p. 13.
23. *De apostasia*, p. 2.
24. *De apostasia*, p. 10
25. *De apostasia*, p. 2.
26. *De apostasia*, p. 1.
27. *De apostasia*, p. 6 and p. 10.
28. *De blasphemia*, p. 7.
29. *De blasphemia*, p. 247–50.
30. *De blasphemia*, p. 9.
31. *De blasphemia*, p. 16.
32. *De blasphemia*, p. 17.
33. *FascZiz*, p. 108 and *De blasphemia*, p. 27.
34. *The letters of John Hus*, ed. M. Spinka (Manchester, 1972), p. 5.
35. *De blasphemia*, p. 89.
36. *Opera Minora*, pp. 258–312, p. 258, Thompson no. 388, 1383–84.
37. *Opera Minora*, pp. 258–312, p. 275, Thompson, no. 388, 1383–84.
38. *De fratribus ad scholares*, p. 18, Thomson, no 392, mid-1382.
39. D. Leader, *History of Cambridge* (Cambridge, 1988), vol. I; Trinity College Dublin, MS A.5.3.
40. *Sermones*, III, p. 254, Thomson, no. 206; Knighton, p. 298.
41. Knighton, p. 290.
42. It has been suggested that this was Peter Stokes, but it could have been Stephen Patrington or Richard Maidstone. See Workman, II, pp. 247–49 and pp. 275–77.
43. *Sermones*, III, p. 246, Thomson, no. 205.
44. See, for example, Bernard of Clairvaux, *Sermones* on the Song of Songs, *Sermo* 64.III.8; *Opera Omnia*, ed. J. Leclercq, C.H. Talbot and H. Rochais, vol. II (Rome, 1958), p. 170; and *Sermones* 64–66 *passim*.
45. T. Wright, *Political Poems and Songs, RS* 14, 2 vols. (1858), A, p. 260.
46. *De fundacione sectarum*, p. 13. Thomson, no. 431, late 1383.
47. Knighton, p. 290. On Purvey see James Crompton, 'Leicestershire Lollards, *Transactions of the Leicestershire Archaeological and Historical Society*, 44 (1968–69), 11–44, pp. 17–18.
48. *De fundacione sectarum*, p. 31. Thomson, no. 431, late 1383.
49. *CivDom* II, p. 1
50. Augustine, *Retractationes*, P. Knoll, *CSEL*, 36 (1902), p. 7.
51. Thomson, no 405, mid-1376 and early 1384.
52. *De servitute civili et dominio seculari*, Thomson, no. 204 on John 1:17.
53. See *CivDom* I, pp. xxii and xxxiv.
54. *De servitute civili et dominio seculari*, p. 146.
55. *De servitute civili et dominio seculari*, p. 158.
56. Thomson, no. 49.
57. *Trialogus*, ed. G. Lechler (Oxford, 1869).
58. The Wyclif Society edition of 1904 by Rudolf Beer was based on three Vienna manuscripts and one Prague manuscript, though eleven manuscripts are now known.

Beer thought the text loosely constructed and incomplete, and suggested that it may represent mere notes taken by a student in a lecture. On the basis of the additional manuscripts Thomson rates it more highly as a piece on its way to being a treatise Wyclif had worked over and was turning into a completed work. Thomson, no. 21, p. 37, *De compositione hominis*, p. xv–xvi, p. 2.
59. Thomson, no. 424, mid-1382
60. Thomson, no. 425, late 1382.
61. *De salutacione angelica*, p. 393.
62. After the Oxford Convocation of Masters had condemned a list of his alleged opinions.
63. Wyclif Sermon xxxii, *Sermones*, III, p. 263, given at Whitsun in ?1378 or ?1384, Thomson, no. 207.
64. This short work was destined, in all probability, for the use of his 'poor priests', who needed urgently and in compact form, the sort of ammunition against their clerical opponents which Wyclif could so effectively supply. Sufficient attention has not been paid to whether Wyclif guided and taught 'poor preachers'. S.Harrison Thomson, 'John Wyclif, the "lost" *De Fide Sacramentorum*', *Journal of Theological Studies*, 33 (1931/2), pp. 359–65, p. 361. The text begins *Illa hostia alba et rotunda*, see Thomson, no. 40. Late 1381?
65. *The Letters of John Hus*, tr. M. Spinka (Manchester, 1972), p. 149.
66. Peter of Blois, later *Letters*, ed. E. Revell, British Academy (London, 1993).
67. John of Salisbury, *Letters*, ed. C.N.L. Brooke and W.J. Millor (Oxford, 1955, repr. 1986 and 1979), 2 vols.
68. *De amore sive ad quinque questiones*, Thomson, no. 393, 1383–84.
69. Thomson, no. 390, early 1382?
70. Thomson, no. 395, early 1383.
71. *Sermones*, III, 1.
72. See *VSS*, vi, vol. I, pp. 107–13 on the levels of Scriptural truth.
73. *Opus Evangelicum*, III, 2, vol. II, p. 7.
74. *VSS*, vi, vol. I, p. 107.
75. *EngWS*, vol. 2, ed. P. Gradon, p. 3.
76. *Opus Evangelicum*, vol. I, p. 1.
77. *Opus Evangelicum*, vol. I, p. 2.
78. James Crompton, 'Leicestershire Lollards, *Transactions of the Leicestershire Archaeological and Historical Society*, 44 (1968–69), pp. 11–44, p. 17. See J. Lelandi, *Antiquarii de Rebus Britannicis Collectanea*, ed. T. Hearne (Oxford, 1715), II, p. 409.
79. *Opus Evangelicum*, vol. I, p. 3.
80. *Opus Evangelicum*, vol. I, pp. 232–34.
81. *Opus Evangelicum*, III, 1, vol. II, p. 5.
82. *Expositio Matt. XXIII*, Thomson, no 372, late 1381. *Expositio Matt.* XXIV, Thomson, no. 373, mid-1383. Both these are polemical pieces, posing questions of genre and date and also questions about their relationship with the *Opus Evangelicum*, which Thomson explores.
83. Text in Anne Hudson, 'The debate on Bible translation', *Lollards and their Books* (London, 1985), p. 71.
84. Text in Anne Hudson, 'The debate on Bible translation', *Lollards and their Books* (London, 1985), p. 71.
85. Thomson, no. 408.
86. *Dialogus*, p. 2.
87. *Dialogus*, p. 2.
88. *Dialogus*, p. 2.

89. *The Lambeth Tract, The works of a Lollard preacher*, ed. Anne Hudson, *EETS*, 327 (2001), p. 73, discusses the opinion of Origen and makes a number of other references to patristic and other authorities.
90. Key texts are Numbers 18:20; Deuteronomy 18:1; Ezekiel 43:28.
91. *Dialogus*, viii, p. 15,
92. *Trialogus*, p. 39.
93. *Trialogus*, p. 326.
94. *Trialogus*, p. 327.
95. *HistAng*, pp. 119–21.
96. 'Sed postea per sententiam universalem Ecclesiae fuit exhumatum et ossa sua fuerunt combusta.' *Eulogium*, III, p. 367.
97. James Crompton, 'Leicestershire Lollards, *Transactions of the Leicestershire Archaeological and Historical Society*, 44 (1968–69), pp. 11–44, p. 17. See J. Lelandi, *Antiquarii de Rebus Britannicis Collectanea*, ed. T. Hearne (Oxford, 1715), II, p. 409.
98. *De citationibus frivolis et aliis versuciis Antichristi*, p. 556, Thomson, no. 413; late 1383?
99. Wyclif was highly vocal against the Crusade of Bishop Despenser of Norwich in 1382–83, see Thomson p. 48 n.4; *De servitute civili et dominio seculari, p. 159; De citationibus frivolis et aliis versuciis Antichristi*, Thomson, no. 413, p. 556; *De dissensione paparum*, Thomson, no. 410, late 1382; *Cruciata*, Thomson, no. 411, late 1382.
100. Letter to Urban VI, p. 2, Thomson, no. 404, 1384. No Vatican evidence of this summons is known to be extant. Thomson discusses the date and whether there was a summons at all, and the fact that this is not strictly a letter but rather a circular, pp. 260–61.
101. *De citationibus frivolis et aliis versuciis Antichristi*, Thomson, no. 413, p. 556; late 1383?
102. Letter to the Bishop of Lincoln, Thomson, no. 396, 1382 to early 1384.
103. Dahmus, *Prosecution*, pp. 140–43.
104. *PW*, vol. II, p. 554.
105. *Trialogus*, vi, p. 262.
106. *De oracione et ecclesie purgatione*, p. 342, Thomson, no. 46, late 1383.
107. *De oracione et ecclesie purgatione*, p. 344.
108. *De oracione et ecclesie purgatione*, p. 347.
109. *De septem donis sancti spiritus*, Thomson, no. 50, late 1383.
110. *De triplici vinculo amoris*, p. 161, Thomson, no. 427, mid to late 1383.
111. *De statu innocentiae*, p. 490.
112. *De perfeccione statuum*, Thomson, no. 426, p. 293.
113. *Responsiones ad argumenta cuiusdam emuli veritatis, Opera Minora*, pp. 258–312, p. 290, Thomson, no. 388, 1383–84.
114. *De perfeccione statuum, PW*, II, Thomson, no. 426, May 1383.
115. Margaret Harvey, *Solutions to the schism: a study of some English attitudes*, 1378–1409 (St. Ottilien, 1983), pp. 43–46.
116. *De Christo et suo adversario Antichristo*, Thomson no. 412, late 1382, a Christology defined by an Antichristology.
117. Thomson, no. 45, late 1382.
118. Bibliography in Thomson, p. 78.
119. Brian Tierney, *Origins of Papal Infallibility, 1150–1350* (Leiden, 1972), p. 105.
120. *De solucione Sathanae, PW*, vol. II, Thomson, no. 435, late 1383–84.
121. Richard Bauckham, *The Tudor Apocalypse* (Sutton Courtenay, 1975), p. 28; see also letter of John Bale printed in H.M. McCusker, *John Bale, Dramatist and Antiquary* (Pennsylvania, 1942), p. 58; and see John Bale, *Selected Works*, ed. H. Christmas, Parker Society (Cambridge, 1849).

Chapter 13

1. *De ecclesia*, chapter I, p. 11.
2. Thomson, no. 32.
3. *De ecclesia*, pp. 564–71.
4. *De ecclesia*, p. 37.
5. *De ecclesia*, p. 290; and see the reference to the *antipapa*, 'Vicar of Lucifer', on p. 309.
6. Anne Hudson, 'The development of Wyclif's Summa Theologie,' *John Wyclif, Logica, Politica, Teologia*, ed. M.F.B. Brocchieri and S. Simonetta (SISMEL, 2000), pp. 57–70, p. 70.
7. M. Spinka, *John Hus' Concept of the Church* (Princeton, 1966), pp. 252ff.
8. See G.R. Evans, *The Church and the Churches* (Cambridge, 1996).
9. This dual view of the faithful persists into modern Roman Catholic Canon Law
10. M. Spinka, *John Hus' Concept of the Church* (Princeton, 1966), pp. 252ff.; and see *Magistri Johannis Hus, Tractatus De ecclesia*, ed. S. Harrison Thomson (Boulder, Colorado, 1956), p. 1.
11. *Opera Minora*, p. 176.
12. *De ecclesia*, xvii, p. 388, referring back to question raised in Chapter v, p. 112.
13. *De ecclesia*, p. 388.
14. *De ecclesia*, pp. 389–90. The mystical eternity of the Church as Christ's body is referred to in *De ecclesia*, p. 391.
15. See Ralph Strode, *Responsiones ad 18 argumenta*, early 1379, *Opera Minora*, pp. 175–200.
16. *Magistri Johannis Hus, Tractatus De ecclesia*, ed. S. Harrison Thomson (Boulder, Colorado, 1956), p. 2.
17. *Opera Minora*, p. 176 bottom.
18. *Responsiones ad argumenta Radulphi Strode*, Thomson, no. 386, early 1379; *Opera Minora*, pp. 175–200. Past and future time meet at the present instant.
19. Brian Tierney, *Origins of Papal Infallibility, 1150–1350* (Leiden, 1972), p. 62.
20. *De ecclesia*, chapter I.
21. E. Talbot Donaldson, *Piers Plowman: the C-Text and its poet* (New Haven, 1949), pp. 202–03.
22. *De gradibus cleri ecclesie*, Thomson, no. 394, late 1382. This is Thomson's hypothesis.
23. *De gradibus cleri ecclesie*, p. 143; Thomson, p. 244.
24. T. Wright, *Political Poems and Songs, RS* 14 (1858), 2 vols., A, p. 255.
25. *CivDom* I, xxxviii, pp. 284–85.
26. *FascZiz*, p. 373.
27. *De ordinatione fratrum*, pp. 100–01. Thomson no. 432, late 1383.
28. E.M. Doyle, 'William Woodford, OFM (c.1330–c.1400). His Life and Works Together with a Study and Edition of His *Responsiones contra Wiclevum et Lollardos*', *Franciscan Studies*, 43 (1983), pp. 17–187, p. 121
29. E.M. Doyle, 'William Woodford, OFM (c.1330–c.1400). His Life and Works Together with a Study and Edition of His *Responsiones contra Wiclevum et Lollardos*', *Franciscan Studies*, 43 (1983), pp. 17–187, p. 122.
30. *Tam religio communis quam privata est a Deo.*
31. E.M. Doyle, 'William Woodford, OFM (c.1330–c.1400). His Life and Works Together with a Study and Edition of His *Responsiones contra Wiclevum et Lollardos*', *Franciscan Studies*, 43 (1983), 17–187, p. 123.

32. *De apostasia*, pp. 1–2.
33. E.M. Doyle, 'William Woodford, OFM (c.1330–c.1400). His Life and Works Together with a Study and Edition of His *Responsiones contra Wiclevum et Lollardos*', *Franciscan Studies*, 43 (1983), 17–187, p. 125.
34. E.M. Doyle, 'William Woodford, OFM (c.1330–c.1400). His Life and Works Together with a Study and Edition of His *Responsiones contra Wiclevum et Lollardos*', *Franciscan Studies*, 43 (1983), 17–187, pp. 137–38.
35. *De nova prevaricancia mandatorum*, Chapter 4, p. 127; Thomson, no. 415; 1375 and 1383, section probably from 1383.
36. Bonaventure, *Collationes in Hexaemeron*, Visio IV, Collatio 3.iii, ed. F. Delorme, *Bibliotheca franciscana Scholastica Medii Aevi* (1934), vol. 8.
37. *De ordine Christiano*, p. 138, Thomson, no. 414, early 1384.
38. Brian Tierney, *Origins of Papal Infallibility,1150–1350: A study on the concepts of infallibility, sovereignty and tradition in the Middle Ages* (Leiden, 1972). His view is disputed, but this study makes a good starting-point.
39. The warmth of Wyclif's regard for Bernard is puzzling in the light of the thrust of this work, so contrary to all Wyclif held to be important.
40. Brian Tierney, *Origins of Papal Infallibility, 1150–1350* (Leiden, 1972).
41. *Magistri Johannis Hus, Tractatus De ecclesia*, ed. S. Harrison Thomson (Boulder, Colorado, 1956), p. 20; cf. Wyclif, *De ecclesia*, p. 17.
42. Bonaventure, *Collationes in Hexaemeron*, Visio IV, Collatio 3.iii, ed. F. Delorme, *Bibliotheca franciscana Scholastica Medii Aevi* (1934), vol. 8.
43. Dahmus, *Prosecution*, p. 81 and p. 148.
44. A. Gwynn, *The English Austin Friars in the time of Wyclif* (Oxford, 1940), pp. 238–39 and pp. 253–55. See Anne Hudson, *Selections from English Wycliffite Writings* (Toronto, 1997).
45. *De potestate pape*, Thomson, no. 34, late 1379.
46. *Foxe's Book of Martyrs*, II, p. 48.
47. *De blasphemia*, p. 8.
48. *Eulogium*, III, p. 354.
49. Thomson, no 49, mid-1383.
50. *De fide catholica*, p. 98, Thomson, no 49, mid-1383.
51. *CivDom* III, p. 13.
52. *CivDom* III, p. 30.
53. *De apostasia*, p. 44.
54. Thomson, no. 429, mid-1383.
55. Bernard of Clairvaux, *De praeceptione et dispensatione, Opera Omnia*, vol. III.
56. *De nova prevaricancia mandatorum*, Chapter 4, p. 127, Thomson, no. 415; 1375 and 1383, section probably from 1383.
57. *De apostasia*, pp. 10–11.
58. *CivDom* III, p. 13.
59. Bernard of Clairvaux, *Sermones* on the Song of Songs, Sermo 66.V.11, Opera Omnia, ed. J. Leclercq, C.H. Talbot and H. Rochais, vol. II (Rome, 1958), p. 185.
60. *Sermones*, vol. III, pp. 230–39 (also surviving as de religione privata, II, *Sermones*, vol. III, pp. 246–48 and *Sermones*, vol. III, pp. 251–57).
61. *Multi augentes religionas privates sunt in hoc procuratores diaboli et sui proximi seductores. Sermones*, vol. III, p. 232.
62. '*Communem religionem christianam quod est religio pure obligans naturam racionalem ad observanciam decem mandatorum,*' *Sermones*, vol. III, p. 233.
63. '*Pseudofrater degens in seculo est dyabolus incarnatus cum adinventis suis signis sensibilibus, desponsatus ad seminandum discordia in militante ecclesia, ex summa cautela*

sathane machinatus,' Descriptio fratris, Thomson, no. 433, 1382–84. PW, II, p. 407.
64. *De quattuor sectis novellis*, Thompson, no. 429, mid-1383.
65. *De novis ordinibus*, p. 324, Thomson, no. 422, mid-1382.
66. *De quattuor sectis novellis, PW*, I, p. 242.
67. *De ordinatione fratrum*, p. 101, Thomson, no. 432, late 1383.
68. *De fide catholica*, pp. 98–99, Thomson, no, 49, mid-1383,
69. *De daemonio meridiano*, Thomson, no. 300, mid-1376.
70. *De condemnacione xix conclusionum, FascZiz*, pp. 481–492, p. 483.
71. The Church in its 'official' pronouncements has always stressed the importance of unanimity in matters of faith. In matters of rite it has allowed local churches (by which it meant dioceses and provinces) to go their own way up to a point. The problem is that liturgy carries a theology within it and a matter of 'order' can also be a matter of faith.
72. *Decrees of the Ecumenical Councils*, ed. Norman P. Tanner (Georgetown, 1990), 2 vols., pp. 231–33.
73. The list of citations of the *Decretum* at the end may have needed a reference book, so this may date from just before he left Oxford in 1381.
74. *De mendaciis fratrum, PW*, II, pp. 405–06, Thomson, no. 419, late 1381.
75. *CivDom* I, p. xxxviii, p. 284.
76. *CivDom* III, p. xxvii, p. 640.
77. *CivDom* I, p. xxxviii, p. 284.
78. *CivDom* II, p. ix, p. 94.
79. *Libellus, FascZiz*, p. 249.
80. *Libellus, FascZiz*, p. 249.
81. *Libellus, FascZiz*, p. 251.
82. *Libellus, FascZiz*, p. 250.
83. *CivDom* III, p. xxvii, p. 639.
84. *CivDom* I, p. ix, p. 94; and *Gloss to Decretum. CivDom* II, p. xi, p. 120.
85. J. Marrone, 'The absolute and the ordained powers of the Pope: an unedited text of Henry of Ghent,' *Mediaeval Studies*, 36 (1974), pp. 7–27.
86. J. Marrone, 'The absolute and the ordained powers of the Pope: an unedited text of Henry of Ghent,' *Mediaeval Studies*, 36 (1974), pp. 7–27, pp. 15–19, Latin text edited pp. 13–17.
87. One most usefully attempted in Hudson, *EngWS*.
88. *EngWS*, commentary vol. 5; *Select English Works*, ed. Thomas Arnold (Oxford, 1869), 2 vols., vol. 2.
89. *Opera Minora*, pp. 354–82.
90. *EngWS*, II, pp. 8–37.
91. *EngWS*, II, p. 328. *Lollard Sermons*, ed. Gloria Cigman, EETS, 294 (1989) show a similar pattern.
92. *EngWS*, II, p. 329.
93. *EngWS*, II, p. 334.
94. *EngWS*, II, p. 335.
95. *EngWS*, II, p. 335.
96. *EngWS*, II, p. 337.
97. *EngWS*, II, pp. 329–30.
98. *EngWS*, II, p. 331.
99. *De nova prevaricancia mandatorum*, Chapter 4, p. 126, Thomson, no. 415; 1375 and 1383, section probably from 1383.
100. Anne Hudson, 'Wyclif and the English language', in *Wyclif in his times*, p. 85.
101. Anne Hudson, 'John Purvey: a reconsideration of the evidence for his life and

writings,' *Viator*, 12 (1981), pp. 355–80, p. 372, discussing M. Deanesly, *The Lollard Bible* (1920), demolished here by Hudson, as are also the arguments of Forshall and Madden.

102. Thomson, no. Gspur.5.

103. Forshall and Madden; and A. Hudson, *English Wycliffite Writings*, Chapter 15.

104. *OxHist II*, p. 222.

105. See Jeremy Catto, '"Fellows and Helpers": the religious identity of the followers of Wyclif', *The medieval Church: universities, heresy and the religious life: Essays in honour of Gordon Leff*, Studies in Church History,*Subsidia*, 11 (Woodbridge, 1999), pp. 141–61.

106. Hudson, *Reformation*, pp. 239–40, suggests that the stilted first version became the more idiomatic later version by a process more complex than Forshall and Madden allowed; and that there was a gaining of confidence as the work began at Genesis and went forward to the New Testament.

107. Forshall and Madden, p. 48; and see A.J. Minnis, '"Authorial intention" and "literal sense" in the exegetical theories of Richard Fitzralph and John Wyclif', *Proceedings of the Royal Irish Academy*, lxxv, C (1975), p. 1. It has been suggested that three things 'are central to the thought of Wyclif and his later followers: a Bible liberated from a corrupt academia and its associated intellectual practices, as well as its perceived values and norms; a Bible self-consciously made accessible to a readership considered – at least theoretically – to be 'simple' and unlearned; the above processes seen as culminating in, indeed constituting, a return to the lost truths of Christ, of the apostles, and of the ecclesia primitiva.' Kantik Ghosh, *The Wycliffite Heresy: authority and the interpretation of texts*, Cambridge Studies in Medieval Literature, 45 (Cambridge, 2002), pp. 1–2, who goes on to refine and nuance this considerably. Ghosh looks at Wyclif's idea of the truth of Scripture in his first chapter.

108. *Prologue* to the Wycliffite Bible, I, Forshall and Madden, p. 1.

109. *Prologue* to the Wycliffite Bible, II, Forshall and Madden, p. 3.

110. Hudson, *Reformation*, p. 231.

111. See Anne Hudson, 'The debate on Bible translation', *Lollards and their Books* (London, 1985), pp. 67, 81, 155–57; and Kantik Ghosh, *The Wycliffite Heresy: authority and the interpretation of texts*, Cambridge Studies in Medieval Literature, 45 (Cambridge, 2002), pp. 86ff.

112. Ullerston's tract is in Vienna, MS Österreichische Nationalbibliothek MS 4133, and summarized in Anne Hudson, 'The debate on Bible translation', *Lollards and their Books* (London, 1985), pp. 71–74.

113. Kantik Ghosh, *The Wycliffite Heresy: authority and the interpretation of texts*, Cambridge Studies in Medieval Literature, 45 (Cambridge, 2002), p. 89.

114. Oxford, Merton College, MS K.2.2.

115. Knighton, p. 242.

116. Hudson, *Reformation*, pp. 99 and 186–87 on women and Lollardy. The reader will have observed the almost complete absence of women in Wyclif's story.

117. Knighton, pp. 242–44.

118. Kantik Ghosh, *The Wycliffite Heresy: authority and the interpretation of texts*, Cambridge Studies in Medieval Literature, 45 (Cambridge, 2002), p. 101 gives this passage.

119. Hudson, *Reformation*, pp. 235ff., on the various marginal and interlinear glosses.

120. Hudson, *Reformation*, pp. 236.

121. Hudson, Oxford, pp. 78–79; and Hudson, *Reformation*, pp. 235–36. See too the Biblical Concordance in British Library, MS Royal 17 Bi. And Sherman M. Kuhn, 'The Preface to a fifteenth-century Concordance', *Speculum*, 43 (1968), pp. 258–73.

122. *Lollard Sermons*, ed. Gloria Cigman, *EETS*, 294 (1989), pp. xliii–v.
123. Knighton, p. 290.
124. 1 Corinthians 14:19 (although Peter says it comes from Hebrews) which Peter paraphrases, *The Later Letters of Peter of Blois*, Letter 42, ed. Elizabeth Revell (Oxford, 1993).
125. Grosseteste on Galatians 5:24, *Lollard sermons*, ed. Gloria Cigman, EETS, 294 (London, 1989), pp. 109–10; Robert Grosseteste, *Expositio in Epistolam Sancti Pauli ad Galatas*, 6:9, ed. James McEvoy and Laura Rizzerio, *CCCM*, 130 (1995), pp. 39–40.
126. Its appropriation, along with other material of his, shows how readily Grosseteste was used by Wycliffite preachers.
127. *Speculum secularium dominorum, Opera Minora*, pp. 74–91, Thomson, no. 409, pp. 74–75.
128. [= holiness].
129. MS Bodleian Library, Bodley 649, sermon quoted ed. Roy M. Haines, 'Our Master Mariner, our Sovereign Lord: a contemporary preacher's view of King Henry V', *Mediaeval Studies*, 38 (1976), pp. 85–96, p. 89.
130. Edited by Anne Hudson and Pamela Gradon.
131. Kantik Ghosh, *The Wycliffite Heresy: authority and the interpretation of texts*, Cambridge Studies in Medieval Literature, 45 (Cambridge, 2002), pp. 112 ff., on these sermons.
132. *OxHist II*, p. 224; *EngWS*, vol. 2, ed. P. Gradon, p. 3.
133. Sermon 14, *EngWS*, II, pp. 532–38; cf. Wyclif *Sermones*, vol. III, p. 17.
134. Sermon 13, *EngWS*, II, pp. 529–30, cf. Wyclif *Sermones*, vol. III, p. 16.
135. Sermon 145, *EngWS*, III, pp. 60–64, p. 60.
136. Sermon 145, *EngWS*, III, pp. 60–64.
137. W.A. Pantin, Documents illustrating the Activities of the General and Provincial Chapters of the English Black Monks 1215–1540, Camden Society, Third Series, 45, 47, 54 (London, 1931–37), esp. III.76–77, and see II.76 and cf. II.11–12.
138. *De officio regis*, p. 193.
139. *Sermones*, vol. IV, Thomson, nos. 31, 37, 38.
140. Hudson, *Reformation*, pp. 63–65.
141. *Trialogus*, p. 379.
142. *Sermones*, vol. III, p. 230.
143. *Chronicon*, p. 190; and see *Eulogium*, vol. III, p. 348 on this point. See, too, R. Bird, *The turbulent London of Richard II* (London, 1949).
144. Alan of Lille, PL 210.114.
145. *Nequam*, p. 84, note 7.
146. *Nequam*, p. 87 from Sermon 3.
147. *Sermones*, vol. III, p. 190, Thomson, no. 199.
148. *Sermones*, vol. III, p. 189, Thomson no. 199.
149. See Hudson, *Reformation*, p. 65, on the question of the language these sermons were preached in.
150. See W. Mallard, 'Dating the *Sermones* Quadriginta of John Wyclif', *Medievalia et Humanistica*, 17 (1966), pp. 86–115 and 'Clarity and Dilemma – the Forty Sermons of John Wyclif', *Contemporary Reflections on the medieval Christian tradition: Essays in Honor of Ray C. Petry*, ed. G.H. Shriver (Durham, NC, 1974), pp. 19–38.
151. Ordered thus in the Wyclif Society edition: Sermons for the liturgical year (Sunday Gospels), vol. I; Sermons for saints' days (Gospels), vol. II; Sermons for the liturgical year (Sunday Epistles), vol. III; Liturgical sequence, mixed Gospels and

Epistles, plus Quadraginta sermons, vol. IV. Most of the *Sermones quadraginta* are between 1375 and 1379.

152. *Sermones*, vol. I, p. iv.

153. *Speculum secularium dominorum, Opera Minora*, pp. 74–91, Thomson, no. 409, p. 76.

154. *Sermones* Quadraginta, 5, *Sermones*, vol. IV, p. 45.

155. *Sermones* Quadraginta, 5, *Sermones*, vol. IV, p. 45.

156. *Trialogus*, II.14, pp. 121–23 and III.7, pp. 150–54, including a discussion of congruent grace.

157. *Trialogus*, II.14, p. 122, Thomson, no. 47, late 1382 or 1383.

158. *Chronicon*, p. 190.

159. Hudson, *Reformation*, p. 63.

160. *Chronicon*, p. 190.

161. R. Bird, *The turbulent London of Richard II* (London, 1949), pp. 63–66; and cf. A. Goodman, *John of Gaunt: the exercise of princely power in fourteenth-century Europe* (Harlow, 1992), pp. 60–61.

162. *HistAng*, II, p. 65; *Chronicon*, p. 349.

163. R. Bird, *The turbulent London of Richard II* (London, 1949), pp. 64–65.

164. Knighton, pp. 260–62; and cf. pp. 276–80.

165. Knighton; and see Hudson, *Selections from English Wycliffite Writings*, pp. 17–18.

166. Knighton, p. 252 note 1, pp. 256ff.; and see Hudson, *Reformation,* p. 201 and n.44; and Hudson, *English Wycliffite Writings,* pp. 17–18 and notes, and pp. 143–44.

167. Knighton, II.171; and MS Bodley 647, f.70.

168. See Miri Rubin, *Corpus Christi, the Eucharist in late medieval culture* (Cambridge, 1991).

169. Chaucer, *Shipman's Prologue*, lines 1173–85, 1188–90.

170. Although the C text, as amended after the beginnings of persecution of the Lollards in the early 1380s, includes additions distancing Langland from the Lollards. Wyclif's teaching of the 1370s about 'dominion' may have been what attracted Langland most, Elizabeth Salter, *Piers Plowman* (Oxford, 1962), p. 12; see also *A Companion to Piers Plowman*, ed. John A. Alford (California, 1988), p. 73.

171. Elizabeth Salter, *Piers Plowman* (Oxford, 1962).

172. For example, *Anglo-Saxon Satirical Poets and Epigrammatists of the Twelfth Century*, ed. T. Wright, RS 59a, 59b (London, 1872).

173. H.G. Richardson, 'Heresy and lay power under Richard II', *EHR*, 51 (1936), 1–28.

174. M. Aston, 'Lollardy and Sedition, 1381–1434', *Past and Present*, 17 (1960), 1–44.

175. E.F. Jacob, *The fifteenth century* (Oxford, 1961), p. 45.

176. Horner, p. 197; and see H.G.Richardson, 'Heresy and lay power under Richard II', *EHR*, 51 (1936), 1–28.

177. MS Lansdowne 409, f.39; and see Margaret Harvey, *English views on the reforms to be undertaken in the General Councils (1400–1418) with special reference to the proposals made by Richard Ullerston* (Oxford DPhil thesis, 1963), p. 22.

178. See Brian Stock, *The implications of literacy* (Princeton, 1983), on the general question of the rise of literacy.

179. Michael Wilks, 'Royal priesthood: the origins of Lollardy', *The Church in a Changing Society: CIHEC Conference in Uppsala* (Uppsala, 1978), pp. 63–70, p. 65.

180. Blackfriars, 1382, *Concilia III*, p. 157.

Conclusion

1. W.W. Shirley, *A Catalogue of the Original Works of John Wyclif* (Oxford, 1865), p. ix.
2. W.W. Shirley, *A Catalogue of the Original Works of John Wyclif* (Oxford, 1865), p. viii.
3. *PW*, I, pp. vi–viii.
4. W.W. Shirley, *A Catalogue of the Original Works of John Wyclif* (Oxford, 1865).
5. *PW*, I, p. vi.
6. *PW*, I, p. viii.
7. R. Buddensieg, *John Wiclif, Patriot and Reformer* (London, 1884), p. 13.
8. R. Buddensieg, *John Wiclif, Patriot and Reformer* (London, 1884), p. 13.
9. *The Letters of John Hus,* tr. M. Spinka (Manchester, 1972), p. 184; and see p. 161.
10. *The Letters of John Hus,* tr. M. Spinka (Manchester, 1972), pp. 137 and 141.
11. Only in later editions did *Foxe* add an account of the history of the primitive church and of dissidents before Wyclif.
12. M. Aston, *Lollards and Reformers. Images and Literacy in Late Medieval Religion* (London 1984), chapter 8, pp. 244–47.
13. *Foxe*, vol. II, pp. 47–48.
14. *Foxe*, vol. II, p. 49.
15. *Foxe*, vol. II, p. 48.
16. *Foxe*, vol. II, p. 49.
17. M. Aston, *Lollards and Reformers. Images and Literacy in Late Medieval Religion* (London 1984). p. 1.
18. *Foxe*, vol. II, p. 49; and see Arnold Williams, 'Chaucer and the Friars', *Speculum,* 28 (1953), pp. 499–513.
19. See M. Spinka, *John Hus at the Council of Constance,* Records of Civilization, Sources and Studies, 73 (1965).
20. Knighton, vol. II, pp. 179 and 186–87. Anne Hudson suggests that there was a deliberate choice on the part of Lollard leaders not to allow individual names to become prominent: Hudson, *Reformation*, pp. 10–11. On the other hand, *EngWS*, II, p. 328, and *Lollard Sermons,* ed. Gloria Cigman, EETS, 294 (1989), suggest some degree of personal if not nameable authorship.
21. *The Letters of John Hus,* tr. M. Spinka (Manchester, 1972), pp. 40, 41, 45, 203.
22. *The Letters of John Hus,* tr. M. Spinka (Manchester, 1972), p. 203.
23. Gordon Leff, 'John Wyclif: the path to dissent', *Proceedings of the British Academy*, 52 (1966), 143–80.
24. See, for example, A. Wilmart, *Auteurs spirituals et texts dévots du moyen âge latin*, Études augistuniennes, 8 (Paris, 1971).
25. The *De religione privata*, I, is an example. Thomson, no. Gdub. 1. Thomson discusses a series of pieces of the fourteenth and fifteenth centuries which survive in manuscripts, often of Prague or Vienna, and a few of which are ascribed to Wyclif in their titles, Thomson, pp. 305–10.
26. For example, in 1571.
27. And *Trialogus*, in Latin, Basle 1525
28. *John Bale's Index of British and other Writers*, (ed.) Reginald Lane Poole and Mary Bateson (London, 1902).
29. Thomson.
30. R. Finucane, *Miracles and Pilgrims* (London, 1977).
31. *The Letters of John Hus,* tr. M. Spinka (Manchester, 1972), p. 203.
32. See Mueller, Wyclif, p. 21, on Hus's assertion that Wyclif's writings were studied at the the University of Prague over some years.

33. *Concilia* III, p. 320.
34. MS Lansdowne 409, f.39v; and see Margaret Harvey, *English views on the reforms to be undertaken in the General Councils (1400–1418) with special reference to the proposals made by Richard Ullerston* (Oxford DPhil thesis, 1963), p. 21.
35. MS Lansdowne 409, f.39; and see Margaret Harvey, *English views on the reforms to be undertaken in the General Councils (1400–1418) with special reference to the proposals made by Richard Ullerston,* (Oxford DPhil thesis, 1963), p. 22.
36. Knighton, p. 298.
37. *Eulogium*, III, p. 355.
38. *FascZiz*, p. 272.
39. *Doctrinale*, II.71; cf. I.626
40. *HistAng*, pp. 324–25, p. 395.
41. *HistAng*, pp. 324–25, p. 395.
42. *PW*, II, p. 478; Thomson, no. 426, May 1383.
43. Knighton, p. 308.
44. Knighton, p. 250.
45. *The letters of John Hus* ed. M. Spinka (Manchester, 1972), pp. 214–15.
46. *The letters of John Hus* ed. M. Spinka (Manchester, 1972), p. 46.
47. Knighton, pp. xxxvii, xliv, 290–92.
48. Knighton, p. 290.
49. Anne Hudson, 'John Purvey: a reconsideration of the evidence for his life and writings,' *Viator*, 12 (1981), pp. 355–80, See, too, James Crompton, 'Leicestershire Lollards, *Transactions of the Leicestershire Archaeological and Historical Society,* 44 (1968–69), 11–44.
50. Emden, BioReg, vol. III, 1536–7. On Purvey's mental powers, see John Purvey, *Haereses et errores* extracted from his *Libellus* haereticus, *FascZiz*, pp. 383–99; and John Purvey, *Recantatio, FascZiz*, pp. 400–07.
51. *FascZiz*, pp. lxviii, 383–89 and 400–07, for his works and his uneasy return to respectability.
52. Anne Hudson, 'John Purvey: a reconsideration of the evidence for his life and writings,' *Viator,* 12 (1981), pp. 355–80, pp. 362–63.
53. Knighton, p. 286.
54. Knighton, p. 288.
55. Knighton, pp. 278–80.
56. *FascZiz*, pp. 329–30.
57. *FascZiz*, pp. 296–97.
58. *FascZiz*, p. 296.
59. Knighton, p. 292; Hudson, *Reformation,* p. 33.
60. Hudson, *Oxford,* p. 75ff.
61. Hudson, *Oxford,* p. 76.
62. Hudson, *Oxford,* p. 76; and on Oldcastle, see *OxHist II*, pp. 242, 247, 252–53.
63. Hudson, *Oxford,* p. 76.
64. There has been a good deal of debate on this point. Wyclif's early modern biographers were keen to portray him as the hero of the Reformation. G. Lechler, *John Wyclif and his English precursors*, tr. P. Lorimer (London, 1885), p. 189, asserts that 'it has long been known that Wycliffe sent out itinerant preachers of the Gospel'. He cites the evidence of Thorpe as proof that Wyclif was actively gathering supporters and sending out preachers while he was still in Oxford, although that is not quite what Thorpe says (ibid., p. 191). A similar view is taken by Lewis Sergeant, *John Wyclif* (London, 1893). See, too, *FascZiz*, p. xl. See the posing of this question by Anne Hudson and additional bibliography, *Premature Reformation*, pp. 62–63.

65. Knighton, pp. 242–43.
66. See Margaret Aston, *Lollards and Reformers* (London, 1984), p. 17.
67. Knighton, p. 298.
68. *Confessio Amantis*, I, line 349 and V, lines 1806–07 and 1869–79, *The Complete Works of John Gower*, ed. G.C. Macaulay (Oxford, 1899–1902), 4 vols.
69. Lay people who tried to live as though under a rule.
70. Chaucer, *The Shipman's Prologue*, ll. 1173, 1183–84.
71. For this reconstruction of the history of the term, see James Crompton, 'Leicestershire Lollards, *Transactions of the Leicestershire Archaeological and Historical Society*, 44 (1968–69), 11–44, p. 11.
72. On the letter of William Courtenay to the Bishop of Lincoln commending him for the zeal with which he is moving *contra eum insultatibus obvietur*, see Dahmus, *Prosecution*, pp. 36 and 138; *Concilia* III, pp. 168–69.

List of abbreviations

The following abbreviations are used in the end notes for speedy reference. Further information on sources is given in the Selected Bibliography.

AHDLMA *Archives d'histoire doctrinale et littéraire du moyen âge*
Bale John Bale, *Scriptorum illustrium maioris Brytanniae... catalogus*, Centuria Sexta (Basle, 1557–59), pp. 450–55
BioReg A.B. Emden, *A Biographical Register of the University of Oxford* (Oxford, 1957–59), 3 vols.
Brinton *The Sermons of Thomas Brinton* (1373–89), *Bishop of Rochester*, ed. Devlin, Camden Society, Third Series, 85–86 (London, 1954)
CCCM *Corpus Christianorum Continuatio Medievalis*
CCSL *Corpus Christianorum Series Latina*
Chaucer Geoffrey Chaucer, *The Canterbury Tales*, ed. Walter W. Skeat, *The Complete Works of Geoffrey Chaucer* (Oxford, repr. 1960).
Chronicon Thomas Walsingham, *Chronicon Angliae*, ed. E.M. Thomson, RS 64 (London, 1874)
CivDom I *De civili dominio*, I, ed. R. Lane Poole, Wyclif Society (London, 1885); late 1375–76
CivDom II *De civili dominio*, vol. II, ed. J. Loserth, Wyclif Society (London, 1900–04); before 1377, probably 1372
CivDom III *De civili dominio*, vol. III, ed. J. Loserth, Wyclif Society (London, 1900–04); before 1377, probably 1372
CivDom IV *De civili dominio,* vol. IV, ed. J. Loserth, Wyclif Society (London, 1900–04); before 1377, probably 1372
Collectanea *Collectanea*, I, ed. C.R.L. Fletcher, OHS, 5 (1885)
Collectanea II ed. Montagu Burrows, OHS, 16 (1890)
Collectanea III ed. Montagu Burrows, OHS, 32 (1896)
CSEL *Corpus Scriptorum Ecclesiasticorum Latinorum*
Cornford Francis Cornford, *Microcosmographia Academica*, ed. G. Johnson (Cambridge, 1994).
Dahmus, Prosecution Joseph H. Dahmus, *The Prosecution of John Wyclif* (New Haven, Conn., 1952)
Doctrinale Thomas Netter, *Doctrinale Antiquitatum Fidei Catholicae Ecclesiae*, ed. B. Bilanciotti (Venice, 1757–59, repr. Farnborough, 1967)
DomDiv *De dominio divino*, ed. R. Lane Poole, Wyclif Society (London, 1890)
EETS *Early English Text Society*
EHR *English Historical Review*
Emden, *Hall* A.B. Emden, *An Oxford Hall in Medieval Times* (Oxford, 1927).
EngWS *English Wycliffite Sermons*, ed. A. Hudson and P .Gradon (Oxford, 1983–96), 5 vols.
Eulogium *Eulogium Historiarum*, ed. Frank Scott Haydon, RS, 91 (London, 1863)
FascZiz *Fasciculi Zizaniorum*, ed. W.W. Shirley, RS 5 (London, 1958)
FitzRalph Richard FitzRalph, *De Pauperie Salvatoris*, ed. R.L. Poole, in Wyclif, *De*

Dominio Divino, Wyclif Society, (London, 1890), pp. 257–76
Forshall and Madden *The Holy Bible: made from the Latin Vulgate by John Wycliffe and his followers*, ed. J. Forshall and F. Madden (Oxford, 1850)
Foxe *Foxe's Booke of Martyrs, being a history of the persecution of the protestants (Acts and Monuments of the Christian church)*, II (1641) ed. A. Clarke and ed. G. Townsend (1843–49), 8 vols.
HistAng Thomas Walsingham, *Historia Anglicana*, ed. H.T. Riley, RS 28A, 28B (London, 1864)
Holmes George Holmes, *The Good Parliament* (Oxford, 1975)
Horner P.J. Horner, 'The King taught us the lesson: Benedictine support for Henry V's suppression of the Lollards', *Medieval Studies*, 52 (1990), pp. 190–220 and pp. 202–205
Hudson, Oxford Anne Hudson, 'Wycliffism in Oxford, 1381–1411, in *Wyclif in his Times*, Anthony Kenny (Oxford, 1986), pp. 67–84
Hudson, *Reformation* Anne Hudson, *The Premature Reformation* (Oxford, 1988)
JEH *Journal of Ecclesiastical History*
Knighton *Martin Knighton's Chronicle*, 1337–96, ed. G.H. Martin (Oxford, 1995)
Leff Gordon Leff, *The Universities of Oxford and Paris in the Thirteenth and Fourteenth Centuries* (New York, 1968)
Little G. Little, *The Grey Friars in Oxford*, OHS, 20 (Oxford, 1891)
Logica *De logica*, ed. M.H. Dziewicki, Wyclif Society (London, 1893–99), 3 vols.
Logica Mod. *Logica Modernorum*, ed. L.M. de Rijk (Assen, 1967), 2 vols.
ManDiv *De mandatis divinis and De statu innocentiae*, ed. J. Loserth and F.D. Matthew, Wyclif Society (London,1922)
Magrath J.R. Magrath, *The Queen's College* (Oxford, 1921)
Mueller *John Wyclif, Tractatus de Universalibus*, ed. Ivan J. Mueller (Oxford, 1985)
MunAcad *Munimenta Academica*, ed. H. Anstey, RS (London, 1868)
Nequam *The Schools and the Cloister: the life and writings of Alexander Nequam*, ed. Hunt, R.W. and Gibson, Margaret (Oxford, 1984)
OHS *Oxford Historical Society*
Opera Minora *Opera Minora*, ed. J. Loserth, Wyclif Society (London, 1913).
OxHist I *The History of the University of Oxford*, . vol. I, *The Early Oxford Schools*, ed. J.I. Catto (Oxford, 1984)
OxHist II *The History of the University of Oxford*, vol. II, *Late Medieval Oxford*, eds. J.I. Catto and Ralph Evans (Oxford, 1992)
Pantin, *Halls* W.A. Pantin, 'The halls and schools of medieval Oxford: an attempt at reconstruction', *Oxford Studies presented to Daniel Callus, OHS*, NS, xvi (1964), pp. 31–100
Parkes, *Books* M.B. Parkes, 'The provision of books', OxHist II, pp. 407–83.
PL *Patrologiae cursus completus… series Latina*, ed. J.P. Migne (Paris, 1864).
PW Rudolf Buddensieg, *John Wiclif's Polemical Works* (London, 1883), 2 vols.
Rex Richard Rex, *The Lollards*, Social History in Perspective (Palgrave, 2002)
RS Rolls Series
RTAM *Recherches de théologie ancienne et médiévale*
SA *Statuta Antiqua Universitatis Oxoniensis*, ed. Strickland Gibson (Oxford, 1931)
Smalley, *English Friars* Beryl Smalley, *English Friars and Antiquity in the early fourteenth century* (Oxford, 1970)
SSLov *Spicilegium Sacrum Lovaniense*
Thomson W.R. Thomson, *The Latin Writings of John Wyclif, An Annotated Catalog* (Toronto, 1983)
TRHS *Transactions of the Royal Historical Society*
VSS *De Veritate Sacrae Scripturae*

Waleys Thomas Waleys, *De modo componendi sermones*, ed. T.M. Charland (Paris/Ottawa, 1936)
Wilkins *Concilia Magnae Britanniae et Hiberniae* (4 vols., London, 1737), vol. III
Workman Herbert B. Workman, *John Wyclif, A study of the English medieval Church* (Oxford, 1926), 2 vols.
Wyclif in his Times *Wyclif in his Times*, ed. Anthony Kenny (Oxford, 1986)

Select bibliography

Sources

Works of John Wyclif

Most of Wyclif's Latin writings are still available only in the Wyclif Society editions (1883–1921). Williell R. Thomson's datings are given for convenience of reference. Unpublished writings and *dubia* and *spuria* are omitted from this list, but details may be found in Thomson. Some of the material in the *Fasciculi Zizaniorum*, ed. Walter W. Shirley, Rolls Series, 4, (London, 1958) is also of Wyclif's authorship.

Ad argumenta Wilelmi Vyrinham determinaciones, Opera Minora, 1913, pp. 415–30; 1378.
'Complaint', I.H. Stein, 'The Latin text of Wyclif's Complaint', *Speculum*, 7 (1932), pp. 87–94.
De actibus animae, ed. Moritz H. Dziewicki, *Miscellanea Philosophica*, I, (London, 1902), pp.1–127; c. 1365.
De amore, ed. J. Loserth, *Opera Minora*, Wyclif Society (London, 1913), pp. 8–10. 1383 or 1384?
De apostasia, ed. Moritz H. Dziewicki, Wyclif Society (London, 1889); late 1380.
De blasphemia, ed. Moritz H. Dziewicki, Wyclif Society (London, 1893); mid-1381.
De Christo et suo adversario Antichristo, De schismate [De dissensione paparum], Polemical Works, ed. R. Buddensieg, Wyclif Society (1883), 2 vols., II, pp. 653–92; late 1382.
De citationibus frivolis, Polemical Works, ed. R. Buddensieg, Wyclif Society (London, 1883), 2 vols., II, pp. 567–76. Late 1383?
De civili dominio, I, ed. R. Lane Poole, Wyclif Society (London, 1885); late 1375–76.
De civili dominio, vols. II–IV, ed. J. Loserth, Wyclif Society (London, 1900–04); before 1377, probably 1372.
De condemnacione xix conclusionum, FascZiz, pp. 481–92; early 1378 to mid-1378.
De contrarietate duorum dominorum, Polemical Works, ed. R. Buddensieg, Wyclif Society (London, 1883), 2 vols., I, pp. 13–80; mid-1382.
De daemono meridiano, Polemical Works, ed. R. Buddensieg, Wyclif Society (London, 1883), 2 vols., II, pp. 417–25; mid-1376.
De dominio divino, ed. R. Lane Poole, Wyclif Society (London, 1890); probably c. 1366.
De duobus generibus hareticorum, Polemical Works, ed. R. Buddensieg, Wyclif Society (London, 1883), 2 vols., II, pp. 431–32; early 1380.
De dyabolo et membris eius, Polemical Works, ed. R. Buddensieg, Wyclif Society (London, 1883), 2 vols., I, pp. 361–74; 1383 or 1384.
De ecclesia, ed. J.Loserth, Wyclif Society (London, 1886); early 1378 to early 1379.

De ente, ed. Moritz H. Dziewicki, Wyclif Society (London, 1909); (parts)1366–68.
De ente, ed. S.H. Thomson (Oxford, 1930); (parts) c. 1365.
De ente praedicamentali, ed. Rudolf Beer, Wyclif Society (London, 1901); c. 1369.
De eucharistia, ed. J. Loserth, Wyclif Society (London, 1892); mid-1380 to late 1380.
De eucharistia conclusiones duodecum, ed. John Lewis, *The History of the Life and Sufferings of the Reverend and Learned John Wiclif*, DD (2nd edition, Oxford, 1820), pp. 318–19; mid-1381 to late 1381.
De eucharistia et penitencia, De eucharistia, ed. J. Loserth, Wyclif Society (London, 1892), pp. 329–43. Early 1383?
De eucharistia minor confessio, FascZiz, pp. 115–32; 10 May 1381.
De fide catholica, ed. J. Loserth, *Opera Minora*, Wyclif Society (London, 1913); mid-1383.
De fide sacramenti (De eucharistia confessio), ed. S.H. Thomson, 'John Wyclif's "lost" *De fide sacramentorum*, *Journal of Theological Studies*, 33 (1932), pp. 359–65. Later 1381?
De fratribus ad scholares, ed. J. Loserth, *Opera Minora*, Wyclif Society (London, 1913), pp. 15–18; mid-1382.
De fundacione sectarum, Polemical Works, ed. R. Buddensieg, Wyclif Society (London, 1883), 2 vols., II, pp. 698–713; late 1383.
De gradibus cleri ecclesiae, ed. J. Loserth, Opera Minora, *Wyclif Society (London, 1913), pp. 140–44. Late 1382?*
De iuramento Arnaldi, ed. Gotthard V. Lechler, *Johann Wyclif und die Vorgeschichte der Reformation, II* (Leipzig, 1873), pp. 573–79; mid-1377.
De logica, ed. Moritz H. Dziewicki, Wyclif Society (London, 1893–99), 3 vols.; 1360–63.
De mandatis divinis and *De statu innocentiae*, ed. J. Loserth and F.D.Matthew, Wyclif Society (London, 1922); 1375– early 1376
De mendaciis fratrum, Polemical Works, ed. R. Buddensieg, Wyclif Society (London, 1883), 2 vols., II, pp. 405–06; late 1381.
De nova prevaricancia mandatorum, Polemical Works, ed. R. Buddensieg, Wyclif Society (London, 1883), 2 vols., I, pp. 116–50. 1375? And late 1383.
De novis ordinibus, Polemical Works, ed. R. Buddensieg, Wyclif Society (London, 1883), 2 vols., I, pp. 323–36; mid-1382.
De octo questionibus pulchris, ed. J. Loserth, *Opera Minora*, Wyclif Society (London, 1913), pp. 12–15. Early 1382?
De officio pastorali, ed. G. Lechler (Leipzig, 1863); early 1379.
De officio regis, ed. A.W. Pollard, Wyclif Society (London, 1887); 1379.
De oracione dominica, ed. J. Loserth, *Opera Minora*, Wyclif Society (London, 1913), pp. 383–92; 1382.
De oratione et ecclesie purgacione, Polemical Works, ed. R. Buddensieg, Wyclif Society (London, 1883), 2 vols., pp. 343–54; late 1383.
De ordinatione fratrum, Polemical Works, ed. R. Buddensieg, Wyclif Society (London, 1883), 2 vols., I, pp. 88–106.
De ordine Christiano, ed. J. Loserth, *Opera Minora*, Wyclif Society (London, 1913), pp.129–39; early 1384.
De paupertate Christi, ed. J. Loserth, *Opera Minora*, Wyclif Society (London, 1913), early 1378.
De peccato in spiritum sanctum, ed. J. Loserth, *Opera Minora*, Wyclif Society (London, 1913), pp. 11–12. Early 1377?
De perfectione statuum, Polemical Works, ed. R. Buddensieg, Wyclif Society (London, 1883), 2 vols., II, pp. 449–82; May 1383.
De potestate pape, ed. J. Loserth, Wyclif Society (London, 1907); late1379.
De quattuor sectis novellis, Polemical Works, ed. R. Buddensieg, Wyclif Society (London, 1883), 2 vols., I, pp. 241–90; mid-1383.

De schismate [De dissensione paparum], *Polemical Works*, ed. R. Buddensieg, Wyclif Society (1883), 2 vols., II, pp. 567–76; late 1382.
De septem donis spiritus sancti, Polemical Works, ed. R. Buddensieg, Wyclif Society (London, 1883), 2 vols., I, pp. 208–230; late 1383.
De servitute civili et dominio seculari, ed. J. Loserth, *Opera Minora*, Wyclif Society (London, 1913), pp. 145–64. Mid-1376? and early 1384.
De simonia, ed. Moritz H. Dziewicki, Wyclif Society *(1898); early 1380.*
De solucione Sathanae, Polemical Works, ed. R. Buddensieg, Wyclif Society (London, 1883), 2 vols., II, pp. 391–400; late 1383 or 1384.
De trinitate, ed. Allen duPont Breck (Boulder, Colorado, 1962); c. 1370.
De vae octupli, ed. J. Loserth, *Opera Minora,* Wyclif Society (London, 1913), pp. 313–53. Late 1381?
De vaticinatione sive de prophecia, ed. J. Loserth, *Opera Minora*, Wyclif Society (London, 1913), pp. 165–74; late 1382.
De veritate sacrae scripturae, ed. R. Buddensieg, Wyclif Society (London, 1905–07), 3 vols; late 1377 to end 1378.
Descripcio fratris, Polemical Works, ed. R. Buddensieg, Wyclif Society (London, 1883), 2 vols., II, p. 407; 1382–84.
Determinacio ad argumenta magistri Outredi, ed. J. Loserth, *Opera Minora*, Wyclif Society (London, 1913), pp. 405–14; 1377–78.
Determinationes contra Kylyngham Carmelitam, FascZiz, pp. 353–476; 1372.
'Dialogus', or 'Speculum Ecclesie Militantis', ed. A.W. Pollard, Wyclif Society, London, 1886). Late 1379?
Epistola missa archiepiscopo cantuariensi, ed. J. Loserth, *Opera Minora*, Wyclif Society (London, 1913), pp. 3–6; mid-1383.
Epistola missa episcopo Lincolniensi, ed. J. Loserth, *Opera Minora*, Wyclif Society (London, 1913), pp. 6–7; 1382 or 1384.
Errare in material fidei quod posit ecclesia militans, ed. S.H. Thomson, 'Three unprinted opuscula of John Wyclif', ed. S.H. Thomson, *Speculum, 3* (1928), pp. 248–53; late 1381.
Exhortacio cuiusdam doctoris, ed. J. Loserth, *Opera Minora*, Wyclif Society (London, 1913), pp. 413–35; 1378.
Expositio in textus Mattei XXIV, ed. J. Loserth, *Opera Minora*, Wyclif Society (London, 1913), pp. 354–82. Mid-1383?
Fasciculi Zizaniorum, ed. W.W. Shirley, *RS* 4 (1958).
John Wyclif, Tractatus de universalibus, ed. Ivan J. Mueller (Oxford, 1985); c. 1373?
Libellus ad parliamentum regis, FascZiz, pp. 245–57; early 1378.
Miscellanea Philosophica, ed. Moritz H. Dziewicki, Wyclif Society (London, 1902), 2 vols.
Opera Minora, ed. J. Loserth, Wyclif Society (London, 1913).
Opus Evangelicum, ed. J. Loserth, Wyclif Society (London, 1895), 2 vols.
Peticio ad regem et parliamentum, ed. I.H. Stein, 'The Latin text of Wyclif's complaint,' *Speculum, 7* (1932), pp. 87–94; 7–22 May 1383.
Polemical Works, ed. R. Buddensieg, Wyclif Society (London, 1883), 2 vols.
Postilla super totam bibliam, some passages ed. in Beryl Smalley, 'John Wyclif's Postilla super totam bibliam, Bodleian Library Record, iv (1953), pp. 186–205; others in Gustav A. Benrath, *Wyclifs Bibelkommentar* (Berlin, 1966).
Purgatorum sectae Christi, Polemical Works, ed. R. Buddensieg, Wyclif Society (London, 1883), I, pp. 298–316; 1382 or 1383.
Questio ad fratres de sacramento altaris, ed. J. Loserth, *De eucharistia*, Wyclif Society, 1892), pp. 347–48. 1381?
Responsio ad quesita regis et concilii de questione utrum licet thesaurum retinere, FascZiz, pp. 258–71; November 1377.

Responsiones ad argumenta cuiusdam emuli veritatis [=Ralph Strode], ed. J. Loserth, *Opera Minora*, Wyclif Society (London, 1913), pp. 258–312; late1383 to mid-1384.
Responsiones ad 44 conclusiones, ed. J. Loserth, *Opera Minora,* Wyclif Society (London, 1913), pp. 201–57; late 1383.
Sermones, ed. J. Loserth, Wyclif Society (1887–89), 4 vols.
Speculum secularium dominorum, ed. J. Loserth, *Opera Minora*, Wyclif Society (London, 1913), pp. 74–91; 1380 or 1381.
Trialogus, ed. G. Lechler (Oxford, 1869); late 1382 to early 1383.
Tractatus de Benedicta Incarnacione, ed. Edward Harris, Wyclif Society (London, 1886); before 1367.

English Wycliffite writings

The Holy Bible: made from the Latin Vulgate by John Wycliffe and his followers, ed. J. Forshall and F. Madden (Oxford, 1850).
Lollard Sermons, ed. Gloria Cigman, EETS, 294 (1989).
English Wycliffite Sermons, ed. A. Hudson and P. Gradon (Oxford, 1983–96), 5 vols.
Select English Works, ed. Thomas Arnold (Oxford, 1869), 2 vols., *Wyclif's Wicket* (Nuremberg, 1546).
Two Wycliffite texts, ed. Anne Hudson, EETS, 301 (1993).
The works of a Lollard preacher, ed. Anne Hudson, EETS, 327 (2001).

Early printed Wyclif material

Trialogus (Basle, 1525).
The Wycket (Nuremberg, 1546).
Two short treatises against begging friars (Oxford, 1608), published by T. James, Bodley's first librarian.

Other ancient, medieval and early modern sources

Abelard, Peter, *Historia Calamitatum*, ed. J. Monfrin (Paris, 1967).
Abelard, Peter, *Commentary on Romans*, CCCM, XI.
Anglo-Saxon Satirical Poets and Epigrammatists of the Twelfth Century, ed. T. Wright, RS 59a, 59b (London, 1872).
Anselmi Opera Omnia, ed. F.S. Schmitt (Rome/Edinburgh, 1938–68), 6 vols.
Aristoteles Latinus, IV, 1–4, ed. L. Minio-Paluello (Paris, 1968).
Aristotle, *Posterior Analytics*, ed. H. Tredennick (Loeb, 1970).
Augustine of Hippo, *De Civitate Dei.*
Augustine of Hippo and his monastic rule, ed. G. Lawless (Oxford, 1987).
Bacon, Roger, *Opera inedita,* ed. J.S. Brewer, RS 15 (London, 1859).
Bacon, Roger, *Compendium studii theologicae*, ed. H. Rashdall (Aberdeen, 1911).
Bale, John, *John Bale's Index of British and other Writers*, ed. Reginald Lane Poole and Mary Bateson (London, 1902).
Bernard of Clairvaux, *De Consideratione, Opera Omnia*, ed. J. Leclercq and H.M. Rochais (Rome, 1963), vol. III.
Bernard of Clairvaux, *De Praeceptione et Dispensatione', Opera Omnia*, ed. J. Leclercq and H.M. Rochais (Rome, 1963), vol. III.

Bernard of Clairvaux, 'Sermones in cantica canticorum', *Opera Omnia*, ed. J. Leclercq, C.H. Talbot and H. Rochais (Rome, 1958), vol. II.
Blund, Johannes, *De Anima*, ed. D.A. Callus and R.W. Hunt (London, 1970).
Boethius, *De Topicis Differentiis*, tr. E. Stump (Ithaca, Cornell, 2nd ed., 1988).
Boethius, Pseudo, *De disciplina scolarium*, ed. O. Weijers (Leiden, 1976).
Bonaventure, '*Sermones dominicales*', ed. Jacques Guy Bougerol, *Biblioteca Franciscana Scholastica Medii Aevi, 27* (1977).
Bradwardine, Thomas, *De Causa Dei,* ed. H. Savile (London, 1618).
Bradwardine, Thomas, *Tractatus de Proportionibus*, ed. and tr. H. Lamar Crosby (Madison, Wisc., 1955).
Bracton, *De Legibus et Consuetudinibus Anglie*, ed. George E. Woodbine (New Haven, 1915–40).
Brinton, Thomas, *The Sermons of Thomas Brinton (1373–89), Bishop of Rochester*, ed. M.A. Devlin, *Camden Society*, Third Series, 85–86 (London, 1954).
Burley, Walter, *De puritate artis logicae tractatus longior,* ed. P. Boehner (New York, 1955).
Chaucer, Geoffrey, *The Canterbury Tales*, ed. Walter W. Skeat, *The Complete Works of Geoffrey Chaucer* (Oxford, repr. 1960).
Collectanea, I, ed. C.R.L. Fletcher, OHS, 5 (1885).
Collectanea, II, ed. Montague Burrows, OHS, 16 (1890).
Collectanea, III, ed. Montague Burrows, OHS, 32 (1896).
Decrees of the Ecumenical Councils, ed. N.P. Tanner (Georgetown, 1990).
Dante, 'Il commento di Cola di Rienzo alla Monarchia di Dante', ed. P.G. Ricci, *Studia Medievalia*, third series, 6ii (1965).
D'Ewes, Sir Simonds, *Two speeches, the first touching the antiquity of Cambridge* (London, 1642).
Documents illustrating the Activities of the General and Provincial Chapters of the English Black Monks 1215–1540, ed. W.A. Pantin, *Camden Society*, Third Series 45, 47, 54 (London, 1931–37, esp. III.76–7).
Donatus, ed. H. Keil, *Grammatici Latini* (Leipzig, 1864), vol. IV.
Durandus de Huesca, '*Une somme anti-Cathare*', *Le Liber contra Manicheos,* ed. C. Thouzellier, *SSLov, 32* (1964).
Dymmok, Roger, *Liber contra xii errores et hereses Lollardum*, ed. H.S. Cronin (London, 1922).
'Epistolae Academicae', 1508–96, ed. W.T. Mitchell, *OHS,* NS, 26 (1980).
'Eulogium Historiarum', ed. Frank Scott Haydon, *RS*, 91 (London, 1863).
Foxe's Book of Martyrs, being a history of the persecution of the protestants (Acts and Monuments of the Christian church), II (1641) ed. A. Clarke and ed. G. Townsend (London, 1843–49), 8 vols.
Gascoigne, Thomas, *Loci e libro veritatum*, ed. J.E. Thorold Rogers (Oxford, 1881).
Geoffrey of Auxerre, *Libellus, PL* 185.
Gilbert of Poitiers, 'Commentary on Boethius, De Hebdomadibus', in *Commentaries on Boethius*, ed. N.M. Häring (Toronto, 1966).
Giles of Rome, (Aegidius Romanus), *De ecclesiastica potestate*, 3.7, ed. R. Scholz (Weimar, 1929).
Gratian, *Decretum Gratiani,* ed. J.P. Migne, PL 187.
Gregory the Great, '*Moralia*', ed. M. Adriaen Tournhout, *CCSL*, 143A (1979).
Grosseteste, Robert, *Commentary on Aristotle's 'Physics'*, ed. Richard C. Dales (Boulder, Colorado, 1963).
Grosseteste, Robert, *Commentary on the Posterior Analytics*, ed. P. Rossi (Florence, 1981).
Grosseteste, Robert, *De Decem Mandatis*, ed. R.C. Dales and E.B. King (London, 1987).
Grosseteste, Robert, *De Cessatione Legalium*, ed. R.C. Dales and E.B. King (London, 1986).

Grosseteste, Robert, *Expositio in Epistolam Sancti Pauli ad Galatas*, 6:9, ed. J. McEvoy and Laura Rizzerio, *CCCM*, 130 (1995).
Guibert of Nogent, *De Vita Sua*, ed. G. Bourgin (Paris, 1906).
Hostiensis, *Summa Aurea* (Lyons, 1588).
Hus, John, *Magistri Johannis Hus, Tractatus de ecclesia*, ed. S. Harrison Thomson (Boulder, Colorado, 1956).
Hus, John, *The Letters of John Hus*, tr. M. Spinka (Manchester, 1972).
John of Hauteville, *Architrenius*, ed. P.G. Schmitt (Munich, 1974).
John of Salisbury, *'Historia Pontificalis', ed. M. Chibnall,* Oxford Medieval Texts *(Oxford, 1986).*
John of Salisbury, *Metalogicon*, ed. J.B.Hall, *CCCM, 98* (1991).
Justinian, *Institutes,* ed. P. Krueger (Berlin, 1869).
Kilwardby, Robert, *De Ortu Scientiarum,* ed. Albert G. Judy (London/Toronto, 1976), Chapters 46–62.
Knighton, Henry, *Chronicon*, ed. J.R. Lumby, *RS 92* (London, 1858).
Knighton's Chronicle, 1337–96, ed. G.H. Martin (Oxford, 1995).
Langland, William, *Piers Plowman* ed. Elizabeth Salter (Oxford, 1962).
Logica Modernorum, ed. L.M. de Rijk (Assen, 1967), 2 vols.
Lollard sermons, ed. Gloria Cigman, EETS, 294 (London, 1989), pp. 109–110.
Luthers Werke (Weimar, 1932), vol. 39II.
Medieval Archives of the University of Oxford, ed. H.E.Salter, OHS, 70 (1920),
Munimenta Academica, ed. H. Anstey, *RS 50* (London, 1868).
Netter, Thomas, *Doctrinale Antiquitatum Fidei Catholicae Ecclesiae*, ed. B. Blanciotti (Venice, 1757–59, repr. Farnborough, 1967).
Ockham, William of, *De predestinatione,* ed. G. Boehner, *Opera Philosphica, II* (1978).
Ockham, William of, 'Expositio Aurea', on Perihermeneias', ed. G. Boehner, Opera Philosphica, II (1978).
Ockham, William of, 'In Librum Primum Sententiarum Ordinatio', ed. G. Gál and S. Brown, *Opera Theologica*, I (Bonaventure, New York, 1967).
Peter of Blois, *The Later Letters of Peter of Blois,* ed. Elizabeth Revell (Oxford, 1993).
Peter Lombard, *Sententie* (Spicilegium Bonaventurianum, 1971).
Priscian, *Institutes,* ed. H. Keil, Grammatici Latini (Leipzig, 1855–58).
Richard of Bury, *Philobiblon,* ed. and tr. E.C.Thomas (London, 1888).
FitzRalph, Richard, *De Pauperie Salvatoris.* ed. R.L. Poole, in *Wyclif, De Dominio Divino*, Wyclif Society, (London, 1890).
Richard Rolle, *Emendatio vitae and orationes ad honorum nominis Ihesu*, ed. Nicholas Watson (Toronto, 1995),
Simon of Tournai, *Disputationes*, ed. J. Warichez, SSLov, 12 (1932)
Snappe's Formulary, ed. H.E. Salter, OHS, 80 (1924).
Speculum Stultorum, Anglo-Saxon Satirical Poets and Epigrammatists of the Twelfth Century, ed. T. Wright, RS 59A, 59B (1872), 2 vols.
Statuta Antiqua Universitatis Oxoniensis, ed. Strickland Gibson (Oxford, 1931).
Swyneshead, Roger, 'Obligationes', ed. Paul V. Spade, *AHDLMA*, 44 (1977), pp. 243–85.
Waleys, Thomas, *De modo componendi sermones*, ed. T.M. Charland (Paris/Ottawa, 1936).
Walsingham, Thomas, *Chronicon Angliae*, ed. E.M. Thomson, *RS* 64 (London, 1874).
Walsingham, Thomas, *Historia Anglicana*, ed. H.T. Riley, *RS* 28A, 28B (London, 1864).
Walter of St. Victor, 'Le contra quatuor labyrinthos Franciae de Gauthier de Saint-Victor', ed. P. Glorieux, *AHDLMA*, 19 (1952), pp. 187–335.
William of Sherwood, *Syncategoremata*, ed. J.Reginald O'Donnell, *Mediaeval Studies*, iii (1941).
William of Sherwood, *Treatise on Syncategorematic Words*, tr. N. Kretzmann (Minneapolis, 1968).

Secondary sources

Alford, John A. (ed.), *A Companion to Piers Plowman* (California, 1988).
Arnold, Ivor D.O., 'Thomas Samson and the Orthographia Gallica', *Medium Aevum*, 6 (1939), pp. 193–209.
Aston, Margaret, 'Lollardy and Sedition, 1381–1434', *Past and Present*, 17 (1960), pp. 1–44.
Aston, Margaret, 'John Wycliffe's Reformation Reputation', *Past and Present*, 30 (1965), pp. 23–51.
Aston, Margaret, *Thomas Arundel* (Oxford, 1967).
Aston, Margaret, *Lollards and Reformers. Images and Literacy in Late Medieval Religion* (London 1984).
Baker, J.H., 'The Inns of Court in 1388', *The legal profession and the common law: historical essays* (London, 1986), pp. 3–6.
Baker. J.H., 'Learning exercises in the medieval Inns of Court and Chancery', *The legal profession and the common law: historical essays* (London, 1986).
Baker, J. H. and Ringrose, J.S., eds. *Catalogue of English Legal Manuscripts in Cambridge University Library* (Boydell, 1996).
Barratt, Alexandra, 'Dame Eleanor Hull: the translator at work', *Medium Aevum*, 62 (2003), pp. 277–96.
Benrath, Gustav A., *Wyclifs Bibelkommentar* (Berlin, 1966).
Bird, R., *The turbulent London of Richard II* (London, 1949).
Boyle, L., 'The curriculum of the Faculty of Canon Law at Oxford in the first half of the fourteenth century', *Oxford Studies presented to Daniel Callus, OHS*, NS, xvi (1964), pp. 135–62.
Brady, Ignatius, 'Background to the condemnation of 1270: Master William of Baglione, OFM', *Franciscan Studies*, 30 (1970), pp. 5–48.
Buddensieg, Rudolf, *John Wiclif, Patriot and Reformer* (London, 1884), p. 13.
Bygott, John, *Lincolnshire*, The County Books Series (London, 1952).
Catto, J.I (ed.), *The History of the University of Oxford*, vol. I, *The Early Oxford Schools*, (Oxford, 1984).
Catto J.I. and Evans, Ralph (eds.), *The History of the University of Oxford*, vol. II, *Late Medieval Oxford* (Oxford, 1992).
Chadwick, Henry, *Boethius* (Oxford, 1981).
Clanchy, M.T., '*Moderni* in Education and Government in England', *Speculum*, 50 (1975).
Clark, M.V., *Medieval Representation and Consent. A study of early parliaments in England and Ireland with special reference to the Modus Tenendi Parliamentum* (repr. New York, 1964).
Cobban, A., *English University Life in the Middle Ages* (London, 1999).
Colish, M., *Peter Lombard* (Leiden, 1994).
Cordeaux, E.H. and Merry, D.H. (eds.), *A bibliography of printed works relating to the University of Oxford* (Oxford, 1968).
Cornford, Francis, *Microcosmographia Academica*, ed. G. Johnson (Cambridge, 1994).
Cronin, H.S., 'John Wycliffe, the Reformer, and Canterbury Hall, Oxford', *TRHS*, Third Series, VIII (1914), pp. 55–76.
Cousin, J., *Recherches sur Quintilian* (Paris, 1975).
Cowdrey, H.E.J., *Lanfranc, scholar, monk and archbishop* (Oxford, 2003).
Cox, J.C., *The Sanctuaries and Sanctuary Seekers of Mediaeval England* (London, 1911).
Crompton, James, 'Fasciculi Zizaniorum', *JEH*, 12 (1961), pp. 35–45 and 155–66.
Crompton, James, 'Leicestershire Lollards', *Transactions of the Leicestershire Archaeological and Historical Society*, 44 (1968–69), pp. 11–44, p.13.

Dahmus, Joseph H., 'Was Wyclif a negligent pluralist?' *Speculum*, 28 (1953), pp. 378–81.
Dahmus, Joseph H., 'John Wyclif and the English Government', *Speculum*, 35 (1960), pp. 51–68.
Dahmus, Joseph H., *William Courtenay* (Pennsylvania, 1966).
Davis, H.W.C., *A History of Balliol College,* revised Davis and R.W. Hunt (Oxford, 1963).
Deanesly, M., *The Lollard Bible* (London, 1920).
Dickens, A.G., *Lollards and protestants in the Diocese of York, 1509–58* (Oxford, 1959).
Doyle, E.M., 'William Woodford, OFM (c. 1330 to c. 1400). His Life and Works Together with a Study and Edition of His *Responsiones contra Wiclevum et Lollardos', Franciscan Studies*, 43 (1983), pp. 17–187.
Emden, Alfred B., *An Oxford Hall in Medieval Times* (Oxford, 1927).
Emden, Alfred B., 'Northerners and Southerners in the organisation of the University to 1509', *Oxford Studies presented to Daniel Callus*, OHS, NS, xvi (1964), pp. 1–30.
Evans, G.R., *The Church and the Churches* (Cambridge, 1996).
Evans, G.R., *Law and Theology in the Middle Ages*(London, 2002).
Evans, G.R., ed. *Medieval Commentaries on the Sentences of Peter Lombard* (Leiden, 2002), vol. I.
Evans, G.R., *Old Arts and New Theology* (Oxford, 1983).
Farmer, D.H., 'New light on Uthred of Boldon', *Benedictines in Oxford*, ed. Henry Wansbrough and Anthony Marett-Crosby, (London, 1997), pp. 116–32.
Finucane, R., *Miracles and Pilgrims* (London, 1977).
Fletcher, John M., 'The Teaching and Study of Arts at Oxford,1400–1520' (Oxford, DPhil thesis, 1961).
Forde, S., 'Nicholas Hereford's ascension day sermon', *Mediaeval Studies*, 51 (1989), pp. 205–41.
Forte, S.L., 'A Study of some Oxford Schoolmen of the middle of the fourteenth century, with special reference to Worcester Cathedral MS F.6.5' (Oxford, BLitt thesis, 1947).
Gairdner, James, *Lollardy and the Reformation in England* (London, 1908), 2 vols.
Ghosh, Kantik, *The Wycliffite Heresy: authority and the interpretation of texts*, Cambridge Studies in Medieval Literature, 45 (Cambridge, 2002).
Gibson, M.T., *Boethius: his life, thought and influence* (Oxford, 1981).
Goodman, A., *John of Gaunt: the exercise of princely power in fourteenth-century Europe* (Harlow, 1992).
Gwynn, Aubrey, 'The Sermon diary of Richard Fitzralph', *Proceedings of the Royal Irish Academy*, xliv (1937), C.
Haines, Roy M., 'Our Master Mariner, our Sovereign Lord: a contemporary preacher's view of King Henry V', *Mediaeval Studies*, 38 (1976), pp. 85–96.
Haines, Roy M., *The Church and Politics in fourteenth century England: the career of Adam Orleton*, c.1275–1345 (Cambridge 1978).
Hanrahan, Michael, 'Defamation as a political contest during the reign of Richard II', *Medium Aevum*, 62 (2003), pp. 259–76.
Harvey, Margaret, 'English views on the reforms to be undertaken in the General Councils (1400–18) with special reference to the proposals made by Richard Ullerston', (Oxford, DPhil thesis, 1963).
Harvey, Margaret, 'Adam Easton and the Condemnation of John Wyclif, 1377', *EHR*, 118 (1998), pp. 321–34.
Harvey, Margaret, The English in Rome, 1362–1420: *Portrait of an Expatriate Community* (Cambridge, 1999).
Hatcher, J., *Plague, Population and the English Economy 1348–1530* (London and Basingstoke, 1977).
Henderson, Bernard William, *Merton College* (1898, repr. Routledge, 1998).

Hinnebusch, William A., *The early English Friars Preachers* (Rome, 1961).
Holland, T.E., 'The origin of the University of Oxford', *EHR* (1891), vol. VI, pp. 238–49.
Holmes, George, *The Good Parliament* (Oxford, 1975).
Hope, Emily Allen, *Writings ascribed to Richard Rolle Hermit of Hampole and materials for his biography*, Modern Language Association of America (New York, 1927).
Hudson, Anne, 'Wycliffism in Oxford, 1381–1411', in *Wyclif in his Times*, ed. Anthony Kenny (Oxford, 1986), pp. 67–84.
Hudson, Anne, *The Premature Reformation* (Oxford, 1988).
Hudson, Anne, 'Aspects of the "publication" of Wyclif's Latin sermons', *Late Mediaeval Religious Texts and their Transmission*, ed. A.J.Minnis (Cambridge, 1994), pp. 121–29.
Hudson, Anne (ed.), Wyclif, *Political ideas and practice: papers by Michael Wilks* (Oxbow, 2000).
Hudson, Anne, 'The development of Wyclif's *Summa Theologie*', *John Wyclif, Logica, Politica, Teologia*, ed. M.F.B. Brocchieri and S. Simonetta (SISMEL, 2000), pp. 57–70.
Hudson, Anne, 'Notes of an Early Fifteenth-Century Research Assistant, and the Emergence of the 267 Articles against Wyclif', EHR, 108 (2003), pp. 685–97.
Hunt, R.W., 'The medieval inventories of Clare College Library', *Transactions of the Cambridge Bibliographical Society*, 1 (1950), p. 125.
Hunt, R.W. ,'Oxford grammar masters in the Middle Ages', *Oxford Studies presented to Daniel Callus,OHS*, NS, xvi (1964), pp. 163–93.
Hunt, R.W., ed. Margaret Gibson, *The Schools and the Cloister: the life and writings of Alexander Nequam*(Oxford, 1984).
Hurley, Michael 'Scriptura sola: Wyclif and his Critics', *Traditio*, 16 (1960), pp. 275–352.
Jacob, E.F., 'Petitions for benefices from English Universities in the Great Schism', *TRHS*, Fourth Series, 27 (1945), pp. 41–59.
Jacob, E.F., 'On the promotion of English university clerks during the later Middle Ages', *JEH*, 1 (1950), pp. 172–86.
Jacob, E.F., *The fifteenth century* (Oxford, 1961).
James, T., *An Apologie for John Wickliffe, showing his conformitie with the new Church of England* (Oxford, 1608).
Jones, John, *Balliol College, a history* (Oxford, 2nd edition, 1997).
Kelly, H.A., 'Trial Procedures against Wyclif and Wycliffites in England and at the Council of Constance', *Huntingdon Library Quarterly*, lxi (1998/1999), pp. 1–28.
Kenny, Anthony, *Wyclif* (Oxford, 1985).
Kenny, Anthony (ed.), *Wyclif in his times* (Oxford, 1986).
Kenny, Anthony, 'The accursed memory: the Counter-Reformation Reputation of John Wyclif', *Wyclif in his times*, ed. A. Kenny (Oxford, 1986), pp. 147–68.
Kibre, P., *Scholarly privileges in the Middle Ages*, Medieval Academy of America, 72 (London, 1961).
Kirp, David L., 'Management 101 at the "New Oxford"', *International Higher Education*, 35 (2004), p. 12.
Kuhn, Sherman M., 'The Preface to a fifteenth-century Concordance', *Speculum*, 43 (1968), pp. 258–73.
Lahey, Stephen E., *Philosophy and Politics in the Thought of John Wyclif* (Cambridge, 2003).
Lambert, M.D., *Franciscan poverty* (London, 1961).
Langbaine, G., *The foundation of the University of Oxford* (London, 1621).
Leff, Gordon, *Bradwardine and the Pelagians* (Cambridge, 1957).
Leff, Gordon, 'Richard FitzRalph's *Commentary on the Sentences', Bulletin of the John Rylands Library, 45 (1963), pp. 390–422.*
Leff, Gordon, *Heresy in the Later Middle Ages. The relationship of heterodoxy to dissent c. 1250 to c. 1450* (Manchester, 1967), 2 vols.

Leff, Gordon, *The Universities of Oxford and Paris in the Thirteenth and Fourteenth Centuries* (New York, 1968).
Little, G., *The Grey Friars in Oxford, OHS, 20* (Oxford, 1891).
Lottin, O., *Psychologie et morale aux xiie et xiiie siècles, vol.V* (Gembloux, 1959).
Lytle, G.F., 'Patronage patterns and Oxford colleges c. 1300 to c. 1530', *The University in Society*, ed. L.Stone (Princeton, NJ, 1975), 2 vols.
Macaulay, G.C., (ed.) *The Complete Works of John Gower* (Oxford, 1899–1902), 4 vols.
Magrath, J.R., *The Queen's College* (Oxford, 1921).
Maitland, F.W., 'Wyclif on English and Roman Law', *The Collected Papers of Frederic William Maitland*, ed. H.A.L. Fisher (Cambridge, 1911), 3 vols.
Maitland, F.W., *The Letters of Frederic William Maitland*, ed. C.H.S. Fifoot (Cambridge, 1965).
Mallard, W., 'Dating the Sermones Quadraginta of John Wyclif', *Medievalia et Humanistica*, 17 (1966), pp. 86–115.
Mallard, W., 'Clarity and Dilemma – the Forty Sermons of John Wyclif', *Contemporary Reflections on the medieval Christian tradition: Essays in Honor of Ray C. Petry*, ed. G.H. Shriver (Durham, NC, 1974), pp. 19–38.
Martin, G.H. and Highfield, J.R.L., *A History of Merton College*, Oxford (Oxford, 1997), p. 100.
McCall, J.P., 'The writings of John of Legnano with a List of Manuscripts', *Traditio, xxiii* (1967), pp. 415–37.
McConica, James (ed.), *The History of the University of Oxford*, vol. III, The Collegiate University (Oxford, 1986).
McCready, W.E., 'Papalists and anti-Papalists: Aspects of the Church/State Controversy in the Later Middle Ages', *Viator, 6* (1975), pp. 241–273.
McFarlane, K.B., *John Wycliffe and the Beginnings of English Nonconformity* (English Universities Press, London, 1952).
McKisack, May, *The fourteenth century, 1307–1399* (Oxford, 1959), pp. 182–207.
Millar, Ronald, *The Masters*, play based on C.P. Snow, *The Masters* (London, 1964).
Minnis, Alastair J., '"Authorial intention" and "literal sense" in the exegetical theories of Richard Fitzralph and John Wyclif', *Proceedings of the Royal Irish Academy, lxxv,* C (1975).
Minnis, Alastair J., *Medieval Theory of Authorship* (Aldershot, 1988).
Montclos, J. de, Lanfranc et Bérengar, SSLov, 37 (Louvain, 1969).
Murphy, J.J., Medieval Rhetoric: a select bibliography (2nd edition, Toronto, 1982).
Murphy, J.J., 'Rhetoric in fourteenth-century Oxford', *Medium Aevum, 34* (1965), pp. 16–17.
Newman, John Henry, *Letters and Diaries*, ed. Ian Ker and Thomas Gornal (Oxford, 1979).
Owst, G., *Literature and Pulpit in Medieval England* (2nd edition, Oxford, 1961).
Pantin, W. A., 'The English Black Monks', *Camden Society,* Third Series, 47 (1933).
Pantin, W.A., *Canterbury College*, Oxford, vol. IV, OHS, NS, 30 (1935).
Pantin, W.A., *Documents illustrating the Activities of the General and provincial Chapters of then English Black Monks 1215–1540, Camden Society*, Third Series 45, 47, 54 (London, 1931–37).
Pantin, W.A., 'Two treatises of Uthred of Boldon on the monastic life', *Studies in Medieval History presented to F.M.Powicke*, eds. R.W. Hunt, W.A. Pantin, R.W. Southern (Oxford, 1948).
Pantin, W.A., 'The halls and schools of medieval Oxford: an attempt at reconstruction', Oxford Studies presented to Daniel Callus, *OHS, NS*, xvi (1964), pp. 31–100.
Paravicini, F. de, *The Early History of Balliol College* (1891).
Parker, J., *The early History of Oxford, OHS*, 3 (Oxford, 1885).

Parkes, M.B., 'The provision of books', *OxHist II*, pp. 407–83.
Peshall, Sir J., *The History of the University of Oxford to the death of William the Conqueror* (Oxford, 1772).
Plassmann, T., 'Bartholomeus Anglicus', *Archivum Fratrum Historicum, 12* (1919), pp. 68–109.
Poole, Austin Lane, *Domesday Book to Magna Carta* (2nd edition, Oxford, 1955).
Poole, Reginald Lane, 'Henry Symeonis', *EHR,* 27 (1912), pp. 515–17.
Post, Gaines, 'Masters' salaries and student fees in the medieval universities', *Speculum,* 7 (1932), pp. 181–98.
Post, Gaines, 'Parisian Masters as a Corporation,' *Speculum, 9* (1934), pp. 421–45.
Pullman, Philip, *Northern Lights* (London, 1996).
Quiller Couch, L.M., ed., *Reminiscences of Oxford, OHS, 22* (1892).
Rashdall, Hastings, 'The friars preacher of the University', *Collectanea, II,* ed. M. Burrows, OHS, 16 (1890), pp. 195–273.
Reeves, M., *The Influence of Prophecy in the Later Middle Ages* (Oxford, 1969).
Rex, Richard, *The Lollards, Social History in Perspective* (Palgrave, 2002).
Ricci, P.G. (ed.), 'Il commento di Cola di Rienzo alla Monarchia di Dante', *Studia Medievalia,* Third Series, 6ii (1965), pp. 679–708.
Richardson, H.G., 'Heresy and lay power under Richard II', *EHR, 51* (1936), pp. 1–28.
Richardson, H.G.,'An Oxford teacher of the fifteenth century', *Bulletin of the John Rylands Library, xxiii,* 2 (1939).
Richardson, H.G., 'Business Training in Medieval Oxford', *American Historical Review, 46* (1941), pp. 259–80.
Robson, J.A., *Wyclif and the Oxford Schools* (Cambridge, 1961).
Roskill, J.S., 'A consideration of certain aspects and problems of the English Modus tenendi parliamentum', *Bulletin of the John Rylands Library, 50* (1968), pp. 411–42.
Roth, F., *The English Austin Friars* 1249–1538 (New York, 1966).
Rubin, Miri, *Corpus Christi, the Eucharist in late medieval culture* (Cambridge, 1991).
Salter, H.E., Medieval Oxford, OHS, 100 (1936).
Scase, Wendy, *Piers Plowman and the New Anticlericalism* (Cambridge,1989).
Shirley, W.W., *A Catalogue of the Original Works of John Wyclif* (Oxford, 1865).
Smalley, Beryl, 'Wyclif's Postilla on the Old Testament and his Principium', *Oxford Studies presented to Daniel Callus, OHS, NS, xvi* (1964), pp. 253–96.
Smalley, Beryl, 'John Wyclif's Postilla super totam bibliam', *Bodleian Library Record, iv* (1953), pp. 186–205.
Smalley, Beryl, *The Study of the Bible in the Middle Ages* (third edition, Oxford, 1983).
Smalley, Beryl, *English Friars and Antiquity in the early fourteenth century* (Oxford, 1970).
Smalley, Beryl, 'The Gospels in the Paris Schools in the late twelfth and early thirteenth centuries, II', *Franciscan Studies, 40* (1980), pp. 298–369, pp. 366–69.
Smalley, Beryl, 'Use of the "Spiritual" Senses of Scripture in Persuasion and Argument by Christian Scholars in the Middle Ages', *RTAM,* 52 (1985), pp. 44–63, p.49.
Snow, C.P., *The Two Cultures and the Scientific Revolution* (Cambridge, 1959).
Southern, R.W., *Robert Grosseteste, the growth of an English Mind in medieval Europe* (Oxford, 1992).
Spade, P.V., *The medieval liar: a catalogue of the insolubilia literature* (Toronto, 1975).
Spinka, M., *John Hus at the Council of Constance, Records of Civilization, Sources and Studies, 73* (1965).
Spinka, M., *John Hus' Concept of the Church* (Princeton, 1966).
Stevenson, W.H., 'The introduction of English as a vehicle of instruction in English Schools', *An English Miscellany presented to Dr. Furnivall* (Oxford, 1901), pp. 421–29
Stewart, J.I.M., *Full Term* (London, 1978).

Stock, Brian, *The implications of literacy* (Princeton, 1983).
Tanner, Norman P., *Decrees of the Ecumenical Councils* (Georgetown, 1990), 2 vols.
Tanner, Norman P., *Heresy trials in the Diocese of Norwich, 1428–31, Camden Society*, Fourth Series, 20 (1977).
Tatnall, Edith C., 'John Wyclif and the Ecclesia Anglicana,' *JEH, 209* (1969), pp. 19–43.
Tatnall, Edith C., 'The Condemnation of John Wyclif at the Council of Constance', *Studies in Church History, vii* (1971), pp. 209–18.
Thomson, S. Harrison, *Writings of Robert Grosseteste* (Cambridge, 1940).
Thomson, Williell R., ed. *The Latin Writings of John Wyclif: an annotated catalog* (Toronto, 1983).
Tierney, Brian, *The Crisis of Church and State, 1050–1300* (Englewood Cliffs, NJ, 1964).
Tierney, Brian, *Origins of Papal Infallibility, 1150–1350* (Leiden, 1972).
Torrell, J.P., *Théorie de la prophetie et philosophie de la connaissance aux environs de 1230, SSLov, 40* (1977).
Ullmann, Walter, *The Origins of the Great Schism* (London, 1948).
Vooght, P. de, *Les sources de la doctrine chrétienne* (Bruges, 1954).
Walsh, K. and Wood, D. (eds.), *The Bible in the Medieval World, Studies in Church History Subsidia, 4* (Oxford, 1985), pp. 237–49.
Walsh, Katherine, *Richard FitzRalph in Oxford, Avignon and Armagh* (Oxford, 1981).
Wansbrough, Henry and Marett-Crosby, Anthony (eds.), *Benedictines in Oxford* (London, 1997).
Weisheipl, J.A., 'Curriculum of the Faculty of Arts at Oxford in the early fourteenth century', *Mediaeval Studies, 26* (1964), 143–185.
Weisheipl, J.A., 'Developments in the Arts Curriculum at Oxford in the early fourteenth century', *Mediaeval Studies, 28* (1966), 151–175.
Wilks, Michael H., *The Problem of Sovereignty in the Later Middle Ages* (Cambridge, 1963).
Wilks, Michael H., 'Royal priesthood: the origins of Lollardy', *The Church in a Changing Society: CIHEC Conference in Uppsala* (Uppsala, 1978).
Workman, Herbert B., *John Wyclif, A study of the English medieval Church* (Oxford, 1926), 2 vols.
Yates, Frances, *The Art of Memory* (London, 1969).

Index

See the relevant entry for aspects of Wyclif's life and work.

A

B

C

D

E

F

G

H

I

J

K

L

law, canon 16, 41, 72, 75, 129, 132, 143, 182, 188, 227, 264, 286, 304

M

N

O

P

Q

R

S

Y

Z